ILLUSTRATED CHECKLIST

BIRDS

OF WESTERN AND CENTRAL AFRICA

HarperCollins*Publishers* Ltd
77–85 Fulham Palace Road
Hammersmith
London W6 8JB

The HarperCollins website address is:
www.**fire**and**water**.com

Collins is a registered trademark of HarperCollins*Publishers* Ltd

TO RIET

First published 2002

1 3 5 7 9 10 8 6 4 2

03 05 07 08 06 04 02

ISBN 0 00 220118 6

Cartography by AWA Graphics, England
Design by White Rabbit Editions, London
Printed and bound in Hong Kong by Printing Express Ltd.

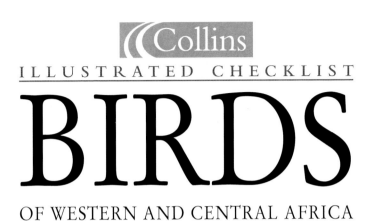

ILLUSTRATED CHECKLIST

BIRDS

OF WESTERN AND CENTRAL AFRICA

BER VAN PERLO

ACKNOWLEDGEMENTS

My brother in Mozambique, Cees van Perlo, played a key role in drawing the maps and compiling the appendix and indices for this book, as he did for *Birds of Eastern Africa* and *Birds of Southern Africa*. I am deeply indebted to him for all his work.

I am also very grateful to Gonçalo Elias, who provided the Portuguese names for this book: not an easy job because many birds appeared not yet to have an official Portuguese name.

Finally, I would like to thank Myles Archibald for the chance he gave me to make this book and Debra Sellman and Katie Piper for their editing work and kind co-operation.

Ber van Perlo
Rotterdam
The Netherlands

CONTENTS

PARTS OF A BIRD

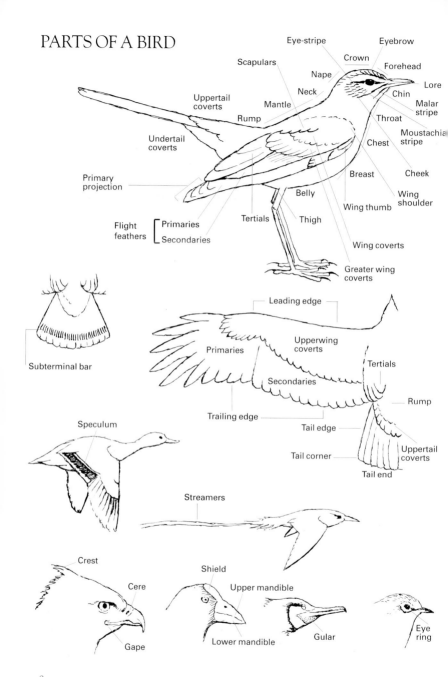

Eye-stripe
Eyebrow
Scapulars
Crown
Nape
Forehead
Neck
Lore
Uppertail coverts
Mantle
Chin
Malar stripe
Rump
Throat
Moustachial stripe
Undertail coverts
Chest
Primary projection
Breast
Cheek
Belly
Wing shoulder
Flight feathers [Primaries / Secondaries]
Wing thumb
Tertials
Thigh
Wing coverts
Greater wing coverts

Subterminal bar

Leading edge
Upperwing coverts
Primaries
Tertials
Secondaries
Rump
Trailing edge
Tail edge
Speculum
Tail corner
Uppertail coverts
Tail end

Streamers

Crest
Shield
Cere
Upper mandible
Gape
Lower mandible
Gular
Eye ring

8

INTRODUCTION

AREA AND SPECIES COVERED

The list in this book is based on *A Contribution to the Distribution and Taxonomy of Afrotropical and Malagasy Birds* (1993), edited by R. J. Dowsett & F. Dowsett-Lemaire, and is supplemented by data from the published volumes of the handbook series *Birds of Africa* and other recent sources (see Bibliography). It mentions all bird species (as known up to 2001) in: the Democratic Republic of Congo, Congo, Gabon, Equatorial Guinea (including Bioco and Annobón), the Central African Republic, Cameroon, Nigeria, Benin, Togo, Ghana, Côte d'Ivoire, Liberia, Sierra Leone, Guinea, Guinea-Bissau, The Gambia, Senegal, Burkina, Mali, Niger, Chad, Mauritania, Cape Verde and São Tomé and Príncipe (see the map on page 14). It provides illustrations, key notes for identification, basic information about habitats, a distribution map for all species and vocalisations for many.

NOMENCLATURE

There is an international established system for scientific names. However, names change constantly, for instance, when scientists think, that – based on new research – species should be split or lumped together.

There is not, however, a similar, generally accepted system for English names; as a consequence names in Central and Western Africa differ in many cases from those used in other parts of Africa. To avoid this problem, this book uses the English and scientific names, as in the first six published volumes of the Handbook series *Birds of Africa*, with some small deviations, mainly in the sparse use of the hyphen. As the last volume of the series is not yet published, the English names are used as they appear in *A Field Guide to the Birds of the Gambia and Senegal* and in other literature mentioned in the Bibliography and List of Further Reading. All the English names are in capitals.

Many people will be familiar with the *Field Guide to the Birds of Western Africa*, written by W. Serle and G. J. Merle and illustrated by W. Hartwig. Some bird names in that guide will be different from those introduced in this book. To avoid confusion, these and many other alternative names are added in the main text, written in lower case between brackets.

The scientific name of a species is composed of two parts: the first one refers to the genus in which similar species are placed together and the second part defines the specific species. For example, there are many buntings that belong to the genus *Emberiza*. The additional *cabanisi* refers to the 'Cabanis's Bunting', as seen in the field. After it became clear that this species has different subspecies (or 'races', a term used in this book for its shortness), the first race ever described was given a name composed of three parts, *Emberiza cabanisi cabanisi*, shortened to 'nominate', a term used in this book. Another race is *Emberiza cabanisi orientalis*, which occurs south-east of the area of the nominate (see caption and map of number 12 on Plate 108).

IDENTIFICATION

Identification of a bird is based upon how it looks ('jizz' or appearance), together with what it does (habits), where we see it (habitat), the chance or probability that we see it there (occurrence) and the sounds it makes (its voice).

JIZZ

What birders call jizz is a difficult-to-define combination of size, relative proportions and body carriage of a bird. Part of a bird's jizz can be its stance (the angle of its body to the flat earth or to a horizontal perch).

APPEARANCE

Each species is illustrated as an adult male in breeding plumage. Other plumages are added when different, in which case the female is normally shown behind the male, in a more horizontal position. The symbols, abbreviations and other indications used in the text and on the plates are as follows:

SYMBOL	EXPLANATION
M	male
F	female
Ad	adult
Imm	immature, any bird, that has
	not yet attained full adult plumage
br	breeding plumage
n-br	non-breeding (or winter) plumage

Many species have a breeding and a non-breeding plumage. Most of these are shown, but in a few cases (some sunbirds, weavers, indigobirds) they are omitted, because the non-breeding plumage of the male closely resembles the normal femal plumage. Every bird that has not attained full adult plumage is called an 'immature' in this book. In a few cases however it was necessary to differentiate further as follows:

ABBREVIATION	EXPLANATION
juv	an immature in its first plumage following the natal down
1stW or (1stS)	an immature in its plumage in the first winter or summer after hatching
2ndW or (2ndS)	an immature in its plumage in the second winter or summer after hatching
sub-ad	an immature in its last plumage before moulting to full adult plumage

Some species have similar looking races, as well as one or more that is more distinct. Only the more recognisable are illustrated and marked (as a, b, c etc) on the plates, mentioned in the text and indicated on the maps.

A colour form is not a race, but a variation of the normal plumage. These forms are represented on the plates when there is a chance of seeing them, for instance where at least 5–15% of the total population of a species is coloured different in some way.

The text opposite the plates gives information about size, main characteristics and differences between similar species. The size is given in centimetres. For most species, size is the total length between tip of bill and end of tail (L); the extra length for tail streamers is in most cases given in brackets e.g. L 12 (+5) cm. For seabirds the size is given as wingspan (W). For a few tall birds the size is height (H).

Because measuring birds is difficult, size data in literature are not uniform. For this reason, sizes above 25 cm are often given in multiples of 5 cm. This enables the user sufficiently to compare the size of a bird he/she wants to identify with the size of other birds.

Full descriptions of feathering and bare parts are not given because the plates contain sufficient information on these areas. Only when these are the most essential features or when they are not visible on the plate are they mentioned.

HABITS

Information about habits – though an important identification tool – has been given sparsely in order to keep the book at an optimal size.

HABITAT

Landscape
The structure of the landscape of Central and Western Africa is determined by the climate, the relative flatness of the area, the soil and by the vegetation.

Climate

The earth travels around the sun with its north-south axis tilted in relation to its plain of orbit. This brings the sun direct overhead the Tropic of Cancer on 23 June, above the Equator on 21 September, above the Tropic of Capricorn on 22 December and again above the Equator on 21 March.

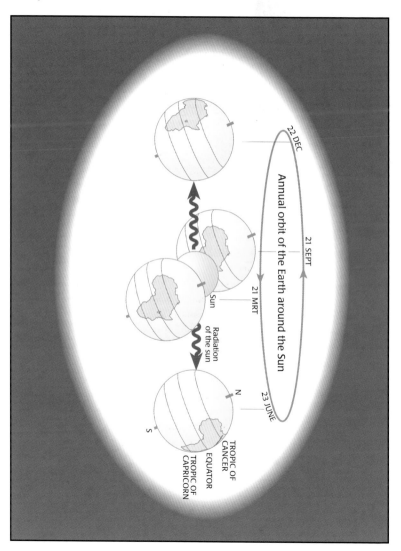

As a result, the intense direct radiation from the sun heats the air in a belt around the earth, that travels to and from the two Tropics and in doing so, passes every place between the tropics twice a year. Within this belt the air warms up at the surface and, on rising, cools at higher altitudes. There the contained moisture condenses to clouds, producing rain.

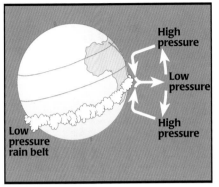

So, every country and place between the tropics has two rainy seasons each year. These follow each other more closely, the nearer to one of the tropics, until they eventually merge. Liberia for instance, 700 km north of the Equator and 2000 km south of the Tropic of Cancer has two wet seasons (in June/July and in September), separated respectively by one dry month (August) and a dry period of eight months (October – May). In Senegal, 1000 km south of the Tropic of Cancer, the two wet seasons follow each other so closely, that they present themselves as one wet season (from mid June to mid November). Meanwhile the northern part of Mauritania, where it is crossed by the Tropic of Cancer, has only one (if any) 'wet' season in July.

The explanation for the occasional thunderstorms in the long dry periods from Senegal to Cameroon and for the (almost) uninterrupted wet season in the rain forest belt is less simple. The air in the low pressure rain belt flows at high altitudes to the north and to the south, forming high pressure areas above respectively the Sahara and the Namib Desert and Kalahari. There the air, rained-out underway, descends, warms up again and, by doing so, becomes even drier, thus creating the desert conditions in these areas. This hot, dry air flows back to the belt of low pressure, but as a result of the earth's rotation these winds, called Tradewinds, are deviated and blow from NE to SW, north of the equator and from SE to NW, south of it.

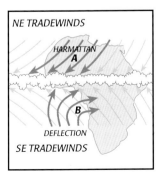

The NE wind is called the Harmattan in Western Africa and is characterised by hot, dry and very dusty weather conditions. Local and global circumstances, such as the existence of the high mountain ranges in eastern Africa and the position of extensive low-pressure areas in the Northern Hemisphere, influence the direction of the SE Trade winds, south of the equator. Over sea (where it becomes saturated by moisture) it is deflected in north-eastern direction for most of the year. Reaching land, it is heated again and rises to heights, where clouds are formed, from which it

13

rains almost every day, especially above The Congo Basin. This moist air also penetrates the countries from Sierra Leone to Nigeria in the form of a wedge, which is often overrun by the dry Harmattan. This results in very unstable weather conditions, which develop to fierce thunderstorms, mainly in the long, dry period between the main rains.

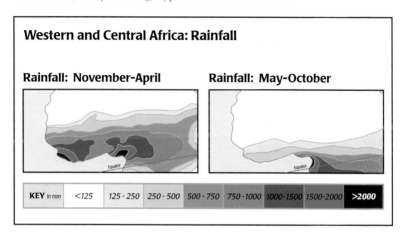

Western and Central Africa: Rainfall

Rainfall: November-April

Rainfall: May-October

| KEY in mm | <125 | 125 - 250 | 250 - 500 | 500 - 750 | 750 -1000 | 1000-1500 | 1500-2000 | >2000 |

Altitude

The area is rather flat, except along the eastern and south-eastern borders of the Democratic Republic of Congo, along the borders in the North, in large parts of Guinea and in the north-western parts of Cameroon. The mountains on the borders with Uganda, Rwanda and Burundi rise to spectacular heights (Mt. Karisimbi >3000 metres), there the weather conditions and the flora are alpine. This is also the case in the highest parts of Katanga, the high laying south-eastern province of the Democratic Republic of Congo. The mountain range in Cameroon is a continuation of the row of volcanic islands in the Gulf of Guinea. Several endemic bird species occur in these isolated highlands and islands.

In Nigeria, Ghana, Ivory Coast, Guinea and the West African countries there are extensive plateaux, which in Guinea rise to 1200 metres and more. In the landscape these plateaux are noticeable by the steep escarpments along their sides, which are very interesting for birders because they guide migration streams and, within a short range, offer a large diversity of habitats, each with its own bird species. In addition, they are favourite places for large raptors, which make use of the strong, uprising winds along their flanks.

Another feature is the 'inzelbergs' (or 'inselbergs'); these are large, bare, rocky, rounded (but sometimes gently sloping, green) hills laying dispersed and isolated in the landscape. Normally they are of very old age (> 570 million years old), protruding through (much) younger geologic formations.

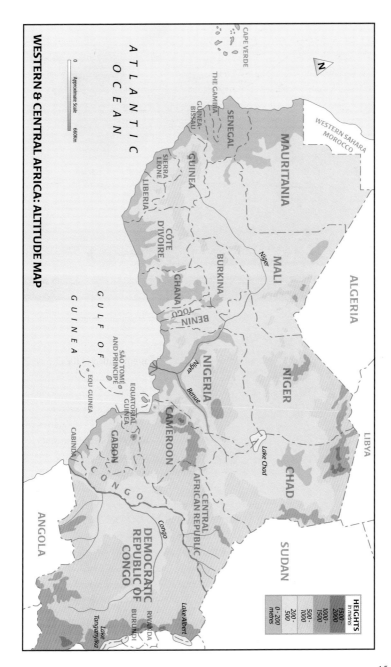

WESTERN & CENTRAL AFRICA: ALTITUDE MAP

Soil

Large parts of the Tropics consist of 'laterite' clays and loess. Their red colour is the result of oxidation of the contained iron particles (rust!). These soils are composed from very fine material, brought there by rivers, wind or volcanoes. Their fertility depends on age; volcanic soils are often very recent and therefore very fertile, but the minerals are easily washed out by penetrating rainwater. In the end, only those nutritional compounds stay behind that can be kept in the biological cycle. This is the reason why rich, luxurious jungle grows on very poor soils and why it deteriorates rapidly after the removal of trees that contain these nutrients.

Vegetation

In relation with the rainfall pattern, there is a gradual transition from the very complex rain forest belt in the south via vast savannah's to the bare desert in the north. The border lines between the different vegetation zones, as drawn on the vegetation map (page 15), are not visible as such in the field. Also, the map might only be approximate: due to the activities of man, the Sahel zone is moving south, while the growth of human population and large-scale logging are responsible for the fragmentation and the disappearance of the rain forest in most of its former range.

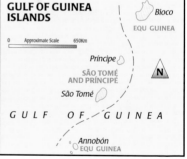

Cape Verde Islands: these are mainly bare or covered by short grass, dry woodland and shrub, while higher slopes are often afforested. SANTO ANTÃO, SÃO NICOLAU, SÃO TIAGO, FOGO and BRAVA are vulcano-shaped; the SÃO VICENTE-group is intermediate.

Gulf of Guinea Islands: BIOCO and ANNOBÓN (parts of Equatorial Guinea) are vulcano-shaped. The lower slopes on the eastern and north side are covered with (neglected) cacao plantations and above 600 metres by mainly forest. SÃO TOMÉ and PRÍNCIPE (together an independent state) are similar in character.

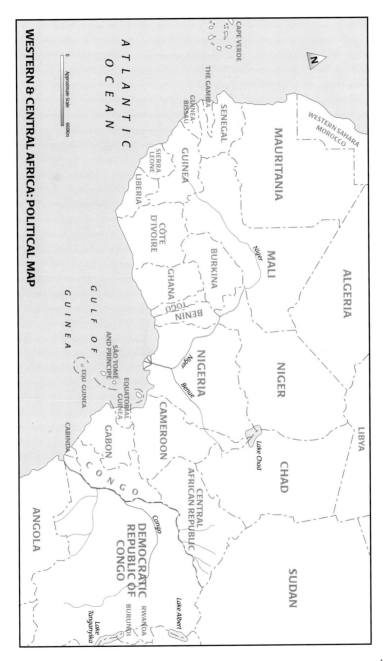

WESTERN & CENTRAL AFRICA: POLITICAL MAP

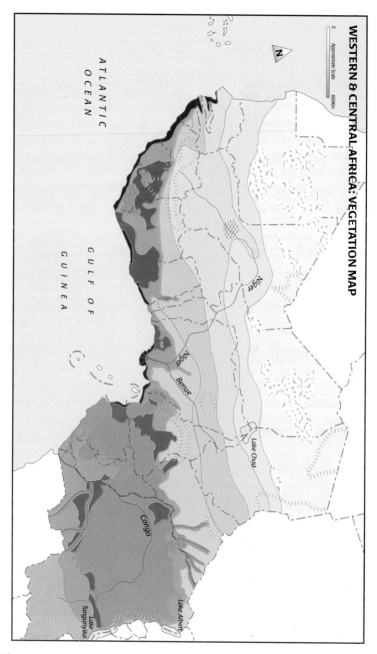

WESTERN & CENTRAL AFRICA: VEGETATION MAP

N

0   660Km
Approximate Scale

ATLANTIC
OCEAN

GULF OF
GUINEA

Niger

Niger

Benue

Lake Chad

Congo

Lake
Tanganyika

Lake Albert

KEY TO VEGETATION MAP

Lowland Forest: a tall, multilayered, evergreen habitat in which the canopy of tall trees is continuous and completely closed.

Degraded Forest: lowland forest, that recently is severely cut up by roads, cultivation, mining etc.

Forest Savannah Mosaic: area where the original forest is fragmented by older cultivation.

Miombo: type of woodland, where trees of the genus *Brachystegia* dominate. Restricted to southern Africa.

Guinea Savannah, southern zone: mainly woodland, 13–17 metres high, in which trees of the genuses *Combretum Terminalia* and *Vitex dominate*, with underneath a continuous grass cover, 2–4 metres high and with only a few shrubs.

Guinea Savannah, northern zone: areas with a grass cover, 1.5 metres high and with more or less tree cover, mainly of the species *Isoberlinia*.

Sudan Savannah: plains with scattered Baobab, some low other tree species, a grass cover up to 1 metre high and with scattered thorn scrub.

Sahel Zone: undulating sand plains, partly stabilised by low bushy acacias.

Desert: bare habitat where only after the rare rains a short living plant cover occurs.

Mangrove and other types of swamp woodlands.

Montane grassland.

Sand Dunes

Alpine Vegetation

Inland Niger Delta

Areas with mountain slopes and escarpments.

TREE ILLUSTRATIONS

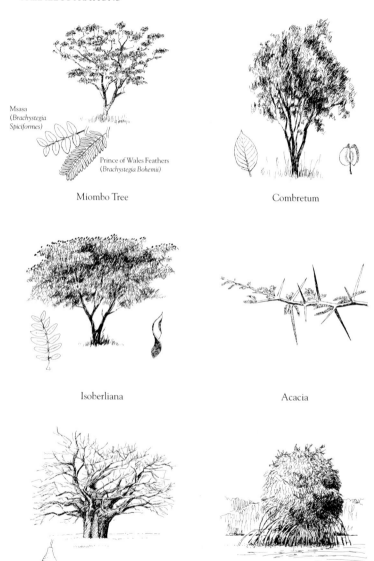

Msasa
(*Brachystegia
Spiciformes*)

Prince of Wales Feathers
(*Brachystegia Bohemii*)

Miombo Tree

Combretum

Isoberliana

Acacia

Baobab

Mangrove

SOME HABITATS MENTIONED IN THIS BOOK:

Terrestrial environments

There is a strong similarity between the maps for rainfall and the vegetation map. In the wettest areas there is forest; from there the cover with trees and grass diminishes in relative to the decline in rainfall. In the desert years may pass without any rainfall at all.

Forest: see key to symbols of vegetation map. Often forest is found in narrow 'galleries' along rivers amidst other vegetation types,

Woodland: is any other habitat in which trees dominate, usually in areas with lower rainfall. Woodland is (and looks) drier than forest,

Miombo: see key to symbols of vegetation map,

Wooded area: is a place with some trees, but where bush, scrub or grass tend to be more dominant,

Bush: areas dominated by normally thorny shrubs, with more or less dense undergrowth of grass,

Scrub: low bush, often impenetrable,

Riverine belt: any growth along a river or stream that is richer in trees, bush or other vegetation than its surroundings. The most lush form is tropical gallery forest which resembles rainforest,

Savannah: plains dominated by grasses, with scattered tree(-groups), bush and/or scrub,

Cultivation: in this book is an area of small-holder plots.

Aquatic environments

West Africa holds many very important wetlands, not only for African herons, storks, ibises, ducks, waders and reed warblers etc, but also for millions of migrants from other parts of the world.

Lake Chad: a large inland lake, that unfortunately is slowly drying up,

Floodplains: larger areas, that are flooded during the wet season, especially at the Niger, the Gambia and the Senegal Rivers,

Inundations: smaller areas, that are temporarily put under water by man

Swamps, natural and artificial lakes, ponds, dams

Estuaries: system of watercourses, comprising a split-up river mouth under tidal influence of the sea (e.g. Senegal and Gambia rivers and the Congo river),

Delta: system of fanning-out watercourses, built-up at the mouth of large river (e.g. the Niger),

Inland Niger Delta, Mali: a system of streams, lakes and swamps at both sides of the Niger,

Mangrove (swamps): strips with tree species of the genus *Rhizophora*, growing on salt mud flats at sea and salt water, with many bowed aerial roots.

OCCURRENCE

Range, status and season determine the possibility of seeing a species in a certain area. This information can be found on the DISTRIBUTION maps (after the plates). The shaded areas are an indication of the RANGE of a species. The presence of most MIGRANTS depends on the northern or tropical seasons, but beware that individual birds, that may stay behind when all other members of that species return for instance to their breeding grounds in Europe or Asia.

Range

The maps give the range of the species. However the very small scale of the maps and the differences in accuracy of the consulted information about distribution make it only possible to give an indication of where a certain species might be seen.

Status

Each map contains information about the status of a species. However, due to the scale of the maps it was not possible to differentiate very much, so that local occurrence might deviate from the indication on the maps. See also the introduction to the maps directly following plate 109.

In the main, text information about status is only given as R (rare) and V (vagrant), when appropriate. A species is rare when its range is very restricted or its total population very small. A vagrant lives in other parts of the world, reaches the region only by accident and hence has been seen less than about five times. The west coast of Africa is especially well known for vagrants, mainly from America.

A question mark (?) in the text and on the maps means that occurrence of the species in Central and Western Africa is insufficiently substantiated. In a few cases the symbol (I) is used for introduced species.

Season

The presence of a species in its indicated range depends in many cases on the seasonal rhythm in Europe, Africa and other parts of the world. Roughly speaking, birds can be divided into 'residents' and 'migrants'. In this book residents are species that are present in a certain area throughout the year. Part of the year, however, there are also species present that only come to breed. They disperse to other areas outside the breeding season or breed elsewhere, but come in to escape from the temporarily unfavourable conditions (winter or drought) in their breeding quarters. These migrants can be divided into northern (or Palaearctic) migrants from Europe, Western Asia and North Africa (indicated as NM on the maps), Intra-African migrants (AM), migrants from other parts of the World (EM from eastern regions, SM from the South and WM from the America's) and vagrants (V).

Text and Map Key	EXPLANATION
NM (northern migrant)	Migrant from Europe, North Africa and Western Asia
AM (African migrant)	African migrants from within or outside the area
EM, WM, SM (eastern, western, southern migrant)	Migrants coming from Asia, America or the Nearctic

If a symbol (NM, AM, WM, EM or RES) is put between brackets it is in combination with another symbol; in these cases the symbol without brackets is more dominant. For instance RES/(NM) indicates a resident species, of which numbers are slightly augmented in the period of the northern winter. Normally, it concerns different races of these species.

Where the symbol RES is used in combination with (AM), it often relates to a 'concertina-migrant'. In the migration patterns of African migrants a distinction can be made between migration from other parts of Africa (often from outside the area) and 'concertina' migration, especially in West Africa. Concertina migration can be described as the pattern in which birds from the more northern savannah zones go to southern zones to breed or to feed (in the dry season) and birds from the southern forest and woodland zones going north for the same sort of reasons.

In the text the symbols R, V, (?), (I) and those for migrants are combined where appropriate. NM.R for instance means that the species is a rare migrant from Europe.

Bird Waves

It pays to look around for 'bird waves', especially in woodland. Suddenly one or two birds are sighted and, waiting patiently, more and more birds appear of several, sometimes many species, that wander together through all layers of the vegetation.

Endemism

This is a fascinating phenomenon. An endemic is a species that occurs only in an area with well-defined boundaries like a continent, a country, an island or a habitat. In this book only the endemic birds of countries are marked E at the end of the relevant caption, followed by the name of the country (between brackets) in which they occur.

VOICE

Information about song and call is given for many birds, especially for those with a hidden way of living (those that live in forests and swamps and those that are active at night), those that are difficult to identify from appearance only (nightjars, swifts, larks, pipits and cisticolas) and those that are well known for their vocal abilities (thrushes and warblers).

Note, however, that not the whole vocabulary could be given and that voice examples could not be found for every species. In the vocalisations only in a few cases has distinction been made between calls and song. The most striking sound has been given as a transcription in italics between quotation marks. This is a hazardous endeavour because these transcriptions may well look confusing and even funny. However if the reader can overcome his or her embarrassment and tries to pronounce the transcriptions in the given speed and pitch he or she might have found another tool to confirm an identification, which is the only reason why they are included. Attention has been paid to pitch, loudness, sound quality, length and structure. General pitch has been given on a rough subjective scale:

Description	EXPLANATION
Extreme low	As low as you can imagine (e.g. large owl)
Very low	(e.g. Feral Dove)
Low	Pitch of an average man's voice (e.g. Corncrake)
Mid-high	Pitch of an average woman's voice (e.g. Glossy
Starlings)	
High	(e.g. Common Bulbul)
Very high	(e.g. Mousebird)
Extreme high	So high that the sound is just within human hearing
	range (ear-reach) (e.g. most Sunbirds)

LOUDNESS is generally indicated by general terms such as soft, loud and crescendo. Louder parts of the calls are put in capitals.

SOUND QUALITY has been described in terms like shrieking, magpie-like, liquid etc. Often songs and calls are compared to those of other birds like reed warblers (for example the well-known Eurasian Reed Warbler *Acrocephalus scirpaceus*, 79.4) or to the miaowing of a domestic cat.

LENGTH: if a transcription ends on '-' the call or song goes on with at least three similar notes, syllables or phrases.

STRUCTURE: the way in which notes follow each other is described in terms like accelerated, staccato and unstructured, and by the way the parts of a transcription are connected. For instance, in '*treet treet treet*' each syllable is well separated, '*treet-treet-treet*' sounds as one 'word' and '*treettreettreet*' as almost a trill.

A 'strophe' is a recognisable complete part of a bird's repertoire that can be dissected successively into phrases, syllables and notes. Strophes can, however, be as short as one note.

A special feature of the song and/or call of many bird species is that it is given in duet. This means that two birds (normally a female and a male) produce sounds that might follow each other so closely or are interwoven so harmoniously that the resulting song or call sounds as though it is from a single bird.

Plate 1

1   SECRETARY BIRD *Sagittarius serpentarius*   H 90 cm. Unmistakable. Habitat: dry open-bushed and wooded natural and cultivated areas.

2   OSTRICH *Struthio c. camelus*   H 210 cm. Unmistakable. Habitat: dry, open plains and semi-desert. Voice: very low, lion-like, well separated '*who who whoooi*' gliding down at the end (heard in early morning and in the evening).

Plate 2

1   **WANDERING ALBATROSS** *Diomedea exulans*   W 330 cm. Goes through 7 stages from juv to
ad plumage, each time with more white to body and wings; stages 1 (juv), 3 (imm), 5 (subad) and 7
(ad) shown. Note all-white back of stages 5, 6 and 7 and all-white tail feathers of stage 7 (ad).
Habitat: open sea. V

2   **YELLOW-NOSED ALBATROSS** *Diomedea chlororhynchos*   W 205 cm. Ad nominate (with
pale-grey head, from southern Atlantic) and imm (with all-black bill) of race *bassi* (with white
head, from Indian Ocean) shown. Note yellow on upper mandible of ad. Black leading edge on
underwing wider than trailing edge. Habitat: open sea. V

3   **SOUTHERN GIANT PETREL** *Macronectes giganteus*   W 195 cm. Two colour forms (a and
uncommon b) shown. Bill pale-yellow with greenish tip. Eye colour often pale, not black. Looks
hump-backed in flight. Habitat: open sea, seashore, harbours. V

4   **ASCENSION FRIGATEBIRD** *Fregata aquila*   W 200 cm. Ad ♂ is completely black, including
upperwings and legs. The ♀ occurs as white-bellied (a) or as all-black (b) form, both with black
legs, but has red toes and a complete pale-brown collar, separating head from rest of body. Juv has
all-white head, which, in following stages, becomes increasingly spotted and blotched black.
Habitat: open sea. V

5   **MAGNIFICENT FRIGATEBIRD** *Fregata magnificens*   W 230 cm. Note the pale wing bar. The
♂ from ♂ 4 by range (and size); the ♀ from 4 (white-bellied ♀ form) by less extended white on
belly; ♀♀ and most imms have three rows of narrow white tips to feathers in armpits and lack the
pale-brown collar of 4. Habitat: open sea. R

ad

1

ad

juv

1

sub ad

2   ad

1   imm

2   imm

3

a

b

1

imm

4   ♀ a

♂

5 ♀   ♂

4

♀ b

4

imm

imm

5

sub ad

Plate 3

Upper- and underside of 1, 2, 6, 8 and 12 shown

1 **SOFT-PLUMAGED PETREL** *Pterodroma mollis*   W 90 cm. Dark (a, rare) and pale (b) forms shown. From 2 and 3 by darker cheeks and fuller collar. Intensity of upper- and underwing pattern depends on light conditions. Habitat: open sea. R

2 **FREIRA** *Pterodroma m. madeira*   W 90 cm. Not safely separable from (1 and) 3, but is said to be smaller with much smaller, finer bill, reduced eye spot and somewhat paler crown and forehead. Habitat: open sea. (Race of 1). R

3 **GON-GON** *Pterodroma m. feae*   W 90 cm. From 1 by incomplete breast band, but otherwise very hard to separate from 1 and 2. Habitat: near Cape Verde, where it breeds between September and April. (Race of 1). E, Cape Verde.

4 **BULWER'S PETREL** *Bulweria bulwerii*   W 65 cm. Note long pointed tail, small head, pale bar on upperwing. Erratic flight close to sea surface. Habitat: open sea. R

5 **PINTADO PETREL** *Daption capense*   W 85 cm. Unmistakable. Singly-large flocks often near trawlers. Habitat: open sea, but also sighted near shore. V

6 **CORY'S SHEARWATER** *Calonectris diomedea*   W 115 cm. Note yellowish dark-ringed bill, clean white underwing, pale cap and lack of hind collar. Varying amount of white on lower rump. Habitat: open sea often near coast.

7 **CAPE VERDE SHEARWATER** *Calonectris diomedea edwardsii*   W 105 cm. From 6 by longer tail and shorter wings. Habitat: open sea. (Race of 6). E, Cape Verde.

8 **GREAT SHEARWATER** *Puffinus gravis*   W 110 cm. Note large body and small head with thin black (not yellowish) bill. From 6 and 7 by blacker cap, separated from back by white collar, dark undertail coverts, dark smudge on belly and different underwing pattern. Habitat: open sea. R

9 **SOOTY SHEARWATER** *Puffinus griseus*   W 105 cm. Note complicated black-and-white underwing pattern, showing from distance as a grey central area. The secondaries, seen from above, form a pale bar along the trailing edge of the wing. Habitat: open sea. Also near coast. R

10 **MANX SHEARWATER** *Puffinus puffinus mauretanicus*   W 80 cm. From 11 by greyer, more contrasting underparts. Flight action (rapid flutters interspersed by short glides) as 12, but often with longer glides. Habitat: open sea, coastal areas. R

11 **YELKOUAN SHEARWATER** *Puffinus puffinus yelkouan*   W 85 cm. See 10. Habitat: open sea. (Race of 10). V

12 **LITTLE SHEARWATER** *Puffinus assimilis*   W 60 cm. Races *boydi* (a, with dark undertail coverts and rather wide black trailing edge to underwing, endemic on Cape Verde) and *baroli* (b) shown. Underwing almost completely white. Habitat: open sea. R

Plate 4

Upper- and underside of 3, 4, 5, 6, 7 and 8 shown

1   **RED-BILLED TROPICBIRD** *Phaethon aethereus*   W 105 cm. Ad from 2 by different mantle and rump pattern. Imm has large black area on outerwing, buff-orange, dark-tipped bill and in neck connected eye stripes. Habitat: open sea. R

2   **WHITE-TAILED TROPICBIRD** *Phaethon lepturus*   W 90 cm. Some adults have overall apricot wash. Imm from imm 1 by short eye stripe. Habitat: open sea. R

3   **WILSON'S STORM PETREL** *Oceanites oceanicus*   L 17 cm. Note straight held out wings. From 7 by less forked tail. White on uppertail coverts extends further down to lower belly. Yellow webs of feet diagnostic (only visible from very short distance). Feet project in flight. Swallow-like, gliding flight, usually in flocks. Habitat: normally at open sea. NM

4   **WHITE-FACED STORM PETREL** *Pelagodroma marina*   L 20 cm. Nominate (a, breeds on Canary Islands) shown and race *eadesi* (b, with whiter neck, endemic on Cape Verde). Note white eyebrow and grey rump. Gregarious. Habitat: open sea.

5   **BLACK-BELLIED STORM PETREL** *Fregetta tropica*   L 20 cm. Normally with black stripe down belly (a), but some without (b). Note broad black leading edge to wing and dark wrist patch on underwing. Dances and bounces over waves. Habitat: open sea. Note: White-bellied Storm Petrel *Fregetta grallaria*, which has not been seen yet in the area, very similar to b, but without dark tips to underprimary coverts. V

6   **BRITISH (or European) STORM PETREL** *Hydrobates pelagicus*   L 15 cm. White underwing stripe diagnostic. Feet do not project in flight. Often in large flocks. Habitat: open sea, occasionally inshore. NM

7   **MADEIRAN STORM PETREL** *Oceanodroma castro*   L 20 cm. Difficult to separate from 3 and 8, but pale band across upperwings less pronounced; more distinct white rump patch than 8 without dark central line. Also more steady flight (with quick wing beats), interspersed with short glides on slightly downward angled wings. Habitat: open sea.

8   **LEACH'S STORM PETREL** *Oceanodroma leucorhoa*   L 20 cm. White rump does not extend to belly. Does not patter on water surface. Flight erratic. Normally solitary. Habitat: open sea. NM

9   **GUILLEMOT** *Uria aalge*   L 40 cm. Less compact than 10 with longer, sharper bill and (in flight) protruding feet. Habitat: at sea. V

10   **RAZORBILL** *Alca torda*   L 40 cm. See 9, from which it differs further by blacker head. Habitat: at sea. V

Plate 5

1   **NORTHERN GANNET** *Sula bassana*   W 170 cm. White tail and white secondaries of ad diagnostic. Note the few white secondaries and the partly white tail of imm. Mainly juveniles seen, which are not safely separable from juv 2. Habitat: open sea. NM

2   **CAPE GANNET** *Sula capensis*   W 165 cm. Note black tail and all-black flight feathers. Long gular stripe diagnostic, but this feature (also present in 1stW) very difficult to see. Imm's in all stages have blacker rump than 1 and never any white secondaries. Habitat: open sea. AM

3   **BROWN BOOBY** *Sula leucogaster*   W 140 cm. Ad is brown-black above and has white restricted to underparts. Note pale underwing area of juv, contrasting with darker flanks. Habitat: open sea.

4   **RED-FOOTED BOOBY** *Sula sula*   W 150 cm. White form (a) shown and very rare dark, white-tailed form (b); many other colour forms known, but red legs diagnostic. Note black cap of ad (a) and whitish underparts of juv, contrasting with mainly dark underwing. Habitat: open sea. V

5   **MASKED BOOBY** *Sula dactylatra*   W 150 cm. From 1 and 2 by yellowish (not bluish) bill, red (not creamy) eyes and lack of yellow on head and nape. Note also full black trailing edge of wings, touching body. Imm has brown head, white collar and rather pale underwing. Habitat: open sea. V

1

imm

juv

2

a

4

imm

b

imm

3

imm

5

imm

Plate 6

1   **CAPE CORMORANT** *Phalacrocorax capensis*   L 65 cm. From 3 by smaller size, blacker, less scalloped plumage and brighter yellow gular pouch in br plumage. Habitat: vagrant from southern Africa, where it is restricted to coastal waters. Feeds at sea but may enter estuaries. V

2   **LONG-TAILED (or Reed) CORMORANT** *Phalacrocorax africanus*   L 55 cm. N-br plumage (not shown) lacks crest. Imm extensively whitish below. Prefers perching in trees, not on the ground. Habitat: inland rivers, lakes, marches, inundations with fringing vegetation and trees. Rarely near the coast. RES.(AM)

3   **GREAT (or White-breasted) CORMORANT** *Phalacrocorax carbo*   L 90 cm. Races *lucidus* (a, throughout the area), *maroccanus* (b, coastal Mauritania) and *sinensis* (c, North Africa, not yet reported from the area) shown. N-br plumage without white thighs. Habitat: large lakes and rivers with open banks and shores; also in lagoons, estuaries, marshes and inundations.

4   **DARTER** *Anhinga rufa*   L 80 cm. Perches in trees, often with wings held half open. Habitat: mainly along fresh water bodies with fringing vegetation, sometimes in coastal lagoons. RES.(AM)

5   **GREAT WHITE(-breasted) PELICAN** *Pelecanus onocrotalus*   L 155 cm, W 315 cm. From 6 by whiter plumage and more colourful bare parts. Underwing black-and-white. Imm has dark bar across underwing coverts. Often seen fishing in co-operating, synchronising groups. Habitat: large freshwater lakes, but also in estuaries.

6   **PINK-BACKED PELICAN** *Pelecanus rufescens*   L 125 cm. Smaller and less white than 5. Flight feathers, seen from below, only slightly darker than underwing coverts. Fishes solitary. Habitat: any large open water.

Plate 7

1 **YELLOW-BILLED STORK (or Wood Ibis)** *Mycteria ibis* L 95 cm. Yellow bill diagnostic. Black tail in flight often not visible. Habitat: any area with fish, especially at larger waterbodies.

2 **AFRICAN OPEN-BILLED STORK** *Anastomus lamelligerus* L 95 cm. Unmistakable, especially if 'open' bill is seen. In flight all-black below. Gregarious, especially in breeding season. Habitat: feeds on snails and freshwater mussels, which it opens with its specially adapted bill at water edge, often in wooded areas. RES.(AM)

3 **BLACK-HEADED HERON** *Ardea melanocephala* L 95 cm. Black crown and legs diagnostic. Note contrasting black-and white underwing pattern in flight. Imm from imm 6 by grey (not white) thighs, dark (not yellowish) legs and some rufous on neck. Habitat: open grassy areas, farmlands, forest clearings near lakes, marshes, estuaries, coastal areas. Occasionally breeds in towns. Often found away from water. RES.(AM)

4 **PURPLE HERON** *Ardea purpurea* L 90 cm. Nominate (a) and race *tournei* (b, endemic on Santiago, Cape Verde) shown. Skulking behaviour and slender streaked head and neck diagnostic. Imm is rufous and tawny. Habitat: reed beds along rivers, lakes, dams, ponds, occasionally on coastal mud flats. NM.RES

5 **GOLIATH HERON** *Ardea goliath* L 140 cm, H 150 cm. Large size and rufous (not black) crown diagnostic. Imm (not shown) as ad but overall slightly more rufous (less so than imm 4). Habitat: shallow water of lakes, rivers, creeks, marshes, mangroves. RES.(AM)

6 **GREY HERON** *Ardea cinerea* L 100 cm. White crown, yellow bill and yellowish (or pinkish) legs diagnostic. Imm from imm 3 by white thighs and yellowish upperlegs. Note uniform grey underwing in flight. Habitat: open or reedy margins and nearby areas of lakes, rivers, marshes, estuaries. (RES).AM.NM

7 **MARABOU** (Stork) *Leptoptilos crumeniferus* W 260 cm, L 150 cm. Very large. Flies with retracted head and neck (unlike other storks). Habitat: dry natural areas, but also in towns and wherever it can feed on fish, wounded, small or young animals, carrion and refuse. RES.(AM)

8 **BLACK STORK** *Ciconia nigra* L 95 cm. Red legs and black rump of ad diagnostic. Imm from 11 by absence of red bare skin on head. Note that black leading edge on underwing widens slightly outwards. Parties of up to 4. Habitat: tall grass, reeds and herbage near streams and other small water bodies, but also in open, dry grassland. NM

9 **WHITE STORK** *Ciconia ciconia* L 100 cm. Unmistakable. Habitat: any open area with large insects, mice, frogs and other small prey. NM

10 **WOOLLY- (or White-)NECKED STORK** *Ciconia episcopus* L 85 cm. Black band across breast and belly diagnostic. Long white undertail coverts conceal black tail in flight. Solitary, but may be gregarious at dusk. Habitat: open shores of all types of large and small water bodies; also in grassland. RES.(AM)

11 **ABDIM'S STORK** *Ciconia abdimii* L 75 cm. White rump diagnostic. Very gregarious. Habitat: open grassland, farmlands, often near settlement. RES.AM

12 **SADDLE-BILLED STORK** *Ephippiorhynchus senegalensis* L 145 cm. Note different eye colour of ♂ and ♀. Habitat: any shallow water and swampy area.

Plate 8

1 **RUFOUS-BELLIED HERON** *Ardeola rufiventris* L 60 cm. Note pale chin of ♀. Skulking. Habitat: swamps, inundations, reedy edges of lakes and swamps. Voice: rasping '*graak*' and other grunts. R

2 **SQUACCO HERON** *Ardeola ralloides* L 40 cm. Well camouflaged, but shows surprisingly white wings on take-off (a). Habitat: fringing vegetation of marshes, pans, lakes, slow streams. RES.NM

3 **MALAGASY POND HERON** *Ardeola idae* L 45 cm. In its restricted range in central Africa only seen in n-br plumage (br plumage probably not seen outside Madagascar). From 2 by much heavier streaking. Less skulking than 2. Habitat: wooded marshes. EM.R

4 **WHITE-CRESTED TIGER HERON (or Bittern)** *Tigriornis leucolophus* L 65 cm. On first sight resembles a long-necked 16. Differs from all other herons by finely barred plumage. Erectile crest normally hidden. Evasive. Habitat: marshy woodland, undergrowth near forest streams.

5 **BLACK-CROWNED NIGHT HERON** *Nycticorax nycticorax* L 55 cm. Not really secretive. Often gregarious. Nocturnal. Habitat: lake edges, rivers with bordering trees, bush, papyrus, reed beds. Voice: mid-high, pushed-out, short barking '*wha wha*'. (RES). NM

6 **WHITE-BACKED NIGHT HERON** *Gorsachius leuconotus* L 55 cm. Note exceptional large eyes. Ad and imm from imm 5 by grey head and darker eyes. Nocturnal. Habitat: dense waterside undergrowth near slow streams and lakes. Voice: low, crow-like '*cra cra cra cra*' or '*craak-craak-craak-craak*'.

7 **DWARF BITTERN** *Ixobrychus sturmii* L 25 cm. Note small size, black eyes, dark appearance. Largely nocturnal. Habitat: thick reedy cover with some trees and shrub in or near marshes, lakes, streams, inundations, flooded woods. Voice: mid-high, dull '*roap-roap-roap*'. RES.(AM)

8 **LITTLE BITTERN** *Ixobrychus minutus* L 35 cm. Nominate (a, NM) and race *payesii* (b, resident, with more rufous to sides of head and neck) shown. Pale wing patches especially striking in flight. Imm (not shown) has even more buffy feather edges on back than ♀. Skulking. Habitat: marshes, wet grasslands. Voice: mid-high dark regular '*roa roa roa*'. RES.(NM)

9 **GREEN(-backed or Striated) HERON** *Butorides striatus* L 40 cm. Well camouflaged, when seen among vegetation, but not necessary secretive. Hunts by day. Habitat: waterbodies with dense fringing vegetation, open coastal mud flats. Voice: mid-high '*tsjah tsjah tsjah*' when flushed.

10 **CATTLE EGRET** *Bubulcus ibis* L 55 cm. Note short robust bill. More compact flight silhouette than 13. Normally forages near cattle and game; also at grass fires. Flies to roost in low-flying V-formations. Habitat: breeds in reed beds and trees near water edges. RES.AM

11 **GREAT (White) EGRET** *Egretta alba* L 95 cm. Note black gape line extending up behind eye. Habitat: margins of large waters. RES.NM

12 **BLACK EGRET (or Heron)** *Egretta ardesiaca* L 65 cm. Note black legs with yellow feet, characteristic head profile with long plumes and black eyes. Unfolds wings repeatedly (like a fast-opening umbrella) to shut off glare when fishing (a). Habitat: lake margins, river edges, marshes, inundations. Occasionally at the seaside. RES.(AM)

13 **LITTLE EGRET** *Egretta garzetta* L 65 cm. Yellow feet (and eyes) diagnostic. Normal white (a) and rare black (b) forms shown. Note slender, mainly black bill. Habitat: shallow fresh water, estuaries, seashore pools. RES.NM

14 **YELLOW-BILLED (or Intermediate) EGRET** *Egretta intermedia* L 65 cm. From 11 by smaller size, shorter bill and yellow upperlegs. From 13 by heavier jizz, all-yellow bill, yellow upperlegs. Gape does not extend beyond eye. Habitat: swampy areas, inundation, flood plains, edges of inland waters, occasionally on mudflats in estuaries. RES.(AM)

15 **WESTERN REEF EGRET** *Egretta gularis* L 60 cm. White (a) and dark (b) forms shown. Note heavy, yellow, slightly decurved bill and extension of yellow on legs. Habitat: coastal mud flats, rarely at lakes. RES.(AM)

16 **EURASIAN BITTERN** *Botaurus stellaris* L 65 cm. In flight with rufous wings and far protruding feet, neck more extended than shown when flying over reed beds. Habitat: at edges of lakes and rivers in bordering trees, papyrus, reeds. Voice: extreme low, pushed-out, booming '*uhthooo uhthooo*'. NM.RES.R

Plate 9

1   **EURASIAN SPOONBILL** *Platalea leucorodia*   L 90 cm. See 2. Imm from imm 2 by pale brown, not dull flesh-coloured bill. Habitat: shallow parts of larger water bodies. RES.NM.R

2   **AFRICAN SPOONBILL** *Platalea alba*   L 90 cm. From 1 by mainly red naked parts. Imm as n-br 1, but with duller-coloured bill and legs and black tips to flight feathers. From white egrets in flight by outstretched neck. Habitat: shallow parts of permanent and seasonal inland waterbodies and estuaries. RES.(AM)

3   **OLIVE (or Green) IBIS** *Bostrychia olivacea*   L 70 cm. Nominate (a) and small race *bocagei* (b, from São Tomé) shown. Difficult to see in its forest habitat. Habitat: open places in forests. Voice: mid-high '*wa waa waa wá-waa*'. R

4   **SPOT-BREASTED IBIS** *Bostrychia rara*   L 45 cm. Note spotting to throat and upperbreast. Habitat: in or close to forests. Voice: very noisy at dusk '*kakkak kakkak - *'. R

5   **HADADA** *Bostrychia hagedash*   L 75 cm. Note white cheek stripe and red ridge of bill. Very vocal in flight. Habitat: cultivated areas, lawns, moist grasslands, marshes, wooded streams. Voice: mid-high, loud, raucous '*haaah hahah haah hahah*'.

6   **WALDRAPP** *Geronticus eremita*   L 80 cm. Unmistakable. Habitat: dry, rocky, rather bare open areas. NM.R

7   **GLOSSY IBIS** *Plegadis falcinellus*   L 65 cm. Slim, long-legged and -necked jizz diagnostic. Habitat: swamps, flood plains, lake margins and dams. Voice: normally silent. NM.(RES)

8   **SACRED IBIS** *Threskiornis aethiopicus*   L 75 cm. Note red stripe and narrow black trailing edge to underwing. Habitat: wetlands, farmland, sewage ponds, coastal beaches, offshore islands. Voice: normally silent, occasionally in flight mid-high '*kreh kreh *'.

9   **SHOEBILL** *Balaeniceps rex*   L 150 cm. Unmistakable. Habitat: large swamps with high papyrus or reeds. R

10   **HAMERKOP** *Scopus umbretta*   L 55 cm. Builds very large nests, which are however often taken over by owls, kestrels, geese, ducks, pigeons, monitor lizards or snakes. Habitat: muddy margins of lakes, rivers, streams, dams, ponds and creeks.

11   **GREATER FLAMINGO** *Phoenicopterus ruber*   L 140 cm. Larger and paler than 12 with pink (not dark red) bill and in flight with more extensively pink upperwing and pinker underwing. Habitat: shallow lakes, salt pans, estuaries, lagoons.

12   **LESSER FLAMINGO** *Phoeniconaias minor*   L 100 cm. Dark bill diagnostic. In flight with triangular pink patch on upperwing. Habitat: larger inland lakes. Also in estuaries, lagoons. AM.(RES).R

1

2   imm

imm

a   3   b   6

4   n-br   7

8

5   11

9   10   12

Plate 10

1   **BEAN GOOSE** *Anser fabalis*   L 75 cm. Note rather dark head, directly connected with orange-and-black bill and absence of belly barring. (Habitat): only known from the Niger Delta. V

2   **GREATER WHITE-FRONTED GOOSE** *Anser albifrons*   L 70 cm. From 1 by belly barring. Note pink bill, separated (but only in ad) by white ring from rather dark head. Habitat: normally in delta wetlands. V

3   **BRENT GOOSE** *Branta bernicla*   L 55 cm. Blackish appearance with paler belly and white undertail coverts diagnostic. Note white barring to back and wings of imm shown in flight. Habitat: normally sleeps at sea, from where it flies inland to graze. V

4   **SPUR-WINGED GOOSE** *Plectropterus gambensis*   L 100 cm (♂), 75 cm (♀). Rests by day at large water bodies or in wetlands, grazes in grasslands and floodplains early morning, late evening and even at night. Habitat: large water bodies and wetlands. (AM)

5   **COMMON SHELDUCK** *Tadorna tadorna*   L 65 cm. Unmistakable. Habitat: could be seen in any type of wetlands. V

6   **RUDDY SHELDUCK** *Tadorna ferruginea*   L 65 cm. Black neck collar of ♂ (shown in flight) absent in n-br plumage. Habitat: dry areas with small water bodies or streams. V

7   **EGYPTIAN GOOSE** *Alopochen aegyptiacus*   L 70 cm. Always in pairs. Gregarious outside breeding season. The ♀♀ are smaller than ♂♂, otherwise similar. Habitat: rivers, streams, lakes, dams, ponds, normally not in saline waters. Voice: mallard-like husky scraped '*sruuuh sruuuh sruuuh*' of ♂ with '*kah-kah-kah-kah*' of ♀, uttered by both with extended neck.

8   **KNOB-BILLED DUCK (or Goose)** *Sarkidiornis melanotos*   L 75 cm (♂), 60 cm (♀). Unmistakable. The ♂♂ much larger than ♀♀. Note white rump patch of ♀ (as shown in flight) which is much darker in ♂. Habitat: wetlands, often near or surrounded by woodland. RES.AM

9   **LITTLE GREBE (or Dabchick)** *Tachybaptus ruficollis*   L 20 cm. Bill shape with yellowish spot at corner diagnostic. Underparts pale brown, not white as 10 and 11. No wing bar in flight. Habitat: quiet rivers, lakes, dams, pans, ponds, pools. Voice: very high fast whinnying trill. RES.(AM)

10   **GREAT CRESTED GREBE** *Podiceps cristatus*   L 50 cm. African race *infuscatus* (a, with none or hardly any difference between br and n-br plumage) and nominate (b, vagrant from North Africa and Europe) shown. Unmistakable. In flight white forewing connected via tertials with white secondaries. Habitat: larger cool inland water bodies. Voice: low and mid-high raucous growls and grunts, but normally rather quiet. R

11   **BLACK-NECKED GREBE** *Podiceps nigricollis*   L 30 cm. Note red eye. Habitat: lakes, dams, pans, swamp, ponds; can be found even at sea. Voice: very high chattering '*weet-weet-weereet*'. V

12   **RED-THROATED DIVER** *Gavia stellata*   L 60 cm. Note uptilted bill. From grebes by habitat and in flight by absence of white on wings. Habitat: at sea. V

13   **JACKASS PENGUIN** *Spheniscus demersus*   L 60 cm. Only African endemic penguin. Habitat: straggler from its breeding grounds (offshore islands near Namibia and SW South Africa). Voice: very much as braying of donkey. V

Plate 11

1 **AFRICAN BLACK DUCK** *Anas sparsa* L 55 cm. Evasive; swims between and under fringing vegetation. In pairs. Habitat: well-wooded streams with stony bottoms especially in mountainous areas, but at night moves often to large open waters. Voice: mid-high, loud, Mallard-like '*wrah-wrah-wrah*' by ♀. R

2 **EURASIAN WIGEON** *Anas penelope* L 50 cm. Note bill shape and bent neck of ♀ when comparing with other ducks. Habitat: shallow, sheltered, open (parts of) lakes and dams. Also in brackish and saline water. Voice: high, sweet, gliding-down, short whistle '*fiiuuuw*'. NM.R

3 **AMERICAN WIGEON** *Anas americana* L 50 cm. The ♀ (and n-br ♂) from ♀ 2 (and n-br ♂ 2) by slightly paler and greyer head, more rufous flanks and whiter armpits. Habitat: as 2, but prefers freshwater habitats. V

4 **GADWALL** *Anas strepera* L 55 cm. The ♂ is rather grey. Bill of n-br ♂ and ♀ more slender and darker than Mallard. Habitat: wetlands with some open water. Voice: as Mallard. NM.R

5 **HOTTENTOT TEAL** *Anas hottentota* L 35 cm. Note white cheek with dark smear and bluish (not red) bill. Habitat: shallow water with fringing, reedy vegetation, sewage ponds. Also on large open dams. Voice: very high, dry, chuckled '*kèhèhè-hèhèh*'. R

6 **RED-BILLED TEAL** *Anas erythrorhyncha* L 45 cm. Unmistakable. Habitat: open shallow fresh lakes, dams and inundations with submerged, floating and fringing vegetation. Voice: high, Mallard-like '*pjehpjeh-pjèèh-pjèèh*'.

7 **CAPE TEAL (or Cape Wigeon)** *Anas capensis* L 45 cm. Note pale head and red, black-based bill. Habitat: mainly brackish waters, sewage ponds, alkaline lakes. Voice: extremely high, smooth '*feeeweeet*' and Mallard-like '*wèèk-wèèk-wèèk--*'. (AM).RES.R

8 **YELLOW-BILLED DUCK** *Anas undulata* L 55 cm. Yellow bill very striking and diagnostic. Habitat: 1500 m. Lakes, dams, rivers, estuaries, pools and sewage ponds. Voice: as Mallard. (AM)

9 **MALLARD** *Anas platyrhynchos* L 60 cm. Most sightings supposed to be escapees, but an occasional vagrant from Europe might be possible. N-br ♂ (not shown) as ♀, but darker and plainer. Voice: well-known duck gaggling. (I).(NM).R

10 **GREEN-WINGED, (Common or European) TEAL** *Anas crecca* L 40 cm. Nominate (a) and vagrant race *carolensis* (b, with white stripe across breast and without white lines around cheek patch) shown. Note small size. The ♀ has hazel (not red) eye. Voice: very high, short, cricket-like '*crick crick*'. NM.R

11 **NORTHERN PINTAIL** *Anas acuta* L 50 (+10) cm. Note slim graceful profile. Rear end of ♀ and n-br ♂ is finely speckled contrasting with scalloped flanks. N-br ♂ from ♀ by more contrasting-patterned bill and in flight, by different upperwing colouring (similar to ♂ br plumage). Habitat: dams, ponds, estuaries, other fresh and brackish waters. Voice: very high liquid rattled '*krruh krruh-krruh*' and short whistled '*fiu-fiu-fiu*'. NM

12 **GARGANEY** *Anas querquedula* L 40 cm. Note small size and graceful profile. N-br ♂ as ♀, but with face pattern less well defined and upperwing pattern as in br plumage. The ♀ has pale streak above and below eye. Habitat: mainly sheltered, shallow parts of freshwater lakes, dams, estuaries. Voice: low dry wooden short rattled '*crrrruh*' of ♂ and mid-high loud hoarse cackling of ♀.

13 **BLUE-WINGED TEAL** *Anas discors* L 40 cm. White crescent-shaped mark in front of eye diagnostic (♂). Head of ♀ rather plain, not so contrasting as ♀ 12. Forewing of both ♂ and ♀ bluer than 12, secondaries without white trailing edge. Habitat: vagrant from America, where frequent in shallow marshes and mud flats. V

14 **CAPE SHOVELER** *Anas smithii* L 50 cm. The ♂ has a yellow eye, the ♀ (only shown in flight) a black eye. From ♀ 15 (and n-br ♂ 15) by all-black bill. Habitat: inundations, sewage ponds and other (often alkaline) water bodies. Voice: Mallard-like '*wèèk-wuhwuhwuh*'. V

15 **NORTHERN SHOVELER** *Anas clypeata* L 55 cm. The ♂ shows only in br plumage a black bill as shown. Larger-billed than 14. N-br ♂ as ♀ (including bill colour), but with yellow eyes. Habitat: shallow fresh lakes, pools, inundations, marshes. Voice: mid-high, rattling '*raptaptap*' and low '*ko-krop-kok-kerop*'. NM

Plate 12

1   **WHITE-FACED WHISTLING (or Tree) DUCK** *Dendrocygna viduata*   L 50 cm. Erect stance combined with white face diagnostic. Highly gregarious. Habitat: large rivers, lakes, sewage ponds, dams with some floating vegetation. Also in swampy areas. Voice: extremely high, lashing, rapid, fluted '*weehweeh-weeh*'. RES.AM

2   **FULVOUS WHISTLING (or Tree) DUCK** *Dendrocygna bicolor*   L 45 cm. Note erect stance and white uppertail coverts. Pairs or small flocks. Habitat: large rivers, lakes, dams, inundations, other waterbodies with some floating vegetation. Voice: not very vocal, high '*tuwée*' ('*tu-*' separated from or as an undertone to '*-wée*'). RES.(AM)

3   **BLACK-BELLIED WHISTLING (or Tree) DUCK** *Dendrocygna autumnalis*   L 50 cm. Only shown in flight. From 1 and 2 by upperwing pattern; note also red bill and legs. (Cape Verde; no map). V (from America).

4   **WHITE-BACKED DUCK** *Thalassornis leuconotus*   L 40 cm. Note white spot at bill base. White back and rump only visible in flight. Habitat: secluded parts of lakes, dams, pools with some floating and fringing vegetation. Voice: extremely high '*witleeet*' or drawn-out '*ooowouw*'.

5   **AFRICAN PYGMY GOOSE** *Nettapus auritus*   L 30 cm. Unmistakable. In flight (not shown) with white secondaries. Habitat: quiet clear waters with some floating and emergent vegetation. Voice: very high, fluted, short '*feewée-feewée-tutukwéet*' or rapid, liquid '*ripripripripri*'.

6   **MARBLED TEAL** *Marmaronetta angustirostris*   L 40 cm. Very pale appearance with dark eye patch diagnostic. In flight upperwings are all-grey. Habitat: shallow freshwater and brackish lakes with fringing and emergent vegetation. NM.R

7   **BLACK SCOTER** *Melanitta nigra*   L50 cm. Note pale cheeks of ♀, visible at long range. Habitat: normally in coastal waters. Voice: (heard at night from passing migrants overhead) high, short, fluting whistles '*peeuw peeuw - - *'. NM.R

8   **SOUTHERN POCHARD** *Netta erythrophthalma*   L 50 cm. The ♂ differs from ♀ 10 by dark belly and red eye, ♀ by pale crescent on face sides. Habitat: clear deep lakes with reedy margins. Voice: high soft fluted '*rrrhew rrrhew rrrhew*' of ♂ and mid-high raucous '*rrah rrah*' of ♀.

9   **COMMON POCHARD** *Aythya ferina*   L 50 cm. The ♀ lacks clear white markings on head and undertail. Habitat: lakes, dams and open water in marshes. Voice: as Mallard but more growling '*graaa graaa graaa*'. Also a very high, liquid squeaking. Note: it is possible, that the Red-crested Pochard *Netta rufina* turns up in western Mauritania or Senegambia. Differs from 9 by larger head and red bill, brown back and white flanks. NM.R

10   **FERRUGINOUS DUCK** *Aythya nyroca*   L 40 cm. Note white undertail coverts and –in flight- isolated white belly patch; ♀ (with black eye!) is less brilliant chestnut. Habitat: lakes, often between floating vegetation. Voice: Mallard-like, but more rolling. NM.R

11   **LESSER SCAUP** *Aythya affinis*   L 40 cm. Note grey back of ♂ and absence of crest. The ♀ from ♀ 12 by (larger) white bill base. (Cape Verde; no map). V (from America).

12   **TUFTED DUCK** *Aythya fuligula*   L 45 cm. Mixed flocks of white-bellied ♂♂ and dark ♀♀ makes confusion with 8 improbable. The ♀ from ♀ 9 by all-black undertail coverts. Habitat: open water of deep lakes, dams, rivers. Voice: very short, compressed, melodious shiver '*wfirr*'. NM.R

13   **MACCOA DUCK** *Oxyura maccoa*   L 50 cm. Note uniform dark-brown wings and shape and stance of tail. The ♀ has pale horizontal lines below eye. N-br ♂ (not shown) as ♀. Habitat: fresh (sometimes alkaline), shallow lakes with emergent vegetation. Voice: very low, dry, drawn-out, rattling '*purrrrrrr*'.

14   **HARTLAUB'S DUCK** *Pteronetta hartlaubii*   L 50 cm. From most other ducks by habitat. Blue forewing diagnostic. Birds in the D. R. of Congo may have extensive white to head (a). Habitat: well-wooded streams especially in forests. Voice: very low soft raucous muttered '*rra-rra-rra-rra--*'.

Plate 13

1   **BAT HAWK** *Macheiramphus alcinus*   L 45 cm. Note striking large, yellow eyes. Hunts small bats and other prey at dusk in open spaces among trees or buildings or at cave mouths. Perches in daytime quietly in well-foliaged trees. Habitat: forest edges, woodland, lakesides, seashores, towns. Voice: very high sharp fluted '*wiiiu-wiiiu-wiiiu-wiiiu*' slightly rising in pitch and volume. Also high '*wikkeh-wikkeh-wikkeh-wikke-wik-wik*'.

2   **HONEY BUZZARD** *Pernis apivorus*   L 55 cm. From most raptors by lack of dark eyebrow (or overshadowing ridge) which gives this species a rather pigeon-like expression. In flight normally with closed tail. The ♀ in flight from ♂ by darker undersecondaries (compared with primaries) and less well defined black wing tip feathers. Many colour forms exist of which normal (a) and dark (b) examples shown. Resembles in flight many other raptors, especially some buzzard species, but note the smallish protruding head and the tail pattern in which one bar seems missing (not so in imm). Imm (not shown perched) has yellow cere, dark eye and different tail pattern. Habitat: forest edges, open woodland. Voice: very high sharp '*fiéeeeh*'. NM

3   **BLACK-SHOULDERED KITE** *Elanus caeruleus*   L 35 cm. Note conspicuous black shoulder patch. Hovers frequently, but perches also on posts, power lines and dead branches. Habitat: open wooded and bushed areas, cultivation, plantations, suburbs. Voice: rather silent. RES.(AM)

4   **AFRICAN SWALLOW- (or Scissor-)TAILED KITE** *Chelictinia rioccourii*   L 30 cm. Unmistakable. Imm from imm 3 by absence of blackish shoulder. Habitat: semi-desert and open or bushed and wooded habitats with some grass cover. AM

5a **YELLOW-BILLED KITE** *Milvus migrans parasitus*   L 55 cm. From 5b by yellow bill (ad only) and darker head. Manoeuvres dextrously with strongly bent wings and constantly twisting tail. Habitat: roadsides, suburban gardens, refuse sites. Voice: very high, quavering '*pih-urrrrrr*' slightly higher than 5b. (Race of 5b). RES.(AM)

5b **BLACK KITE** *Milvus m. migrans*   L 55 cm. Black bill and pale head of ad diagnostic. Habitat: as 5a. Voice: very high, quavering, slow, trilled '*pihurrrrrr*' ('*pih-*' lashing short). NM

6   **RED KITE** *Milvus milvus*   L 55 cm. Nominate (a) shown and race *fasciicauda* (b, with less red, undeep forked tail; from Cape Verde). Nominate is deeply forked; both show large white patches at carpal joints on underwing. Habitat: open woodland. Voice: much less vocal than 5a and 5b: high, miaowing '*pieeeooh peeeoh*'. R.V

Plate 14

1 **AFRICAN FISH EAGLE (or West African River Eagle)** *Haliaeetus vocifer* L 65 cm. Unmistakable. Habitat: large lakes, rivers, inundations, estuaries, seashore. Voice: free, triumphant, Herring Gull-like '*wááák wááa wáaa kaa-ka-ka*', given from tree top or in soaring flight, often in an unsynchronised duet of ♂ and ♀.

2 **VULTURINE FISH EAGLE (or Palm-Nut Vulture)** *Gypohierax angolensis* L 60 cm. Note pink bare skin around eye. Imm has rounded tail (not wedged as 6) and pale band along wing coverts. Habitat: open forest (and plantations) with oil palms (the fruits of which it eats). Voice: very high, drawn-out, whistled '*feeeeeh*', often rising in pitch.

3 **OSPREY** *Pandion haliaetus* L 55 cm. Note in flight wings characteristically bent at wrist. Ad from most other raptors by (long) eye stripe. Imm (not shown) from ad by paler eye stripe and more striped head and underparts, from imm 1 by pale eye and longer tail. NM.(RES)

4 **LAMMERGEIER** *Gypaetus barbatus* L 110 cm. Very large with long narrow wings and wedge-shaped tail. Habitat: cliffs, gorges and adjacent country. R

5 **HOODED VULTURE** *Necrosyrtes monachus* L 70 cm. Note thin bill and dark underparts. Imm has dark down (no feathers) on head and neck. Habitat: any habitat, including at urbane refuse sites.

6 **EGYPTIAN VULTURE** *Neophron percnopterus* L 65 cm. Note all-white (ad), wedge-shaped tail. Imm from 5 and from 15.5 by longer feathers of crown and nape. Note: ad and imm show some resemblance to 2. Habitat: arid or dry, open and wooded country near cliffs. Often near cattle enclosures. Also in towns and villages.

Plate 15

1   **EUROPEAN GRIFFON** *Gyps fulvus*   L 100 cm. From 2 by pale (not black) bill and from 3 also by much paler and buff colouring of both ad and imm (however this not very visible in flight). Unlikely to occur south of the Equator. Note differences in colouring and patterning of underwing coverts between 1, 2 and 3. Habitat: high cliffs and surrounding country. NM.R

2   **CAPE VULTURE** *Gyps coprotheres*   L 115 cm. Note very large size and pale brown appearance. Ad from 3 by pale eyes, pale blue bare skin, dark centres of first row of upperwing coverts. Imm shows pink (not brownish) bare neck. Unlikely to occur north of the Equator. Habitat: cliffs in otherwise flat country. V

3   **AFRICAN WHITE-BACKED VULTURE** *Gyps africanus*   L 95 cm. From 1 by white underwing coverts and from 2 by darker, greyish-brown (not tawny-brown) colouring and blackish bare skin. First row of upperwing coverts is only narrowly edged pale. White rump patch in flight diagnostic. Imm in flight very similar to imm 4, which has slightly more tapered wings and reddish, not greyish bare skin. See also imm 14.6. Habitat: open bushed and wooded habitats.

4   **RUEPPELL'S GRIFFON** *Gyps rueppellii*   L 90 cm. Overall scaly appearance, also visible in flight on underwing coverts, diagnostic. Imm not safely separable from other imm griffons; in mixed groups from imm 1 and 3 by darker down on neck and slightly paler bill. Imm 2 has more distinct reddish neck. Habitat: open, bushed and wooded habitats. Generally in more arid areas than 3.

5   **WHITE-HEADED VULTURE** *Aegypius occipitalis*   L 80 cm. Solitary. The ♂ has all flight feathers dark brown (as shown in flight). From 6 by much smaller size and by pink bill and legs. Habitat: dry open and sparsely wooded grasslands.

6   **LAPPET-FACED VULTURE** *Aegypius tracheliotus*   L 100 cm. Note black feather garlands on breast. Large size and aggressive, dominant behaviour at carcasses make it unmistakable. Imm (only shown in flight) has dark trousers. Habitat: dry, scrubby and lightly wooded plains.

Plate 16

1 CONGO SERPENT EAGLE *Dryotriorchis spectabilis* L 60 cm. Nominate (a) shown and race *batesi* (b, spots restricted to flanks). Note long tail, short wings, black throat stripe, very large eyes. Habitat: mid- and ground strata of dense forest.

2 BATELEUR *Terathopius ecaudatus* L 55 cm. Note unique flight silhouette with very short tail. Habitat: soars over dry plains and bushed and wooded country.

3 BROWN SNAKE EAGLE *Circaetus cinereus* L 70 cm. Note large size, broad face with large yellow eyes and erect stance on top of tree or post. Like all snake eagles in flight with broad wings, sharply bent at wrists. Habitat: dense thornbush and woodland with some large trees. Voice: very high sharp piercing yelps *'tjark tjark tjark'*. Note: snake eagles are often called harrier-eagles in other guides. RES.(AM)

4 SMALLER (or Western) BANDED SNAKE EAGLE *Circaetus cinerascens* L 55 cm. Tail pattern diagnostic. Barring on underparts not very pronounced. Cere and gape yellow. Normally perches in (not on) dead or poor-leafed trees. Habitat: riverine belts and forests patches in open country. Voice: mid-high, toy trumpet-like *'uh kruruh'*, high descending *'ko-ko-ko-ko-ko-koh'*.

5a BEAUDOUIN'S SNAKE EAGLE *Circaetus gallicus beaudouini* L 65 cm. Very similar to 5b but note the narrow, dense barring below and more distinct barring of tail and flight feathers. Imm is paler (with almost white head) than imm 5b (from which otherwise very difficult to separate) and 5c. Habitat: prefers more wooded habitats than 5b and 5c. Note: 5a, 5b and 5c differ from 4 by grey cere and pale legs. (AM)

5b EUROPEAN (or Short-toed) SNAKE EAGLE *Circaetus g. gallicus* L 65 cm. From 5a by irregularly barred, almost blotched underparts. Imm from imm 5a by more barred underparts and less defined tail bars. Habitat: dry, stony and lightly wooded plains and hillsides, often near water. Voice: very high or low, short, almost human whistles *'fiu fiu fiu'*. NM

5c BLACK-BREASTED SNAKE EAGLE *Circaetus gallicus pectoralis* L 65 cm. Perches conspicuously. May hover. Habitat: dry, stony, lightly wooded plains and hillsides often near water. Voice: high (or low), sometimes accelerated, whistled *'fiuu fiuu fiuu - '*. (AM)

Plate 17

1   **NORTHERN (or Hen) HARRIER** *Circus cyaneus*   L 45 cm. Less slender than 2 and 3. The ♂ from 2 by better defined separation of grey chest from whitish belly and in flight by more extensively black primaries especially seen from above; from ♂♂ 2 and 3 by more obvious white rump patch. The ♀ very much like 2 and 3, but bulkier, broader-winged, more heavily striped below and with less obvious white lower eyelids. In flight shows 5 (not 4) projecting primaries, giving more rounded wing tip impression. Imm striped on pale rufous underlay below. Habitat: dry open natural and cultivated plains. NM

2   **PALLID HARRIER** *Circus macrourus*   L 40 cm. Note upright stance and long legs. Wing tip falls short of tail tip when perched. Imm from imm 3 by more pronounced facial disc separated by whitish line from more extensively dark-brown neck. Habitat: as 3, but occasionally in more wet areas. NM

3   **MONTAGU'S HARRIER** *Circus pygargus*   L 50 cm. Wingtip reaches tail tip when perched. From 2 by shorter legs, greyer plumage, more black in wings (including a wing bar), some chestnut streaking on underparts and underwings. The ♀ from ♀ 2 by paler facial disc, which is not separated by white line from streaks on sides of neck. The ♀ has also paler secondaries below than ♀ 2, while neatly arranged barring on underwing coverts is more chestnut. Habitat: dry open natural and cultivated plains even at high altitudes. NM

4   **MARSH HARRIER** *Circus aeruginosus*   L 50 cm. Note unbarred tail and flight feathers. Pale heads of ♂, ♀ and imm sharply demarcated from rest of body. The ♂ has grey wings and tail, ♀ and imm show dark underwing. Imm from ♀ by dark eye and absence of pale breast band. Habitat: marshes, reed beds, tall grass. NM

5   **AFRICAN MARSH HARRIER** *Circus ranivorus*   L 45 cm. Ad from 4 by less pale head and barred flight feathers and tail. Note pale breast band of imm. Habitat: larger swamps; also in grass- and farmland.

Plate 18

Upper- and underside of 3 and 4a shown in flight.

1 **AFRICAN CUCKOO FALCON (or Hawk)** *Aviceda cuculoides* L 40 cm. Note crest both of ad and imm. Perches conspicuously and flies from tree to tree in light, kite-like fashion. Habitat: forest edges, woodland, riverine belts, cultivations, Voice: very high, gliding-down '*píeuuh*' and staccato '*pi-pi-peh-*' with '*fieuuh*' from a pair. RES.(AM)

2 **GRASSHOPPER BUZZARD** *Butastur rufipennis* L 35 cm (♂), 40 cm (♀). Rather pot-bellied. Red wings, normally also visible when perched, diagnostic. Habitat: more or less wooded areas. AM

3 **LIZARD BUZZARD** *Kaupifalco monogrammicus* L 35 cm. Heavy-headed jizz. Note black streak down throat centre, white uppertail coverts and black tail with normally one white bar as shown in flying birds or two as in perched birds. Normally perches in exposed position. Habitat: forest edges, woodland, thornbush, cultivated areas, farmland. Voice: very high, liquid '*weee-weee-weee-weee-weee*' in display flight.

4 **GABAR GOSHAWK** *Micronisus gabar* L 30 cm. Rather thickset. Normal (a) and dark (b) forms shown. Note dark eye, pale grey breast, white rump and white edge to secondaries and tail sides. Dark form from dark 19.2 by absence of white streaks on tail shafts and by showing some barring on flight feathers. Imm shows pale eyes. Hunts from cover. Habitat: woodland, open thornbush and scrub, suburban gardens, villages.

5 **DARK CHANTING GOSHAWK** *Melierax metabates* L 50 cm. Note erect stance on top of bush or low tree. Fine barring makes rump in flight look grey. Habitat: open thornbush and woodland. Voice: high, loud, fluted '*wiooh wiooh wiooh wiooh -*' (each '*wiooh*' sharply descending).

6 **AFRICAN HARRIER HAWK (or Gymnogene)** *Polyboroides typus* L 60 cm. Raids on weaver nests and extracts nestlings from tree holes with special adapted, very flexible legs. Habitat: forest edges, moist wooded areas, suburbs. Voice: very high, plaintive '*phuweeee*'.

Plate 19

Upper- and underside of 1, 2 and 3 shown in flight.

1   **LONG-TAILED HAWK** *Urotriorchis macrourus*   L 60 cm. Unmistakable, when properly seen in its normal, densely foliaged habitat. Habitat: forest canopies.

2   **OVAMBO SPARROWHAWK** *Accipiter ovampensis*   L 30 cm (♂), 35 cm (♀). Note small head and dark-eyed appearance. Legs, cere and eyelids maybe red, pink or yellow (form with red bare parts shown). Throat indistinctly barred grey. Small white streaks on tail shafts diagnostic even for rare black form (a). Normal (b) and rufous (c) imm forms shown, both with brown, almost black eyes. Hunts from cover or from exposed perch. Habitat: open woodland, thornbush, eucalyptus and other exotic plantations. AM.RES

3   **RUFOUS-CHESTED SPARROWHAWK** *Accipiter rufiventris*   L 30 cm (♂), 35 cm (♀). Rufous underparts and brown upperparts diagnostic. Imm has irregular streaked (not barred) underparts. Secretive. Habitat: forests, woodland, plantations including surrounding open country. R

4   **AFRICAN GOSHAWK** *Accipiter tachiro* (toussenelii group)   L 35 cm (♂), 45 cm (♀). Plumage, especially of ♀, often more brown than grey. Note white barring (brown as for ♀) of tail. Black form (a) from 5b by more brownish plumage and grey barred tail. Imm is heavily blotched and barred below. Skulking. Habitat: in and near forests, dense thornbush and other woodland, riverine belts, suburban gardens. Voice: high sharp '*whip*' in flight or from perch. Rather vocal.

5   **BLACK (or Great) SPARROWHAWK** *Accipiter melanoleucus*   L 45 cm (♂), 55 cm (♀). Normal (a) and dark (b, only occurring in the Congo's) forms may be paired. Imm ♂♂ are probably rufous (c) below, imm ♀♀ white (d). Adults from 24.3 (and 24.6) by dark eye, unfeathered lower legs and absence of crest. May soar, but in general is rather secretive, though not shy. Habitat: forests, woodland, exotic plantations, suburbs.

Plate 20

Upper- and underside of 1, 3, 4, 5 and 6 shown in flight

1 **CHESTNUT-FLANKED SPARROWHAWK (or Goshawk)** *Accipiter castanilius* L 30 cm (♂), 35 cm (♀). Note white spots to tail, not to rump. Rather like African Goshawk (19.4) but flanks unbarred chestnut and underwing barred black-on-white. Also resembles Rufous-chested Sparrowhawk (19.3), but that species is without bars below, has white eyebrows, but no white on tail. Habitat: dense forests. R

2 **LEVANT SPARROWHAWK** *Accipiter brevipes* L 35 cm (♂), 40 cm (♀). Note dark, almost black wing tips. Very similar to Shikra (6, with similar dark eyes) but larger and paler. Compare also underwing coverts. Habitat: dry, wooded grass-and farmland. V

3 **RED-THIGHED (or Western Little) SPARROWHAWK** *Accipiter erythropus* L 25 cm (♂), 30 cm (♀). All-black above except conspicuous white rump. Yellow-eyed imm shows fine barring below. Habitat: dense forests.

4 **AFRICAN LITTLE SPARROWHAWK** *Accipiter minullus* L 25 cm (♂), 30 cm (♀). Less black above than 3 and finely barred, not uniform white and pink-rufous below. Imm has tail spots too, but less white on rump. Habitat: woodland and thornbush, less in forests than 3.

5 **EURASIAN SPARROWHAWK** *Accipiter nisus* L 30 cm (♂), 40 cm (♀). Note white eyebrow, yellow eye, barred underwing coverts and barred tail (without white) of ♂. The ♀ has white eyebrow and blacker (less chestnut-brown) barring of underparts than 2. Habitat: woodland and nearby open country. NM.R

6 **SHIKRA** *Accipiter badius* L 30 cm (♂), 35 cm (♀). Note red eyes with contrasting yellow cere and legs. Central tail feathers unbarred, in ♀ with darker tip. Imm is mainly barred on underparts. May perch exposed. Habitat: woodland and thornbush with tall-grassed parts.

Plate 21

1 **AUGUR BUZZARD** *Buteo augur* L 50 cm (♂), 55 cm (♀). Unmistakable. Melanistic form (not shown, all black except rufous tail) occasionally seen in NE parts of the D. R. of Congo. Imm's normally have irregular black markings to sides of face, throat, breast and flanks. Habitat: hilly open areas, woodland, cultivations, suburbs. Voice: in flight high '*kjow-kjow-kjow-kjow*'.

2 **MOUNTAIN BUZZARD** *Buteo oreophilus* L 40 cm (♂), 45 cm (♀). (Formerly known as Forest Buzzard *Buteo tachardus*). Rather small. Normally coloured brown without any rufous. Underparts spotted (not streaked, striped or barred). From 3 by indistinct terminal bar on underside of tail. Habitat: in and around mountain-forests. Voice: in flight high, short, slightly descending '*piuuh*'.

3 **COMMON BUZZARD** *Buteo buteo* L 45 cm (♂), 55 cm (♀). Race *vulpinus* (a, Steppe Buzzard with b, imm) shown, race *bannermanni* (c, from Cape Verde) and nominate (d, Common Buzzard, NM, vagrant south to Liberia, pale form). Very variable (except *bannermanni*, which is monotypic), different colour forms in flight shown. Only the rufous-tailed forms more or less safely attributable to Steppe Buzzard, but beware of the brown form (e, in flight) of this race which is not separable of the normal form of Common Buzzard (h, in flight). Steppe Buzzard (widespread) normally has a pale chestnut-brown tail with broad terminal bar and some faint barring. From 4 by less distinct pale panel on upperwing. Dark form (g) differs from dark form of 4 by size and different jizz (Long-legged Buzzard is large and heavy with smallish, rounded head). Note streaked (not barred) underparts of imm with narrowly barred tail (not with broad terminal bar). Common Buzzard (d) is rare and only seen in the most western parts of West Africa. Habitat: open natural and cultivated areas with at least a few lookout posts. Voice: in flight very high, sharp, rapidly descending, whistled '*níau*'. NM a,d.

4 **LONG-LEGGED BUZZARD** *Buteo rufinus* L 50 cm (♂), 65 cm (♀). Normal (a, variable) and very rare dark (b) forms shown. Note bulky, pale-headed appearance with unbarred cinnamon tail and (in flight) dark wrist patches on underwing. Ad from imm 3 by unstreaked underparts, which normally are more or less rufous. Tail of imm shows only narrow evenly spaced bars. Very pale panel on upperwings diagnostic, even in dark form (not shown). Habitat: semi-desert and other open areas. Voice: rather silent; rarely loud explosive descending '*íau*'. NM

5 **RED-NECKED (or –tailed) BUZZARD** *Buteo auguralis* L 40 cm (♂), 45 cm (♀). Note characteristic reddish glow. Imm is mainly brown with only one broad terminal tail bar. Habitat: forest edges, heavily wooded areas.

Plate 22

1   **GOLDEN EAGLE** *Aquila chrysaetos*   L 80 cm (♂), 90 cm (♀). Not unlike 2, but ad without white on mantle. Note the relative short secondaries in flight, giving a curved form to the trailing edge of the wings. Imm (1stW) very distinctive, overall dark with striking white basal half of flight and tail feathers; following year-stages with irregular, partly white flight feathers as shown. Habitat: dry, open and more or less wooded areas. Roosts on cliffs or trees. NM.R

2   **IMPERIAL EAGLE** *Aquila heliaca*   L 80 cm (♂), 85 cm (♀). Ad (darker than 1) soars with closed tail and with wings held flat (not raised in a slight V as 1). Underwing coverts and tail of juv even-coloured (without white, but with whitish edges). Imm from 3 (but not from 4) by almost uniform pale rump and uppertail coverts and darker, irregular patterned underwing coverts. Habitat: hilly, open, bushed and wooded country. Note: shown is nominate with only partly white scapulars. Race *adalberti* from Spain, with white extending along leading edge of wing (sometimes treated as an independent species) is unlikely to be seen. NM.V

3   **STEPPE EAGLE** *Aquila r. orientalis*   L 70 cm (♂), 85 cm (♀). Note gape extending just behind middle of eye and tawny nape. In flight faint barring of flight feathers and tail visible. Bases of primaries form paler panel on upperwing than those of 4. Imm (1stW) has diagnostic broad whitish edge to underwing coverts. This band disappears gradually in following years (see 3dW in flight). Note shaggy trousers of Steppe Eagle and next species, but normally is darker and larger than 4. Steppe Eagle perches more often on the ground than 4. Habitat: dry open bushed and wooded country. Note: there are two records of the race *nipalensis* in Senegal and one in the D. R. of Congo, which is even bigger than *r. orientalis*, but no useful field marks described. NM.R

4   **TAWNY EAGLE** *Aquila r. rapax*   L 65 cm (♂), 80 cm (♀). Several colour forms, of these dark (a) and pale (b) forms shown. Gape stops just under middle of eye. Imm from imm 3 by narrower pale-edged secondaries and wing coverts (also visible on perched birds). Note also the less obvious upperwing panels on soaring bird and (near-)absence of visible barring of flight feathers and tail. From spotted eagles (next plate) by oval (not round) nostrils. Habitat: as 3.

5   **WAHLBERG'S EAGLE** *Aquila wahlbergi*   L 55 cm (♂), 60 cm (♀). Many colour forms exist, of these most common a (perched), and b shown. From other eagles by much smaller size and better visible barring of flight feathers and tail. Note large black eyes, black lores and rather long tail. May show slight crest. Flies with closed tail, which – together with long straight wings – gives cross-form to flight silhouette. Imm (not shown) as ad but feather edges are paler and head and neck more streaked. Habitat: no preferred habitat, but not in true forest. AM

Plate 23

1 **LESSER SPOTTED EAGLE** *Aquila pomarina* L 60 cm (♂), 70 cm (♀). From 2 (perched and in flight) by less homogeneously coloured wings in which flight feathers are slightly darker then coverts. Ad (in flight) from ad 2 by contrasting white, narrow U-shaped patch on rump and more extensive white bases of flight feathers. Both ad and imm in flight from 2 by double white carpal crescents on underwing. From 22.3 and 22.4 also by tight trousers. Habitat: open woodland. NM.R

2 **GREATER SPOTTED EAGLE** *Aquila clanga* L 65 cm (♂), 75 cm (♀). Ad and imm very much like 1, but is (much) darker, heavier-bodied, larger- and broader-winged and normally with upper- and undercoverts darker than flight feathers (this feature reversed in 1). Imm from imm 1 by more (rows of) larger white wing spots. Adult from dark form of 22.4 by smaller size, purplish gloss to fresh plumage and on ground by longer narrower-trousered legs. Habitat: as 1. Note: there is a very rare form *fulvescens*, which is very similar to the pale form of 22.4, but with different jizz (smaller, neater, more slender bill). NM.V

3 **VERREAUX'S EAGLE** *Aquila verreauxii* L 75 cm (♂), 90 cm (♀). Note narrow-based rounded wing form in flight silhouette. Imm reaches full ad plumage after 5 years, in first stage starting to be black on face sides. Habitat: bushed and wooded mountain sides with cliffs and rocky ravines.

4 **MARTIAL EAGLE** *Polemaetus bellicosus* L 80 cm. Ad shows fine black spotting on underparts and has fully feathered legs. Imm (which differs from imm snake eagles by fully feathered legs) is very pale below with narrow barring of flight feathers and tail. Habitat: semi-desert, more or less wooded and bushed areas. Voice: in display flight very high '*fju-wírr*' and '*fwee-fwee-fwee-*'.

5 **CROWNED (Hawk) EAGLE** *Stephanoaetus coronatus* L 80 cm. Note orange gape, large yellow toes with enormous claws, short wings, long tail. Perched imm from imm 4 by whiter head, yellow mouth corner, different tail pattern and spotted leggings. Habitat: forest, wooded areas. Voice: very high excited '*puwéepuwéepuwée-*', undulating in pitch and volume, synchronised with up-and-down display flight.

Plate 24

1   **LONG-CRESTED (Hawk) EAGLE** *Lophaetus occipitalis*   L 50 cm (♂), 55 cm (♀). Unmistakable. Habitat: forest edges, swampy, bushed grassland, cultivation, suburban gardens. Voice: high drawn-out '*feeeeeh*'.

2   **BOOTED EAGLE** *Hieraaetus pennatus*   L 45 cm (♂), 55 cm (♀). Normal (a) and less common dark (b) forms shown. Note characteristic upper-wing and mantle pattern of perched and flying bird. When seen head-on in flight, shows white spots at base of wings ('head lights', but these also present on some other birds of prey like e.g. 6 or 13.2, honey buzzard). Habitat: forest, dry woodland, open or slightly bushed and wooded hilly country, desert. Normally at higher elevations. Voice: very high, staccato, sustained '*djip-djip-djip-djip- - -*'. NM.AM

3   **CASSIN'S HAWK EAGLE** *Spizaetus africanus*   L 55 cm (♂), 60 cm (♀). Note short-winged and long-tailed jizz. Sparsely spotted and streaked (mostly around legs). In flight shows clean white underparts, contrasting with dark underwing coverts. Imm is spotted, not streaked below. Ad from 19.5 by feathered lower legs. Rarely seen except soaring low over forest. Habitat: forest canopy.

4   **AFRICAN HAWK EAGLE** *Hieraaetus spilogaster*   L 65 cm (♂), 80 cm (♀). Note large size, feathered legs, rounded wings (in flight). Imm from imm 5 by (normally) paler underparts and darker upperparts; in flight however not safely separable, but 5 (as migrant) restricted to Mauritania. Perches in cover, but can be seen soaring freely, especially in morning. Habitat: open woodland, thornbush with some large trees often near streams and rocky hillsides. Voice: Fish Eagle-like, slightly rising '*kee-kee-kee-*' (6-7x). AM.RES

5   **BONELLI'S EAGLE** *Hieraaetus fasciatus*   L 70 cm (♂), 75 cm (♀). Ad shows diagnostic white patch on mantle and a black band of varying width on underwing. Juveniles almost entirely ginger-orange below with darker wing tips. In following stages this colour is gradually replaced by white and black until the ad stage (as shown) is reached. NM.R

6   **AYRES'S HAWK EAGLE** *Hieraaetus ayresii*   L 45 cm (♂), 55 cm (♀). White forehead of ad diagnostic, but small crest often hidden. Note heavily barred underwings and tail. In flight with white 'head lights' as 2. The very rare dark ♀ form (a) might have white eyebrows, often connected over bill. Often confused with 3, which hunts however from perch, while *hieraaetus* hawk eagles (4, 5 and 6) spend most of the time in soaring flight. Habitat: canopy of forest and woodland. Voice: very high pushed-out '*fuweéh fuweéh - *'. RES.AM.R

Plate 25

1 **PYGMY FALCON** *Polihierax semitorquatus* L 18 cm. Perches shrike-like on top of small tree or post. Habitat: more or less bushed areas and semi-desert.

2 **FOX KESTREL** *Falco alopex* L 40 cm. Underwing coverts very pale rufous with white, (dark-tipped) flight feathers, the whole underwing contrasting strongly with dark-red body. Habitat: mountains and semi-desert with rocky hills. RES.(AM)

3 **COMMON (or Rock) KESTREL** *Falco tinnunculus* L 35 cm. Migrant nominate shown (a, in northern winter period outnumbering local races. Also recorded from Sal, Cape Verde); also resident races *rufescens* (b, darker coloured, in most of Sub-Saharan Africa), *neglectus* (c, endemic in part of Cape Verde) and *alexandri* (d, also endemic on some of the islands of Cape Verde). The ♂ and ♀ of the races *neglectus* and *alexandri* are less different from each other than a and b, where the ♀♀ differ from ♂♂ by strongly barred tail, brown heads and subdued colouring. Not often seen hovering, the African breeze normally not being strong enough. Habitat: open or lightly wooded country often near cliffs or tall buildings. NM.RES

4 **LESSER KESTREL** *Falco naumanni* L 30 cm. Normally in flocks. Pale claws diagnostic. Often together with other falcons. From 2 (with which it occurs in mixed flocks) by wing tip reaching tail tip, when perched. The ♀ from ♀2 by slightly protruding central tail feathers. Habitat: open bushed and wooded areas, short grass- and farmland. Flocks may roost in towns. NM

5 **SOOTY FALCON** *Falco concolor* L 30 cm. Wing extends slightly beyond tail tip. Note white chin, black moustache, absence of barring on underwing. From 6 by longer wings, darker cheeks, indistinct striping. Very rare deep-black form not shown. Normally hunts small birds from perch at dusk. Habitat: mainly cliffs in deserts. R

6 **GREY KESTREL** *Falco ardosiaceus* L 30 cm. Note absence of moustachial stripe, faint barring of flight feathers below. Wing tip shorter than tail when perched. Hunts at dusk from perch or in low flight over ground. Habitat: more or less wooded grassland often near palms and water.

7 **DICKINSON'S KESTREL** *Falco dickinsoni* L 30 cm. Barred tail and white rump (not visible on plate) diagnostic. Head paler than breast and mantle. Hunts from perch. Habitat: open woodland, plantations, edges of flood plains. Often near palms. R

8 **RED-NECKED FALCON (or Kestrel)** *Falco chicquera* L 30 cm. Note reddish head and pale grey, finely barred upperparts. Tail of perched bird protrudes far beyond the wing tip. Flies (and hunts) in very swift flight without gliding. Habitat: open tall-grassed or swampy areas. Prefers places with *Borassus-palms* (a palm species with a characteristic swelling, concentrated halfway its height).

9 **AFRICAN HOBBY** *Falco cuvieri* L 30 cm. Note rufous underparts. Darker above than 10. Habitat: forest edges, open landscapes with scattered trees, densely populated rural areas. RES.(AM)

10 **(European) HOBBY** *Falco subbuteo* L 30 cm. Note slim build, rufous undertail coverts, streaked belly and underwing, short tail. Fast flier; may overtake swallows, but catches also flying termites, dragon flies and other insects. Habitat: forest edges, thornbush, more or less wooded natural and cultivated areas. NM

Plate 26

1   **EASTERN RED-FOOTED FALCON** *Falco amurensis*   L 30 cm. Perched ♂ is almost inseparable from ♂ 2, but is paler below, which makes black eye area more conspicuous. In flight white underwing coverts diagnostic. The ♀ resembles several other falcons, but note red legs and eye ring. Imm from imm 2 by slightly whiter underparts. Habitat: open country. V

2   **RED-FOOTED FALCON** *Falco vespertinus*   L 30 cm. All-black underwing of ♂ diagnostic. The ♀ resembles several other chestnut falcons but is much paler grey above and has red legs. Flight kestrel-like with much gliding, but hardly any hovering. Hunts in groups, catching mainly insects. Habitat: dry open areas, cultivated lands. NM

3   **ELEONORA'S FALCON** *Falco eleonorae*   L 35 cm. Blackish underwing diagnostic. Both normal (a) and dark form (b) appear dark, with long tail and exceptional long and narrow wings. Easy graceful flight with soft wing beats, alternated with smooth gliding. The ♀♀ of both forms (not shown) have bluish, not yellow ceres and eye ring. Imm from imm 25.9 by contrasting pale flight feathers below and denser breast striping (appearing as a dark breast band). Habitat: vagrant, normally only (occasionally) seen in eastern parts of Africa, when it migrates (probably at great heights) from Mediterranean breeding quarters to Madagascar. V

4   **MERLIN** *Falco columbarius*   L 25 cm. Often compared in size and flight characteristics with a large grey- (♂) or brown- (♀) backed thrush. In swift, direct flight smaller and more compact than kestrels. Habitat: any open country with plenty of small birds (its prey). V

5   **BARBARY FALCON** *Falco pelegrinoides*   L 35 cm (♂), 55 cm (♀). Note rufous on nape and sides of face (but less so than 7) and general pale appearance. Habitat: desert and semi-desert. V

6   **PEREGRINE FALCON** *Falco peregrinus*   L 35 cm. Migrant nominate shown (a, NM without any trace of rufous and more grey than black above); also the races *minor* (b, RES throughout, small-sized with black cheek and heavy barring below), *brookei* (c, often with traces of rufous to crown and with pinkish wash below) and *madens* (d, with irregular rufous-brown colour, from Cape Verde). Race *calidus* (rare winter visitor, not shown) is larger, paler grey above and whiter below with scarcer barring and spotting. Note compact build, short wings and tail when perched, pointed wings in flight. Imm's of race b have yellowish-green bare parts, unlike imm's of other races, which have these parts bluish. Flight with rather fluttering wing beats but extremely fast in attack and pursuit. Habitat: open country, sea coast, city centres. Often near cliffs or high buildings. RES b,d. NM aR. Vc

7   **LANNER FALCON** *Falco biarmicus*   L 40 cm. More frequent than 6. The ♀♀ are larger, browner above and more spotted below than ♂♂. Chestnut crown and nape of ad ♂ (whitish on imm) diagnostic. In flight rather pale with diagnostic narrow blackish bar on underwing. Habitat: open country often near cliffs and buildings. May enter cities.

8   **SAKER** *Falco cherrug*   L 45 cm (♂), 60 cm (♀). Note pale (not buff-rufous) crown. From 7 by larger size, browner overall colouring, paler head, with only trace of moustachial streak and with spotted (not barred) tail. Mainly dark legs and wide blackish bar on underwing diagnostic. Habitat: marshes and lake margins with nearby trees. V

Plate 27

1 **WHITE-BREASTED GUINEAFOWL** *Agelastes meleagrides*   L 40 cm. White collar diagnostic. Imm (not shown) darkish brown with sharply demarcated white belly and undertail coverts. Habitat: forest undergrowth. R

2 **BLACK GUINEAFOWL** *Agelastes niger*   L 40 cm. From 3, 4 and 5 by lack of white spots. Habitat: dense forest. R

3 **PLUMED GUINEAFOWL** *Guttera plumifera*   L 45 cm. Nominate (a) and race *schubotzi* (b, with pink cheek) shown. Often difficult to separate from 4, but with longer erect crest and grey (not bluish-purple) naked skin. Range overlaps only in the Congo's with range of 4. Habitat: dense forest. R

4 **CRESTED GUINEAFOWL** *Guttera pucherani*   L 50 cm. See 3. Habitat: dense undergrowth of forest and woodland. Voice: low, speeded-up cackles and rattles like '*tetrut-tetrut-trrrueh*'.

5 **(Grey-breasted) HELMETED GUINEAFOWL** *Numida meleagris*   L 55 cm. Several races occur, of these *galeata* (a, with purple upperbreast and mainly bluish-white naked parts of head) and *marungensis* (b) shown. Only guineafowl outside forest. Habitat: dry natural and cultivated areas with more or less tree cover, shrub and bush. Voice: high fluted '*puweeet puweeet puweeet*' ('*pu-*' barely audible). Note: wiped out in Nigeria and Liberia.

6 **CONGO PEACOCK** *Afropavo congensis*   L 65 cm. Unmistakable. Habitat: undergrowth of tall forest. E, D. R. of Congo

7 **STONE PARTRIDGE** *Ptilopachus petrosus*   L 25 cm. Note bantam-like posture. Habitat: rocky hillsides with dense scrub, tall grass cover and more or less bush.

8 **BARBARY PARTRIDGE** *Alectoris barbara*   L 35 cm. Unmistakable. Note flank pattern. Habitat: dry, grassy and scrubby areas to bare semi-desert. R

9 **LATHAM'S FOREST FRANCOLIN** *Francolinus lathami*   L 20 cm. From 10 by head pattern and buff underparts. Habitat: dense forests.

10 **NAHAN'S FRANCOLIN** *Francolinus nahani*   L 20 cm. From 9 also by red (not yellow) legs. Habitat: dense forests. R

11 **CRESTED FRANCOLIN** *Francolinus sephaena*   L 35 cm. Note prominent white eyebrow, red legs and, in flight, black tail. Habitat: dry bushed and shrubbed areas with some grass cover. Voice: mid-high loud scraping '*kurrk-krí-kurrk-krí*' (higher '*krí*' of ♂ in duet with ♀). R

12 **SCALY FRANCOLIN** *Francolinus squamatus*   L 30 cm. Note red legs and bill and uniform overall colouring. Habitat: tall grassy glades and forest edges. Voice: very high, hoarse, running-up '*skreetch-uh-skreetch-uh-skreetch-*'.

13 **RING-NECKED FRANCOLIN** *Francolinus streptophorus*   L 25 cm. Note yellow legs, white chin and white-and-black barred collar and breast. Habitat: grassy, sparsely bushed and wooded, rocky hillsides. R

Plate 28

1   **RED-NECKED FRANCOLIN** *Francolinus afer*   L 35 cm. Races *cranchii* (a), *harterti* (b) and *melanogaster* (c) shown. Red legs and bare head parts diagnostic. Habitat: forest patches, other bushed and wooded natural and cultivated areas with long grass. Voice: mid-high, indignant, hurried, descending '*kúkukruk-kúkukruk-kúkukruk*' or '*corrúpt-corrúpt-corrúpt*'.

2   **HANDSOME FRANCOLIN** *Francolinus nobilis*   L 35 cm. From 27.12 in same range by red bare eye ring and rather rufous overall feathering. Habitat: montane forest with dense undergrowth, bamboo, giant heath and moorland.

3   **CAMEROON MOUNTAIN FRANCOLIN** *Francolinus camerunensis*   L 35 cm. As 1 (except naked throat) but with different range and different habitat. Habitat: dense forest undergrowth. E, Cameroon.

4   **AHANTA FRANCOLIN** *Francolinus ahantensis*   L 35 cm. Rather unmarked appearance, striped white on dull brown with orangish bill and legs. Habitat: forest edge and other dense growth.

5   **DOUBLE-SPURRED FRANCOLIN** *Francolinus bicalcaratus*   L 30 cm. Note prominent white eyebrow. From 6 by absence of bare skin around eye and greenish (not orange) bill and legs. The ♀ (without) spurs shown. Habitat: any type of grassland, farmland, woodland, but not in forest.

6   **HEUGLIN'S FRANCOLIN** *Francolinus icterorhynchus*   L 30 cm. Note yellowish bare skin behind eye, orange bill and unmarked belly-centre. Habitat: open and bushed grass- and farmland.

7   **HILDEBRANDT'S FRANCOLIN** *Francolinus hildebrandti*   L 35 cm. Note scaly underparts of ♂, rufous underparts of ♀ and red legs of both. Habitat: rocky hillsides with rough grass and patches of dense scrub. R

8   **CLAPPERTON'S FRANCOLIN** *Francolinus clappertoni*   L 35 cm. Note bare red eye area, rufous crown and nape, scaly mantle and wings and (in flight) pale buff wing-patch. From 1 by absence of naked red throat. Habitat: rocky hillsides and dry, lightly wooded and bushed habitats.

9   **SHELLEY'S FRANCOLIN** *Francolinus shelleyi*   L 35 cm. From 10 by all-buff chin and throat and greyer underparts. As 10 and 11 with much rufous in opened wing. Habitat: stony more or less wooded and bushed habitats, often with rocky outcrops. Voice: very high sharp fluting '*wukwuk-weekweek-wukwuk-weekweek--*' ('*weekweek*' higher in pitch). R

10   **REDWING FRANCOLIN** *Francolinus levaillantii*   L 40 cm. Note throat pattern. From 9 by more rufous (not pale brown-buff) overall colouring. Habitat: stony sloping grass- and farmland, woodland with scrub, tall grass and reedy spots. Voice: very high sharp '*tikitiktiktik-let's-GO-then*'.

11   **FINSCH'S FRANCOLIN** *Francolinus finschi*   L 35 cm. Only red-winged francolin without black head marking. Habitat: grassland near forest and woodland, at higher altitudes also on bare slopes. R

12   **WHITE-THROATED FRANCOLIN** *Francolinus albogularis*   L 25 cm. Red wings as 9, 10 and 11 but with other jizz and smaller bill. Note whitish chin. Habitat: dry open areas with some grass cover often near forest and water.

13   **COQUI FRANCOLIN** *Francolinus coqui spinetorum*   L 25 cm. From 27.13 by absence of eye stripe, by blotched upperparts and paler underparts. Habitat: grassy, more or less wooded and bushed areas. Voice: very high sharp: '*keh-kwee-keh-kwee-keh-kwee-*' or very high '*keh-krih keh-ker-riiiii*'.

14   **SCHLEGEL'S FRANCOLIN** *Francolinus schlegelii*   L 25 cm. From 13 by different range, more extensive black barring below and darker, reddish upperparts. Habitat: wooded grasslands. R

Plate 29

1   **COMMON QUAIL** *Coturnix coturnix*   L 18 cm. Nominate (a) and redder race *erlangeri* (b) shown. The ♂ from ♀ 2 by long white streaks along flanks. Note pale wings in flight. Flight as all quails with rapid wing beats, interspersed with short glides. Habitat: dry areas with grass or crops of varied height. Voice: very high liquid staccato rapid '*get-me-then get-me-then*'. NM a.RES b

2   **HARLEQUIN QUAIL** *Coturnix delegorguei*   L 18 cm. The ♂ from 3 by white eyebrow. Note black streaks on back and head of ♀. Slightly gregarious. Habitat: lightly bushed grass- and farmland. Voice: very high, clicked, irregular '*witwit witwit-wit witwit witwit witwit-wit*'. AM?.RES

3   **(African) BLUE QUAIL** *Coturnix chinensis adansonii*   L 15 cm. The ♂ from other quails by red wings, ♀ from other ♀♀ quails by barred (not streaked) underparts. Not gregarious. Habitat: moist open grassland near swamps. Voice: mid-high, descending, hoarse '*wéhwehweh wéhwehweh -- *'. RES.(AM)

4   **LITTLE (African or Kurrichane) BUTTON-QUAIL** *Turnix sylvatica*   L 14 cm. From 5 by absence of black rump in flight. Habitat: tall grass- and farmland. Voice: strange, very low, hollow, slightly crescendoing '*woooooo wooooooooooh* '. RES.AM

5   **BLACK-RUMPED BUTTON-QUAIL** *Turnix hottentotta*   L 14 cm. From quails by more rufous plumage and creamy eye. Long buff streaks along scapulars diagnostic. Looks long-necked in flight and shows area of pale upperwing coverts. Habitat: short, partly bare grassland and floodplains. Voice: strange, very low, pumping, regular '*wuh-wuh-wuh-wuh--*'. RES.(AM)

6   **QUAIL-PLOVER** *Ortyxelos meiffrenii*   L 12 cm. Said to resemble a small courser (33.4-5) by its upright stance. In flight not unlike a large butterfly. Habitat: normally in dry habitats with some grass cover and more or less bush. RES.AM

7   **RED-CHESTED FLUFFTAIL** *Sarothrura rufa*   L 16 cm. See 9. The ♀ from ♀ 10 by being finely barred (not striped) below, from ♀ 9 by larger, bushier tail, from ♀♀ 8 and 11 by brown, not rufous-orange tail. Habitat: marshy reed beds and papyrus swamp, thick herbage and tall grass near rivers and pools. Voice: mid-high hooted '*hoo hoo hoo hoo -*' often in duet with very high contra-song '*piu piu piu -*' ('*hoo*' and '*piu*' alternating). Also a call resembling alarm cry of Black-tailed Godwit (35.3). Note: flufftails are called 'pigmy rails' in '*Serle*'.

8   **WHITE-SPOTTED FLUFFTAIL** *Sarothrura pulchra*   L 15 cm. Note pale eye of ♂ and ♀. Habitat: swampy forest and surrounding areas with tree cover. Voice: high, hurried, hooted '*poopoopoopoopoo*', mid-high, fluted, rapid, slightly speeded-up '*poo-poo-poo-poo-poo-*' and very fast, high '*tutitititi*'.

9   **BOEHM'S (or Streaky-breasted) FLUFFTAIL** *Sarothrura boehmi*   L 15 cm. The ♂ from 7 by whitish chin and belly. The ♂ and ♀ have very short tail and pale lower mandible. Habitat: short wet grassland, inundations and river margins. Voice: mid-high level rhythmic hooted '*hooh hooh hooh-*', also with shorter intervals and '*uhooh-uhooh-uhooh-*' ('*u-*' as very low undertone). R

10   **CHESTNUT-HEADED FLUFFTAIL** *Sarothrura lugens*   L 15 cm. Black-tailed ♂ from 7 and 9 by absence of rufous on throat, ♀ from other ♀♀ flufftails by streaked (not barred or blotched) plumage. Habitat: tall wet grassland near marshes, woodland or forest. Voice: long sequence of slowly speeded-up '*oohoohooh-*' slightly rising in pitch and volume and trailing off at the end. Also mid-high '*ooeh ooeh ooeh -*' (2 x '*ooeh*' per 3 sec). R

11   **BUFF-SPOTTED FLUFFTAIL** *Sarothrura elegans*   L 16 cm. From 8 by barred tail. The ♀ lacks clear diagnostic features. Habitat: forest, bamboo, dense bush, cultivation, gardens with undercover. Voice: low, hollow, level, crescendoing '*hooooooooooo-*' (3 sec) and extreme low, hollow, rolling '*rurururu-*'.

12   **SPOTTED CRAKE** *Porzana porzana*   L 20 cm. Note yellow bill with pink base and extensive white spotting above and below. Secretive. Habitat: dense reeds and herbage in shallow parts of marshes, inundations, ponds. Voice: usually silent in Africa. Very high, lashing '*wheet wheet wheet wheet -*'. NM.R

13   **STRIPED CRAKE** *Aenigmatolimnas marginalis* L 20 cm. Note rufous undertail and flanks. Habitat: dense reeds and herbage in marshes, inundations and similar areas. Voice: mid-high, dry, fast, prolonged, mechanical trill, '*trrrrrrrr--*'.

▶

14 **LITTLE CRAKE** *Porzana parva* L 20 cm. Note green legs and pink-based bill. The ♂ and ♀ dissimilar. Longest primary projection of all crakes. Habitat: swamps and other places with reeds and tall grass. Voice: e.g. high starting unexpected '*purrrr purrrr --* ' or nasal '*pweet pweet pweet pweet-pweet-pweetpweetpweet*' (accelerated to a slow rattle). NM.R

15 **BAILLON'S CRAKE** *Porzana pusilla* L 18 cm. From 14 by darker overall colouring, absence of pink bill base, different leg colour. Note white-centred black markings above. The ♂ and ♀ (not shown) similar, but ♀ paler below. Habitat: reed beds and dense tall vegetation in wet places. Voice: low short dry rattle, decelerated just at the end. RES.NM.R

16 **BLACK CRAKE** *Amaurornis flavirostris* L 20 cm. Note yellow bill and red legs. Normally not secretive or shy. Habitat: edges of reedbeds, papyrus, shrubbery al lake margins, dams, ponds, streams. Voice: high, excited chuckling, closely followed by a very low grunt '*rettretretretretret-growl*'.

Plate 30

1 **GREY-THROATED RAIL** *Canirallus oculeus* L 30 cm. Unmistakable, but in its dense habitat difficult to get a good view of. In flight with dark-brown, strikingly barred white flight feathers. Habitat: undergrowth along forest streams. R

2 **NKULENGU RAIL** *Himantornis haematopus* L 45 cm. Note large size, black lore and red legs. Habitat: undergrowth along forest streams. Voice: low, rhythmic '*boom tuckeh-heh boom tuckeh-heh*', actually an inseparable duet. (Name of the species is supposed to imitate its call).

3 **(European) CORNCRAKE** *Crex crex* L 30 cm. Most obvious feature are the reddish wings in flight. In good side view unmistakable. Habitat: grass plains and areas near marshes and rivers. Voice: low, dry, double rattle '*crexcrex crexcrex -*'. NM.R

4 **AFRICAN CRAKE** *Crex egregia* L 25 cm. From 3 by darker brown plumage without rufous and by seemingly longer head and bill. Habitat: moist grassland, inundations and swamps; often in dry habitats, but not in forests. Voice: mid-high, loud, cackling '*ceck-ceck-ceckceckceck-*'. RES.AM

5 **AFRICAN WATER RAIL** *Rallus caerulescens* L 30 cm. From 4 by long red bill. Secretive. Habitat: reed beds of marches, lake margins, stream banks. Voice: very high, slowed down, slightly lowered, piping trill ending in mid-high '*- piu piu piu* '.

6 **PURPLE SWAMPHEN** *Porphyrio porphyrio* L 45 cm. Larger than most swamp birds. From 7 and 8 also by heavy bill, concolorous with red frontal shield. Habitat: large swamps and shallow lakes with reeds, papyrus and floating vegetation. Voice: raucous repeated goose-like grunts, shrieks and cackles. Note: (still) often called the Purple Gallinule, which name is reserved for 8.

7 **ALLEN'S GALLINULE (or Reed-Hen)** *Porphyrio alleni* L 25 cm. Note small size, blue shield and red legs. Shield in n-br plumage is almost brown. Imm from imm 8 by prominent buffy scaling on upperparts. Habitat: marshes, inundations with tall grass and other vegetation. Voice: high raucous '*kreeg-kreeg-kreeg-*' or '*tuk tuk tuk -*'. RES.AM

8 **PURPLE GALLINULE (or King Reed-Hen)** *Porphyrio martinica* L 35 cm. (See 'note' under 6). Distinguished by large size, pale blue shield, yellow legs and yellow-tipped bill. Imm from imm 7 by almost yellow bill and far less buffy scaling above. Habitat: vagrant from America; very few records from West Africa, but in southern Africa more frequent, arriving there as sub-ad with blue feathering coming through on underparts. Voice: cackling '*tuk-tuk-tuk-*' (6x or more). V

9 **COMMON MOORHEN** *Gallinula chloropus* L 30 cm. Note bill pattern and red 'garters' around upperlegs. Habitat: fresh lakes, ponds, marshes with fringing vegetation. Voice: high sharp fast tinking: '*bekbekbek*' or '*wek wek wek -*'. RES.(NM)

10 **LESSER MOORHEN** *Gallinula angulata* L 25 cm. Smaller than 9 with less pronounced white stripe along upperflank. Imm from imm 9 by absence of well-defined flank stripe. Secretive. Habitat: dams, ponds, swamps, flood plains. Voice: very high, bouncing '*peek peek peek -*' or hurried '*treek-treek-treek*'.

▶

11   **RED-KNOBBED COOT** *Fulica cristata*   L 45 cm. From 12 by less deep intrusion of black into bluish (not pinkish) bill. Habitat: all types of quiet freshwater bodies. Voice: mid-high, coughing '*uhurk uhurk -*'. RES.(AM)

12   **EURASIAN COOT** *Fulica atra*   L 40 cm. Black face feathering points deep into pinkish-white (not bluish) upper mandible. Neck held more bent than Red-knobbed Coot. Note white trailing edge to wings in flight. Habitat: fresh, brackish and salt lakes with some floating and emerged vegetation. NM

13   **AFRICAN FINFOOT** *Podica senegalensis*   L 65 cm. Nominate (a) shown and darker, less spotted race *camerunensis* (b). Red bill (and feet) diagnostic. Swims with 'pumping' head movements. Habitat: quiet rivers, streams, pools with fringing vegetation and overhanging trees. Mid-high, dry, bouncing '*crut crut-crut crut crut*'.

Plate 31

1   **DEMOISELLE CRANE** *Anthropoides virgo*   L 95 cm. Rather similar to 4, especially in flight, but black on foreneck further down, with less bushy tail and with shorter neck. Habitat: dry, lightly wooded, short-grassed plains, marshes, open farmland, lake edges and riverbanks. NM.R

2   **GREY CROWNED CRANE** *Balearica regulorum*   H 95 cm. From 3 by paler neck and upperparts and by different cheek pattern. Habitat: roosts and nests in or near wet places but feeds in open or wooded grass- and farmland.

3   **BLACK CROWNED CRANE** *Balearica pavonina*   L 100 cm. From 2 by different colour pattern of cheeks. Habitat: breeds in marshes but feeds in natural and cultivated areas with tall grass. Note: the birds seen outside the areas, indicated on the map (e.g. in the valleys of the Nigerian rivers) are probably escapees from feral stock.

4   **COMMON CRANE** *Grus grus*   L 115 cm. See 1. Imm's have pale rufous (not black) head. Habitat: open areas, away from trees and shrub. V

5   **WATTLED CRANE** *Bugeranus carunculatus*   H 125 cm. Note black belly in flight. Habitat: shallow water of wet, wide-open areas. R

6   **DENHAM'S (or Stanley's) BUSTARD** *Neotis denhami*   H 75 cm. Note facial pattern, large black-and-white area on folded wing, tawny-rufous hindneck. Habitat: slightly wooded, natural and cultivated areas.

7   **NUBIAN BUSTARD** *Neotis nuba*   H 55 cm. Note buff crown and black chin. Habitat: semi-desert, often with some scrub. R

8   **ARABIAN (or Sudan) BUSTARD** *Ardeotis arabs*   L 90 cm. No black visible on folded wing. Habitat: semi-desert and other dry open areas with some grass cover, trees and thickets. RES.AM

9   **HOUBARA** *Chlamydotis undulata*   L 60 cm. Black, fluffy stripe down sides of neck diagnostic. In flight with extensive white on wings. Habitat: dry, open and scrubby areas. R

10   **BLACK-BELLIED BUSTARD** *Eupodotis melanogaster*   H 55 cm. From 11 and 12 by striking long thin neck and legs, narrow black stripe running up front of neck, extensively white outer wing.. The ♀ from ♀ 11 by underwing pattern. Habitat: tall grassland with some trees and lightly wooded farmland. (AM)

11   **WHITE-BELLIED (or Senegal) BUSTARD** *Eupodotis senegalensis*   H 45 cm. Nominate (a) shown and race *mackenziei* (b, with buff-brown neck and without buff breast band). The ♀ from ♀ 10 by other jizz with much shorter neck and legs and pale underwing. Habitat: grassy, lightly bushed and wooded parts (often near streams) of natural and cultivated areas. (AM)

12   **SAVILE'S BUSTARD** *Eupodotis savilei*   H 45 cm. Note black stripe down chin. Reddish crest normally concealed. Habitat: bush- and woodland with open places. Note: the very similar Crested Bustard *Eupodotis ruficrista* does not occur in the area; all previous records refer to Savile's Bustard. R

Plate 32

1   **AFRICAN JACANA (or Lily-Trotter)** *Actophilornis africana*   L 30 cm. Imm (with white, not rufous underparts of ad) much larger than 2. Habitat: swamps, lakes, ponds, slow streams with floating vegetation. Voice: high, often descending, yelping '*wetwetwetwet-wetwet-wet-wet-*' or mid-high '*weh-weh-weh-weh-*'.

2   **LESSER JACANA** *Microparra capensis*   L 15 cm. Ad from imm 1 by much smaller size, paler upperparts and chestnut (not dark brown) nape. Habitat: as 1. Voice: very high, fast, angry '*didititititi--*'. R

3   **EURASIAN OYSTERCATCHER** *Haematopus ostralegus*   L 45 cm. Unmistakable. Habitat: open sandy and rocky shores (mainly) at sea. NM

4   **AFRICAN BLACK OYSTERCATCHER** *Haematopus moquini*   L 45 cm. Unmistakable. Habitat: at or very near to the seashore. (?)

5   **EURASIAN AVOCET** *Recurvirostra avosetta*   L 40 cm. Unmistakable. Habitat: feeds and rests knee-deep in water along lake edges, estuary streams, seashore. RES.NM

6   **COMMON (or Black-winged) STILT** *Himantopus himantopus*   L 40 cm. The ♂ (a) has upperparts glossy greenish black, while these parts in ♀ (b) are deep dark brown. In br plumage normally with white head, in n-br plumage with brownish head, like imm. Sometimes in br plumage with variable, not sex-related black head markings (see flying ♂). Habitat: shallow lakes, estuaries, inundations. Rarely at the open sea coast. RES.NM

7   **SPOTTED THICK-KNEE** *Burhinus capensis*   L 45 cm. From 9 by spotted upperparts. Note conspicuous large eye, absence of grey in wing, small white spots on flight feathers. Habitat: open dry rocky river beds and other arid more or less wooded natural and cultivated areas. Voice: very high, slightly undulating, yelping '*wuuiwuuiwuui--*' at night. AM.RES

8   **STONE CURLEW** *Burhinus oedicnemus*   L 45 cm. Very similar to 9 and 10, but with double white wing bar. Note also the absence of grey on wing. Habitat: sandy lake and riverbanks. NM.R

9   **WATER THICK-KNEE** *Burhinus vermiculatus*   L 40 cm. Note grey-and-white wing bar. Habitat: prefers wetter habitats than 7. River banks, lakeshores, estuaries, and lagoons. Voice: very high, sharp '*tjuutjuutjuu-*' (15-20x) first half speeded-up and rising, second half decelerated and falling off, heard at night.

10   **SENEGAL THICK-KNEE** *Burhinus senegalensis*   L 40 cm. Very similar to 9, but lacking the white upper wing bar and with more yellow on bill. Habitat: sandy lake and riverbanks.

Plate 33

1   **RUFF, REEVE** (♀) *Philomachus pugnax*   L 30 cm (♂), 24 cm (♀). The ♂♂ attain spectacular br plumages (a few examples a, b and c given), which are however not (fully) seen in Africa. Note orange legs. From 2 by (much) larger size and diagnostic white oval patches at either side of rump. Note the few br tertials of the ♀ br plumage as shown. Habitat: river banks, lake edges, dams, inundations. NM

2   **BUFF-BREASTED SANDPIPER** *Tryngites subruficollis*   L 18 cm. Imm (shown on plate) as ad, which has narrower pale feather edges. Note plump, small-headed, short-billed jizz. Pale ring as white 'lips' around bill base. Habitat: marshes and short grassland. V

3   **EGYPTIAN-PLOVER** *Pluvianus aegyptius*   L 20 cm. Unmistakable. Habitat: sandy river banks, lakeshores.

4   **TEMMINCK'S COURSER** *Cursorius temminckii*   L 20 cm. Note orange(-rufous) crown, small black breast patch, all-black flight feathers. Habitat: dry more or less bushed habitats, bare fields, burnt ground. Voice: high hooted unhurried '*hak hak hak zunk*' ('*zunk*' slightly lower and inhaled). (AM)

5   **CREAM-COLOURED COURSER** *Cursorius cursor*   L 25 cm. Note gradual paling from throat to undertail coverts. Habitat: desert, semi-desert and open and bushed grass- and farmland. AM.RES

6   **BRONZE-WINGED (or Violet-tipped) COURSER** *Cursorius chalcopterus*   L 25 cm. Note large, red-rimmed eye. Beautiful purple tips of flight feathers not visible in folded wing. Nocturnal, hence the large eyes. Habitat: more or less wooded and bushed areas. Voice: strange, high, peacock-like, repeated '*miau-eh*' at night. AM.RES

7   **COLLARED (or Common) PRATINCOLE** *Glareola pratincola*   L 25 cm. Note diagnostic white trailing edge to wing in flight. Underwing is dark reddish (but this not always well visible). Wings not longer than tail, when perched. Habitat: open areas near lakes, rivers, seashore. NM.RES

8   **BLACK-WINGED PRATINCOLE** *Glareola nordmanni*   L 25 cm. Note absence of white trailing edge to wing in flight. From 7 also by darker appearance and black underwing. Tail of perched bird shorter than wing tip. Habitat: open sandy areas with some grass near lakes, rivers. Rarely at the sea coast. NM.(RES)

9   **GREY PRATINCOLE** *Glareola cinerea*   L 19 cm. Much paler than similar-sized 10. Catches insects in swallow-like fashion; active at the end of the day. Habitat: sand bars in rivers and lakes.

10   **ROCK PRATINCOLE** *Glareola nuchalis*   L 18 cm. Nominate (a) shown and race *liberiae* (b, with chestnut, not white neck). Note white cheek and bar on underwing. Habitat: rocky river- and lakeshores, occasionally also on sandy and muddy beaches. RES.AM

Plate 34

Note: lapwings are often called plovers in other bird guides.

1 **LONG-TOED (or White-faced) LAPWING** *Vanellus crassirostris*   L 30 cm. Unmistakable. Habitat: floating vegetation at lake shores and calm river banks, large swamps, inundations.

2 **BLACK-HEADED LAPWING** *Vanellus tectus*   L 25 cm. From 9 by different head pattern and black stripe down chest. As 3 with a short crest, other features very different. Habitat: semi-desert with some grass cover. Sometimes far from water.

3 **NORTHERN LAPWING** *Vanellus vanellus*   L 30 cm. Note long crest, blackish upperparts, broad rounded wings and rufous undertail coverts. Habitat: normally in moist grasslands of any size, even in forest clearings. V

4 **WHITE-TAILED LAPWING** *Vanellus leucurus*   L 25 cm. Note long-legged jizz and pale unmarked head. Habitat: mainly in dry, open and short-grassed areas. Also at riversides. V

5 **BROWN-CHESTED (Wattled) LAPWING** *Vanellus superciliosus*   L 25 cm. Imm from imm 6 and 7 by smaller size, bulkier build, less projecting primaries. Habitat: dry short grassland, bare fields, often near river- and lakeshores. AM.RES

6 **LESSER BLACK-WINGED LAPWING** *Vanellus lugubris*   L 22 cm. Note sharp demarcation of white on forehead. Wing pattern diagnostic. Imm lacks distinct eyebrow. Habitat: dry open short grassland with some shrub at lower altitudes. (In Serle: Senegal Lapwing).

7 **AFRICAN WATTLED LAPWING** *Vanellus senegallus*   L 35 cm. Nominate (a) shown and race *lateralis* (b, with black band across belly). Note large size. From 8 by more uniform colouring. Habitat: bare, muddy, sandy or short-grassed ground near marshes and lakes, ponds and rivers. (In Serle: Senegal Wattled Lapwing). RES.(AM)

8 **WHITE-HEADED (or –crowned) LAPWING** *Vanellus albiceps*   L 30 cm. From 7 by all-white underparts and different upperwing pattern. Habitat: sandy river banks in forested areas. RES.(AM)

9 **CROWNED LAPWING** *Vanellus coronatus*   L 30 cm. Imm (not shown) from ad by yellow (not red) bare parts. Noisy. Habitat: drier areas with more or less short grass cover and some shrub and trees. Often at airfields, golf courses. Voice: high loud grating '*kreeep*' or '*kree-kree-kree-kreeip*', especially in flight.

10 **SPUR-WINGED LAPWING** *Vanellus spinosus*   L 25 cm. Recalling crestless 3, but normally unmistakable. Habitat: bare, sandy or muddy and grassy lakeshores and riverbanks. RES.(AM)

11 **BLACKSMITH LAPWING** *Vanellus armatus*   L 30 cm. Unmistakable. Habitat: dry or muddy or marshy shores of lakes, dams, ponds, lagoons, swamps. Voice: extreme high, metallic '*tink-tink--*' (hence the species name).

Plate 35

Flying birds in n-br plumage

1   **SHORT-BILLED DOWITCHER** *Limnodromus griseus*   L 30 cm. This and next species resemble small godwits (3 and 4) by their long bills, which they use in snipe-like fashion when feeding; note however the colour of their legs (green, not red or black) and more buff overall colouring. This species is very difficult to separate from 2, but is in br plumage more spotted than barred below and in n-br plumage slightly less pale and less extensively grey on breast. Habitat: 1 and 2 are vagrants from America and are found there in shallow wetlands, with a preference by 1 for salt and brackish waters. Voice: mellow '*tududu*' as opposed to high, shrill '*keek*' of 2 (main diagnostic feature). WM.V

2   **LONG-BILLED DOWITCHER** *Limnodromus scolopaceus*   L 30 cm. See 1. WM.(?)

3   **BLACK-TAILED GODWIT** *Limosa limosa*   L 40 cm. Note long legs and neck, absence of streaking on n-br plumage, white wing bar and underwing, black tail. Habitat: all types of inland and coastal wetlands. Voice: silent in Africa. NM

4   **BAR-TAILED GODWIT** *Limosa lapponica*   L 40 cm. In n-br plumage from 3 by finely striped upperparts and neck. Note slightly upturned bill, barred tail, absence of wing bar. Habitat: rarely away from the sea coast. Voice: high '*witwit witwitwit*'. NM

5   **GREATER GOLDEN PLOVER** *Pluvialis apricaria*   L 30 cm. From 7 by golden-yellow (not whitish-grey) tone above in all plumages and from 6 and 8 by white inner underwing (diagnostic). Looks paler than 6 and 8 above by being spotted black on golden-yellow, rather than spotted golden-green on black. Habitat: grass plains, farmland, fresh and brackish wetlands. NM.R

6   **PACIFIC GOLDEN PLOVER** *Pluvialis fulva*   L 25 cm. See 8. Note also the very long legs and heavy bill. Habitat: normally in freshwater habitats in coastal regions. Note: In *Birds of Africa* 6 and 8 are treated as races of one species: Lesser Golden Plover *Pluvialis fulva*. EM.R

7   **GREY PLOVER** *Pluvialis squatarola*   L 30 cm. From 6 in n-br plumage by larger size and heavier bill. Note diagnostic black armpit. Habitat: mainly sea shore, lagoons, rarely at lakes and pools. NM

8   **AMERICAN GOLDEN PLOVER** *Pluvialis dominica*   L 30 cm. In br and n-br plumage with larger dark centres to feathers of upperparts which make this species look darker, less bright than 6. Primary projection beyond tertials shows 4 primaries, while 6 shows 3 (but beware of wing moult). Bill finer than that of 6. Habitat: in America is short grassland away from the coast. WM.R

9   **SLENDER-BILLED CURLEW** *Numenius tenuirostris*   L 40 cm. Note small size and white ground colour with black stripes broken in spots. Habitat: as 11. NM.V

10   **EURASIAN CURLEW** *Numenius arquata*   L 55 cm. Larger and longer-billed than all other shorebirds. Habitat: sea and lakeshores, estuaries, sand dunes, riverbanks, grassland. Voice: high, beautiful, liquid, mellow, slightly trilled '*fruuw-fuui-fuuui*'. NM

11   **WHIMBREL** *Numenius phaeopus*   L 45 cm. Note white streak over middle of crown, diagnostic dark streaks on head above and below eyebrow. From 10 also by smaller size, darker upperparts and flight feathers. Habitat: mainly seashore and other coastal areas. Voice: diagnostic call sounds as high, rapid '*bibibibibibi*' (± 7x 'bi'). NM

1

n-br

n-br

3

n-br

5

n-br

6

n-br

2

n-br

n-br

4

7

n-br

n-br

8

9

10   11

Plate 36

Flying birds in n-br plumage

1   **THREE-BANDED PLOVER** *Charadrius tricollaris*   L 18 cm. Note long eyebrows forming complete circle around cap, grey (brown in imm) face sides and narrow white wing bar. Habitat: edges of ponds, streams, sewage ponds. Rarely at salt water. AM.RES

2   **FORBES'S (Banded) PLOVER** *Charadrius forbesi*   L 19 cm. Eyebrows only connected at nape, not on forehead. From ad 1 by brown face sides and absence of wing bar. Note long tapered jizz. Habitat: open more or less grassy places away from water, but occasionally on mud flats at lake and river sides. RES.AM

3   **EURASIAN DOTTEREL** *Charadrius morinellus*   L 20 cm. Br plumage distinctive. In n-br plumage from all other plovers (except 1 and 2) by long white eyebrow and faint white bar across breast. Habitat: dry, sandy and stony planes, but also at the coast. V

4   **LITTLE RINGED PLOVER** *Charadrius dubius*   L 15 cm. From 5 and 6 by pale legs and eye ring, absence of wing bar and all-black bill (except base of lower mandible in br plumage). Habitat: lake margins; avoids the seashore. NM.(RES)

5   **SEMIPALMATED PLOVER** *Charadrius semipalmatus*   L 17 cm.. Very similar to 6, but with smaller white spot behind eye, thin pale eye ring and white wing bar less pronounced on outer wing. Breast band normally less bulging to sides of breast. (Vagrant to Cape Verde; no map). V

6   **RINGED PLOVER** *Charadrius hiaticula*   L 16 cm. Note orange-pink bill base and legs. From 4 (and 5) by absence of eye ring. Imm has dark breast patches (forming almost a collar) and pinkish (not yellow) legs. Habitat: seashore, lake edges, riverbanks. Occasionally away from water. NM

7   **KITTLITZ'S (Sand) PLOVER** *Charadrius pecuarius*   L 16 cm. From most other small plovers by absence of dark breast band or patches. Note diagnostic buff breast and isolated white throat. Habitat: dry short grass near lakes and dams, sandy and muddy edges of lakes and streams.

8   **GREAT SAND PLOVER** *Charadrius leschenaultii*   L 22 cm. From 9 by larger size, taller stance, heavier bill, paler and longer legs, feet protruding in flight. Habitat: open seashore and other open sandy and muddy coastal places. Occasionally at lakes. Voice: call more trilling than 8. V

9   **MONGOLIAN PLOVER** *Charadrius mongolus*   L 19 cm. Normally with small (or absent) white spots before eyes. Smaller, darker-legged and finer-billed than 8. Also with shorter projecting feet in flight. Habitat: as 9. V

10   **CASPIAN PLOVER** *Charadrius asiaticus*   L 22 cm. Note tall slender profile, small head, thin bill, long legs. Prominent eyebrow gives capped appearance. In flight shows dusky underwing, little white at tail sides and protruding feet. Long-winged in flight and with long primary projection after landing. Habitat: prefers dry places even in coastal areas; short grass, burnt ground, sand dunes. NM.R

11   **KENTISH PLOVER** *Charadrius alexandrinus*   L 16 cm. In winter plumage very similar to 12, but with white ring around neck . Note interrupted black necklace of br ♂. In all plumages with striking white hindneck and dark brownish-grey upperparts. Habitat: muddy beaches at the coast, lagoons. NM.(RES)

12   **WHITE-FRONTED (Sand) PLOVER** *Charadrius marginatus*   L 20 cm. No black on breast or chest. White hindcollar absent. Tail projects beyond wing tip. Habitat: sandy and rocky seashores. Also at lake and riverbanks.

Plate 37

Flying birds in n-br plumage

1   **SPOTTED REDSHANK** *Tringa erythropus*   L 30 cm. Note large size, slender build, prominent white eyebrow (n-br), long red base to lower mandible. Streaked rump and tail looks grey in flight. Pale finely speckled secondaries look paler than rest of (opened) upperwing. From red-legged 2 by more slender jizz with longer bill and legs. Habitat: muddy and marshy pools and riverbanks. NM

2   **COMMON REDSHANK** *Tringa totanus*   L 30 cm. Note compact build, red legs, black-tipped bill. White wedge on back and broad trailing edge to upperwing are diagnostic. Habitat: short grass near and at edges of lakes, ponds, streams, seashore, creeks, estuaries. Voice: in flight high '*tjuu-wuh*'. Alarm call: '*tiutiutiu-*'. NM

3   **COMMON GREENSHANK** *Tringa nebularia*   L 30 cm. Note large size, grey-and-white colouring, upturned pale-based bill, green legs, long white rump wedge. Habitat: muddy shores, riverbanks, pools, lagoons. Voice: high melodious '*tjuutjuutjuu-*' (3x '*tjuu*' or more). NM

4   **MARSH SANDPIPER** *Tringa stagnatilis*   L 30 cm. Note fine needle-like bill, very white underparts, dark wing shoulders in n-br plumage. From 3 by finer more slender build and fine needle-like bill. Habitat: muddy and marshy lake shores, riverbanks, streams, pools. Voice: very high, sharp '*tsjik tsjik tsjik-tsjik-*' when flushed. NM

5   **LESSER YELLOWLEGS** *Tringa flavipes*   L 25 cm. Yellow legs diagnostic. Bill as long as head and straight. Habitat: vagrant from America, where it is found in all types of coastal and inland wetlands. V

6   **GREEN SANDPIPER** *Tringa ochropus*   L 20 cm. Note compact jizz with short neck and legs, white eye ring and narrow black lore. In flight looks very dark above (also on underwing) with square white rump patch (more contrasting than on 8). Habitat: sheltered pools, streams, creeks, sewage ponds. Voice: when flushed '*weereet-weet-weet*', louder than 8. NM

7   **SOLITARY SANDPIPER** *Tringa solitaria*   L 20 cm. Very similar to 6, but note diagnostic dark rump and banded tail sides. Habitat: vagrant from America; normal habitat there are marshes, muddy shores of streams and ponds. Record in the Central African Republic now rejected, possible vagrant to Cabinda. V

8   **WOOD SANDPIPER** *Tringa glareola*   L 20 cm. Note slender profile, yellowish-green legs, long diffuse eyebrow. From 6 by less black colouring, longer legs, more slender build, less contrasting white rump and in flight by further protruding feet; different call diagnostic. Habitat: secluded parts of marshes, inundations, pools, creeks, sewage ponds. Voice: very high, staccato, slightly descending '*tri-tri-ti-tit*'. NM

9   **TEREK SANDPIPER** *Xenus cinereus*   L 25 cm. Note yellow-based upturned bill, yellow legs and black V-mark (faint in n-br plumage) on back. White trailing edge to upperwings as 2, but not a white wedge into back. Habitat: seashore, muddy lake, creek and river edges. NM.R

10   **UPLAND SANDPIPER** *Bartramia longicauda*   L 30 cm. Long protruding tail and thin neck diagnostic. No or little white to tail and rump. Habitat: vagrant from American fields and prairies. V

Plate 38

Flying birds in n-br plumage

1   **BROAD-BILLED SANDPIPER** *Limicola falcinellus*   L 17 cm. Note striped head, kinked bill, greenish legs. From other stints by slower feeding action. Habitat: muddy and sandy sea and lake shores. NM.R

2   **LEAST SANDPIPER** *Calidris minutilla*   L 14 cm. Note short, pale legs (in flight not protruding). From 1 and 3 by dark legs, from 1 by less striped head and from 5 by greyer plumage in n-br plumage and more colourful plumage in br plumage. As 4 (which see) with short or no primary projection. Often with almost complete breast band. Habitat: from the actual sea shore to inland wetlands. WM.R

3   **LITTLE STINT** *Calidris minuta*   L 14 cm. In n-br plumage very difficult to separate from other small stints, but often with whiter head and forehead. Agile with fast feeding action. Habitat: more at fresh water bodies than at the actual sea shore. NM

4   **LONG-TOED STINT** *Calidris subminuta*   L 14 cm. Note seemingly long tertials and pale base to lower mandible. Dark crown touches down to bill (unlike 2, which has white eye brows connected over bill). In flight with protruding toes. From other small stints by longer neck when stretched in alarm. Note yellowish legs. Habitat: normally at muddy lake edges. V

5   **SEMIPALMATED SANDPIPER** *Calidris pusilla*   L 14 cm. Note blunt tip and rather deep base of bill in br plumage. Normally greyer than other stints and without white lines on mantle. Short webs between toes (difficult to see) diagnostic. Habitat: coastal mud flats. WM.V

6   **TEMMINCK'S STINT** *Calidris temminckii*   L 14 cm. Note uniform grey breast and upperparts, green-yellowish (not black as 7) legs, white sides to tail. Habitat: marsh pools, muddy lake edges. Unlikely to be found at the sea shore. NM

7   **BAIRD'S SANDPIPER** *Calidris bairdii*   L 17 cm. Note pale spots above lores, long tapered jizz with wing tips clearly projecting beyond tail, brown, scalloped (not grey-scalloped) upperparts and streaked breast of n-br plumage. Habitat: inland and coastal areas, shallow pools, lagoons, edges of marshes. V

8   **WHITE-RUMPED SANDPIPER** *Calidris fuscicollis*   L 17 cm. Note streaked flanks, long wings clearly projecting beyond tail, slightly decurved bill, unmarked upperparts of n-br plumage, flesh-coloured base of lower mandible. In flight white rump diagnostic. Habitat: coastal mudflats, estuaries, inland pools, marshes. V

9   **PECTORAL SANDPIPER** *Calidris melanotos*   L 19 cm. Note sharp demarcation between white underparts and grey breast. Bill has pale base and there is a faint wingbar in flight. Habitat: marsh, wet grassland, muddy water edges. Rarely at the coast. NM.R

10   **DUNLIN** *Calidris alpina*   L 18 cm. From 11 in n-br dress by shorter bill which is curved at tip, absence of eyebrow and shorter legs. Note black stripe through middle of rump in flight. Habitat: normally in coastal areas but is seen at inland dams. NM

11   **CURLEW SANDPIPER** *Calidris ferruginea*   L 19 cm. Note white rump in flight, long legs and gradually curved bill. N-br plumage with little or no streaking on breast. Habitat: prefers coastal areas, but occasionally found also at muddy fresh water and alkaline lake sides, dams, pans, inundations. NM

12   **PURPLE SANDPIPER** *Calidris maritima*   L 21 cm. Note robust, short-legged jizz, projecting tail, dark upperparts and broadly streaked breast. Habitat: rocky sea shores. V

13   **RED KNOT** *Calidris canutus*   L 25 cm. Note large size, greenish legs and finely barred flanks of n-br plumage. In flight shows seemingly grey rump and unmarked tail. From 11 by larger, heavier jizz and straight, shorter bill. Habitat: sea shore and other coastal habitats. NM

14   **SANDERLING** *Calidris alba*   L 19 cm. Winter plumage is very pale with darker shoulder. Br plumage (rarely seen in Africa) often less colourful than shown. Conspicuous white wing bar in flight. Habitat: actual sea shore. Runs up and down the beach with each advancing and retreating wave. NM

Plate 39

1   **GREATER PAINTED-SNIPE** *Rostratula benghalensis*   L 24 cm. Note large eyes, down-curving bill and pale line by which the wings seem to be separable from the body. Normally skulking and crepuscular. When flushed flies away with dangling feet. Habitat: muddy places in fringing vegetation of lakes, dams, ponds, slow rivers. Voice: mid-high rather pigeon-like '*wakkuh-wakkuh*' or '*ukruk ukruk*'.

2   **AFRICAN SNIPE** *Gallinago nigripennis*   L 30 cm. Note very long bill, short wings, dark upperparts, contrasting white belly. White outer tail feathers with some black barring. When flushed rises explosively and steeply calling '*tsjuk*' and zigzags (but less so than 4) away at low level before dropping into cover within 100–200 m. Habitat: moorland, marshes, grassy lakes shores and inundations at higher elevations. Voice: ♂♂ produce quivering roars, produced by spread tail in display flight. AM.R

3   **GREAT SNIPE** *Gallinago media*   L 30 cm. Note striking white wing bars, obvious belly barring, spotted (not striped) neck sides. When flushed at 5–10 m shoots away at shallow angle silently or with soft '*itch-itch*', flies in straight line and disappears abruptly in cover within 30–50m. Habitat: swamp and lake edges, also in short wet grass away from water. NM

4   **COMMON SNIPE** *Gallinago gallinago*   L 25 cm. From 2 by less contrast between upper- and underparts, shorter bill and relative longer wings. Tail predominantly rufous with narrow white margins. When flushed at 10–15 m rises steeply and explosively, calls '*tweek*' 1-2 x while zigzagging away; sometimes circles around before dropping into cover within 200–300 m. Habitat: marches, grassy lake shores, inundations. NM

5   **JACK SNIPE** *Lymnocryptes minimus*   L 19 cm. Note small size, double eyebrow, dark line through crown and absence of white or rufous in tail. Difficult to flush but if so, it rises silently and flies straight away over only 50–100 m before dropping in cover again. Habitat: swamps, short-grassed lake shores, inundations. NM

6   **COMMON SANDPIPER** *Actitis hypoleucos*   L 20 cm. Imm shown, differing from ad by more barred, not slightly striped upperparts. Tail projects beyond wing tip. Note white patch in front of folded wing. Prominent white wing bar in flight diagnostic. Habitat: short grass near and at edge of lakes, ponds, streams, sea shore, creeks, estuaries. Voice: extreme high sharp '*feetfeetfeet*' when flushed. NM

7   **SPOTTED SANDPIPER** *Actitis macularia*   L 19 cm. As 6 with projecting, but shorter tail and more compact build. Imm from 6 by shorter tail, normally with more yellow legs, shorter bill, less white to secondaries and therefore shorter wing bar, less prominent patches to sides of breast. Habitat: at all types of water bodies, including the Ocean. (Cape Verde; no map). V

8   **RUDDY TURNSTONE** *Arenaria interpres*   L 23 cm. Note characteristic jizz (drawn-in head, hunched body, short legs). Black crescents on sides of breast (br and n-br) diagnostic. Habitat: normally at rocky sea shores. NM

9   **WILSON'S PHALAROPE** *Phalaropus tricolor*   L 23 cm. Straggler from America. Swims less and forages more on land than 10 and 11. Rather plump yet graceful. In n-br plumage shows long thin bill, grey, not black eye patch, yellow legs (black in br plumage), no wingbar, diagnostic white rump without central stripe. Habitat: in America normally at inland waters, marshes. WM.V

10   **RED-NECKED PHALAROPE** *Phalaropus lobatus*   L 18 cm. From 9 and 10 by short needle-like bill. N-br plumage is darker above than 11, so white wing bar in flight is better defined and more striking. Habitat: open sea, large lakes, occasionally at pools and sewage ponds. NM.R

11   **GREY PHALAROPE** *Phalaropus fulicarius*   L 20 cm. From 10 by less slender jizz and stubbier bill. Habitat: normally at open sea, rarely on inland waters. NM.WM.R

1

♂ ♀

6

6

7

7

imm

7

n-br

8

2

9

br ♀ br ♂

3

n-br ♀

4

10

br ♀ br ♂

n-br ♀

5

br ♀ 11

11

n-br ♀ br ♂

Plate 40

1 **SOUTH POLAR SKUA** *Catharacta maccormicki*   L 55 cm. Note rather small, contrasting patterned black bill. Underparts not striped or mottled except some striping on imm throat. Habitat: seashore. Note: most skuas occur in several colour forms (pale, intermediate and dark), only pale forms (except dark form of 3) shown. V

2 **GREAT SKUA** *Catharacta skua*   L 60 cm. From 1 by heavier bill and more striped-blotched underparts. Note hooded appearance of ad. Imm has rufous (not pale brown) underparts. Habitat: normally at sea. NM.R

3 **POMARINE SKUA** *Stercorarius pomarinus*   L 55 cm (excluding tail streamers). Normal and dark (a) forms shown. Lengthened blunt twisted tail feathers diagnostic, but these are often missing in worn plumage. Black of under-wing 'drips' over flanks. In n-br plumage head and breast densely barred brown. Note double concentric white band on outer underwing of n-br ad and imm. Habitat: seashore.

4 **ARCTIC SKUA** *Stercorarius parasiticus*   L 45 cm (excluding tail streamers). Rare greyish imm (a) and normal imm (b) forms shown. Note pointed tail feathers and faint chest-band. N-br plumage as imm plumage but under wing-coverts plain brown, not barred. Imm often with pale rusty neck. Habitat: seashore. NM.R

5 **LONG-TAILED SKUA** *Stercorarius longicaudus*   L 35 cm (excluding tail streamers). No chest-band and with pale buff throat in br plumage. N-br plumage as imm plumage but belly paler and under wing-coverts unbarred. Intermediate form is rare, but dark form does not exist in this species. Imm very much like imm Arctic Skua but neck less rusty and middle tail-feathers slightly lengthened. Habitat: seashore. NM.R

6 **YELLOW-LEGGED GULL** *Larus cachinnans*   L 60 cm. Only silver-backed large gull in the area (8a has darker upperparts). Habitat: normally only occurring at the sea coast. Note: in *Birds of Africa* erroneously a race of Herring Gull *Larus argentatus*. R

7 **KELP GULL** *Larus dominicanus*   L 60 cm. Wingtip in flight not blacker than rest of wing. Note large stocky build with short wings and colour of legs (paler than 8); 2 out of every 3 birds have dark eye as shown, rest have creamy eye as 8. Juv has all-black bill, 2dW shows some white parts in and near armpit. Habitat: sea beach and nearby areas. Voice: high almost double-toned '*tjik tjik-tjik-tjik-*'. V

8 **LESSER BLACK-BACKED GULL** *Larus fuscus*   L 55 cm. Paler race *graellsii* (a) and nominate (b) shown. Note black wing tips of a, sharply demarcated from dark grey remainder of upperwing. Habitat: mainly at the coast, but also along larger rivers. Voice: call is less sharp than that of 6. NM

9 **GREAT BLACK-BACKED GULL** *Larus marinus*   L 75 cm. Larger, more robust and broader-winged than 6 and 8. 2dW from imm's 6, 7 and 8 by bicoloured bill and pale inner primaries. Habitat: normally only at the seashore. V

1

2

imm

1

2

imm

ad

3

a

imm

imm

n-br

br ♂

4

a

imm

b

n-br

2nd S

n-br

2nd S

5

imm

n-br

2nd S

n-br

6

2nd S

n-br

7

n-br

1st S

b

2nd W

2nd W

8

a

n-br

b

2nd W

a

b

9

n-br

2nd W

2nd W

Plate 41

Perched birds in n-br plumage, flying adults in br plumage

1 **AUDOUIN'S GULL** *Larus audouinii* L 50 cm. Large, but smaller than 40.6. Note red bill and black eye. Br and n-br plumage similar. Imm with U-shaped white rump. Habitat: rocky sea coast, sandy beaches. NM.R

2 **MEW (or Common) GULL** *Larus canus* L 45 cm. In br plumage with all-yellow bill. Note large white windows at wing tip. Imm with faintly marked rump and coarsely marked underwing. Habitat: all types of larger coastal and inland waters. V

3 **RING-BILLED GULL** *Larus delawarensis* L 50 cm. From 2 by pale eye and smaller window at wing tip. Imm very much as imm 2, but black tail band less well cut and grey on upperwing paler. Habitat: vagrant from inland and coastal North America. V

4 **GREY-HEADED GULL** *Larus cirrocephalus* L 40 cm. Note the diagnostic creamy eyes of ad, bright red legs and dark underwing. From 13 by white mirrors at wing tip. Drawn-out head profile as 10. Habitat: normally at the sea shore and larger inland waters.

5 **LAUGHING GULL** *Larus atricilla* L 40 cm. Darker than any other gull on this plate. From 11 (with similar head pattern in br plumage) by proportionally larger bill, far less white on primaries, no white between black wing tip and grey rest of wings. In n-br plumage less clearly hooded than 11. Habitat: vagrant from America; there normally in coastal areas. V

6 **MEDITERRANEAN GULL** *Larus melanocephalus* L 40 cm. Generally no black at wing tip or only on outer web of first primary. Subadults (not shown) have more black at wing tips. Habitat: seashore. V

7 **LITTLE GULL** *Larus minutus* L 25 cm. Note black underwing and all-grey upperwing of ad; 2dW plumage (not shown) may have some black at wing tip. Black-billed imm has similar M-mark on upperparts as imm 12. Habitat: normally in coastal habitats. NM.R

8 **BONAPARTE'S GULL** *Larus philadelphia* L 30 cm. Note fine, black bill and red legs in all plumages. Black at wing tips restricted to edges. Habitat: vagrant from inland and coastal America. V

9 **SABINE'S GULL** *Larus sabini* L 35 cm. Yellow-tipped bill and striking wing pattern diagnostic. Note that imm (unlike several other imm gulls) lacks white hind collar. Habitat: open sea but also at inland waters not too far from the sea. WM.R

10 **SLENDER-BILLED GULL** *Larus genei* L 45 cm. Shape of head, with forward-placed bill, may be best identification feature. Habitat: coastal areas. RES.NM

11 **FRANKLIN'S GULL** *Larus pipixcan* L 35 cm. Black wing tip separated from grey by white band, but this band reduced or absent in 1st and 2dS birds. N-br ad and imm have partial black or grey hood. Up perwing of imm from imm 5 by greyer less brownish colouring. Habitat: vagrant from America, where normally in marshes, lakes with fringing vegetation, also at the sea coast. Feeds often away from water on grass- and farmland. V

12 **BLACK-LEGGED KITTIWAKE** *Rissa tridactyla* L 40 cm. Yellow bill and short legs diagnostic. Note small 'cut-of' triangled wing tips in flight. Imm from imm 7 by interruption of M-mark on back and pure white (not grey) crown. Habitat: open sea. NM.V

13 **BLACK-HEADED GULL** *Larus ridibundus* L 35 cm. In all ad plumages with red bill and legs. Shows a characteristic widening white leading edge to upperwing. Imm as imm 4 but shows more white on primaries. Habitat: prefers coastal habitats but may also be found at inland waters, farmland, refuse dumps. NM

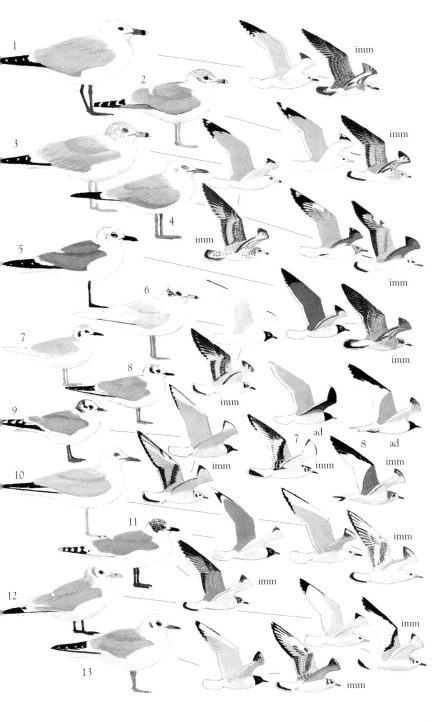

Plate 42

Perched birds in n-br plumage, flying adults in br plumage.

1   **COMMON TERN** *Sterna hirundo* L 35 cm. From 2 by heavier build, longer bill, longer legs. N-br ad often shows reddish bill base. Note dark wedge between mid-grey outer and pale-grey inner primaries. Br ad from 3 by absence of pink wash below and shorter streamers. Imm normally has bi-coloured bill. Habitat: at sea shore. Rarely inland. Voice: '*kee-er*' ('kee' high and sharp). RES.NM

2   **ARCTIC TERN** *Sterna paradisaea*   L 35 cm. Note short legs, short bill, long tail (reaching wing tip or just beyond), narrow dark trailing edge to primaries, 'translucent' flight feathers. In br plumage greyer below than 1. Note all-red bill and white cheek separated from greyer underparts. Imm has rather uniform grey upperparts in flight. Habitat: more offshore than inshore. May however wander inland. Voice: mid-high '*eeeehr*' lowered at the end. NM

3   **ROSEATE TERN** *Sterna dougallii* L 40 cm. From 1 by longer tail and paler upperparts. In br plumage (outside Africa) shows only during a few weeks an all-red bill. Note wedge-shaped darker leading edge of wing. Wing of imm rather pale without much contrast; scapulars (just not visible on plate) rather dark. Habitat: sea shore. Voice: as 2 but different from 1, very high '*weewee*'. NM

4   **DAMARA TERN** *Sterna balaeanarum*   L 23 cm. Note black bill and legs, grey rump and tail, black cap (of br ad). Habitat: prefers inshore coastal waters. Voice: very high almost sparrow-like '*sree-sreeetiti*'. (RES).AM

5   **LITTLE TERN** *Sterna albifrons*   L 24 cm. Flies with fast wing beats. Note small size, white rump and tail and dark first 3–4 primaries of ad. Black tip of bill in br plumage may be absent. Imm (especially juv) shows contrasting white secondaries. Habitat: sea shore. Voice: very high '*peel peee peee*'. RES.NM

6   **BRIDLED TERN** *Sterna anaethetus*   L 35 cm. In br plumage black cap contrasting with dark upperparts. Note long tail, projecting beyond wing tip. White eyebrow extends behind eye. N-br ad has brown (not black) cap. Habitat: sea shore. EM.RES

7   **SOOTY TERN** *Sterna fuscata*   L 45 cm. Cap and upperparts concolorous black, white eyebrow short. N-br ad shows some white spotting on crown. Note dark underparts of imm. Habitat: sea shore. WM.RES.R

8   **WHISKERED TERN** *Chlidonias hybridus*   L 25 cm. Note grey rump of ad and dark saddle of imm (similar to white-rumped imm 9). From 9 in n-br plumage by longer wings and deeper wing beat. Habitat: open inland waters, occasionally at sea shore. Feeding behaviour as 9 but also plunge-dives. Voice: mid-high '*scratchscratch scratch*'. NM

9   **WHITE-WINGED BLACK TERN** *Chlidonias leucopterus*   L 23 cm. N-br ad and imm show white rump, shorter bill and longer legs than 8 and 10. From 10 by absence of breast patches and less black on head and nape (in n-br plumage). Habitat: lakes, but can be seen feeding on insects away from water; does not plunge-dive but snatches food from water surface. NM

10   **BLACK TERN** *Chlidonias niger* L 23 cm. Br ad has diagnostic pale underwings and reddish-black legs. N-br plumage and imm darker than 8 and 9; note also the characteristic dark patch to breast sides of n-br ad and imm, grey rump and (in n-br plumage) extensive black cap extending below eye. Habitat: inshore areas near the coast. NM

Plate 43

Perched birds in n-br plumage, flying adults in br plumage

1   **CASPIAN TERN** *Sterna caspia*   L 50 cm. Note (top-)heavy jizz, striking red bill, normally with subterminal dark spot (often absent in br plumage). N-br ad and imm usually with densely spotted forehead. Bill relatively longer and heavier than 3. Imm less well marked on upperwings than other imm large terns. Habitat: seashore. Voice: mid-high, raucous, pressed-out '*pfweeet*'. RES.NM

2   **SWIFT (or Greater Crested) TERN** *Sterna bergii*   L 50 cm. Note chrome-yellow bill and white forehead, even in br plumage. Note dark upperwing of imm.. Habitat: seashore and nearby areas. EM.V

3   **ROYAL TERN** *Sterna maxima*   L 50 cm. From 1 by shorter, less deeply red bill. Heavier built, longer-legged and paler above than 4. Note strongly patterned upperwing of imm. Habitat: seashore and nearby areas. WM.AM.RES

4   **LESSER CRESTED TERN** *Sterna bengalensis*   L 45 cm. Note very pale orange bill, grey rump and uppertail. In n-br plumage from similar 3 by more black behind eye. Habitat: seashore. NM.R

5   **SANDWICH TERN** *Sterna sandvicensis*   L 45 cm. Note slender, black, yellow-tipped bill and flat crown. In flight with outerwing paler than innerwing. Imm shows all-black bill. Habitat: offshore, but can also be seen in coastal areas. NM

6   **GULL-BILLED TERN** *Sterna nilotica*   L 40 cm. Note short black bill, rounded head, long legs, all-grey, very pale upperparts. Imm and n-br ad show little black behind eye. Flight straight, less buoyant than other terns. Habitat: seashore, inland lakes, wetlands. Voice: high, rasping, pushed-out '*kureet*' and mid-high, bleating chatters. RES.NM

7   **BLACK NODDY** *Anous minutus*   L 35 cm. From 8 by sharply demarcated white cap. Imm (not shown) as ad but with some pale edging to feathers of upperparts. Habitat: normally at offshore islands. AM.R

8   **LESSER NODDY** *Anous tenuirostris*   L 30 cm. From 7 by gradual transition between white forehead and darker cheek and chin. Habitat: mainly at open sea. V

9   **BROWN NODDY** *Anous stolidus*   L 40 cm. From 7 and 8 by larger size, pale-centred underwing, dark tail (darker than rump) and pale wing bar. Imm (not shown) with less white cap and pale edges to feathers of upperparts. Habitat: normally at offshore islands. AM

10   **AFRICAN SKIMMER** *Rhynchops flavirostris*   L 40 cm. Characterised by unique fishing method in which bill snaps shut when longer lower mandible (ploughing through water surface) touches fish (a). Habitat: large rivers, lakes, lagoons with sandbars.

Plate 44

1 **LICHTENSTEIN'S SANDGROUSE** *Pterocles lichtensteinii* L 30 cm. Note uniform barred appearance of ♀, without any orange to chin. Habitat: arid, hilly, rocky, lightly wooded areas with some scrub. (Drinks just before sunrise or just after sunset but not in large flocks). R

2 **FOUR-BANDED SANDGROUSE** *Pterocles quadricinctus* L 30 cm. Note unmarked chin, throat and chest of ♀. Habitat: open and bushed areas with some grass cover. Also in scrubbed coastal dunes. (Drinks at sunset; otherwise mainly nocturnal). AM

3 **CROWNED SANDGROUSE** *Pterocles coronatus* L 28 cm. Note orange throat of ♀. The ♂ from ♂ 4 by black bill base and clean belly. Habitat: desert and other areas with sparse vegetation. (Drinks in the morning). RES.NM.R

4 **SPOTTED SANDGROUSE** *Pterocles senegallus* L 30 (+5) cm. Note spotted, not barred appearance of ♀ and dark narrow line on underbelly. The ♂ with black restricted mainly to undersecondaries. Habitat: dry, stony areas. (Drinks in the morning). NM.RES

5 **CHESTNUT-BELLIED SANDGROUSE** *Pterocles exustus* L 30 (+5) cm. The ♀ from ♂♂ 1 and 2 by plain, not black-and white forehead and elongated tail. Note all-dark underwing of both ♂ and ♀. Habitat: sparsely grassed areas. (Comes to drink in early to mid-morning). AM

6 **AFRICAN GREEN PIGEON** *Treron calva* L 30 cm. Several races: those in eastern and southeastern parts of the D. R. of Congo (not shown) have red (not yellow) legs. Habitat: forest edges, cultivation, suburbs (wherever it finds wild figs to eat). Voice: combination of mid-high frog-like grunts, short fast rattles and other sounds.

7 **SÃO TOMÉ GREEN PIGEON** *Treron sanctithomae* L 30 cm. Overall more dark-grey than green. Habitat: tree crowns of forests and plantations. E, São Tomé.

8 **BRUCE'S GREEN PIGEON** *Treron waalia* L 30 cm. From 6 by grey, not green head. Habitat: dry, wooded grassland, towns, villages and other places with fruiting figs. Voice: starts like creaking door and continues like the yelping of a small dog wanting to be let out.

9 **ROCK PIGEON** *Columba livia* L 35 cm. Shown in the plate is race *gymnocyclus* of the original Rock Pigeon (or Dove); race *targia* of central Sahara lacks red eye ring and has grey, not white rump. (In many cities in Africa and in the rest of the world Feral Pigeons are found, which are descendants of this Rock Dove; they have accepted the urban buildings as a replacement of the rocky cliffs in their original natural habitat and often still show basic features as black wing bars and purple-green neck patches). Habitat: dry areas with cliffs, canyons, rocky hills.

10 **SPECKLED (or Rock) PIGEON** *Columba guinea* L 40 cm. Shows striking white rump in flight. Habitat: areas near cliffs and buildings including towns and villages. Voice: mid-high (or high) slightly rising 'coocoocoo-) (10–20x 'coo') or 'roocoocoo roocoocoo-'.

11 **WOOD PIGEON** *Columba palumbus* L 40 cm. Note white neck spot and wing bars. Habitat: normally in forests and stands of tall trees. Vagrant to the area. Voice: 5-syllable series of coos with emphasis on first and short pause before 4th: 'CU-coocoo coocoo'. V

12 **AFEP PIGEON** *Columba unicincta* L 35 cm. Large forest pigeon with striking pale tail bar in flight. Habitat: forest canopies. Voice: hurried low 'oooh-oooh-oooh-oooh' (each 'oooh' falling off).

13 **CAMEROON OLIVE PIGEON** *Columba sjostedti* L 35 cm. Highland species of Mt Cameroon and Bioco. Note all-grey, not white-naped head and black feet. From 14 by different range. Habitat: forest.

14 **OLIVE (or Rameron) PIGEON** *Columba arquatrix* L 40 cm. Very dark with yellow bare parts. Habitat: canopy of forests and plantations. Voice: low rattled drawn-up 'kukurururu kukukururu' and scolding shrieked 'ku-reeeet' ('ku-' very short and low).

15 **WHITE-NAPED PIGEON** *Columba albinucha* L 40 cm. Note white-grey nape, tail pattern and unspotted wings. Feet red. Habitat: canopies and mid-strata of montane forests, especially in palms.

16 **SÃO TOMÉ OLIVE PIGEON** *Columba thomensis* L 40 cm. Very dark, including head and undertail. Habitat: forest. E, São Tomé.

▶

Plate 44 (continued)

17 **SÃO TOMÉ BRONZE-NAPED PIGEON** *Columba malherbii*   L 30 cm. From 45.11 by white eye and chestnut, not whitish undertail coverts. Habitat: forests and plantations.

18 **WESTERN BRONZE-NAPED PIGEON** *Columba iriditorques*   L 30 cm. Note tail-pattern. Habitat: forest canopies. Voice: mid-high '*oohooroo*', high '*oo-hooroo*' and high '*oohoo-oohoo-oohoo*' (each '*oohoo*' gliding down).

19 **STOCK DOVE** *Columba oenas*   L 35 cm. From 9 by dark eye, restricted black in wings and concentrated green patches to sides of neck. Habitat: normally in areas with large trees; vagrant to Niger. V

Plate 45 (continued)

BLACK-BILLED WOOD DOVE *Turtur abyssinicus*   L 20 cm. Note black bill. Habitat: woodland, dry scrubland, thickets, wooded swamp edges and cultivation. Voice: high, slowly descending '*oo ooooh oovoovoo oovoovoo oocoovoovoovoo*'.

EMERALD- (or Green-)SPOTTED WOOD DOVE *Turtur chalcospilos*   L 20 cm. From 13 by much darker bill. Habitat: any type of woodland. Voice: as 13 but with more double-notes '*ookoo ookoo ookoo* '.

TAMBOURINE DOVE *Turtur tympanistria*   L 25 cm. Strikingly white below. Habitat: forest, scrub- and woodland, plantations, suburbs. Voice: as 12 and 14 but whole sequence starts at a lower pitch.

BLUE-HEADED WOOD DOVE *Turtur brehmeri*   L 25 cm. Unmistakable, note orange rump patch in flight. Habitat: forest floors and ground strata. Voice: mid-high call, starting very slowly, gradually descending '*pioe pioe pioe pioe pioe-pioe poopoopoopoopoo*' (ending in a near-trill).

Plate 45

1   **EUROPEAN TURTLE DOVE** *Streptopelia turtur*   L 30 cm. Note black-and-white striped neck patches. Shown is very pale race *arenicola* from NW Africa (not the Eurasian nominate, occasionally found in the area, which differs from 3 by white-striped neck patch, grey-vinous breast and belly and with strikingly white-cornered tail). Habitat: found in thornbush. Voice: mid-high guttural level '*gruurrr gruurr gruuuurrr*' or '*krukrurrr-gruuuu*'. NM

2   **DUSKY (or Pink-breasted) TURTLE DOVE** *Streptopelia lugens*   L 30 cm. Note all-black neck patches. No white in tail. Habitat: edges of montane forests, suburbs, woodland. Voice: low raucous repeated '*kkroarrr-kroarrrr -*'.

3   **ADAMAWA TURTLE DOVE** *Streptopelia hypopyrrha*   L 30 cm.. From Eurasian race of 1 by solid black neck patches, grey terminal band to tail and rufous underparts, sharply demarcated from grey upperbreast. Habitat: in or near forest patches, woodland and stands of large wild or planted trees. Voice: as 1 (which is normally silent in Africa). (AM)

4   **AFRICAN COLLARED (or Rose-grey) DOVE** *Streptopelia roseogrisea*   L 30 cm. Note very pale greyish-pink appearance. Large white tail corners. Habitat: open and bushed semi-desert with more or less grass cover. Voice: mid-high, unhurried, gliding '*cook-crrrooooooh*'. (AM)

5   **AFRICAN MOURNING DOVE** *Streptopelia decipiens*   L 30 cm. Note red-rimmed eye and black white-edged neck patch. Race *ambigua* from SE parts of the D. R. of Congo has yellow, not mainly red iris. In flight from other similar doves by narrow white terminal tail band, from 6 by more grey in wing. Dark tail base not visible when tail is folded. Habitat: dry wooded areas with some grass often near streams. Also in gardens. Voice: e.g. combination of high '*woodurrrr*' and short '*woo*' or low '*durrrr*'.

6   **RED-EYED DOVE** *Streptopelia semitorquata*   L 30 cm. Red colour of eyes only visible at close range. Note small greyish tail corners and dark tail feather bases, visible when tail is closed. Upperwing without grey. Habitat: forest edges, woodland, suburbs. Voice: high hurried '*koo-koo-kookookookoo*' or '*frur kookoo*'.

7   **RING-NECKED (or Cape Turtle) DOVE** *Streptopelia capicola*   L 25 cm. Note small pale black-eyed appearance and large white tail corners. From 4 by different range, grey rump and wider black half-collar. Habitat: forest edges, open woodland, suburbs. Voice: very high sustained '*wikwirrik-wuk-*'.

8   **VINACEOUS DOVE** *Streptopelia vinacea*   L 25 cm. More pink than 7. Tail-feathers, except central pair, white with dark brown base. Belly and under tail-coverts not so white as 7. Habitat: dry, more or less wooded and bushed natural and cultivated habitats. Voice: very high, almost rattling, hollow, fast '*rurururu-*' and high, fast '*weeweewee-weeweeru-*'. RES.AM

9   **LAUGHING DOVE** *Streptopelia senegalensis*   L 25 cm. Note buff-rufous black-speckled throat patch, pale rufous colouring of upperparts, broad grey wing bar in flight, large white tail corners. Habitat: suburbs, cultivation near settlement, more or less bushed grassland. Voice: '*ooh-wuwuwu*' ('*ooh*' very short).

10   **EURASIAN COLLARED DOVE** *Streptopelia decaocto*   L 30 cm. Expanding its range from the North African coast southwards. Might have reached Niger. Note absence of (or hardly any) pinkish wash and weak uppertail pattern. (No map). (?)

11   **LEMON (or Cinnamon) DOVE** *Columba larvata*   L 25 cm. The ♀♀ (not shown) duller than ♂♂. Races *inornata* (a) and *jacksoni* (b) shown, latter with more rufous than grey belly and with grey (not coral red) eye ring. Note plain, unmarked wings. Habitat: undergrowth and floor of dense mountain forests, parks and suburban gardens. Voice: high, hollow '*woop woop -*' (2 x '*woop*' per 3 sec).

12   **NAMAQUA DOVE** *Oena capensis*   L 25 cm. Normally in pairs, showing white rump patch when flushed. Habitat: semi-desert, dry more or less bushed and shrubbed areas. Voice: high hollow '*uhwhooo*' or '*uh-rhoo-rhoo*'. (AM)

13   **BLUE-SPOTTED (or Red-billed) WOOD DOVE** *Turtur afer*   L 20 cm. From 14 by red yellow-tipped bill. Habitat: rather moist forest. Voice: high starting, very slow, lazy, hesitating, slowly speeding up and descending with a bouncing finale '*oo oo oo oo oo oo oo-oo-oo-ookookookookoo*'.

◀

Plate 46

1   **NARINA'S TROGON** *Apaloderma narina*   L 30 cm. See 2 and 3. Habitat: more or less open forests and suburban gardens. Voice: low, loud, crescendoing, hooting 'oooh-oh-oooh--oooh-oh- oh-oh'.

2   **BARE-CHEEKED TROGON** *Apaloderma aequatoriale*   L 30 cm. From 1 by yellow, less extensive bare parts on face sides and by some barring at base of tail feathers, seen from below. Habitat: lowland rainforests. Voice: descending, crescendoing series of 6-8 notes 'ooh-ooh-ooh- - - -'. R

3   **BAR-TAILED TROGON** *Apaloderma vittatum*   L 30 cm. From 1 and 2 by darker head and uppertail and more distinct wing barring. Barred undertail diagnostic. Unobtrusive. Habitat: mid-strata of montane forests. Voice: high loud crescendoing yelping 'hoo-hoo-hoo-hoo-hoo-hoo-hoo-hoo-hoo-hoo'.

4   **SPECKLED MOUSEBIRD** *Colius striatus*   L 35 cm. Rump is concolorous with rest of upperparts. Other races (not shown) have no or little white to cheeks. Habitat: open forest, wooded grassland, orchards, suburbs.

5   **RED-BACKED MOUSEBIRD** *Colius castanotus*   L 35 cm. From 4 by chestnut rump and different range. Habitat: dry wooded and bushed grasslands. R

6   **RED-FACED MOUSEBIRD** *Urocolius indicus*   L 35 cm. Note thin long tail and red bare parts. Eye may be black (shown), pale blue or yellow. Habitat: wooded scrub- and bush, plantations, gardens. R

7   **BLUE-NAPED MOUSEBIRD** *Urocolius macrourus*   L 35 cm. Note blue neck patch, pale bluish rump and upper tail-coverts. Imm without blue nape. Habitat: dry, more or less wooded and bushed, natural and cultivated areas.

8   **RED-HEADED LOVEBIRD** *Agapornis pullaria*   L 13 cm. Note black eye, red bill and pale blue rump. Habitat: moist wooded areas at lower altitudes.

9   **BLACK-COLLARED LOVEBIRD** *Agapornis swinderniana*   L 13 cm. Yellow-necked (a) and red-necked (b) forms shown. Note dark blue rump. Habitat: forests and connected well-wooded streams. R

10   **GREY PARROT** *Psittacus erithacus*   L 30cm. Nominate (a) shown and smaller race *timneh* (b, with darker, less red tail and tail coverts and with reddish upper mandible). Unmistakable. Habitat: forests.

11   **ROSE-RINGED PARAKEET** *Psittacula krameri*   L 40 cm. Unmistakable. Habitat: wooded grassland, scrub, marshes and any habitat with large trees, except true forest.

12   **RED-FRONTED (or -headed) PARROT** *Poicephalus gulielmi*   L 30 cm. Note brilliant green plumage with darker (not pale grey as ♂15) face and wings, red forehead and shoulder, yellowish-green rump. Habitat: forest canopy.

13   **NIAM-NIAM PARROT** *Poicephalus crassus*   L 23 cm. Mainly green with grey extending to breast and yellow underwings. Habitat: wood patches and tree stands in further open country.

14   **MEYER'S PARROT** *Poicephalus meyeri*   L 22 cm. Note blue-green lower breast. From 13, 16 and 17 by smaller yellow area on underwing. Upperparts mainly brown. Yellow on forehead sometimes missing. Habitat: more or less wooded grassland.

15   **BROWN-NECKED (or Cape) PARROT** *Poicephalus robustus*   L 35 cm. Note pale olive head, red 'socks', red on shoulder. Not all ♀♀ have reddish forehead as shown. Imm without any red. Habitat: forest at mid-high altitudes and woodland.

16   **SENEGAL (or Yellow-bellied) PARROT** *Poicephalus senegalus*   L 25 cm. Nominate (a) shown and race *versteri* (b, more extensive orange below). Habitat: all types of woodland, especially with baobab.

17   **RUEPPELL'S PARROT** *Poicephalus rueppellii*   L 23 cm. Brown with yellow shoulder, yellow underwing coverts and blue belly without any green. Blue of ♀ deeper. Habitat: dry grassy thornbush, woodland. (?)

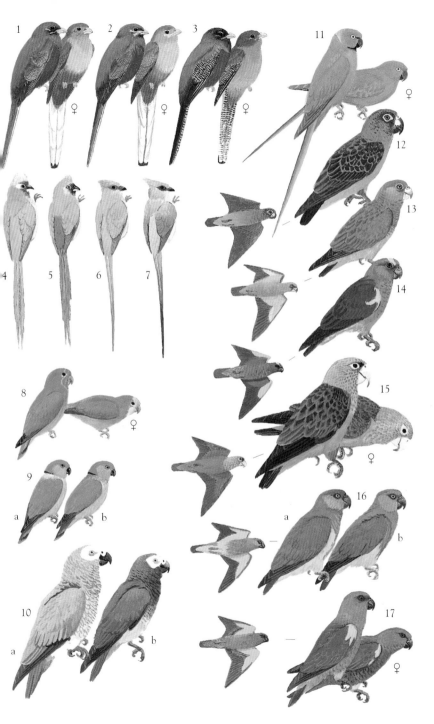

Plate 47

1 **GREAT BLUE TURACO** *Corythaeola cristata* L 75 cm. Unmistakable. Habitat: canopies of forests, riverine belts, forest remains.

2 **WESTERN GREY PLANTAIN-EATER** *Crinifer piscator* L 50 cm. From 3 by plain tail and short stripes on upperparts. Habitat: all types of wooded, natural or cultivated areas.

3 **EASTERN GREY PLANTAIN-EATER** *Crinifer zonurus* L 50 cm. Note white windows in tail and upperwing. Habitat: open woodland, cultivated areas and suburban gardens.

4 **BARE-FACED GO-AWAY BIRD** *Corythaixoides personata* L 50 cm. Unmistakable. Habitat: more or less wooded, natural and cultivated areas. R

5 **GREY GO-AWAY BIRD** *Corythaixoides concolor* L 50 cm. Unmistakable. Note erectile crest (a). Habitat: thornbush, dry open woodland. Voice: mid-high miaowing gliding-down '*meeeh*'. Note: the name Go-away bird is derived from the call of the East-African White-bellied Go-away Bird '*g'wa*'.

6 **ROSS'S TURACO** *Musophaga rossae* L 50 cm. From 7 by different head pattern. Habitat: canopy of forest remains, miombo, gardens. Often near streams. Voice: high short slowed-down cackled '*rutututut-tut tut*'.

7 **VIOLET TURACO** *Musophaga violacea* L 50 cm. As 6, but with different head pattern and more southern range. Habitat: near streams in natural and cultivated areas with high trees.

8 **RWENZORI TURACO** *Musophaga johnstoni* L 40 cm. Race *johnstoni* (a) shown and race *kivuensis* (b, without bare yellow skin around eye). Habitat: montane forests and bamboo. R

9 **SCHALOW'S TURACO** *Tauraco schalowi* L 40 cm. High crest makes it unmistakable. Habitat: forest and woodland.

10 **GREEN TURACO** *Tauraco persa* L 45 cm. Nominate (a) shown and race *buffoni* (b, without white below eye). From 14 by white in front of eye, pink bill and blue tail. Habitat: mid-strata and canopy of rather dense forests and woodland. Voice: high loud barking '*wah-wah-wraah-wraah-wraah-wraah*'.

11 **BLACK-BILLED TURACO** *Tauraco schuetti* L 40 cm. Nominate (a) shown and race *emini* (b, mainly green, not purplish). Note white line along crest (and black bill). Habitat: forest canopies. Voice: mid-high sustained '*wahweh-wahweh-wahweh-*' (like barking of small dogs).

12 **RED-CRESTED TURACO** *Tauraco erythrolophus* L 40 cm. From 13 by white line along crest and different range. Habitat: forests. V

13 **BANNERMAN'S TURACO** *Tauraco bannermani* L 40 cm. No other red-crested turaco in its range. Habitat: mountain forests. E, Cameroon

14 **YELLOW-BILLED (or Verreaux's) TURACO** *Tauraco macrorhynchus* L 40 cm. Nominate (a) shown and race *verreauxii* (b, without white in crest). From very similar 11 in same range by absence of white above black lore and paler bill. Habitat: forest canopies.

15 **WHITE-CRESTED TURACO** *Tauraco leucolophus* L 40 cm. Unmistakable. Habitat: leafy canopy at montane forest edges. Also in wood-, bush- and scrubland.

Plate 48

1   **GREAT SPOTTED CUCKOO** *Clamator glandarius*   L 40 cm. Not striped below. Note black streak through eye of ad and red primaries of imm. Habitat: dry more or less wooded and bushed natural and cultivated areas. Voice: high slightly chattered 'rrrrrri--' or very high loud rattled sharp 'ririririririririri'. RES.NM?

2   **JACOBIN (or Black-and-white) CUCKOO** *Oxylophus jacobinus*   L 35 cm. Note white wing bar across primary bases of this and next species. Habitat: dry grassland with scattered trees and bush. Voice: very high piped 'piu piu piu piu - -' (each 'piu' gliding down) or 'tjiu-tjiu-weet'. AM

3   **AFRICAN STRIPED CUCKOO** *Oxylophus levaillantii*   L 35 cm. From 2 by streaks on throat and upperbreast. Habitat: forest edges, wooded swamps, dense bush, gardens. Voice very high piped 'piu piu piu - -' (each 'piu' gliding off) or high chattered rattle 'chachacha- -'. RES.AM

4   **THICK-BILLED CUCKOO** *Pachycoccyx audeberti*   L 35 cm. Imm from 1 by whitish head and barred tail. Habitat: miombo, thornbush, riverine belts. Voice: extreme high lashing 'weeehwit weeehwit'.

5   **YELLOWBILL (or Green Coucal)** *Ceuthmochares aureus*   L 35 cm. Note small size with heavy yellow bill. Solitary and skulking. Habitat: dense undergrowth at forest edges and connected riverine belts. Voice: song starts with extreme high staccato 'tic's', then changes to mid-high scolding 'kah-kah-kah-' which ends in a trill. Many variations of this series. Also very high 'fu weeeh'.

6   **YELLOW-THROATED CUCKOO** *Chrysococcyx flavigularis*   L 20 cm. Note unbarred upperparts of ♀. Outer tail-feathers mainly white. Habitat: forest canopies. Voice: very high, fluting, slightly falling-off 'fee-wee-peepeepeepeepee'.

7   **AFRICAN EMERALD CUCKOO** *Chrysococcyx cupreus*   L 20 cm. Note regular barring of ♀. Habitat: forest glades and edges, woodland, and bush, cultivation, suburbs. Voice: very high, mellow, liquid, affirmative 'hello Judy'.

8   **KLAAS'S CUCKOO** *Chrysococcyx klaas*   L 15 cm. The ♀ from ♀ 7 by white eye stripe. Habitat: forest patches, parks and gardens. Voice: very high fluted plaintive 'It's not true dear' or 'weeeetuh-weeeetuh-weeeetuh'.

9   **DIEDERIK (or Didric) CUCKOO** *Chrysococcyx caprius*   L 20 cm. Note white spots, arranged in a wedge on closed wing. Normal (a) and uncommon rufous (b) imm forms shown. Habitat: forests and other more or less wooded and bushed areas, including cultivation and gardens. Voice: very high fluted 'it is not good so' or 'weet-weet-weetrr'.

10   **RED-CHESTED CUCKOO** *Cuculus solitarius*   L 30 cm. Chestnut breast of ♂ may be unbarred and brighter rufous. From 11b by pale upperparts, grey (not rufous) chin and throat, imm from ad 11b by absence of rufous. Often heard but seldom seen. Habitat: forest belts, cultivations, suburbs. Voice: very high loud fluted staccato unhurried 'it-will-rain it-will-rain' (emphasis on first syllable). RES.(AM)

11   **BLACK CUCKOO** *Cuculus clamosus*   L 30 cm. Nominate (a, savannah belt) and race *gabonensis* (b, forest areas) shown. Underwing barred as 10. Habitat: canopy at forest edges, woodland, bush- and scrubland, gardens. Voice: mid-high fluted unhurried 'fiufiuu-fiuu' of ♂ together with hurried rising 'wowowowikkewikkewikkewikke' of ♀.

12   **COMMON (or European) CUCKOO** *Cuculus canorus*   L 35 cm. From 13 by less barred tail (seen from below) and darker underwing, from 14 and 15 by larger size and white (not pale buff) undertail coverts. Rufous (a) form of ♀ rare. Imm (not shown) from imm 13 by unbarred rump; also rufous and grey imm forms known. Habitat: more or less wooded and bushed habitats. Voice: silent in Africa. NM

13   **AFRICAN CUCKOO** *Cuculus gularis*   L 35 cm. See 12. Bill base often rather extensively yellow than variation of this feature makes it not reliable enough for diagnosis and separation from 12, 14 and 15. Note barred rump of imm. Habitat: hilly dry more or less wooded and bushed areas. Voice: mid-high rather level 'ku-koo ku-koo ku-koo'. AM

14   **ASIAN LESSER CUCKOO** *Cuculus poliocephalus*   L 25 cm. From 12 and 13 by smaller size and blackish uppertail coverts. A very rare rufous morph of ♀ exists (not so of 15). Differences in voice not helpful, because 12, 14 and 15 are probably silent in Africa. Habitat: forest edges and dense undergrowth in woodland, and bush. Voice: probably silent in Africa. High descending yelping rapid 'djipdjipdjipdjip'. EM

▶

15 **MADAGASCAR LESSER CUCKOO** *Cuculus rochii* L 30 cm. No rufous ♀ form known. Often shows less undertail barring than 14. As 14 with dark uppertail coverts. Habitat: forest, woodland and bushed areas. Voice: high liquid yelping rapid '*woopwoopwoop-wop*' (lower in pitch than 14). R

16 **OLIVE LONG-TAILED CUCKOO** *Cercococcyx olivinus* L 35 cm. Very difficult to separate from 17 and 18, but upperparts slightly more bronzy and underparts less heavily barred. Imm as imm's 17 and 18. Note, that 17 has a restricted range in eastern parts of the D. R. of Congo and prefers forests in montane areas. Habitat: lowlands. Less restricted to dense forest than 18. Voice: mid-high fluted sustained '*fiuw-fiuw-fiuw- -*' (each '*fiuw*' with slight inbuilt tremolo), or high very lazy '*it will rain*'. R

17 **BARRED LONG-TAILED CUCKOO** *Cercococcyx montanus* L 35 cm. Note restricted range. Habitat: prefers montane forest edges. Voice: high loud '*weet-weet-weet-weh*' or long sequence of slowly rising '*fjuu-fjuu-fjuu-fijuu-fijuu- -*' (up to 20x '*fijuu*').

18 **DUSKY LONG-TAILED CUCKOO** *Cercococcyx mechowi* L 35 cm. From 16 by slightly heavier belly baring and less buffy chest sides and from 17 by preference for lowlands, from 16 and 17 by voice. Habitat: mainly lowland forest. Undergrowth near streams. Voice: very high climbing lashing '*pu wee wir*' (reminding of 10), fluted descending rapid '*tijuwtijuwtijuw-tijuw-tijuw-*' and other whistles.

Plate 49

1 **SPOTTED EAGLE OWL** *Bubo africanus* L 50 cm. Nominate (a) shown and dark-eyed race *cinerascens* (b, which might be an independent species). Note fine barring. May have orange (instead of normal yellow) eyes. Habitat: open forest, rocky desert, woodland, suburbs. Voice: low, drawn-out '*hoooi hoooi*'

2 **SHELLEY'S EAGLE OWL** *Bubo shelleyi* L 65 cm. Very large. Note dark, barred appearance. Habitat: lowland forest. R

3 **FRASER'S EAGLE OWL** *Bubo poensis* L 55 cm. Note overall barring and contrastful marked head. From 2 by paler face, crown and upperparts. Habitat: forests. Voice: high, crescendoing, plaintive '*uuuuuuuh*' and very low, pigeon-like rolling '*rrrrru rrrrru*'.

4 **VERREAUX'S (or Giant) EAGLE OWL** *Bubo lacteus* L 65 cm. Note greyish appearance and pink eyelids. Habitat: well-wooded streams, other areas with some large trees. Voice: extreme low '*prooh prooh prooh*', each '*prooh*' very short.

5 **AKUN EAGLE OWL** *Bubo leucostictus* L 50 cm. From other large owls in same range by yellow eyes, except 1 which is paler, finer barred, less contrasting marked and has a mainly different habitat (and range). Habitat: lowland forest.

6 **DESERT EAGLE OWL** *Bubo bubo desertorum* L 55 cm. (Often treated as an independent species, different from extralimital Eurasian Eagle Owl *Bubo bubo ascalaphus*). Note very pale colouring. Habitat: rocky desert and sparsely wooded semi-desert. Voice: low, pigeon-like '*oohoo*'. R

7 **VERMICULATED (or Bouvier's) FISHING OWL** *Scotopelia bouvieri* L 55 cm. From 8 and 9 by yellow bill and white underparts. Habitat: forests ribbons along streams.

8 **RUFOUS FISHING OWL** *Scotopelia ussheri* L 50 cm. From 9 by unbarred upperparts. Habitat: forest along rivers and lakes, mangroves. R

9 **PEL'S FISHING OWL** *Scotopelia peli* L 70 cm. Unmistakable. Habitat: well-forested streams and lakes. Voice: extreme low sinister '*hoop ho hoop ho –*'.

10 **COPPERY-TAILED COUCAL** *Centropus cupreicaudus* L 50 cm. Note brown (not rufous) mantle and all-black (not barred) uppertail coverts. From 11 by absence of blue gloss on head and mantle, from 14 by darker mantle, gradually merging into neck and crown. Habitat: reed beds, papyrus, tall grass, shrubbery. Voice: low piping rapid slightly descending '*poo-poo-poo-pup-pup-pup-pup*' as water running from a bottle. R

11 **BLUE-HEADED COUCAL** *Centropus monachus* L 45 cm. Note buff wash to underparts. Difficult to separate from 14 in same range, but larger, with heavier bill, less reddish-rufous upperparts; from 12 by unbarred uppertail coverts. Note blue sheen on head and neck. Imm has faintly streaked uppertail coverts and pale-streaked brown crown. Habitat: reed beds, shrubbery, at riverbanks or in forest clearings. Voice: e.g. mid-high hollow piping '*poo-poo-poo-poopoo-poo*'.

▶

12 **GABON COUCAL** *Centropus anselli* L 50 cm. Note buff underparts. Habitat: dense undergrowth of swampy forest, old cultivations. Voice: mid-high hooting slightly descending '*foo-foo foo fooh fooh foo*' or very high '*fooh-fooh-fooh-fooh-wukwukwukwukwuk-wooh wooh wooh wooh*' ('*wukwuk-*' part very high).

13 **BLACK-THROATED COUCAL** *Centropus leucogaster* L 50 cm. Only coucal with black chin and white belly. Habitat: forest undergrowth.

14 **SENEGAL COUCAL** *Centropus senegalensis* L 40 cm. Dark (a, with rufous underparts) and 'normal' (b) forms shown. Note absence of blue gloss, bright rufous mantle and unbarred uppertail coverts. Habitat: rather dry bush, forest edges, swamps. Voice: as 10 but at mid-high pitch.

15 **WHITE-BROWED COUCAL** *Centropus superciliosus* L 45 cm. From imm coucals (except 16, which lacks eye stripe) by white black-edged feathers of nape and neck. Habitat: areas with high grass, reeds and some trees; in north-east of range: semi-desert. Voice: mid-high hollow '*uhuhuhuhurrrrrruhuhuhuh*' with a lower trill in the middle.

16 **BLACK COUCAL** *Centropus grillii* L 35 cm. From 14a by black belly and darker upperparts. Note absence of eyebrow in n-br plumage. Habitat: marshes, inundations with some bush and shrub. Voice: mid-high, mellow '*wukwuk wukwuk wukwuk*'.

Plate 50

1 **BARN OWL** *Tyto alba* L 35 cm. Nominate (a) shown and races *detorta* (b, Cape Verde) and *thomensis* (c, São Thomé). Note upright stance. Does not perch on the ground. Habitat: near caves, buildings, Hamerkop nests; not in true forest. Voice: very high loud shivering '*wrururururu*' and drawn-up shrieking '*frrrruuuui*'.

2 **AFRICAN GRASS OWL** *Tyto capensis* L 35 cm. From 5 by high-legged build and absence of dark wrist patches on underwing. Habitat: moist grass- and moorland. Voice: high shriek '*frieeet*' and low Mallard-like '*kweh kweh kweh kweh*'. R

3 **SHORT-EARED OWL** *Asio flammeus* L 40 cm. Active all day. Habitat: open marshes and wet grasslands. Voice: soft, pushed-out '*booh-booh-booh-booh-*'. NM.R

4 **LONG-EARED OWL** *Asio otus* L 45 cm. Note long upright stance especially when disturbed but may perch also with fluffed-out feathers and no visible ear plumes. Habitat: montane forest edges and giant heath. R

5 **MARSH OWL** *Asio capensis* L 35 cm. Note seemingly large dark (not yellow as in 3) eyes, buff window on upperwing, crouched stance. Active in twilight at sunrise and sunset. Will come to and circle intruder. Habitat: short grassland, marches, swamps. Voice: mid-high snipe-like '*krèèh*', mid-high duck-like barked '*ruururu*', loud explosive shrieks. (AM)

6 **CONGO BAY OWL** *Phodilus prigoginei* L 30 cm. Note reddish upperparts and short tail. Habitat: open montane forest. E, D. R. of Congo.

7 **LITTLE OWL** *Athene noctua* L 25 cm. Example shown of several pale desert races. Note short tail and rather long legs. May hunt by day. Habitat: rocky country and dry areas with scattered trees, shrub and some grass cover. Voice: high, melancholy '*Wjooo Wjooo -*' ('*Wj-*' rapidly lowered in pitch) and alarm '*kip-kip-kip*'. R

8 **MANED (or Akun Scops) OWL** *Jubula lettii* L 40 cm. Note reddish glow and maned appearance. Intermediate forest owl, larger than 10–18, smaller than *Bubo* owls 49.1–5. Habitat forest, especially along rivers. R

9 **WHITE-FACED SCOPS OWL** *Otus* (or *Ptilopsis*) *leucotis* L 30 cm. Nominate (a, Northern White-faced Scops Owl) and race *granti* (b, Southern White-faced Scops Owl) shown, sometimes considered to be two separate species. Note orange eyes and pale grey feathering. Habitat: large trees in woodland. Voice: mid-high cooing '*bbbbb-woouow*' ('*bbbbb*' as a slow trill).

10 **SANDY SCOPS OWL** *Otus icterorhynchus* L 20 cm. From 12 and 13 by rather unmarked and more white-spotted than black-streaked plumage. Not in same range as 11. Voice: a series of descending whistles. R

11 **SÃO TOMÉ SCOPS OWL** *Otus hartlaubi* L 20 cm. Only small owl on São Tomé. Might occur on Príncipe. Habitat: forests and plantations. E, São Tomé.

▶

Plate 50 (continued)

12 **AFRICAN SCOPS OWL** *Otus senegalensis*   L 20 cm. As 13 very variable in colour. 'Ears' not always obvious. Habitat: more or less wooded habitats including gardens. Voice: very high '*prriur prriur - -*' with 4 seconds intervals. ,

13 **COMMON SCOPS OWL** *Otus scops*   L 20 cm. From 12 only distinguishable by voice. As 12 very variable in colouring (examples a and b shown) and stance (thickset or slender).. Habitat: more or less wooded habitats, including gardens. Voice: high, clear '*hjuuhhjuuh - hjuuhhjuuh*' (with 2 sec between each). NM

14 **RED-CHESTED OWLET** *Glaucidium tephronotum*   L 20 cm. Unmistakable by dark upperparts and reddish breast patches. May hunt by day. Habitat: forests. Voice: high, mellow, gliding, hooting '*too-too-too-*' (2–30 times) or '*tutju tutju-*' or '*huu-huu-huu-p*'. R

15 **PEARL-SPOTTED OWLET** *Glaucidium perlatum*   L 20 cm. Note streaking (not barring) below, long tail, pseudo-face at back of head (a). Often seen by day. Habitat: open woodland, bush with some trees. Voice: high '*puukpuukpuuk- - - -*', sustained for 20–30 seconds and very high piercing descending '*piiiuuu*' (like fireworks).

16 **AFRICAN BARRED OWLET** *Glaucidium capense*   L 25 cm. Miombo race *ngamiame* (a) and forest race *castaneum* (b, with plain mantle and spotted crown) shown. The forest race *etchecopari* (not shown) from western Africa has dark, almost unmarked upperparts and partly spotted (forehead) and partly barred (crown and nape) head. Habitat: more or less dense forest often near water. Voice: very high staccato '*pjuipjuipjuipjui- - -*' (each '*pjui*' descending) and very high '*wruhwruhwruh- - -*'.

17 **CHESTNUT-BACKED (or Sjöstedt's) OWLET** *Glaucidium sjostedti*   L 25 cm. From other owlets by reddish mantle, from 18 by more and larger white spots on upperwing. Habitat: forest interior. R

18 **ALBERTINE OWLET** *Glaucidium albertinum*   L 20 cm. From 16b by buff, not white edge to mantle and less white spots on upperwing. Habitat: montane forest. R

19 **AFRICAN WOOD OWL** *Strix woodfordii*   L 35 cm. Plumage variable from pale brown via russet to dark brown, dark form shown. Note black eyes set in white face and barring below. Habitat: forest, plantations, suburbs. Voice: high and mid-high barking '*woo-woo woorrrorrwoo*'.

Plate 51

The identification of nightjars can be made somewhat easier by checking their ranges (see maps) and their nocturnal songs (see 'voice'). There are two basic song types: either a short liquid melodious whistle (type A) or a very long sustained churr (B). Most nightjars are either whistlers or churrers. The presence and form of white (or buff) markings on wings and tail might be helpful e.g. for identifying traffic victims.

1 **BROWN NIGHTJAR** *Caprimulgus binotatus* L 22 cm. Plain, dark red-brown coloured with pale edge to the scapulars. Habitat: forest canopy. Voice: long series of '*glu-glu-glu- - -*' given from high branch (song type B). R

2 **RED-NECKED NIGHTJAR** *Caprimulgus ruficollis* L 30 cm. Note extension of white in tail. From 3 and 8 by paler and greyer forewing, from other similar nightjars by different range. Habitat: open woodland. Voice: slow churr '*kutok-kutok-kutok- -*', but normally silent in West Africa. NM.R

3 **EUROPEAN NIGHTJAR** *Caprimulgus europaeus* L 25 cm. Note bright first row of white spots along wing coverts, enhanced by dark forewing. Tawny neck bar not obvious. Generally rather dark and grey. Perches lengthwise on tree branches. Habitat: bushed and wooded, natural and cultivated areas. Voice: rarely heard in Africa. Sings from tree branch mid-high '*rrrri-------*' narrowed to '*rrru----*', at irregular intervals sustained for up to 5 minutes (song type B). NM

4 **EGYPTIAN NIGHTJAR** *Caprimulgus aegyptius* L 25 cm. Pale and rather uniform coloured. No or hardly any white in tail and opened wing. Habitat: desert and semi-desert. Voice: mid-high, sustained, rapid '*corrcorrcorrcorrcorr-*' like a car engine ticking over. NM.EM

5 **GOLDEN NIGHTJAR** *Caprimulgus eximius* L 25 cm. Unmistakable. Habitat: dry areas without trees. Voice: very long, low, monotonous churr.

6 **MOUNTAIN NIGHTJAR** *Caprimulgus poliocephalus* L 25 cm. Note dark appearance. The ♂ has two outer pairs of tail feathers mostly white (buff in female). Habitat: prefers higher altitudes. Open forests, moist woodland. Voice: sings from dead tree branch or telephone line very high fluting '*pieuj pjurrr*' (song type A). (?)

7 **FIERY-NECKED NIGHTJAR** *Caprimulgus pectoralis* L 24 cm. Note strikingly large head. The ♂ from 6 by less pale neck and collar, from 9 by moister habitat and different voice. Habitat: wooded areas including gardens. Voice: sings from tree perch high '*tjuuu-tuwirrrr*'.

8 **BLACK-SHOULDERED NIGHTJAR** *Caprimulgus nigriscapularis* L 25 cm. Note rather rufous-brown colouring and dark forewing. Habitat: rainforests, dense woodland and moist bush. Voice: high, liquid '*tjuuu tjuderrr*' ('*tjuuu*' drawn up '*tjuderrr*' short) (song type A).

9 **RUFOUS-CHEEKED NIGHTJAR** *Caprimulgus rufigena* L 24 cm. From 3 by tawny hind collar. Little overlap with range of 7. Habitat: dry woodland, thornbush, scrub desert. Voice: sings from ground (occasionally from perch) low sewing machine-like '*rrrrrr----*' (song type B) sustained for several minutes, preceded by soft '*tjuw tjuw tjuw –*'. AM.R

10 **SLENDER-TAILED NIGHTJAR** *Caprimulgus clarus* L 30 cm. From 52.8 (with similar white (♂) or buff (♀) edge to secondaries) by duskier, less rufous colouring, shorter tail and slower song tempo. Habitat: dry wooded and bushed areas. Voice: sings from ground high staccato sustained '*riririri-------*' (song type B) like a rapid sewing machine.

11 **SOMBRE (or Dusky) NIGHTJAR** *Caprimulgus fraenatus* L 25 cm. More brownish, less rufous then other nightjars. Note black and white scapulars. Very restricted range. Habitat: rocky outcrops in dry areas with scattered scrub and some grass cover. Voice: low, rapid rattle '*rrrrrrr------*' like a fast electric sewing machine. R

12 **PRIGOGINE'S NIGHTJAR** *Caprimulgus prigoginei* L 20 cm. Very rare, only a ♀ ever found. Small, rather rufous Habitat: probably forest. Voice: not known. R

Plate 52

1   **RWENZORI NIGHTJAR** *Caprimulgus ruwenzorii*   L 20 cm. As 51.6 a highland species, but smaller, with less white in tail and smaller wing spots. Habitat: highlands; forest edges and glades. Voice: extra high, piercing '*piee-pirrrr*'. R

2   **SWAMP (or Natal) NIGHTJAR** *Caprimulgus natalensis*   L 24 cm. Note rather crude blotching above and all-white (or buff in ♀) colouring of outer 2 pairs of tail feathers. Habitat: damp grassy places near swamps. Also in woodland. Often associated with palms. Voice: sings from ground high staccato '*kukukuk----*' as small river boat (song type B) sustained for up to 30 seconds and high level '*wuwirrrrr*' (song type A) with '*wu*' as very short undertone at beginning.

3   **PLAIN NIGHTJAR** *Caprimulgus inornatus*   L 25 cm. Rather unmarked; occurs in different colour forms (a, b and c) in accordance with the local soil colour (tawny, brown and grey forms shown). Habitat: dry, wooded and bushed areas with more or less grass cover. Voice: sustained churr. AM.RES

4   **FRECKLED (or Rock) NIGHTJAR** *Caprimulgus tristigma*   L 30 cm. Note large size, dark uniform freckling with pale edge to scapulars and characteristic habitat. Rests by day on bare rock (never in trees). Probably nests also on flat roofs in cities. Habitat: bare (or sparsely overgrown) rocky outcrops and ravines. Voice: sings from ground very high staccato '*whewwhew whewwhew whewhew --*' (resembling very slow song type B) sustained for up to 30 seconds.

5   **BATES'S NIGHTJAR** *Caprimulgus batesi*   L 30 cm. Note large, very dark rufous and grey-capped appearance. The ♀ with rufous-brown (not grey) crown and without white in tail and wings. Habitat: rainforests. Voice: loud, rapid '*whow-whow-whow-*' (5–20 times) (song type B).

6   **SQUARE-TAILED (Gabon or Mozambique) NIGHTJAR** *Caprimulgus fossii*   L 24 cm. Note all-white outer tail feathers (of next pair only terminal half is white); the ♀ has these markings more buffy. Habitat: grassy and sandy areas often at woodland edges near lakes and rivers. Voice: sings from ground (and maybe from tree perch) mid-high rapid staccato rattle, irregular alternating between '-*ru*-' (10–20x) and '-*ri*-' (20–30x) as '*rururuririri----*' (song type B) sustained for up to 2–3 minutes. (Records in Ivory Coast and Ghana of this species refer probably to 7, next species). AM.RES

7   **LONG-TAILED NIGHTJAR** *Caprimulgus climacurus*   L 25 (+10) cm. Brown race *sclateri* (a, southern half of range) and grey nominate (b, northern half) shown. White spots also on outer primaries. Rather similar to 51.7, which however is less rufous and has a very restricted range. Habitat: semi-desert, bushed and wooded grassland, extensive fields, open woodland. Voice: sings from ground high (sometimes low) very fast rattled '*rrrrr-----*' (song type B), faster than sewing machine. AM

8   **STANDARD-WINGED NIGHTJAR** *Macrodipteryx longipennis*   L 25 cm. Note pale eyebrow. In n-br plumage looking small without white in wing or tail. Buff scapulars and hind-collar. Habitat: bushed and more or less wooded habitats. Voice: extra high, sharp, sustained twitter '*tititititititititi----*' with slight decelerations. AM.RES

9   **PENNANT-WINGED NIGHTJAR** *Macrodipteryx vexillaria*   L 30 cm. N-br plumage of ♂ retains most of the black-and-white wing pattern but without pennants. The ♀ as ♀ 8 with pale eyebrow, but with relative longer tail and more pointed wings. Habitat: woodland often in stony hilly areas. Voice: sings in flight or from low perch extreme high insect-like shivering phrases of irregular length '*sisisisisisi----*'. AM.RES

Plate 53

Upper- and underside shown, except of 9.

1   **SCARCE SWIFT** *Schoutedenapus myoptilus*   L 17 cm. Note tightly closed tail, narrow wings, contrasting black eye patch. Best identified in mixed flocks by voice. Habitat: rocky mountains and cliffs, but feeds mainly over forests. Voice: combination of high rapid running-up '*wutwutwut*' with diagnostic '*tiktik tikkerik*' (reminding of Blacksmith Lapwing 34.11). R

2   **SCHOUTEDEN'S SWIFT** *Schoutedenapus schoutedeni*   L 17 cm. With similar jizz as 1, but with uniform dark plumage. Very rare, voice and habitat not known, but probably a highland species. E, D. R. of Congo.

3   **SÃO TOMÉ SPINETAIL** *Zoonavena thomensis*   L 14 cm. Very small. Habitat: flutters around large trees in forest clearings and plantations, constantly twittering. E, São Tomé and Príncipe.

4   **BLACK (or Chapin's) SPINETAIL** *Telacanthura melanopygia*   L 14 cm. Note mottled throat and fluttering flight. Habitat: forest edges, dry woodland, especially near baobab. Voice: high dry sparrow-like '*tsju tsjrrrsjrr*'.

5   **MOTTLED(-throated) SPINETAIL** *Telacanthura ussheri*   L 14 cm. Note white belly-patch (not so in very similar 54.10), connected with larger rump patch and wing shape. Habitat: forest edges and dry woodland, especially near baobab. Voice: very high, dry '*tchu-tchu tchrrrchrrr*' or mid-high rattling '*rururururururururu*'.

6   **CASSIN'S SPINETAIL** *Neafrapus cassini*   L 15 cm. Larger than 7, with same extreme short tail, but with narrower white band across tail base and different range. Habitat: lakes and forest in and near forest. Voice: extra high, soft, twittering cries.

7   **BAT-LIKE (or Böhm's) SPINETAIL** *Neafrapus boehmi*   L 10 cm. Note diagnostic seemingly tail-less appearance, white underparts and rump, characteristic wing shape. Slow erratic bat-like flight around trees. Habitat: open woodland especially near baobab. Voice: very high twittered fast trill '*tsrrirririririritweeh*'. R

8   **SABINE'S SPINETAIL** *Rhaphidura sabini*   L 12 cm. Note bluish sheen over upperparts. Black tail concealed between white coverts. Habitat: rainforest edges, often over water. Voice: extreme high, sharp '*tititututu-tu-tu-tu*'.

9   **AFRICAN PALM SWIFT** *Cypsiurus parvus*   L 17 cm. Note pale very slim long-tailed silhouette. Habitat: any area with palm trees. Voice: extreme high twittered chatter '*twirrr*' or '*srrrr*'.

10   **ALPINE SWIFT** *Tachymarptis melba*   L 22 cm. Note white throat and belly. Habitat: breeds in rocky mountains and cliffs, but travels daily far afield. Voice: extreme high very fast '*swiswiswiwitititi*', slowed-down at the end. NM.RES

11   **MOTTLED SWIFT** *Tachymarptis aequatorialis*   L 22 cm. Note large size and mottling below. Mantle darker than head and rump. Habitat: as 10. Voice: extreme high sweeping '*tcheeet tcheeet –*'.

Plate 54

Upper- and underside shown.

1   **AFRICAN BLACK SWIFT** *Apus barbatus*   L 18 cm. Race *sladeniae* (a, very black, from Bioco and W. Cameroon) shown and nominate (b, with whitish chin). Separation of pale throat-patch from breast gradually scalloped. Belly, rump and underwing feathers slightly pale-fringed. Inner secondaries (seen from above) paler than rest of upperparts. Habitat: rocky mountains and cliffs. Voice: extreme high sharp screams '*tsjieeeah tsjieeeeah –*' (each '*tsjieeeeah*' longer than 4 sec and falling off in '*-ah*'). R

2   **NYANZA SWIFT** *Apus niansae*   L 15 cm. All-black with small, well-defined, sometimes finely striped, throat-patch. Browner than other swifts (except 3, which is more bulky in shape and has different range). Habitat: breeds in rocky caves and buildings. Voice: as Eurasian Swift. R

3   **PALLID SWIFT** *Apus pallidus*   L 15 cm. In mixed flocks looks paler than other swifts. Note large throat patch extending up to forehead giving very pale head-on view. Mantle darkest part above. Broader-winged and bulkier than other swifts. Habitat: towns, coastal areas, oases and highlands. There are a few breeding colonies in the Sahara, but otherwise mainly a migrant from northern Africa and southern Europe. Voice: from 5 by less extreme high, shorter, but shriller shrieks '*sreeh sreeh*'. AM

4   **BATES'S SWIFT** *Apus batesi* L 14 cm. (Also called the Black Swift, which is too similar to the name of 1). Small, with a deeply forked tail and a strong gloss over upperparts. Habitat: rocky, hilly rainforest. Voice: not known. R

5   **EUROPEAN SWIFT** *Apus apus* L 15 cm. Note sooty black colouring with paler throat patch. Rather uniform upperparts. Habitat: any open area. Voice: extreme high sharp hurried screams '*tsjeetsjee tsjee*' (each '*tsjee*' slightly falling of). NM

6   **WHITE-RUMPED SWIFT** *Apus caffer* L 15 cm. Note slender silhouette, deeply forked tail, narrow white crescent across rump which is connected with white rear edges of secondaries. Habitat: 'steals' nests from swallows under rocks, bridges, roofs. Voice: mid-high short rather sparrow-like chatter '*prep-prep-prip- - -*' or very high short shrieks. (AM)

7   **PLAIN SWIFT** *Apus unicolor* L 15 cm. Small, streamlined all-black swift, with only obscure throat patch and more erratic flight than 5. Habitat: breeds in sea cliffs outside the area. Wintering grounds not known, probably on SW Morocco. Voice: as 5. V

8   **ALEXANDER'S SWIFT** *Apus alexandri* L 13 cm. Small, shallow-forked, rather pale below with dark saddle above. Habitat: over any habitat in Cape Verde. Voice: as 5, but higher pitched. E, Cape Verde.

9   **HORUS SWIFT** *Apus horus* L 15 cm. Looks stout, as a fork-tailed version of 10. White of rump extends down to lower flanks. Habitat: prefers higher altitudes. Breeds in sand cliff tunnels, 'stolen' from bee-eaters, kingfishers or martins. Often seen over water. Voice: high plover-like fluted '*piu-purrr piu-purrr*'. R

10   **LITTLE SWIFT** *Apus affinis* L 12 cm. Note white rump and very short square tail. Often seen as screaming intertwining 'balls' of many birds high over towns. Habitat: breeds under overhanging roofs, bridges and rocks. Voice: extreme high fast '*pir-r-r-r-r pirr-r-r-r*' (each syllable bouncing down). AM.(NM)

Plate 55

1   **AFRICAN GIANT KINGFISHER** *Megaceryle maxima*   L 40 cm. The ♂ less rufous below than ♀. Habitat: streams, ponds, lagoons with overhanging trees and shrub. May be seen at garden pools. Voice: mid-high loud resounding nasal shrieks '*kaai-kaai-kaai- - -*'.

2   **PIED KINGFISHER** *Ceryle rudis*   L 24 cm. The ♂ has a double, ♀ a single (interrupted) breast collar. Plunge-dives from hovering flight. Habitat: lakes, dams, rivers, creeks, estuaries, lagoons; even at the open sea shore.

3   **HALF-COLLARED KINGFISHER** *Alcedo semitorquata*   L 19 cm. Note black bill, pale but brilliant colouring. From 4 by overall paler colouring; from 5- 8 by blue cheeks. Habitat: rivers, streams, lakes, lagoons, normally with overhanging trees. Voice: extreme high staccato '*tseep tseep-tseep tseep*'. R

4   **SHINING-BLUE KINGFISHER** *Alcedo quadribrachys*   L 19 cm. From 3 by darker colouring and plain, less spotted wings. Habitat: ponds, streams in forests; also at wooded reedy fringes of lakes, rivers. Voice: extreme high irregular '*sweep sweep sweep-sweep-*' (just within ear reach).

5   **WHITE-BELLIED KINGFISHER** *Corythornis leucogaster*   L 13 cm. Nominate (a) shown and race *nais* (b, from Príncipe; note full breast band and blue cap touching eye). All races have white stripe through middle of belly. Habitat: dense swampy forests near streams.

6   **MALACHITE KINGFISHER** *Corythornis cristata*   L 13 cm. From most other small blue kingfishers by blue cap touching eye. Normally not found in forest habitats. May show crest. Habitat: reed beds, papyrus, shrubbery along lakes, dams, ponds, rivers, streams, creeks. Voice: very high, sharp '*tsip tsip-tsip -*' of ♂, short trilled '*trwwwi*' of ♀.

7   **AFRICAN DWARF KINGFISHER** *Ceyx lecontei*   L 10 cm. Note diagnostic rufous crown and nape. Tiny forest species, normally away from water. Habitat: dense forest undergrowth. Voice: extreme high, irregular '*see see see*'.

8   **AFRICAN PYGMY KINGFISHER** *Ceyx picta*   L 12 cm. From other small kingfishers by long, rufous-violet streak behind eye. Habitat: ground strata of dry wood-, bush- and scrubland, tall-grassed forest glades, lake and river edges. Feeds on insects, taken from ground, rarely catches fish in water. Voice: very high, mumbled, fast trill '*trrrt-trut trrrrrrrtrrrrrit -*' or extreme high '*tseet tseet*'. AM.RES

9   **GREY-HEADED (-hooded or Chestnut-bellied) KINGFISHER** *Halcyon leucocephala*   L 20 cm. Nominate (a) shown, white-headed race *actaeon* (b, Cape Verde) and race *pallidiventris* (c with pale underparts). Imm from ad 10 black mantle, from 11 by more overall dark bill and less blue body plumage. Habitat: woodland, bush. Voice: very high up-and-down warbled '*tsi-tsi-tsi-tju-tji-tji-tju*' or '*tsjurrr-tsjurrr*'.

10   **WOODLAND (or Senegal) KINGFISHER** *Halcyon senegalensis*   L 21 cm. Nominate (a) shown and race *cyanoleuca* (b, with black mark behind eye). From 11 by paler plumage without blue breast band or black wrist patch on underwing. Habitat: dry open woodland, bush often near streams. Voice: very high fast trill '*tiu trrrrrrriueh*' and fast high chatter. AM.RES

11   **BLUE-BREASTED KINGFISHER** *Halcyon malimbica*   L 25 cm. From 10 by blue breast band and black carpal patch on underwing. Habitat: forests, riverine belts. Voice: extreme high loud fluted sharp '*tiu-titititititiutiutiu*'. RES.(AM)

12   **BROWN-HOODED KINGFISHER** *Halcyon albiventris*   L 20 cm. Note streaked head (not capped as 14) and buff underwing. The ♀ browner above than ♂. Habitat: open forests, wooded areas, suburbs, especially near ponds and streams. Voice: very high short sharp fast chatter '*wi-wuwuwu*'.

13   **CHOCOLATE-BACKED KINGFISHER** *Halcyon badia*   L 20 cm. Unmistakable. Habitat: undergrowth at well-wooded streams. Voice: mid-high fluted unhurried '*weeh fu-fee-fee-fee tenk fju fjuh*' (central part highest-pitched).

14   **STRIPED KINGFISHER** *Halcyon chelicuti*   L 17 cm. Unobtrusive when perched, but striking blue in flight. Flight feathers (seen from below) of ♀ plain grey without black and with small carpal patch. Habitat: open woodland, bush, often away from water. Voice: very high short fluted '*tee*', '*trrrrr*' or '*twee tweetwee*'. Also a duet of ♂ and ♀ sounding as one short phrase '*tee-wuh*'. RES.(AM)

Plate 56

1 **BLACK BEE-EATER** *Merops gularis*   L 20 cm. From all other bee-eaters, except 2, by habitat. Habitat: forest interiors.

2 **BLUE-HEADED BEE-EATER** *Merops muelleri*   L 20 cm. Unmistakable. Habitat: forest edges and interiors.

3 **RED-THROATED BEE-EATER** *Merops bullocki*   L 20 cm. From 4 by green, not white forehead, all-pink throat and different range. Habitat: bushed grassland along streams near sand cliffs.

4 **WHITE-FRONTED BEE-EATER** *Merops bullockoides*   L 24 cm. Note striking white forehead, white chin, pink throat and blue lower underparts. Habitat: wooded and bushed areas, swamp edges, other open areas, not too far away from sand cliffs, where it breeds. R

5 **BLACK-HEADED BEE-EATER** *Merops breweri*   L 25 (+8) cm. Unmistakable. Habitat: along edges and open patches in forests, woodland and plantations. R

6 **SWALLOW-TAILED BEE-EATER** *Merops hirundineus*   L 20 cm. Unmistakable. Habitat: wooded and bushed grassland.

7 **CINNAMON-CHESTED (or –breasted) BEE-EATER** *Merops oreobates*   L 20 cm. Note green (not rufous) wings and white cheeks. Only little or no rufous in tail. Habitat: more or less open montane forests, cultivation, roadsides, suburban gardens and parks.

8 **BLUE-BREASTED BEE-EATER** *Merops variegatus*   L 20 cm. As 9 but yellow throat looks paler due to more white below black ear coverts. Habitat: generally in more moister habitats than 9. Humid grassy areas at forest edges or lake sides.

9 **LITTLE BEE-EATER** *Merops pusillus*   L 17 cm. See 8. Habitat: bush and forest edges often near water.

10 **ROSY BEE-EATER** *Merops malimbicus*   L 24 (+4) cm. Unmistakable. Habitat: forest and high woodland, normally not far away from large rivers and lakes.

11 **CARMINE BEE-EATER** *Merops nubicus*   L 40 cm. Nominate (a) shown and race *nubicoides* (b). Habitat: wooded and bushed, natural and cultivated areas, including roadsides. AM

12 **LITTLE GREEN BEE-EATER** *Merops orientalis*   L 25 cm. Race *viridissimus* shown; yellow-throated forms in Chad (not shown) may form a separate race *flaviviridis*. No rufous in wing. Habitat: dry woodland and bushed areas with scarce grass cover; sometimes near watersides and other less dry areas.

13 **BOEHM'S BEE-EATER** *Merops boehmi*   L 21 cm. Note rich russet head. Not gregarious. Hawks insects in short sallies from perch. Habitat: forest edges near rivers and streams. R

14 **WHITE-THROATED BEE-EATER** *Merops albicollis*   L 20 (+10) cm. Unmistakable. Habitat: normally in wooded and bushed areas, also in forests, plantations, gardens. RES.AM

15 **EUROPEAN BEE-EATER** *Merops apiaster*   L 30 cm. Often heard and seen passing overhead in loose seemingly aimless flying flocks. Habitat: more or less wooded areas, suburbs. Voice: high melodious liquid short fluted '*prjuur*' and '*iup*'. NM

16 **BLUE-CHEEKED BEE-EATER** *Merops persicus*   L 25 (+6) cm. From 17 by different coloured crown and less pale overall green plumage. Blue cheeks not obvious. Habitat; open wooded and bushed grassland, lake and swamp edges. Voice: high short '*pjuur-pjuur*' sharper than 15. AM.RES

17 **MADAGASCAR (or Olive) BEE-EATER** *Merops superciliosus*   L 25 (+6) cm. From 16 also by deep rufous underwings. Note dark-brown cap. Habitat: as 16. AM

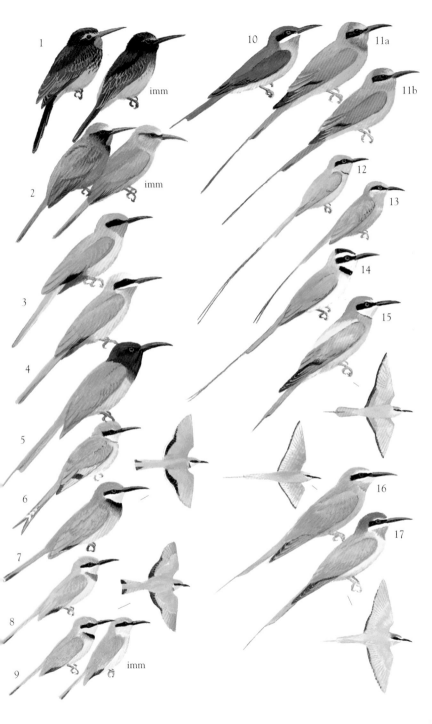

Plate 57

1   **EUROPEAN ROLLER** *Coracias garrulus*   L 30 cm. Note absence of white eyebrow (ad). All flight feathers black (not partly blue). Crown (especially of imm) often more green than blue. Habitat: forest edges, more or less wooded and bushed, natural and cultivated areas. NM

2   **ABYSSINIAN ROLLER** *Coracias abyssinica*   L 30 (+15) cm. Mantle darker than other rollers. Ad with broken-off tail streamers and imm from 1 by blue flight feathers. Habitat: semi-desert and open, more or less wooded and bushed areas, including gardens. RES.AM

3   **LILAC-BREASTED ROLLER** *Coracias caudata*   L 30 (+10) cm. Ad from 4 by different form of streamers and less dark wings. Habitat: dry bushed and wooded natural and cultivated areas including suburbs.

4   **RACKET-TAILED ROLLER** *Coracias spatulata*   L 30 (+10) cm. Nominate (a) shown with purple restricted to sides of breast, and race *weigalli* (b, rare in the extreme east of the D. R. of Congo, but might be a youth form of nominate). In flight shows rufous of tertials extended onto coverts, merging into purple. Habitat: open woodland. R

5   **BLUE-BELLIED ROLLER** *Coracias cyanogaster*   L 29 (+ 6) cm. Unmistakable. Habitat: all habitats with mosaics of open spaces and large trees, forest edges, riverine belts. Often in palm trees.

6   **RUFOUS-CROWNED (or Purple) ROLLER** *Coracias naevia*   L 35 cm. Vinaceous-purple-crowned nominate (a) shown and green-crowned race *mosambica* (b, in flight). All primaries of b are black below, but are partly white in a. Large and shaggy jizz. Habitat: dry areas with tall trees and bush. RES.AM

7   **BROAD-BILLED ROLLER** *Eurystomus glaucurus*   L 25 cm. Note short yellow bill, shallow-forked tail and purple underparts. From 8 by azure-blue undertail coverts and absence of blue chin spot. Habitat: forest glades and edges, wet woodland, grass- and farmland with scattered trees near streams and marshes. Voice: low raucous rather frog-like 'draaaf-draaaf-'. RES.AM

8   **BLUE-THROATED ROLLER** *Eurystomus gularis*   L 25 cm. Nominate (b) shown and race *neglectus* (a, with more extensive purple underparts). From 7 by blue chin, brown undertail coverts and (in flight) paler-based flight feathers. Habitat: less intensively cultivated areas with forest patches. Voice: very high slightly hoarse 'hew hew hew –'.

9   **GREEN (or Red-billed) WOOD HOOPOE** *Phoeniculus purpureus*   L 40 cm. Race *marwitzi* (a) shown and *guineensis* (b, which is darker with violet neck and larger white spots in wings and tail). Small parties. Habitat: open woodland, bush, well-wooded streams, suburbs. Voice: mid-high to high magpie-like fast excited chatters sounding as 'chachachacha----'.

10   **WHITE-HEADED WOOD-HOOPOE** *Phoeniculus bollei* L 35 cm. Nominate (a) shown and race *jacksoni* (b, with whiter head). Imm has dark head, but no white in tail and wing. Habitat: montane forest interiors and edges (canopies), often along streams. Voice: very high, liquid chatters 'chachachachacha-'.

11   **FOREST WOOD-HOOPOE** *Phoeniculus castaneiceps*   L 30 cm. Nominate (a, with chestnut head and upperbreast) shown and race *brunniceps* (many forms, of which b, dark-headed and c, white-headed form depicted). Note almost straight black bill. Habitat: forest canopies, not on the ground. Voice: extra high, fast, trilling cackling 'tritrutritritritritrutritri-' and high, slightly hoarse fluting 'wuut-wuut-wuut-wuut-wuut- wuut-wuut'.

12   **BLACK WOOD-HOOPOE** *Phoeniculus aterrimus*   L 25 cm. Note short tail and rather straight bill. From 13 by white primary coverts and absence of spots in tail, (but beware of races in the D. R. of Congo, which have white spots on outer tail feathers). Habitat: dry wooded and bushed areas. Voice: high, fluting, slightly rising and descending 'weetweetweetweetweetweetweet'.

13   **(Greater) SCIMITARBILL** *Phoeniculus cyanomelas*   L 30 cm. Note strongly decurved bill and silent behaviour. May show a few white primary coverts (not shown). Habitat: dry bush, thornbush. Voice: very high fluted 'pwuupwuu', each 'pwuu-' slightly lashed-up. R

14   **HOOPOE** *Upupa epops*   L 30 cm. African races (a) are rich cinnamon and ♂♂ have more white in wings than migrant nominate (b), which is overall paler. Note that ♀♀ of African races show as many wing bars as b. Habitat: normally foraging on short grass in more or less bushed and wooded areas including suburbs. Voice: mid-high regular hooted hurried 'oopoop oopoopoop opoop –'. RES.NM

Plate 58

1 **YELLOW-CASQUED WATTLED HORNBILL** *Ceratogymna elata* L 65 cm. From 2 by smaller casque, different cheek colouring and more white in tail. Habitat: forest, riverine tree belts, plantations.

2 **BLACK-CASQUED WATTLED HORNBILL** *Ceratogymna atrata* L 80 cm. Only white at outer tail tips. Habitat: moist lowland forest, riverine belts, plantations. Voice: low hoarse fast chattering (often partly breaking up two octaves) or Herring Gull-like screams in flight.

3 **PIPING HORNBILL** *Ceratogymna fistulator* L 60 cm. Nominate (a) shown and races *sharpii* (b, with white outertail feathers and mainly white secondaries) and *duboisi* (c, with higher, longer ridge along bill and all flight feathers white or mainly white). Note dark central patch to bill. Habitat: moist forests. Voice: mid-high rapid fast magpie-like chattering (up to 5 sec).

4 **TRUMPETER HORNBILL** *Ceratogymna bucinator* L 65 cm. Note red orbital skin and all-blackish bill. Habitat: montane rivers and connected riverine belts. Voice: mid-high loud resounding bleating slightly lowered '*weeeeee*' and excited '*wèhwèhwèhwèh*'. R

5 **BLACK-AND-WHITE-CASQUED HORNBILL** *Ceratogymna subcylindricus* L 75 cm (♂), 70 cm (♀). Note bi-coloured upper mandible of ♂. From 3b-c by less white, confined to second half of outer tail-feathers. Only outer primaries all-black. Habitat: forest and surrounding wooded areas, including gardens.

6 **BROWN-CHEEKED (or White-thighed) HORNBILL** *Ceratogymna cylindricus* L 70 cm. Nominate (a) shown and race *albotibialis* (b, with different bill form and colouring, more extensive white underparts and different colour around eye). Note white-black-white pattern of tail. Habitat: montane dense forests.

7 **RED-BILLED DWARF HORNBILL** *Tockus camurus* L 35 cm. The ♀ with smaller casque along upper ridge of bill. Habitat: dense swampy lowland forests. Voice: Very high tooting '*toot-toot-toot-toot-toot-toot-toot-toot*' (descending 4 notes from beginning to end).

8 **CROWNED HORNBILL** *Tockus alboterminatus* L 50 cm. Note white line between bill and head, yellow eye and all-brown upperparts. Habitat: more or less dense forests and woodland. Voice: very high, shrieking, rapid '*wutweetweetweetweet-*' descending at the end.

9 **PALE-BILLED HORNBILL** *Tockus pallidirostris* L 45 cm. From 10 by yellow bill and plain brown rump. Habitat: dry miombo.

10 **AFRICAN GREY HORNBILL** *Tockus nasutus* L 50 cm. Race *epirhinus* (a, with reduced casque) shown and nominate (b, with prominent casque). From 9 in flight by white stripe through middle of rump. Habitat: dry more or less wooded areas with some bush. Voice: high unhurried piping '*pi-pi-pi-pi-piu-piu-plee-plee-plee*' (middle part extreme high) and high fluted '*tuuu-tjuh tuuu-tjeh*'.

11 **RED-BILLED HORNBILL** *Tockus erythrorhynchus* L 45 cm. Note small size, white head and red bill. Feeds on the ground. Habitat: dry, more or less wooded and bushed areas. Voice: high to mid-high excited rapid hoarse yelping '*wekwekwekwek------*' (up to 25 sec) at the end falling-off.

12 **AFRICAN PIED HORNBILL** *Tockus fasciatus* L 50 cm. Nominate (a) shown and race *semifasciatus* (b, with no or less red to bill and with different tail pattern). Habitat: forest and surrounding areas. Voice: very high rather short phrases '*fjuk-fjuk-fjuk-fjukfjuk-fjukfjukfjuk*'.

13 **BLACK DWARF HORNBILL** *Tockus hartlaubi* L 35 cm. Nominate (a) shown and race *granti* (b, with rows of white wing spots). Upperparts with bottle-green wash. Catches insects in rather flycatcher-like fashion. Habitat: forest canopies. Voice: high, mellow, staccato '*week-week-week-week-week-week*'.

14 **WHITE-CRESTED HORNBILL** *Tockus albocristatus* L 65 cm. Nominate (a, with white cheeks and crown) shown and races *macrourus* (b, with white head, throat and neck) and *cassini* (c, with black cheeks and white wing spots). Habitat: dense forests and surrounding areas. Voice: very high yelping, gliding up to extra high '*eeeoouuww*' ('*-uww*' lashing).

▶

15 **SOUTHERN GROUND HORNBILL** *Bucorvus cafer* L 105 cm. Note white outer wings which are only visible in flight. Habitat: wooded and bushed areas. Voice: extreme low booming '*ohooh ohooh ohooh ohooh*' often in bi-vocal duet of ♂ and ♀. R

16 **ABYSSINIAN GROUND HORNBILL** *Bucorvus abyssinicus* L 105 cm. From 15 by black eyes. Shares the white outerwings in flight. Casque is open at front. Habitat: arid or dry, open, wooded and bushed areas with more or less grass cover.

Plate 59

1 **SPECKLED TINKERBIRD** *Pogoniulus scolopaceus* L 10 cm. Note pale eye and chequered colouring. Habitat: forest edges and glades.

2 **WESTERN GREEN TINKERBIRD** *Pogoniulus coryphaeus* L 9 cm. Note long yellow-green streak from crown to tail and greenish throat. Habitat: forest and wooded areas.

3 **YELLOW-FRONTED TINKERBIRD** *Pogoniulus chrysoconus* L 9 cm. Note pale (not bright) yellow wings. Birds in southern parts of the D. R. of Congo might have orange, not yellow forehead. Habitat: woodland, more or less wooded and cultivated areas. Voice: high regular uninterrupted: '*puk-puk-puk - - -*' sustained for very long periods.

4 **YELLOW- (Lemon- or Golden-) RUMPED TINKERBIRD** *Pogoniulus bilineatus* L 10 cm. Note distinctive head pattern. See also 5. Habitat: forest, woodland, cultivation, suburbs. Voice: high or mid-high regular slow or hurried wooden '*pook-pook-pook - - -*' (a '*pook*' in every 3–7 is often left out) or mid high hooting trilled '*prrru-prrru-prrr - - -*'.

5 **YELLOW-THROATED TINKERBIRD** *Pogoniulus subsulphureus* L 10 cm. From 4 mainly by voice, but also by less pronounced colour contrast between throat and rest of underparts. Habitat: montane forest clearings. Voice: very high, sustained, hurried '*puck-puck-puck-puck-*' (a '*puck*' in every 2–7 is left out); also rapid '*puckpuckpuckpuck------*'.

6 **RED-RUMPED TINKERBIRD** *Pogoniulus atroflavus* L 13 cm. Note yellow face lines and red rump. Habitat: forests. Voice: low, monotonous, hollow '*hoot hoot hoot - -*' or high '*trrri trrri trrri*'.

7 **SPOT-FLANKED BARBET** *Tricholaema lacrymosa* L 13 cm. Note pale eye of ♂ (♀ has darker reddish-brown eye), absence of red to forehead, unspotted upperparts (only edges of flight feathers and tips of greater coverts are yellow), boldly spotted flanks. Habitat: woodland, bush, forest patches, often near water.

8 **MIOMBO PIED BARBET** *Tricholaema foreheadata* L 15 cm. From smaller 3 by spotted underparts. Habitat: miombo, open grassland with some trees and shrub, other more or less open woodland.

9 **HAIRY-BREASTED BARBET** *Tricholaema hirsuta* L 15 cm. Race *ansorgei* (a) shown, nominate (b, with black chin and white moustachial stripe) and race *angolensis* (c, overall rather uniform spotted and striped). Habitat: forests and nearby areas. Voice: mid-high regular fast rapid or slow '*hoothoothoothoot-*'.

10 **YELLOW-BILLED BARBET** *Trachyphonus purpuratus* L 25 cm. Nominate (a) shown and race *goffinii* (b, with black, not yellow bare skin around eye and with plain, dull yellow underparts). Race *togoensis* (Togo-area, not shown) as a, but with plain underparts. Often perches quietly in unbarbet-like upright stance. Habitat: dense forest undergrowth, often at edges and glades, near streams. Voice: mid-high or very high monotonous '*hoot hoot -*' (2 seconds between '*hoots*').

11 **YELLOW-BREASTED BARBET** *Trachyphonus margaritatus* L 21 cm. From larger 12 by brown (not black), uniform spotted upperparts, black forehead and whitish underparts. Habitat: more or less wooded dry areas, often along water courses. Voice: high, loud, jubilant '*tiuu tiuu tiuu trutru - -*' in an excited, unsynchronised, sustained duet.

12 **CRESTED BARBET** *Trachyphonus vaillantii* L 23 cm. Note red forehead and yellow underparts. Habitat: dry open woodland, bush, riverine belts, even in suburbs. Voice: very high coppery long trill '*prrrrrrruh*' and similar slightly hoarse fluting '*wuutwuutwuutwuutwuutwut*'. R

Plate 60

1 **NAKED-FACED BARBET** *Gymnobucco calvus* L 16 cm. Blackish naked face as 2 and 3. From 2 by more yellow, less horn-coloured bill, white chin, yellow hair tuft under bill, not in nostril, darker rump. From 3 by pale bill, slightly paler underparts, which contrast more with dark wing. Breeds in colonies, often together with 2 and 4. Habitat: forests. Voice: mid-high, hesitating, bouncing, accelerated '*hoot-hoot-hootootoot*'.

2 **BRISTLE-NOSED BARBET** *Gymnobucco peli* L 15 cm. Very similar to 1, sometimes nesting in the same tree! Less common than 1 and 4. Habitat: forests.

3 **SLADEN' BARBET** *Gymnobucco sladeni* L 15 cm. Range different from that of 1 and 2. From 4 in same range by dark eye, naked face, smaller size. Habitat; forests. R

4 **GREY-THROATED BARBET** *Gymnobucco bonapartei* L 18 cm. Note pale eye, black bill, grey head. Larger than 2 and 3. Habitat: forest glades. Voice: very high rapid sharp chatters and trills.

5 **ANCHIETA'S BARBET** *Stactolaema anchietae* L 17 cm. Note yellow face and single white wing patch. Habitat: open woodland, riverine belts.

6 **WHYTE'S BARBET** *Stactolaema whytii* L 18 cm. From 5 by smaller white-yellow area to forehead, darker wing (with 2 white patches per opened wing) and white-streaked underparts. Double wing patch diagnostic. Habitat: miombo. Voice: high hooted sighing regular '*hoo-hoo-hoo- - -*'.

7 **YELLOW-SPOTTED BARBET** *Buccanodon duchaillui* L 15 cm. Note long, yellow eyebrow. Habitat: montane forest canopies. Voice: high, owl-like, hollow '*rrrrruu*' and very high, loud, shivering, fast '*bibibiwi-bibibiwi*'.

8 **VIEILLOT'S BARBET** *Lybius vieilloti* L 15 cm. From 9 by different range and far less black around red face mask. Habitat: dry, more or less wooded and scrubbed, natural and cultivated areas. Voice: strange, rather low piping, scops owl-like '*hoot-hoot hoot hoot-hoot-hoot-hoot-*', magpie-like chatters and high goose-like shouts.

9 **BLACK-COLLARED BARBET** *Lybius torquatus* L 20 cm. Unmistakable. Not in same range as 8 and 10. Habitat: woodland, grass- and farmland with scattered trees. Voice: mid-high, miaowing, hurried '*tjauw-tjauw-tjauw-*' or high loud bouncing '*-beedidder-*' often given in duet.

10 **BLACK-BILLED BARBET** *Lybius guifsobalito* L 15 cm. Note striped wing coverts and red head, including chin. Habitat: open, more or less wooded and bushed, natural and cultivated areas, mostly at higher elevations.

11 **WHITE-HEADED BARBET** *Lybius leucocephalus* L 15 cm. Unmistakable. Habitat: dry open woodland, bush, gardens, cultivation, often near water. Voice: high loud sharp chattering shrieks '*peek-peek-peek-peek-*' or tinkling chattered '*pi-pi-pi-pi-peh*'.

12 **BLACK-BACKED BARBET** *Lybius minor* L 15 cm. Nominate (a, with brown upperparts) and race *macclounii* (b) shown. Note pale bill, pinkish belly with black belt. Habitat: woodland, bush and scrub, farmland with trees and hedges. R

13 **DOUBLE-TOOTHED BARBET** *Lybius bidentatus* L 25 cm. Eye colour may vary between dark brown (shown) and yellow. From 14 by pink wing bar, absence of black breast band, more extensive red underparts. Habitat: understorey at forest edges, riverine belts, cultivation, more or less wooded natural and cultivated grasslands. Voice: mid-high, tinkerbird-like, sustained '*pook-pook-pook- -*'.

14 **BEARDED BARBET** *Lybius dubius* L 26 cm. See 13. Range generally just north of 13. Habitat: as 13, but more in upper storeys.

15 **BLACK-BREASTED BARBET** *Lybius rolleti* L 30 cm. Note white bill. Red restricted to centre of belly. Habitat: dry open woodland, plantations and farmland with scattered trees, normally at higher elevations. R

Plate 61

1 **LYRE-TAILED HONEYGUIDE** Melichneutes robustus L 20 cm. Unmistakable, when properly seen. Habitat: forest, plantations. Voice: soft extreme high shrill 'feefeefeefeefeefeefee---'. Produces also a mechanical 'song', produced by vibrations of its tail, sounding as a loud sequence of bleating toy trumpet-like 'mehèh-mehèh-' slightly speeded-up as the bird flies around over the forest canopy.

2 **CASSIN'S HONEYBIRD** Prodotiscus insignis L 9 cm. Not in same range as 3. From 4 by grey chin and by tail pattern. As all honeybirds and honeyguides rather pot-bellied and with white in tail normally concealed (but often visible in flight). Note short bill. Habitat: treetops in forests and surrounding areas.

3 **GREEN-BACKED (or Slender-billed) HONEYBIRD** Prodotiscus zambesiae L 9 cm. From 2 by paler belly, thin white eye ring and different range. May have small dusky tips to white tail feathers. Habitat: forest edges, woodland. R

4 **WAHLBERG'S (or Sharp-billed) HONEYBIRD** Prodotiscus regulus L 13 cm. Note pale chin, dusky colouring and blackish T-pattern on tail. Habitat: woodland, plantations, cultivation. Voice: dry insect-like trill 'shriiiiiii' (7 sec). R

5 **ZENKER'S HONEYGUIDE** Melignomon zenkeri L 13 cm. Rather brownbull-like (see plate 71), but with white in tail. From 6 by less yellow feet and bill, darker underparts, less white in tail and less bright upperparts. Habitat: forests. R

6 **YELLOW-FOOTED (or Serle's) HONEYGUIDE** Melignomon eisentrauti L 13 cm. See 5. Habitat: forests. R

7 **GREATER (or Black-throated) HONEYGUIDE** Indicator indicator L 20 m. Note white cheek and pink bill of ♂, yellow underparts of imm, conspicuous yellow upperwing coverts and white-streaked rumps (of ♂ and ♀) in flight. Habitat: well-wooded areas, even in suburbs. Voice: very high unhurried sharp 'weet-threeee' ('weet' lashing), endlessly repeated.

8 **WILLCOCKS'S HONEYGUIDE** Indicator willcocksi L 11 cm. In face only faint malar stripe and no white between eye and bill. Note pale olive-green (not grey or brown) underparts and narrow dark stripes to lower flanks. Habitat: montane forests and connected well-wooded streams. Voice: extra high, fluting 'uweew-uweew-uweew-' (each 'uweew' slightly swept up). R

9 **PALLID (or Eastern) HONEYGUIDE** Indicator meliphilus L 10 cm. Note plain golden-olive upperparts (extremely golden individual shown), pale loral spot, absence of moustachial stripe; shows faint or no streaks on lower flanks. Paler below and with less white in tail than most other honeyguides. Habitat: miombo, thornbush. Voice: calls from favourite tree, changing perches. R

10 **DWARF HONEYGUIDE** Indicator pumilio L 10 cm. Note striking white loral spot. Crown and nape rather green. Note white moustachial stripe. Flank striping faint. Habitat: moist montane forests. R

11 **THICK-BILLED HONEYGUIDE** Indicator conirostris L 15 cm. Overall rather dark. No or faint loral spot. Faint black striping to lower flanks. Habitat: dense forests and connected well-wooded streams, normally at higher elevations.

12 **LEAST HONEYGUIDE** Indicator exilis L 11 cm. Note dark-centred golden feathers of upperparts, white loral spot, distinct moustachial stripe and streaks to flanks. Habitat: forest. Voice: extreme high sharp 'weew-weew-weew-' (each 'weew' slightly lashed-down).

13 **LESSER HONEYGUIDE** Indicator minor L 15 cm. Note dark narrow moustachial stripe, sharply demarcated grey cheek and pale underparts. Habitat: forest edges, woodland, scrubland, cultivation, grassland with scattered trees. Voice: very high level staccato 'weew-weew-weew- -'.

14 **SCALY-THROATED HONEYGUIDE** Indicator variegatus L 19 cm. From 15 by fine white streaks to head, whitish unstreaked belly and finely streaked undertail coverts. Habitat: forest, woodland, wooded grassland. Voice: very high rather short drawn-up trill 'rrrrrruh' at 1 min intervals. R

15 **SPOTTED HONEYGUIDE** Indicator maculatus L 20 cm. From 14 by plain forehead and crown. Coarsely scalloped green on underparts from chin to under tail-coverts. Habitat: montane forest and surrounding areas.

Plate 62

1   **NORTHERN (or Eurasian) WRYNECK** *Jynx torquilla*   L 15 cm. Unobtrusive. Note the long stripe through eye and down neck. Normally feeds on the ground, but may climb tree trunks (without support of tail). Habitat: more or less wooded grassland, farmland and gardens. Voice: high, rapid, bleating '*tjutjutjutju*' (often running up). NM

2   **RUFOUS-BREASTED (or Red-throated) WRYNECK** *Jynx ruficollis*   L 19 cm. Perches crosswise like 1. Forages more on ground than on tree trunks and branches. Habitat: open more or less wooded natural and cultivated areas. Voice: high bleating '*pjuuuut - pjuuut - pjuuut*'.

3   **AFRICAN PICULET** *Sasia africana*   L 8 cm. Only as long as a finger. The ♂ from ♀ by rufous forehead. Very active, difficult to follow. Often in mixed bird waves. Only uses its feet, not its tail, for support. Climbs trunks, twigs, grass stems. Habitat: undergrowth at forest edges. Voice: extreme high, barely audible '*srrrrrrreeh*'.

4   **FINE-SPOTTED WOODPECKER** *Campethera punctuligera*   L 22 cm. From other similar woodpeckers by finely spotted underbreast and spotted, not barred or striped upperparts. Habitat: more or less open woodland and areas with scattered trees. Voice: excited, sharp, high, slightly barbet-like '*weh-weh-weh-weh- -*' in duet of ♂ and ♀.

5   **BENNETT'S WOODPECKER** *Campethera bennettii*   L 19 cm. Note clean cheeks and chin (♂), buffish brown in ♀. Habitat: open woodland and scrub. Voice: mid-high excited cackled '*rrrrrru-ti-wee-ti-wee-ti-wee-ti- -*' ('*rrrrr-*' running up). R

6   **NUBIAN WOODPECKER** *Campethera nubica*   L 20 cm. Note heavily striped cheeks, barred upperparts and densely spotted sides of upperbreast. The ♀ has long white-spotted malar stripe. Not in same range as 5. Habitat: woodland and other more or less wooded habitats. Voice: mid-high, loud, excited, accelerated '*weetweetweetweet--*' (lasting 4 sec) often in duet. R

7   **GOLDEN-TAILED WOODPECKER** *Campethera abingoni*   L 20 cm. Striped above and below, not spotted or barred. From 5 by boldly streaked face and almost black throat and upperbreast. Habitat: forest, woodland, often near streams. Voice: mid-high bleating '*puwee*' ('*pu-*' as undertone) or nasal rapidly lowered '*weeeeh*'.

8   **GREEN-BACKED (or Little Spotted) WOODPECKER** *Campethera cailliautii* L 16 cm. Similar to 9, but greener above with less black tail; ranges overlap only in Ghana and Togo. Note short bill, absence of moustachial stripe. Habitat: forest edge, woodland, thornbush. Voice: very high, questioning '*weeh?*'.

9   **LITTLE GREEN (or Golden-backed) WOODPECKER** *Campethera maculosa*   L 16 cm. See 8. The ♀ from ♂ 8 by absence of red in crest. Habitat: forest glades and edges. Voice: high sharp '*puweeh puweeh puweeh*' with emphasis on higher '*weeh*'.

10   **TULLBERG'S (or Fine-banded) WOODPECKER** *Campethera tullbergi*   L 20 cm. Nominate (a) shown and race *taeniolaema* (b, which is finely banded below, not spotted). Note plain upperparts. Nominate is only woodpecker with some red at wing bent; note also the fine spotting below, which separates it from other green-backed woodpeckers in its montane habitat. Race b is only woodpecker barred from chin to under tail-coverts. Habitat: canopy of moist montane forests.

11   **BUFF-SPOTTED WOODPECKER** *Campethera nivosa*   L 15 cm. Overall rather dark. Note densely spotted and barred underparts. From 11 by absence of brown ears. Habitat: forests. Voice: short, soft rattle '*prruh prruh prruh*'.

12   **BROWN-EARED WOODPECKER** *Campethera caroli*   L 19 cm. Note dark colouring and diagnostic brown ear coverts. Habitat: forest, riverine belts, plantations. Voice: high drawn- and puffed-out rising then lowered '*piuuuuiih*'.

Plate 63

1   **LITTLE GREY WOODPECKER** *Dendropicos elachus*   L 13 cm. Very pale coloured and short tailed. Note red rump. Habitat: sparsely-wooded, dry areas.

2   **CARDINAL WOODPECKER** *Dendropicos fuscescens*   L 14 cm. Note very small size and erectile crest. Striped, not barred or spotted below. From 1 by darker appearance, different habitat and, in general, different range, from 3 by weakly barred mantle and white (not pale green) underparts. Habitat: forest, other wooded and bushed habitats. Voice: extreme high rapid sharp twittered 'tu-teetee tle-tu-tee-tutee' or dry high thrush-like 'shree-shree-shree-'.

3   **SPECKLE-BREASTED WOODPECKER** *Dendropicos poecilolaemus*   L 13 cm. Note plain golden-green mantle, unmarked belly and golden-yellow rump. Habitat: more or less wooded and bushed, natural and cultivated areas, normally at higher elevations. Voice: high, sharp, rasping, speedy 'tethree-tethree-tethree'.

4   **ELLIOT'S WOODPECKER** *Dendropicos elliotii*   L 16 cm. Nominate (a, with unmarked upper- and underparts) shown and race johnstoni (b, with buff face sides and streaked underparts). No similar species in its range. Habitat: dense forest. R

5   **FIRE-BELLIED WOODPECKER** *Dendropicos pyrrhogaster*   L 24 cm. No similar woodpecker with black ears, red crown (♂ only) and red rump in its range. Habitat: forests.

6   **YELLOW-CRESTED WOODPECKER** *Dendropicos xantholophus*   L 23 cm. The ♂ is only woodpecker with yellow crown and rump, latter also in ♀. Wing barring mainly visible in flight. Habitat: forest and surrounding areas. Voice: very high shrill excited chattered trills like 'tierrrr tierr tu-tu-tu-tu-twi'.

7   **GABON WOODPECKER** *Dendropicos gabonensis*   L 14 cm. Nominate (a) shown and race lugubris (b, with different patterning of face sides and underparts. Might be an independent species: Melancholy Woodpecker). Intermediate race reichenowi from Nigeria not shown. Upperparts, including primaries and rump, all-green. Forehead brown. From 62.12 by different patterned underparts. Open forests; also in natural and cultivated areas with tree-stands and scattered trees. Voice: very high, level trill 'rrrrrrri'.

8   **GREY WOODPECKER** *Dendropicos goertae*   L 19 cm. Note pale grey head and underparts and barred wings and tail. Habitat: open forests, more or less natural and cultivated areas, gardens. Voice: very high angry sharp chattered 'ti-ti-ti-tri-tri-tri-tri-tri'.

9   **OLIVE WOODPECKER** *Dendropicos griseocephalus*   L 17 cm. From 8 by less barring (absent in tail) and tawny (not grey) underparts. Habitat: dense forest. Voice: high plaintive pushed-out 'wweewit wweewit wheewit'. R

10   **BEARDED WOODPECKER** *Dendropicos namaquus*   L 25 cm. Note large size and brownish-green, all-barred (except head) appearance. Habitat: dry woodland, bush, with some large trees. Voice: high, loud, rapid, slightly descending 'klu-klu-klu-klu-klu-klu-klu'. R

11   **BROWN-BACKED WOODPECKER** *Picoides obsoletus*   L 14 cm. Note neat face pattern. Rump barred white (not red or orange-yellow as 1-3). Habitat: open, more or less wooded and bushed habitats. Voice: mid-high, hurried, sharp, nasal 'tui-tui-truh-tui'.

Plate 64 (continued)

17   **SUN LARK** *Galerida modesta*   L 14 cm. Note striking long eyebrow, short crest, rather stout bill, black moustachial stripe and heavy breast streaking. Some rufous in opened wing. Habitat: open, flat or hilly areas, often with rocky outcrops and occasional stands of large trees. Also on pasture land, bare fields and airstrips. Voice: very high, rather sharp, twittering 'sritisrititwee'.

Plate 64

1 **GREY-HEADED BROADBILL** *Smithornis sharpei* L 17 cm. Note rufous breast sides and absence of wing bars. Habitat: lower strata in forest.

2 **RUFOUS-SIDED BROADBILL** *Smithornis rufolateralis* L 12 cm. The ♀ from ♀ 1 by wing bars. Habitat: forest canopy, often near streams. Voice: high, rather level, toy trumpet-like '*trrrui*'.

3 **AFRICAN BROADBILL** *Smithornis capensis* L 14 cm. Note absence of rufous breast sides. Hawks insects from perch or gleans them from underside of leaves. Habitat: undergrowth of forest and dense woodland. Voice: low toy trumpet-like '*prrrueh*'.

4 **AFRICAN GREEN BROADBILL** *Pseudocalyptomena graueri* L 12 cm. Perches quietly (unlike e.g. agapornis species, 46.8-9) and hawks insects. Habitat: mainly mid-strata and canopies of montane forests, bamboo. R

5 **AFRICAN PITTA** *Pitta angolensis* L 20 cm. From 6 by buff (not green) breast and in flight by slightly larger white wing spots. Habitat: floor under dense shrub patches in wooded areas. Voice: strange, compressed '*puwee*' ('*pu-*' low and frog-like, '*-wee*' very fluting). AM.RES

6 **GREEN-BREASTED PITTA** *Pitta reichenowi* L 15 cm. See 5. Habitat: montane forest floors. Voice: high, fluting, pressed-out, short '*fjull fjull fjull*'. R

7 **FISCHER'S SPARROW LARK** *Eremopterix leucopareia* L 12 cm. Note rusty-tawny, black-bordered crown of ♂; ♀ from ♀ 9 by buffy-rufous sides to face. Habitat: dry areas with some short grass. R

8 **BLACK-CROWNED SPARROW LARK** *Eremopterix nigriceps* L 12 cm. Note white frontal patch and unstriped back. The ♀ is rather plain, coloured rich-brown without black on belly. Habitat: open areas with some grass cover near streams, dry rivers or seashore. Voice: extra high hurried '*puweet-wee puweet-wee puweet-wee*'.

9 **GREY-BACKED SPARROW LARK** *Eremopterix verticalis* L 13 cm. Note white crown (not forehead) of ♂. The ♀ from other ♀♀ sparrow larks by white eyebrow. Habitat: open sandy or stony grasslands with some bush. Voice: (in flight) very high sharp pleasant variations of '*weeweewurwee*'. R

10 **CHESTNUT-BACKED SPARROW LARK** *Eremopterix leucotis* L 12 cm. Note chestnut upperparts of ♂ and buff-and-chestnut wing coverts of ♀. Habitat: as 9. Voice: (in flight) unstructured flow of very fast compressed partly muttered partly clear strophes '*wwwuchi twwuee - *'. RES.AM

11 **TEMMINCK'S HORNED LARK** *Eremophila bilopha* L 17 cm. Unmistakable. Habitat: dry, sparsely grassed flat semi-desert. R

12 **HOOPOE LARK** *Alaemon alaudipes* L 20 cm. Large and slender. Striking wing pattern only visible in flight. Habitat: sandy plains with hardly any vegetation. Voice: slowly rising, almost human whistle, with sudden accelerations and decelerations '*piuu-piuu-piuu piuu-piuu- *'.

13 **RUFOUS-RUMPED LARK** *Pinarocorys erythropygia* L 20 cm. Note rufous tail, rump and flanks. From 14 by different range. Habitat: wooded grassland, burnt ground, bare fields. Voice: high, sharp, fluted, descending '*tuuuu-tuuuu*' and '*tee-tiuu-tee-tui-tee*'. AM.RES

14 **DUSKY LARK** *Pinarocorys nigricans* L 18 cm. Note dark, almost black appearance with striking face pattern. From breast-spotted thrushes by shorter bill and pale-edged wing feathers. Flicks wings frequently when foraging on the ground. Habitat: open grassy thornbush, woodland. Voice: in flight high rasping '*sreeeeh-sreeeh-sreeeh*'. AM.R

15 **THEKLA LARK** *Galerida malabarica* L 17 cm. From 16 by rustier rump. Habitat: more stony, rocky areas than 16. V

16 **CRESTED LARK** *Galerida cristata* L 17 cm. Note conspicuous crest. Very similar to 15, but with slightly larger and more elongated, shaggier crest, longer bill and rusty underwing. Habitat: flat, sandy, partly grassed areas with some occasional bush and trees; also bare fields and roadsides. Voice: extra high, hurried '*tuchee-tuchee-tuwee*'. RES.NM

◀

Plate 65

Note: in coastal Cabinda the extralimital Sabota Lark *Mirafra sabota* is found, which lacks the typical red Mirafra wing patch. It shows a pronounced, long, white eyebrow, a black moustachial and a (fainter) malar stripe.

1   **SINGING BUSH LARK** *Mirafra cantillans*   L 13 cm. Note slightly striped rump. Red in wings disappears with wear. From 2 (small overlap in range) by paler plumage and less pronounced two-toned bill, from 3 by darker, less contrasting middle tail feathers. Habitat: open and more or less bushed areas. Voice: very high, continuous '*tjip-tjip-tjip-*' larded with trills, chatters and short flutes (airborne or perched).

2   **WHITE-TAILED BUSH LARK** *Mirafra albicauda*   L 13 cm. Very restricted range. Note black-marked upperparts, bicoloured bill, white outer tail-feathers and rufous in wing. Habitat: open and sparsely bushed habitats. Voice: long sequences of harsh and mellow whistles, without trills. R

3   **KORDOFAN LARK** *Mirafra cordofanica*   L 17 cm. Note pale-rufous plumage and pronounced tri-coloured tail. Habitat: open plains with scarce grass and some bush. R

4   **RUFOUS-NAPED LARK** *Mirafra africana*   L 17 cm. Not all races depicted, *chapini* (a), *malbranti* (b), *stresemanni* (c) and *bamendae* (d) shown, but even within the races very variable. From 5 by buff not white outer tail feathers. Crest diagnostic. Habitat: open and bushed, partly bare or overgrazed grassland and pasture land. Voice: extreme high short sharp yet sweet whistle '*tee-tjuih*' or '*tiu-uweek*' given from boulder or bush top.

5   **ANGOLA LARK** *Mirafra angolensis*   L 17 cm. From 4 by sharper, longer bill, white outer tail feathers, smaller red wing patch, barred tertials. Occupies a restricted range, only overlapping in SE with range of 4. Habitat: montane grassland, moist valleys. R

6   **RUSTY BUSH LARK** *Mirafra rufa*   L 13 cm. Rather plain and darkish without the typical well-defined rufous *mirafra* wing patch. Note the reddish, striped breast. Habitat: open grassy plains, rocky areas with some bush, open woodland.

7   **FLAPPET LARK** *Mirafra rufocinnamomea*   L 14 cm. Not all races depicted, *buckleyi* (a) and *schoutedeni* (b) shown. Note buff (not white) outer tail feathers and red in wing. Habitat: woodland, wooded grass plains. Voice: dry short burst of wing flaps (not unlike distant motorbike exhaust) during high air cruise, sometimes with very high up-and-down short twitter '*wit-wee-tree-weeh*'.

8   **DESERT LARK** *Ammomanes deserti*   L 14 cm. Note the characteristic tail pattern in which black merges in red base (see also 9, which prefers a different habitat). Habitat: arid, stony and rocky plains or hillsides with sparse grass cover and occasionally some scrub. Voice: very high '*tsruee*' ('*tsru-*' drawn back, '*-ee*' very short and sharp).

9   **BAR-TAILED LARK** *Ammomanes cincturus*   L 14 cm. Note clear cut, black, subterminal band in tail. Habitat: prefers true desert, generally avoids rocky, sloping areas.

10   **RASO LARK** *Alauda razae*   L 13 cm. Extreme restricted range on one of the Cape Verde islands. Note long bill (shorter in ♀). Habitat: open plains and valleys with some vegetation. E, Cape Verde.

11   **EURASIAN SKY LARK** *Alauda arvensis*   L 18 cm. From all other larks by white trailing edge to wings. Note erectile crest and long hind-claw. Habitat: may show up in any type of open, natural or cultivated, moist or arid country. Vagrant to Mauritania. V

12   **GREATER SHORT-TOED LARK** *Calandrella brachydactyla*   L 13 cm. Small area of stripes restricted to sides of upperbreast. Note short primary projection. Habitat: dry areas, bare fields and overgrazed grassland. Voice: mid-high, liquid, hurried twitter '*trititituitwee*'. NM

13   **LESSER SHORT-TOED LARK** *Calandrella rufescens*   L 13 cm. Note small size and pale appearance. From 12 by more extensive breast streaking and longer primary projection. Habitat: stony grass plains. Voice: sustained medley of trills, rattles, whistles and twitters. NM.R

14   **RED-CAPPED (or African Short-toed) LARK** *Calandrella cinerea*   L 15 cm. Note red crest (not always erected) and diagnostic shoulder patch. Habitat: dry bare more or less grassed and scrubbed areas. Voice: very high unstructured unhurried connected short twitters including '*sweeeh*' and sharp descending '*tweeeeeh-*'. RES.AM

▶

15 **DUNN'S LARK** *Eremalauda dunni*   L 13 cm. Note strong bill, pale reddish plumage, short primary projection and mainly black tail. Habitat: flat, sandy desert.

16 **SPIKE-HEELED LARK** *Chersomanes albofasciata*   L 15 cm. Note short tail with white corners, thin bill, erect stance. Habitat: grass- and shrubland, sparsely grass-covered gravel plains. Voice: sings in short phrases just after take-off, plover-like sharp very fast '*wuutwuutwuut*'. R

17 **THICK- BILLED LARK** *Ramphocoris clot-bey*   L 17 cm. Unmistakable; ♀ shown, the ♂♂ with more black to face sides and underparts, imm's with black only in wings. Habitat: stony desert. R

6   **PREUSS'S CLIFF SWALLOW** *Hirundo preussi*   L 14 cm. From 15 and 17 by absence of rufous on throat, rump and undertail coverts. From 67.10 by less 'clean', less sharply demarcated appearance. Red spot behind eye difficult to see. Habitat: natural and cultivated plains with wood near streams and/or settlement. R

7   **SOUTH AFRICAN CLIFF SWALLOW** *Hirundo spilodera*   L 14 cm. Similar to 15 which see. Absence of tail spots diagnostic. Habitat: grasslands not too far from buildings, bridges or buildings. Voice: very high '*sree-titirrrrrr*'. AM

8   **FOREST SWALLOW** *Hirundo fuliginosa*   L 14 cm. Note compact build. From short-tailed saw-wings (next plate) by less fluttering, more swift and purposeful flight. Habitat: rainforest. AM.R

Plate 66

1   **RED-CHESTED SWALLOW** *Hirundo lucida*   L 15 cm. Similar to 3, but note much larger white tail spots, large chestnut throat patch, dusky under wing-coverts and white underparts. Habitat: montane grassland, marshes, lakes and rivers. See note under 7.

2   **ANGOLA SWALLOW** *Hirundo angolensis*   L 15 cm. Similar to 3 which see. Note dusky underwing coverts. Habitat: open and bushed habitats, river edges, lakes, swamps, forest, settlement.

3   **BARN (or European) SWALLOW** *Hirundo rustica*   L 16 (+5) cm. From 2 by unbroken breast band, longer tail streamers, paler underparts. Habitat: can be seen anywhere except in true forest. Voice: mid-high happy nasal twitters combined with inhaled trills. NM

4   **WHITE-THROATED SWALLOW** *Hirundo albigularis*   L 16 cm. Note white throat, unbroken, black breast band, chestnut forehead. Habitat: open grass plains, inundations, dams, rivers, settlement. Voice: extreme high soft '*sreeeeeeh sreeeeeeeh*' in flight. AM.R

5   **ETHIOPIAN SWALLOW** *Hirundo aethiopica*   L 14 cm. Note interrupted throat-collar and pure white underparts. Habitat: open areas near woodland and settlement, often at higher elevations, but also in coastal areas. RES.(AM)

6   **WIRE-TAILED SWALLOW** *Hirundo smithii*   L 13 (+10) cm. Note very thin tail streamers (difficult to see in flight and in ♀ much shorter), pure white underparts, interrupted black ring between belly and undertail coverts, red cap. Habitat: forest edge, woodland, grassland, settlement, often near rivers and lakes. Voice: very high '*twitwit srièèh*' in short phrases.

7   **RED-BREASTED SWALLOW** *Hirundo semirufa*   L 20 cm. Note black cheek. Chin and under wing-coverts as rufous as (or only slightly paler than) rest of underparts. Habitat: open and bushed habitats with some scattered trees, often near water. Voice: mid-high, sharp, explosive '*tit-ti-tri-uooh*'. Note: nomenclature of 1 and 7 in literature is confusing, but 1 is always called 'Red-chested', while all other combinations of 'rufous', 'red' 'chested' and 'breasted' apply to 7.

8   **MOSQUE SWALLOW** *Hirundo senegalensis*   L 17 (+7) cm. Nominate, in flight, shown (a, similar to, but paler than not-depicted race *saturatior* from Nigeria region) and race *monteiri* (b, with white windows in undertail, missing in a). From 7 by white chin, cheeks and upperbreast and white underwing coverts. Habitat: forest edge, open woodland with baobab. Voice: mid- and very high nasal miaowing '*twit*' and '*treeek*' or '*truuuih*'. AM

9   **BLACK-AND-RUFOUS SWALLOW** *Hirundo nigrorufa*   L 15 cm. Appears all-black in the field. Note absence of rufous to rump. Habitat: grass plains, open woodland, marsh edges. R

10   **GREATER STRIPED SWALLOW** *Hirundo cucullata*   L 14 (+5) cm. Note pale chestnut cheek, hardly or not striped throat. Habitat: open grassland. Avoids woodland and forest. Voice: mid-high unhurried '*trrit-trrit-treet-treet*'. AM

11   **LESSER STRIPED SWALLOW** *Hirundo abyssinica*   L 13 (+4) cm. Face sides more orange than in 10. Striped throat and chin looks uniform dark if seen from a distance. Habitat: open forests, woodland, dry bushed grass- and farmland, areas near cliffs and buildings (needed for nesting), often near water. Voice: high often reed warbler-like '*wit weet witwit-*'. AM

12   **PIED-WINGED SWALLOW** *Hirundo leucosoma*   L 13 cm. Unmistakable. Habitat: dry, grassy plains with large trees, around settlement, open forest.

13   **PEARL-BREASTED SWALLOW** *Hirundo dimidiata*   L 14 cm. From 67.10 by absence of white rump, less strong gloss on upperparts and dark feet. Habitat: more or less wooded and bushed habitats, often near swamps and settlement. Voice: mid-high nasal '*sreet*', '*sreet-sreet*' or '*sriauw-sriauw*'. R

14   **RED-RUMPED SWALLOW** *Hirundo daurica*   L 14 (+4) cm. Note rufous neck isolating black cap from mantle and diagnostic black undertail coverts. Habitat: rocky hill sides. Voice: mid-high nasal '*weet-weet*'. NM.RES

15   **RED-THROATED CLIFF SWALLOW** *Hirundo rufigula*   L 13 cm. From 17 by white spots in tail, darker uniform rufous rump, clean throat, less obvious breast band Habitat: as 17.

◀

Plate 67

1 **AFRICAN RIVER MARTIN** *Pseudochelidon eurystomina* L 15 cm. Note red eyes and yellow bill of this aberrant swallow. Habitat: over and near large waters and rivers; nests in flat sand bars and grassy plains near water. R

2 **BROWN-THROATED SAND MARTIN** *Riparia paludicola* L 13 cm. Pale-bellied (a, perched) and dark (b, in flight) forms shown. Note uniform brown face sides, absence of dark eye patch, absence of white spots in tail. Forms small colonies in tunnels, excavated in sand banks and cliffs. Habitat: areas near rivers, lakes and dams. Voice: mid-high rasping shrieks and liquid twitters. RES.(AM)

3 **CONGO SAND MARTIN** *Riparia congica* L 13 cm. Restricted range. From 4 by less defined breast band, from 2a by pale throat. Habitat: over large rivers and nearby forests.

4 **COMMON SAND MARTIN** *Riparia riparia* L 13 cm. Brown cheek separated from crown and nape. Very gregarious, forms colonies in river banks and sand cliffs. Habitat: anywhere near water except in forests and dense settlement. Voice: mid-high slightly rasping hurried twitters. NM

5 **BANDED MARTIN** *Riparia cincta* L 15 cm. Note white under wing-coverts, short white eyebrow, distinct breast band. Habitat: open and bushed grassland, marshes, dams and ponds, normally at higher elevations. Voice: mid-high, reed warbler-like, hurried twittering. AM

6 **BRAZZA'S MARTIN** *Phedina brazzae* L 11 cm. Note dark underwing coverts and striped underparts (looking uniform dark from some distance). Habitat: riverine belts with sand banks. R

7 **GREY-RUMPED SWALLOW** *Pseudhirundo griseopyga* L 12 (+2) cm. Note grey rump, weak blue gloss, dark brown head, absence of white in tail. Habitat: sheltered areas with some grass, often near water. Voice: mid-high shrieking '*shree free wih shree*'.

8 **CRAG MARTIN** *Hirundo rupestris* L 15 cm. Under wing-coverts are darkest area of underparts. White tail spots only visible in opened tail. Habitat: areas near cliffs and buildings up to high elevations. NM.R

9 **ROCK MARTIN** *Hirundo fuligula* L 13 cm. Variable, examples (a and b) shown. From 2 by white spots in tail (difficult to see unless spread tail is seen against dark background e.g. tree or cliff). Singly or in small colonies. Habitat: near cliffs, houses, bridges. Voice: very high shrill '*sreeh*' and '*tusjirr*'. RES.NM

10 **COMMON HOUSE MARTIN** *Delichon urbica* L 14 cm. Only swallow with pure white rump. Normally seen in flocks (often with other swallows) over any type of country. Habitat: shows some preference for rocky cliffs or high structures. Voice: very high sharp yet liquid '*pri-wip prrri-wrip*'. NM

11 **WHITE-THROATED BLUE SWALLOW** *Hirundo nigrita* L 15 cm. Note large white windows in tail. Habitat: along forest streams, rivers.

12 **BLUE SWALLOW** *Hirundo atrocaerulea* L 15 (+6) cm. From 13–16 by very long thin tail streamers (these in ♀ however much shorter) and blue-black plumage. Habitat: open bushed and wooded grassland near swamp or forest edges, often at high altitudes. Voice: high reed warbler-like rapid '*weetweetweetweetweet----*' mixed with short chirps and twitters. R

13 **MOUNTAIN SAW-WING** *Psalidoprocne fuliginosa* L 14 (+3) cm. Uniform dark blackish brown. From 15 (in area where ranges overlap) by black, not pale or dark grey underwing coverts. Habitat: forest and forest clearings. Also in other natural and cultivated areas with large trees. R

14 **WHITE-HEADED SAW-WING** *Psalidoprocne albiceps* L 14 (+4) cm. The ♀ lacks white crown or shows only a broken white eyebrow. Flight slow, often low over vegetation. Habitat: forest glades, woodland, sparsely wooded areas.

15 **BLACK SAW-WING** *Psalidoprocne pristoptera holomelaena* L 14 (+4) cm. Not all races depicted, *petiti* (a, with white underwing coverts) and *ruwenzori* (b, with blackish underwing) as examples shown. Flight slow and steady with much gliding low over vegetation. Also hawks from perch. Habitat: forest glades and edges, more or less open woodland, marshes, often near settlement. Voice: very high '*priuuuw sreeeuw sreeeoh*'.

16 **FANTI SAW-WING** *Psalidoprocne obscura* L 14 (+6) cm. Note green gloss (difficult to see in flight). Individuals without long tail streamers often seen. Habitat: areas near forests.

17 **SQUARE-TAILED SAW-WING** *Psalidoprocne nitens* L 13 cm. Note absence of gloss and square tail. Very difficult to separate from imm's 13–16 and 66.18, which all however have more or less forked tails. Habitat: forest interior and edges.

Plate 68

1 **YELLOW WAGTAIL** *Motacilla flava*   L 17 cm. Shows double wing bar and greenish, not yellow rump in flight. Undertail coverts yellow, but this feature is not always well-developed, especially not in 1stW ♀♀. Often near grazing cattle. Visiting races are: nominate (a, most common), *flavissima* (b), *thunbergi* (c), *iberiae* (d), *cinereocapilla* (e), *feldegg* (f), *superciliaris* (g), *lutea* (h), *beema* (i) and *melanogrisea* (j, vagrant). Habitat: short grass. Voice: soft very high *'sree-sree'*. Note: several races, especially *feldegg*, might prove to be independent species. NM

2 **GREY WAGTAIL** *Motacilla cinerea*   L 18 cm. Only wagtail with yellow rump. White wingbar only visible in flight. Conspicuously long-tailed. Habitat: wooded rocky mountain streams. Voice: very high *'twitwit weet'* (*'weet'* just within ear reach). NM.R

3 **WHITE WAGTAIL** *Motacilla alba*   L 19 cm. From other wagtails by white (br) or pale (n-br) forehead and face sides. Habitat: river banks, lake shores, large lawns, sewage ponds. Voice: extreme high compressed *'teeweet teeweet'*. NM

4 **AFRICAN PIED WAGTAIL** *Motacilla aguimp*   L 20 cm. Unmistakable. Imm from ad 6 by more white in wing and more distinct collar. Habitat: edges of rivers, lakes, lagoons, golf courses, lawns. Voice: very high liquid very short strophes like lashed-up *'tweeet'* or sharp rapid *'kwik-wik treet'*.

5 **MOUNTAIN (or Long-tailed) WAGTAIL** *Motacilla clara*   L 19 cm. Lacks any yellow; delicately marked with black and pure grey above. Habitat: mountain streams. Voice: extreme high descending *'sreeeeeh'* or *'treederup'*.

6 **CAPE WAGTAIL** *Motacilla capensis*   L 19cm. From 2 by brown, not yellow rump and white wing bars, from imm 4 by less white in wing. Habitat: wet open woodland, grass- and pasture land, swamp, lake edges. Voice: *'sweep tèdèdjèh'* (*'sweep'* very high, *'tèdèdjèh'* rattling and low). R

7 **TREE PIPIT** *Anthus trivialis*   L 14 cm. As n-br 8 but less distinctly streaked on mantle and with unstreaked rump and heavier bill. Habitat: woodland, suburbs, at higher altitudes. Voice: extreme high thin nasal *'tsjee'*. Note: it is possible, that Olive-backed Pipit *Anthus hodgsoni* occurs as a vagrant to the area, separable from Tree Pipit by black cheek spot (see inset a). NM

8 **RED-THROATED PIPIT** *Anthus cervinus*   L 15 cm. Horizontal stance. From all other pipits by reddish glow to head. Note contrasting pattern of mantle; often one mantle stripe seems paler than others. Habitat: lake and sea shores, moorland, wet grass. Voice: high, thin *'sièèh'*. NM

9 **MEADOW PIPIT** *Anthus pratensis*   L 15 cm. Note warm (n. br) plumage. From 7 by heavier streaking to lower flanks and diffuse eyebrow. Habitat: open grassy areas; normally avoids dry areas. NM

10 **TAWNY PIPIT** *Anthus campestris*   L 15 cm. Note pale plumage, almost unstreaked upperparts, plain breast. Habitat: dry, short grassland often with some bush and trees. Voice: high, sharp, short *'tchuwi'*. NM

11 **BUSH(-veld) PIPIT** *Anthus caffer*   L 13 cm. From 12 by less dark upperparts, white outer tail feathers, faint malar stripe and streaking below which is restricted to breast. Habitat: open woodland, bush with sandy patches. Voice: high rather nasal *'mèètjeh mèètjeh mèètjeh mèètjeh- - -'*. R

12 **SHORT-TAILED PIPIT** *Anthus brachyurus*   L 12 cm. Skulks between grass, reluctant to be flushed. Note thin short tail and indistinct eyebrow; outer tail feathers greyish brown. Habitat: open woodland, grassy hill sides. Voice: call sounds like high partly grating *'fuweeh fuweeh'*. R

13 **LONG-BILLED PIPIT** *Anthus similis*   L 18 cm. Note large size, long bill, rather plain plumage. More greyish above than 14 with less pronounced lores. Habitat: stony, sparsely covered slopes. Voice: high monotonous well-spaced *'tjuip tree tjip tjiip three'*.

14 **RICHARD'S PIPIT** *Anthus novaeseelandiae*   L 16 cm. Note erect slender stance and white outertail feathers. From 13 by heavier striping. Habitat: any open area. Voice: very high, liquid, rapid, level *'tjee-tjee-tjee'*; song is a level fast twittering *'twee-twee-hwee-hwee-hwee-hwee'*. (NM).RES.R/RES

15 **PLAIN-BACKED PIPIT** *Anthus leucophrys*   L 17 cm. From plain-backed 17 and 19 by darker warm brown plumage, fainter breast streaking and buff (not pale brown) outer tail feathers. Habitat: dry hilly areas with short grass. Voice: high unstructured *'tjee tjup tree swee tjup'*.

16 **MOUNTAIN PIPIT** *Anthus hoeschi*   L 18 cm. As 14 but less slender. Outertail feathers buff. Habitat: montane grasslands. Voice: very high call *'tuwee tuwee'*. Song as 14 but shorter. AM.R

▶

17 **BUFFY PIPIT** *Anthus vaalensis* L 18 cm. Note pale plumage, very erect stance, unstreaked upperparts and faint streaking on breast. Habitat: dry bare or sparsely grassed areas. Voice: very high rapid '*truuh*' as part of an unstructured well-spaced sequence. AM

18 **STRIPED PIPIT** *Anthus lineiventris* L 17 cm. Well-streaked, especially below. Note long dark cheeks. Habitat: rocky, wooded slopes often near water. Voice: high, rich, loud song in short strophes '*witwitweetwit-witwitweeh*'. R

19 **LONG-LEGGED PIPIT** *Anthus pallidiventris* L 17 cm. Note white underparts and pale brown outer tail feathers. Habitat: open places in forest and woodland. Voice: extreme high '*pweet pweet pirriweet piuu-pweet pirreweet*'.

Plate 69

1 **WESTERN WATTLED CUCKOO-SHRIKE** *Lobotos lobatus* L 18 cm. Not unlike some orioles (plate 97), but with black bill, orange wattles and different jizz. Habitat: rainforest. R

2 **EASTERN WATTLED CUCKOO-SHRIKE** *Lobotos oriolinus* L 18 cm. From 1 by green rump, yellow underparts and without yellow in wings. Not in same range as 1. Habitat: rainforest. R

3 **GREY CUCKOO-SHRIKE** *Coracina caesia* L 21 cm. Note uniform grey plumage. Habitat: montane forest, well-wooded streams. Voice: extreme high '*shreeu*' with slow twittering just within ear reach.

4 **GRAUER'S CUCKOO-SHRIKE** *Coracina graueri* L 20 cm. Unmistakable. Not in same range as 6. Habitat: forest at higher elevations. E, D. R. of Congo.

5 **BLUE CUCKOO-SHRIKE** *Coracina azurea* L 20 cm. Unmistakable, but can look black in shade. Habitat: canopy of forest and woodland.

6 **WHITE-BREASTED CUCKOO-SHRIKE** *Coracina pectoralis* L 25 cm. The ♀ from 3 by almost white underparts. Habitat: open miombo and other woodland at lower altitudes. Voice: very high '*shree-shree witwit –* ' ('*witwit*' much lower).

7 **RED-SHOULDERED CUCKOO-SHRIKE** *Campephaga phoenicea* L 18 cm. Unmistakable, but some ♂♂ rather similar to individuals of 8a with dark yellow-orange shoulders. The ♀ from ♀ 8 by greyer upperparts and less yellow on underside of tail feathers. Habitat: more or less wooded and bushed areas. RES.(AM)

8 **BLACK CUCKOO-SHRIKE** *Campephaga flava* L 18 cm. All-black form (a, common) and yellow-shouldered form (b, less common) shown. Note predominantly white (black-barred) underparts of ♀. Gleans insects from foliage. Floppy undulating flight. Often in mixed bird parties. Habitat: open forests, plantations, other wooded and bushed habitats. Voice: extreme high silvery short insect-like trill '*srrrrri*'. AM.R

9 **PETIT'S CUCKOO-SHRIKE** *Campephaga petiti* L 19 cm. From 8 by blue sheen. The ♀ from ♀ 8 by yellow and less barred underparts. Habitat: tall trees at forest edges and surrounding areas. Voice: combinations of extreme high '*shreeeeh*' with much lower '*weewee*', '*dee-deeder*' etc. R

10 **PURPLE-THROATED CUCKOO-SHRIKE** *Campephaga quiscalina* L 20 cm. Note beautiful purple and green (not bluish) gloss. Habitat: montane forests.

11 **GRIMWOOD'S LONGCLAW** *Macronyx grimwoodi* L 20 cm. Overall buff, heavily marked black. From 14 by larger black centres of upperpart and wing feathers, buff, not pink belly and by black streaks instead of a solid black necklace. Habitat: open grassy hills.

12 **YELLOW-THROATED LONGCLAW** *Macronyx croceus* L 20 cm. From 13 by all-white outer tail feathers. Habitat: moist sparsely wooded grassland. Voice: very high '*mièèèèh mioweeh*' combined with low '*cha-cha-cha-cha*'.

13 **FUELLEBORN'S LONGCLAW** *Macronyx fuelleborni* L 19 cm. From 12 by partly (not all-) white outer tail feathers, absence of streaks below necklace and off-yellow underparts. Habitat: short grassland, marshes. Voice: mid-high loud well-spaced fluted notes '*fiu feew feeuw weejeh wut fiu -*'.

14 **ROSY-BREASTED (or Pink-throated) LONGCLAW** *Macronyx ameliae* L 19 cm. Tail corner and outer tail feather all white. The ♂ from 11 by red belly, white margins to wing feathers and solid black necklace, ♀ by rosy (not buffy) underparts. Rather skulking. Habitat: rough grass near lakes, dams, inundations, marshes. Voice: high '*weetjèh-weetjèh- -*'. R

Plate 70

1   **COMMON (or Black-eyed) BULBUL** *Pycnonotus barbatus*   L 18 cm. Shown are races *tricolor* (a), *inornatus* (b, with white vent) and *arsinoe* (c, with faint white mark to ear coverts). Unmistakable. Habitat: forest edges, gardens, more or less wooded and bushed areas. Voice: high happy up-and-down whistled '*I'm coming home*'.

2   **SJÖSTEDT'S HONEYGUIDE GREENBUL** *Baeopogon clamans*   L 18 cm. Note absence of black tips to outer tail feathers, but imm with tail pattern as ad 3. From 3 also by more buffish underparts, paler throat and harsher call. Habitat: along streams and rivers in forest. Voice: nasal very high '*tjuw tjuw*' or rapid '*tititjuweeh*'.

3   **HONEYGUIDE GREENBUL** *Baeopogon indicator*   L 18 cm. From honeyguides (plate 61) by darker plumage without any yellow tones. Only ♂ has pale eye, but ♀♀ with pale eyes may occur too. Habitat: open forest and forest edges. Voice: very high, melodious '*pi-pi-piuuuh*', or *´pipiwiuuuuh*' or '*wee wee wee piuwweeh*', each '*….uuuh*' drawn out and down.

4   **SPOTTED GREENBUL** *Ixonotus guttatus*   L 15 cm. In chattering flocks. Looks all white from below. Note spots on rump. Habitat: forest canopies. Voice: very high, wren-like '*tjitjerk------*'.

5   **GOLDEN GREENBUL** *Calyptocichla serina*   L 15 cm. Note pale, flesh-coloured bill. From other similar bulbuls in its habitat by keeping to the forest canopy. Habitat: forest and other habitats with high trees. Voice: sharp, high '*tjut-twéee tjut-twéee*', last part higher and accentuated.

6   **YELLOW-WHISKERED GREENBUL** *Andropadus latirostris*   L 18 cm. Note conspicuous yellow whiskers of ad. Habitat: forests, forest remains, plantations, large gardens. Voice: mid-high unstructured up-and-down scratching unhurried '*tjash tjesh tjesh-tjush tresh-tjash-*'.

7   **SHELLEY'S GREENBUL** *Andropadus masukuensis*   L 15 cm. Note pale (not white) eye-ring and grey head with dark grey-brown (not grey-blue) crown. Habitat: montane forests and surrounding well-wooded areas. Voice: rather quiet '*wit-wit-wit*'.

8   **CAMEROON MONTANE GREENBUL** *Andropadus montanus*   L 15 cm. Very dark with paler yellowish chin and lower underparts. From other bulbuls in same habitat by uniform plumage and dark brown (not rufous) tail. Habitat: forest undergrowth, often near clearings. R

9   **LITTLE GREENBUL** *Andropadus virens*   L 15 cm. From 10 by yellowish (not greyish) chin, greenish (not olive) mantle, absence of eye ring. Habitat: midstrata and undergrowth of forest. Voice: hurried strophes like mid-high warbling up-and-down '*prrrrk-prrrrk-jterp fuwit*'.

10   **LITTLE GREY GREENBUL** *Andropadus gracilis*   L 15 cm. Note narrow eye ring, greyish throat, yellowish lower belly. Forages rather high in trees. Habitat: forest. Voice: very high up-and-down '*wee-tup-to-wup tjut*'.

11   **ANSORGE'S GREENBUL** *Andropadus ansorgei*   L 15 cm. Similar to 10, but more greyish green, less warm brown. Note white eye-ring, dark grey head and greenish edges of flight feathers. Tail more reddish brown than rest of body. Habitat: midstrata of montane forest. Voice: very high, rapid '*weet-wju-twee*'.

12   **PLAIN (or Cameroon Sombre) GREENBUL** *Andropadus curvirostris*   L 16 cm. Note well-defined grey throat and pale grey eyelids. Habitat: forest understudy. Voice: mid-high fluted '*twwee-tu-dirrrr*' or '*wee-to-wee-hoh*'.

13   **SLENDER-BILLED GREENBUL** *Andropadus gracilirostris*   L 17 cm. Note pale, almost white underparts (only forest greenbul so). Habitat: upper strata of montane forests. Voice: very high descending repeated '*tjiuuuu tjuuu*' and mid-high miaowing drawn-up '*nieau nieau*'.

14   **(Western) MOUNTAIN GREENBUL** *Andropadus tephrolaemus*   L 20 cm. Note white eye-ring and striped cheeks. Habitat: montane forests and bamboo. Voice: high, 3-noted '*it's-not-so-chilly*'. Note: might be a race of 7.

Plate 71

1   **XAVIER'S GREENBUL** *Phyllastrephus xavieri* L 15 cm. Note pale lore, rather yellow underparts and rather dark breast. Habitat: forest undergrowth and nearby wooded habitats. Voice: very high, staccato, fluted '*tju-tee-tu*' and '*tee-tju-tee*'.

2   **BAUMANN'S GREENBUL** *Phyllastrephus baumanni* L 15 cm. Overall drab brown with pale underparts. Tail only slightly rufous. From similar 70.9 in same habitat by much longer bill. Habitat: forest, woodland and other habitats with trees and bush. R

3   **GREY-OLIVE GREENBUL** *Phyllastrephus cerviniventris* L 16 cm. Similar to 7 and 15, but with pale bill. Habitat: forest undergrowth, riverine belts. R

4   **PALE OLIVE GREENBUL** *Phyllastrephus fulviventris* L 16 cm. Overall greenish with rather pale rufous lower underparts. Habitat: forest undergrowth. R

5   **CAMEROON OLIVE GREENBUL** *Phyllastrephus poensis* L 20 cm. No similar greenbul in its restricted range and habitat. Note face pattern. Habitat: montane forest. R

6   **TORO OLIVE GREENBUL** *Phyllastrephus hypochloris* L 15 cm. Very similar to 70.10 and 70.12, but without eye ring, paler below and with finer, longer bill. Habitat: forests. R

7   **NORTHERN BROWNBUL** *Phyllastrephus strepitans* L 15 cm. Note rather rufous appearance with pale eye-ring; 15 is more brown overall with less pronounced rufous rump. Habitat: undergrowth of forest patches, woodland and bush. (?)

8   **GREY-HEADED GREENBUL** *Phyllastrephus poliocephalus* L 19 cm. No other similar greenbuls in its restricted range and habitat except 70.14, which is duller below. Note yellowish corners to tail. Habitat: forests. R

9   **YELLOW-STREAKED GREENBUL** *Phyllastrephus flavostriatus* L 19 cm. Yellow streaking on underparts not apparent in the field. Not shy. Constantly raises or flicks a wing on one side. Habitat: mid- and higher strata of forests. Voice: mid-high reed warbler-like lazy '*terrettjup terrettjup tjup-tjup-tjup-tjup*' or high sharp '*tsjirrup-tsjirrup*'.

10   **SASSI'S OLIVE GREENBUL** *Phyllastrephus lorenzi* L 15 cm. Note well-defined dark cap. Habitat: forests. R

11   **WHITE-THROATED GREENBUL** *Phyllastrephus albigularis* L 16 cm. Note striking white throat. From 72.6 by overall less bright colouring, more slender build, smaller size. Habitat: forest edges, gardens. Voice: high melodious bubbling '*wit-wit-weet-wit-juu tjuu-tjuu*' (first part rapidly chattered).

12   **LIBERIAN GREENBUL** *Phyllastrephus leucolepis* L 15 cm. Solitary. Very restricted range and habitat. Shows only wing spots to flight feathers and to greater (not to other) wing coverts. From 70.4 and nicators (Plate 94) also by rufous tail and rump. Habitat: rain forest. E, Liberia.

13   **CABANIS'S GREENBUL** *Phyllastrephus cabanisi* L 17 cm. Note pale eye, pale yellow underparts, well-developed greenish breast band. Small noisy flocks. Habitat: highland forests.

14   **ICTERINE GREENBUL** *Phyllastrephus icterinus* L 15 cm. Underparts uniform pale yellow without greenish breast band. Eye colour variable. Habitat: forest undergrowth and surrounding wooded areas. Voice: high, rapid, miaowing '*weck-weck weck-weck –*' mixed with low, drawn-out miaowings.

15   **TERRESTRIAL BROWNBUL** *Phyllastrephus terrestris* L 18 cm. From 7 by browner, less rufous plumage, often foraging on the forest ground in small noisy flocks. Habitat: dense forest undergrowth, riverine belts, dense woodland. Voice: sharp rattling reed warbler-like '*cratch-oh-cratch-oh wi-wir*'. R

Plate 72

1   **GREY-HEADED BRISTLEBILL** *Bleda canicapilla* L 20 cm. From 3 by grey head and grey, not pale yellow lore. Keeps close to the ground, often at ant swarms. Habitat: forest interior. Voice: melodious, fluid, rapid '*peeweeweeweeweeh wik wik puweeweehweeh*'.

2   **RED-TAILED BRISTLEBILL** *Bleda syndactyla* L 21 cm. From 1 by bare blue skin above eye, green head and rufous tail. Very shy. Habitat: forest, riverine belts and other habitats with dense undergrowth. Voice: mid-high hurried miaowing '*kiau-kiau-kiau*' and many other repeated thrush-like or magpie-like whistles changing in speed, pitch and volume, often with more or less crescendo.

3   **GREEN-TAILED BRISTLEBILL** *Bleda eximia* L 20 cm. Note yellowish lores and yellow tail corners. Habitat: forest edges and interiors. Voice: very high, twittered, fluted '*titjituu-tuu*' continued with rolls, trills and clear whistles.

4   **EASTERN BEARDED GREENBUL** *Criniger chloronotus* L 20 cm. Note whitish often fluffed-out 'beard' contrasting with dark head, grey-brown breast and reddish tail. Habitat: forests. Voice: mid-high, trilled whistle '*tu-tu-tu-tjiuu*'.

5   **WESTERN BEARDED GREENBUL** *Criniger barbatus* L 20 cm. From 4 by yellow 'beard' and more yellow undertail coverts. Habitat: forest, open forest, gallery forest. Voice: high, fluid '*piuuh-piuuh-piuuh-piuuh*' or '*woo-whiuuuh*' ('*whiuu*'-part higher).

6   **RED-TAILED GREENBUL** *Criniger calurus* L 17 cm. Note pure white frequently puffed-out beard contrasting with cheek and breast, bare blue skin around eye, red tail. Habitat: lower level of forest, riverine belts. Voice: high fluted short repeated '*tutu-tjiuh*' or '*ti-tju-tjieh*'.

7   **WHITE-BEARDED GREENBUL** *Criniger ndussumensis* L 18 cm. From very similar 6 (in same habitat) by paler lore, buffier undertail coverts and different call. Habitat: forest. Voice: call is a hard trill. R

8   **YELLOW-BEARDED GREENBUL** *Criniger olivaceus* L 16 cm. From other yellow-throated greenbuls by all-green underparts (except 9, which has a different range). Quiet and unobtrusive. Habitat: all levels in rainforest. Voice: high, level, rather staccato '*tu-tu-tjúu*'. R

9   **YELLOW-NECKED GREENBUL** *Chlorocichla falkensteini* L 18 cm. No other mainly green, yellow-throated greenbul in its range and habitat. Habitat: thick bush outside forest. Voice: mid-high miaowing chatters like '*tu-tju-tjí-wiuuh*'. R

10   **SIMPLE GREENBUL** *Chlorocichla simplex* L 19 cm. Note broken eye ring and white throat. Shy skulker in foliage. Habitat: as 11. Voice: high short hurried miaowing chatter '*mew-mau-mi-chet-chet*'.

11   **YELLOW-THROATED LEAFLOVE** *Chlorocichla flavicollis* L 21 cm. Race *soror* (a, with white (!) throat) and yellow-throated nominate (b) shown. From 10 by pale eye, absence of eye ring, greener upperparts. Puffs out throat feathers when singing. Noisy flocks. Not shy. Habitat: open forest, riverine belts, abandoned cultivation, large gardens.

12   **YELLOW-BELLIED GREENBUL** *Chlorocichla flaviventris* L 21 cm. Note olive-brown upperparts, yellowish underparts, broken eye ring which is broader above eye. Habitat: forests, riverine belts, coastal shrub. Voice: mid-high miaowing '*tjuk tjuk tjeeh-tjeeh tjee tutje tu-tji-tji-tji-tji –*' (some parts running-up). R

13   **JOYFUL GREENBUL** *Chlorocichla laetissima* L 20 cm. From 12 by more uniform and bright green upperparts and yellow underparts. Habitat: forest. Voice: low hoarse rather excited scattered '*tjuut-tjuut-tjuut-tuu-terre-tuut*'.

14   **PRIGOGINE'S GREENBUL** *Chlorocichla prigoginei* L 19 cm. From 13 by white chin and lore. Habitat: forest patches at higher elevations. E, D. R. of Congo

15   **SWAMP (or White-tailed) PALM GREENBUL** *Thescelocichla leucopleura* L 20 cm. Noisy flocks in swamps. Note white tail tips. Habitat: more or less wooded swamps with palms. Voice: low, slightly rising, rapid miaowing chatters '*whit-tau-wit-tau-wit-wit*'.

16   **LEAFLOVE** *Pyrrhurus scandens* L 20 cm. Note large size, grey head, pale breast (but darker than rest of underparts), buff edging of flight feathers. Habitat: forests, often near streams and swampy places. Also in surrounding areas. Voice: mid-high, melodious, jackdaw-like chatters '*piu-piu piew-pu-pu-pu-pu*'.

Plate 73

1 **ISABELLINE WHEATEAR** *Oenanthe isabellina* L 16 cm. From ♀2 by tail pattern, paler almost translucent outer wing, clean (not dusky) underwing, short eyebrow, white in front of eye, clean pale ear coverts. Wing coverts concolorous with mantle. Habitat: (very) dry areas without or with scarce bush and trees. Voice: (probably silent in Africa). Rich flow of short sweeping phrases with many imitations. NM

2 **NORTHERN (or European) WHEATEAR** *Oenanthe oenanthe* L 15 cm. Nominate (a) shown and race *seebohmi* (b, from NW Africa, with black chin, speckled black in n-br plumage). 1stW birds with more black in folded wing than 1. Note also tail pattern with narrower black band. Habitat: short-grassed areas often with some bush and trees. Voice: (probably silent in Africa). Alarm call low '*tak-tak-phew*' ('*phew*' very high). NM

3 **BLACK-EARED (or Spanish) WHEATEAR** *Oenanthe hispanica* L 15 cm. White- (a) and black-throated (b) forms shown. In n-br plumage not safely separable from 10 but back less dusky. Note narrow black terminal band and mainly black outer tail-feathers. Habitat: bare fields and rocky areas with some short grass cover and trees. NM

4 **RED-BREASTED WHEATEAR** *Oenanthe bottae* L 14 cm. Note very upright stance, buff-orange lower underparts, plain upperparts and short white eyebrow. Habitat: rocky areas with some short grass, up to high elevations. Voice: high, unstructured, scratchy reed warbler-like whistles '*tjickturrr-tjick-tjicktjick-tjirktjirk*'. AM.RES

5 **DESERT WHEATEAR** *Oenanthe deserti* L 15 cm. Note almost white wing shoulder in n-br dress (unlike 1 and 2). Black of wing (in br plumage) connected with black throat. Note almost all-black tail (but white rump). Habitat: dry, flat, stony and sandy areas with sparse vegetation. NM

6 **WHITE-CROWNED BLACK WHEATEAR** *Oenanthe leucopyga* L 15 cm. Imm from ad 8 by more white in tail. Habitat: rocky desert, also near settlement. Voice: high, loud, happy, short, fast whistles '*ratsjsja-sjarara*'. NM

7 **CAPPED WHEATEAR** *Oenanthe pileata* L 17 cm. Unmistakable. Habitat: semi-desert, montane moorland, open coastal shrub. Voice: unhurried sequence of high unstructured rasping and chattered notes.

8 **BLACK WHEATEAR** *Oenanthe leucura* L 16 cm. The ♀ from imm 6 by brown, not slate-black plumage and different tail pattern. Habitat: dry, hilly, rocky country often with some bush or trees. R

9 **MOURNING WHEATEAR** *Oenanthe lugens halophila* L 15 cm. From 10 by white upperbreast, all-white cap, faintly buff undertail coverts. Head of ♀ rather white. Habitat: rocky slopes and slightly bushed areas with patches of rough grass cover. V

10 **PIED WHEATEAR** *Oenanthe pleschanka* L 15 cm. Note tail pattern. Br plumage of ♂ with grey top of crown. Note dusky upperparts of ♀ and 1stW. Habitat: open areas from rocky hill sides to moorland. Voice: very varied repertoire of very short hurried extreme high to mid-high strophes like '*fifi-feeh*' or '*tjap-tjeeh*'. NM.R

11 **WHINCHAT** *Saxicola rubetra* L 13 cm. From ♀ 12 by prominent white eyebrows, white sides to tail base, rump in same colour as mantle. Habitat: open woodland and other more or less wooded natural and cultivated areas. Voice: hurried very high '*juu weeroweet*'. NM

12 **COMMON STONECHAT** *Saxicola torquata* L 14 cm. Not all races depicted, *stonei* (a) and *moptana* (b, with less orange to breast) shown. Note all-black tail and white neck patches. The ♀ has only inconspicuous eyebrows. Habitat: areas with some scattered bush and shrub, moorland, swamp edges. Voice: short nervous rattle '*si-si-ti-tur-rut-tur-rut*'. NM.RES

13 **BLACKSTART** *Cercomela melanura* L 14 cm. Note black tail and grey-brown back. Habitat: dry rocky slopes, often with some scrub and bush. Voice: very high, simple rapid warble '*frrrfrrri-did-not-see*'.

14 **FAMILIAR (or Red-tailed) CHAT** *Cercomela familiaris* L 15 cm. From 13 and 15 by red in tail. Habitat: dry rocky areas, dry river courses, cultivation. Voice: low scratchy unhurried notes interspersed with high '*weet*'.

15 **BROWN-TAILED CHAT** *Cercomela scotocerca* L 13 cm. Note dark brown tail and upright stance. Habitat: dry bushed areas with rocky outcrops.

Plate 74

1 **BLACK REDSTART** *Phoenicurus ochruros* L 15 cm. Unmistakable. 1stW ♂♂ as ♀ or as ♂ (as shown), but without white wing patch. Habitat: rocky slopes with more or less trees; also on buildings in towns and villages. NM.R

2 **COMMON (or European) REDSTART** *Phoenicurus phoenicurus* L 14 cm. The ♂ is unmistakable, ♀ from ♀ 1 by paler plumage without orange wash to underparts. Note constant shivering of tail. Habitat: dry scrub- and woodland often along streams. Voice: (probably silent in Africa). Song composed of very high variations on 'see-see-swee-dji-dji-dji' (last part as a melodious rattle). NM

3 **NIGHTINGALE** *Luscinia megarhynchos* L 15 cm. Note warm brown colouring, almost red tail and large eye. Habitat: dry undergrowth of woodland and scrub. Voice: very rich flow of very variable short phrases with rolls, rattles and the famous crescendo 'tjuu-tjuu- tjuu- tjuu- tjuu-'. NM

4 **SPROSSER** (or Thrush Nightingale) *Luscinia luscinia* L 17 cm. Note large black eye and pale eye ring. Yellowish mouth corner gives face its characteristic expression. Tail is slightly russet-brown. Habitat: thickets, woodland with leafy undergrowth. Voice: can be heard singing in Africa especially in February–March. Very rich flow of very variable well-separated single or repeated liquid notes and harsh fluted or trilling rattles (lacking crescendo of Nightingale). V

5 **BLUETHROAT** *Luscinia svecica* L 14 cm. Nominate (a) shown and race *cyanecula* (b), both as ♂♂ in breeding plumage. N-br plumage of both races the same. Note rufous at tail base. Habitat: reeds, papyrus and shrubbery near water and swamps. NM

6 **RED-TAILED PALM THRUSH** *Cichladusa ruficauda* L 17 cm. From 7 by absence of breast collar. Note upright stance. Forages mainly on the ground. Habitat: palm thickets, palm plantations, gardens. Voice: unhurried sequence of fluted notes rather varying in pitch: 'fiufiuflehweedjubdjubdjubweetweet', ('-djubdjubdjub-') almost a short rattle.

7 **COLLARED PALM THRUSH** *Cichladusa arquata* L 18 cm. From 6 by black line around throat patch and different range. Habitat: riverine palm thickets, palm savannahs. Voice: unhurried sequence of fluted notes and phrases of any length 'weet weet weetweetuhweet'. R

8 **SPOTTED PALM (or Morning) THRUSH** *Cichladusa guttata* L 15 cm. Note drop-shaped black dots in lines to breast. As congeners mainly on the ground. Habitat: dense thickets along dry streams. Voice: high, continuous, 4–5 toned, up-and-down song with short whistles.

9 **WHITE-STARRED ROBIN** *Pogonocichla stellata* L 16 cm. White patches on head (especially the one on throat) normally concealed or hardly visible. Habitat: coastal and montane forest edges. Voice: very high clear single or repeated short phrases often sounding like carefree human whistling.

10 **MIOMBO BEARDED SCRUB ROBIN** *Cercotrichas barbata* L 17 cm. From 11 by paler plumage, red cheek, rufous, not brown or grey flanks, different habitat and range. Habitat: miombo, thick bush and scrub. Voice: very high sharp strophes

11 **FOREST SCRUB ROBIN** *Cercotrichas leucosticta* L 17 cm. Not all races depicted, nominate (a) shown and race *collsi* (b, with grey, not buffish underparts). From 10 by much darker plumage and brown-black tail. Habitat: forest interior often near termite mounts. R

12 **BROWN-BACKED SCRUB ROBIN** *Cercotrichas hartlaubi* L 15 cm. From 13 by darker upperparts and sharply defined wing bars. Habitat: tall grass near forest and cultivation. Voice: very high fluted whistles e.g. 'feetjudeewee'. R

13 **WHITE-BROWED SCRUB ROBIN** *Cercotrichas leucophrys* L 15 cm. In most of its range only scrub robin with streaked breast. Habitat: dense grassy thornbush patches in more or less wooded and bushed areas. Voice: very high loud fluted whistles repeated 2-3x, e.g. 'weeduweet-weeduweet-weeduweet'.

14 **RUFOUS SCRUB ROBIN** *Cercotrichas galactotes* L 15 cm. From 13 by less contrasting wing pattern. Habitat: areas with trees, palms, thickets in dry semi-desert. Voice: high rapid warbling in short strophes 'trrrrti-tu-trrrwiet' (like European Robin). RES.NM

▶

15 **BLACK SCRUB ROBIN** *Cercotrichas podobe* L 20 cm. Unmistakable; note white spots to tips of outer tail feathers and white undertail coverts. Forages mainly on the ground. Habitat: areas with palms, trees and thickets in dry semi-desert. Voice: high, rather short or prolonged thrush-like warbling.

Plate 75

1 **FOREST ROBIN** *Stiphrornis erythrothorax* L 12 cm. Race *xanthogaster* (a) shown and nominate (b, with olive wash on upperparts and more intense orange breast and throat). Race *gabonensis* (not shown) as b, but with sooty grey upperparts. See also 76.5. Note black face and white spot before eye. Habitat: undergrowth of swampy forests. Voice: extra high, sharp hurried whistle '*feetjeetowee*', '*feetjeeweeteewo*' and '*sri-sweep-sreepper-sreep-sreepsreep-sweep*'.

2 **EUROPEAN ROBIN** *Erithacus rubecula* L 14 cm. Very compact. Note sharply demarcated orange breast. Habitat: woodland, plantations, orchards and other small-sealed habitats, often near settlement. Voice: short rather hoarse, inhaled phrases '*phreesreereeweerheeh*'. V

3 **EQUATORIAL AKALAT** *Sheppardia aequatorialis* L 13 cm. Similar to 6 but separated by altitude and voice. Habitat: montane forest undergrowth. Voice: mid-high, simple, rolling flute '*prurr prurr –*'. R

4 **GREY-WINGED ROBIN CHAT** *Cossypha polioptera* L 13 cm. Note narrow white eyebrow and absence of black in tail. Habitat: forest edges, woodland, thickets. Voice: very high, sharp whistling of varied pitch, interspersed with clicks and short tempo changes, often resembling human whistling. R

5 **BOCAGE'S AKALAT** *Sheppardia bocagei* L 14 cm. Race *chapini* (a) shown and race *poensis* (b, with some black below eye, from Bioco). Note dark rufous rump and tail. Habitat: montane forests. Voice: very high fluted loud sharp '*fuu-tji-fuu-tu-weeh*'.

6 **LOWLAND (or Common) AKALAT** *Sheppardia cyornithopsis* L 13 cm. Similar to 3, but distinguished by altitude and song. Note short stumpy bill, greyish cheeks, orange flanks and rump. Habitat: undergrowth of more or less swampy forests. Voice: very high, varied, calm warbling strophes (2–3 sec) with melodious rattles and rolls.

7 **FIRE-CRESTED (or White-tailed) ALETHE** *Alethe diademata* L 17 cm. Nominate (a) shown and more warm brown, less dark race *woosnami* (b). Note orange crown with contrasting grey face sides. Habitat: lowland forests, riverine belts, plantations. Voice: mid-high simple repeated strong whistle '*fuuu fuuu fuuu –*' at the end falling-off or '*fju wèh*'.

8 **RED-THROATED ALETHE** *Alethe poliophrys* L 15 cm. Restricted range. From similar thrush-like birds by small area of orange on throat. Habitat: undergrowth of montane forest and bamboo. Voice: single down-slurred note.

9 **BROWN-CHESTED ALETHE** *Alethe poliocephala* L 15 cm. Note narrow white eyebrow and reddish-brown upperparts. Habitat: forest undergrowth and nearby areas. Voice: high fluted descending slow whistled '*fju-fju-fju-fju-fju-fju-fjufju*'.

10 **MOCKING CLIFF CHAT** *Myrmecocichla cinnamomeiventris* L 21 cm. Several races, of these the black-headed *cavernicola* (a) and the white-crowned race *coronatas* (b, only race so) shown. Unmistakable. Habitat: sloping, well-wooded areas near cliffs, rocky outcrops, buildings. Voice: very varied, extreme high whistles, sunbird-like twitters and melodious nightingale-like strophes.

11 **RUFOUS FLYCATCHER THRUSH** *Neocossyphus fraseri* L 20 cm. From 13 by flycatcher-like stance and more contrasting tail-pattern. Catches insects in short sallies from perch. Habitat: middle and higher levels in forest. Voice: mid-high slightly drawn-out whistle '*uweeeet-uweet-tereet*' (at the end drawn-up) and mid-high lashing '*weeet-wreet-wreet*'.

12 **FINSCH'S FLYCATCHER THRUSH** *Neocossyphus finschii* L 19 cm. From 14 by different stance, paler plumage and less red in wings. Habitat: lower stories of very dense forest.

13 **RED-TAILED ANT THRUSH** *Neocossyphus rufus* L 20 cm. Thrush-like in stance and feeding habits. Note all-rufous tail. Habitat: forests, moist bush- and scrubland. Voice: extra high, trilling '*fi-fi-fi-fi-fi-fi-sruu fjui weee*' ('*-sruu*' rapidly descending, '*weee*' as a high, loud, level whistle).

▶

Plate 75 (continued)

14   **WHITE-TAILED ANT THRUSH** *Neocossyphus poensis*   L 20 cm. Very dark upperparts. Note white tail corners and red bar in flight, formed by red bases of all flight feathers. Thrush-like in stance and behaviour. Habitat: midstrata and undergrowth of forest. Voice: e.g. very high lashed-up '*fueeet*' or mid-high '*weeet-weeet-weeet*'.

15   **WHITE-FRONTED BLACK CHAT** *Myrmecocichla albifrons*   L 14 cm. Race *frontalis* (a) shown and white-shouldered race *limbata* (b). Unmistakable. Habitat: bare, stony places in bushed and wooded areas. Voice: very high, swept-up '*ohweetjee-ohweetjeeh-weetjeeh*', interwoven with imitations, mainly of other birds.

16   **WHITE-HEADED BLACK (or Arnott's) CHAT** *Myrmecocichla arnotti*   L 17 cm. Unmistakable. Habitat: bare patches in miombo and other woodland. Voice: very high canary-like hurried twittering with some rasping notes, as garlands hanging from recurring very high '*-feee-*'. R

17   **CONGO MOOR CHAT** *Myrmecocichla tholloni*   L 17 cm. Note white rump and wing patches. Habitat: open grassland with some trees, bushes and other look-out posts.

18   **NORTHERN ANTEATER CHAT** *Myrmecocichla aethiops*   L 20 cm. Striking white wing patches in flight. Habitat: termite mounds in dry short grassland at higher elevations. Voice: high, loud, rather slow whistle '*pee-pee-pju tju-fju.*'

19   **SOOTY CHAT** *Myrmecocichla nigra*   L 16 cm. From imm 16 by smaller white wing patch, shorter tail, more open habitat. Habitat: open short grassland with termite mounds. Voice: very high sharp calm thrush-like 4 or 5-toned phrase '*tu-tu-tjee-tu-tju*'.

Plate 76 (continued)

16 **GREY GROUND THRUSH** *Zoothera princei* L 22 cm. Note white tail corners. From 17 by slightly larger size, heavier bill and longer tail. Habitat: dense parts of forest, often near streams. R

17 **BLACK-EARED GROUND THRUSH** *Zoothera cameronensis* L 20 cm. Nominate (a, from 16 in same range by tawny underparts) shown and race *graueri* (b, paler with some streaking on breast). Note rather pale brown colouring of upperparts and pale chin and throat. Habitat: groundstrata of lowland forests. R

Plate 76

1   **WHITE-BELLIED ROBIN CHAT** *Cossyphicula roberti*   L 14 cm. Very small. Note white eyebrow and dark middle tail feathers. Habitat: forest understorey. Voice: very high, plaintive song, lasting about 1 minute. R

2   **MOUNTAIN ROBIN CHAT** *Cossypha isabellae*   L 16 cm. Nominate (a, Mt Cameroon) shown and race *batesi* (b, range of species except Mt Cameroon; paler above with black restricted to cheek). From 1 by larger size, orange belly and black cheek. Habitat: ground and understorey in montane forest. Voice: extreme high, shrill '*wheeteetshreeh*' and similar variations.

3   **ARCHER'S ROBIN CHAT** *Cossypha archeri*   L 15 cm. Note absence of black on head, warm overall rufous-brown colouring and white eyebrow. Habitat: undergrowth of montane forests, bamboo and giant heath. Voice: very high '*firra-tweet-tweet-tweet*'.

4   **CAPE (or Common) ROBIN CHAT** *Cossypha caffra*   L 17 cm. Note grey-olive flanks and black cheek, bordered below and above by white. Habitat: suburbs, cultivation, open forests, scrubland. Voice: varied repertoire of connected flutes and whistles.

5   **SANGHA FOREST ROBIN** *Stiphrornis sanghensis*   L 12 cm. Recently discovered new species with very restricted range (should have been placed next to 75.1). From 75.1 by yellow belly. Habitat: forest undergrowth. E, Central African Republic.

6   **BLUE-SHOULDERED ROBIN CHAT** *Cossypha cyanocampter*   L 20 cm. Note shining pale orange underparts and blue shoulder. Habitat: wet forest undergrowth especially along streams. Voice: mid-high to high, liquid, rich, unhurried whistles repeated 1–3 times (like a person happily whistling).

7   **WHITE-BROWED (or Heuglin's) ROBIN CHAT** *Cossypha heuglini*   L 19 cm. Note diagnostic long white eyebrows. Habitat: well-planted gardens, bush, open forest. Voice: high melodious crescendoing strophes, endlessly varied with small skilful tempo changes and interwoven with imitations, mainly of other birds.

8   **RED-CAPPED (or Natal) ROBIN CHAT** *Cossypha natalensis*   L 18 cm. Unmistakable. Habitat: suburbs, forest undergrowth, coastal bush, riverine belts. Voice: '*weeeh rurr*' (call). Song is a flow of rather short phrases with often repeated rich fluted notes incorporating adapted imitations. RES.AM

9   **WHITE-CROWNED ROBIN CHAT** *Cossypha albicapilla*   L 25 cm. From 11 by larger size, darker lower belly and undertail coverts. Race *giffardi* (not shown) has crown black finely speckled white. Habitat: swampy woodland thickets. Voice: rich, rather sharp and slightly hurried fluted phrases, normally without imitations.

10   **WHITE-HEADED ROBIN CHAT** *Cossypha heinrichi*   L 23 cm. No similar bird within its range. Habitat: riverine belts. R

11   **SNOWY-CROWNED ROBIN CHAT** *Cossypha niveicapilla*   L 23 cm. From 9 by chestnut on chin, reaching bill. Habitat: forest edges, undergrowth of moist woodland and gardens. Voice: very rich, liquid, sustained whistling with perfect imitations, mainly of other birds.

12   **ABYSSINIAN GROUND THRUSH** *Zoothera piaggiae*   L 20 cm. Nominate (a) shown and race *ruwenzorii* (b, with orange on head extending until nape). Habitat: groundstrata of montane forests and bamboo. Voice: very high, rather sharp, fluted, slightly hurried '*pi-pi-pji-pju*'. R

13   **CROSSLEY'S GROUND THRUSH** *Zoothera crossleyi*   L 22 cm. Note: may have white tail tips. From 14 by broad black band through eye; from 16 and 17 by absence of black ear mark and generally more orange colour. Habitat: forest. R

14   **OBERLAENDER'S GROUND THRUSH** *Zoothera oberlaenderi*   L 20 cm. Note rufous face and overall warm colouring. Habitat: groundstrata of forests. Voice: high, unstructured, up-and-down '*peeeuu-wip to-three*' and '*riu-riu-reez reep-reep*'. R

15   **ORANGE GROUND THRUSH** *Zoothera gurneyi*   L 22 cm. From 12 by dark ear patch and vertical line through eye. Habitat: montane forests. Voice: high loud piping repeated whistles like '*tu-tu-tu-tir-tjirr*' and other variations (lacking double-toned quality of other thrushes). R

◄

Plate 77

1 **GULF OF GUINEA THRUSH** *Turdus olivaceofuscus* L 23 cm. Nominate (a, São Tomé) shown and race *xanthorhynchus* (b, Príncipe, with yellow bill and legs). Habitat: forest, plantations, woodland with tall trees. E, São Tomé and Príncipe.

2 **GROUNDSCRAPER THRUSH** *Psophocichla litsitsirupa* L 21 cm. From 64.14 by larger size and uniform coloured wings. From other spotted thrushes by unspotted wings. May occasionally flick one wing to show yellow-buff panel on underwing. Habitat: suburbs, cultivation, open woodland, moorland. Voice: short mid-high melodious slightly harsh whistles like '*tiktik-tweed-weeth*'.

3 **SPOTTED GROUND THRUSH** *Zoothera guttata* L 22 cm. From 2 by striking wing bars. Habitat: groundstrata of humid forest and woodland. Voice: high loud plaintive fluted whistles like '*twee-o-twee-twitirik*'. R

4 **KURRICHANE THRUSH** *Turdus libonyanus* L 22 cm. From 7 by prominent beard stripe. Habitat: suburbs, woodland, bush. Voice: very high short fluted far-carrying whistles like '*weetoweet*' or '*weetowee-three*'.

5 **SONG THRUSH** *Turdus philomelos* L 20 cm. Note unstructured face pattern (with faint vertical bar through eye) and small wing spots. Habitat: areas with some trees and bush. NM.R

6 **(West) AFRICAN THRUSH** *Turdus pelios* L 21 cm. Several races, of these *centralis* (a, from 7 by paler plumage and more slender stance), *stormsi* (b, extensive rufous-tawny below) and *nigrilorum* (c, without rufous) shown. Habitat: forests, woodland, gardens. Voice: very high calm sustained (!) far-carrying fluted '*-peeweepeeweetuweetuwee-*' (every part repeated 2–3x).

7 **OLIVE THRUSH** *Turdus olivaceus* L 24 cm. Underparts variable from orange (as shown) to dusky (higher altitudes). Habitat: suburbs, riverine belts, plantations, forests. Voice: high full up-and-down short whistles like almost level '*weet-o-weet-three*'.

8 **RING OUZEL** *Turdus torquatus* L 24 cm. Unmistakable. Note faint breast crescent of 1stW. Habitat: dry mountain slopes and ravines with some trees or shrub. V

9 **MIOMBO ROCK THRUSH** *Monticola angolensis* L 17 cm. The ♂ from 10 by less intensive colouring and spotted mantle, ♀ by well-defined white moustachial stripe. Habitat: miombo. Voice: mid-high rather short '*fiuuu-wirwir*'.

10 **MOUNTAIN (Common or European) ROCK THRUSH** *Monticola saxatilis* L 20 cm. The ♂ has white back-patch; n-br ♂ (not shown) as ♀, but scalloped feathers below with larger, white centres. ♀ with dark and white spots all over. Habitat: open areas with high look-out posts like buildings or telephone wires. NM

11 **BLUE ROCK THRUSH** *Monticola solitarius* L 20 cm. Unmistakable. Note uniform, dark upperparts of ♀ without rufous in tail. Habitat: areas with rocky outcrops. NM.RES

12 **FULVOUS CHATTERER** *Turdoides fulvus* L 20 cm. Note unspotted white throat. Lives in social, noisy, playful flocks of 12–25 birds. Habitat: arid areas with some scrub.

13 **WHITE-RUMPED BABBLER** *Turdoides leucopygius* L 20 cm. Note white rump (only babbler so). Generally very variable in extension of white (and black) especially on head which may be all white, two variations (a and b) shown. Habitat: damp wooded and bushed grassland.

14 **DUSKY BABBLER** *Turdoides tenebrosus* L 20 cm. Note black, sharply demarcated lores. Habitat: dense forest undergrowth near streams. R

15 **BLACKCAP BABBLER** *Turdoides reinwardtii* L 24 cm. Unmistakable. Moves in flocks through dense vegetation. Habitat: thickets, dense patches of bush and tree stands.

16 **BROWN BABBLER** *Turdoides plebejus* L 25 cm. Note absence of black before and around eye. Habitat: more or less wooded and bushed areas. Habitat: wooded and bushed, mostly dry areas, including cultivations and gardens.

17 **ARROW-MARKED BABBLER** *Turdoides jardineii* L 24 cm. Note red-rimmed yellow eye, arrow-marked feathering, uniform brown upperparts. Note: as all babblers in parties of up to 10–20. Habitat: any type of woodland, riverine belts, acacia bush, suburbs.

18 **BLACK-LORED BABBLER** *Turdoides melanops* L 25 cm. Note scaled feathering of head, breast and mantle. Habitat: bushed and wooded areas. R

Plate 78

1 **RUFOUS-WINGED ILLADOPSIS** *Illadopsis rufescens* L 14 cm. Note contrasting white underparts with ill-defined partial breast band. Habitat: forest undergrowth. Note: all illadopsis species live in pairs or small groups and spend most of their time on the forest floor, looking for insects between and under fallen leaves. Voice: rhythmic '*ti-ti-ti-hu-hu-hu*'.

2 **BLACKCAP ILLADOPSIS** *Illadopsis cleaveri* L 14 cm. From 75.9 by uninterrupted grey around cheek. Habitat: forest and forest remains. Voice: very high, sharp, fluting '*tuh-teeeh*' or '*tutu-teeh*'.

3 **SCALY-BREASTED ILLADOPSIS** *Illadopsis albipectus* L 14 cm. Note vague grey around cheek and scalloped breast (some individuals without or reduced scaling!). Solitary or in pairs. Habitat: forest. Voice: very high slightly rising sharp '*piuu-piuu-peeh*' or very high sharp whistled '*fjuu-fjee-fjee*'. R

4 **PUVEL'S ILLADOPSIS** *Illadopsis puveli* L 15 cm. From 1 by full, be it ill-defined breast band. Note grey around eye. Habitat: forest, bush, thickets. Voice: very high, babbling, robin-like '*peehpuhwripeepee*'.

5 **PALE-BREASTED ILLADOPSIS** *Illadopsis rufipennis* L 14 cm. Note greyish face sides. From 6 by white belly. Habitat: dense forest undergrowth. Voice: very high, pure, short whistle '*feeeeeeee*' with very slight tremolo and crescendo.

6 **BROWN ILLADOPSIS** *Illadopsis fulvescens* L 16 cm. Note sharp division between grey cheeks and white chin and uniform tawny-brown underparts. Less on the ground than other illadopsises. In pairs or in small family groups. Habitat: forest. Voice: three-toned soft unhurried mellow fluted '*few-ftwtu*' in inseparable duet of ♂ and ♀. Also e.g. high '*fweeeeh*' or '*djip-djip*' with varied '*pic*' as contra-song.

7 **MOUNTAIN ILLADOPSIS** *Illadopsis pyrrhoptera* L 14 cm. Note very dark colouring with whitish chin, rufous-brown wings and tail. Solitary or in small groups of up to 5. Habitat: montane forest. Voice: very high fluted descending calm: '*one-two-three four*' ('*four*' is very low answer in a duet of ♂ and ♀). R

8 **AFRICAN HILL BABBLER** *Pseudoalcippe abyssinica* L 13 cm. Not all races depicted, nominate (a), *monacha* (b, restricted to Mt Cameroon, with spotted throat) and *atriceps* (c, with almost black crown and cheeks) shown. Social. Note extensive grey on breast. Habitat: undergrowth of damp mountain forests and bamboo. Voice: high, up-and-down, rather unhurried, thrush-like, fluted '*wipiwipwupwiwjopwiwup*'.

9 **GREY-CHESTED ILLADOPSIS** *Kakamega poliothorax* L 15 cm. Unmistakable by beautiful rufous upperparts. Habitat: mountain forest undergrowth. Voice: high, descending thrush- or oriole-like '*pju-pju-pjuwi*' ('j' falsetto). R

10 **SPOTTED THRUSH BABBLER** *Ptyrticus turdinus* L 22 cm. Note triangled spots on breast and otherwise white underparts. Habitat: swampy woodland, riverine belts. Voice: mid-high, melodious, fluted '*wuWutju-tjitjutuditjuw*' and other mellow phrases. R

11 **WHITE-THROATED MOUNTAIN BABBLER** *Kupeornis gilberti* L 20 cm. Note striking white throat and cheeks. In noisy flocks high up in trees. Often together with 71.8. Habitat: edges of montane forest.

12 **RED-COLLARED BABBLER** *Kupeornis rufocinctus* L 20 cm. Unmistakable, when properly seen in canopy. Habitat: montane forest. R

13 **CHAPIN'S BABBLER** *Kupeornis chapini* L 20 cm. Note chestnut panel in wings. Normally occurring in flocks, often together with other forest species. Habitat: forest canopy. R

14 **CAPUCHIN BABBLER** *Phyllanthus atripennis* L 20 cm. Not all races depicted, race *bohndorffi* (a, with grey chin and throat) and nominate (b) shown. Habitat: dense lowland forest undergrowth.

15 **DOHRN'S THRUSH BABBLER** *Horizorhinus dohrni* L 15 cm. Warbler-like in shape and behaviour. One of the most common birds on Príncipe. Habitat: forest, woodland, plantations. E, Príncipe.

Plate 79

1   **CAPE VERDE CANE WARBLER** *Acrocephalus chapini*   L 14 cm. Note dark legs and very short wings. Habitat: man-made environments with some water on Santiago. E, Cape Verde.

2   **AQUATIC WARBLER** *Acrocephalus paludicola*   L 13 cm. Note contrasting head and mantle pattern. Ad shown, the imm lacks spotting on breast. Habitat: in reed beds and sedges along water; also in flooded grassland. NM.R

3   **SEDGE WARBLER** *Acrocephalus schoenobaenus*   L 13 cm. Prominent eyebrow, streaked mantle. Habitat: as 2. Voice: mid-high varied medley of fluted hoarse rattling sharp and sweet syllables repeated 2–20x. NM

4   **EURASIAN REED WARBLER** *Acrocephalus scirpaceus*   L 13 cm. Almost impossible to separate from 6 unless by song (both 4 and 6 sing also in their African winter quarters). Overall warm-coloured, long flat forehead, broken eye ring, rufous tinge to rump. Habitat: reed beds. Voice: mid-high unhurried rasping 'kritteritkrit-tirrr-treetree-karrekarre-treetreet-'. NM

5   **AFRICAN REED WARBLER** *Acrocephalus baeticatus*   L 13 cm. Note general rusty-reddish colouring and brown wings and tail. Habitat: tall grass, reed beds and other lush herbage, not necessarily near water. Voice: high, loud, chattered, sustained, rapid syllables 'krits-krit-tjitji weetkarreweetweet-tri- -', each syllable repeated twice.

6   **MARSH WARBLER** *Acrocephalus palustris*   L 13 cm. Eye-ring dominates eyebrow. May look hippolais warbler-like (80.4–7) especially with raised crest. Very difficult if not impossible to separate from 8 than by voice, but note pale legs (dark in imm). Habitat: thickets, reed beds, tall herbage not necessarily near water. Voice: very high, powerful, rapid warble, each short phrase repeated 3–7 times with perfect imitations and short canary-like rolls like 'weet-weet-o-kree-kree-wee-tic-tic-tic- -'. NM.R

7   **GREAT REED WARBLER** *Acrocephalus arundinaceus*   L 18 cm. Large size, strong bill, creamy eyebrow, faint streaks on throat. Habitat: as 5. Voice: mid-high very loud hoarse unhurried 'karre-karre-keetkeet-weet-'. NM

8   **GREATER SWAMP WARBLER** *Acrocephalus rufescens*   L 17 cm. Drab-brown above, brown-grey below, long bill, short wing, ill-defined eyebrow. Habitat: papyrus. Voice: low to very high unhurried 'tjiptjip-whaaro-pju-pju-pju'.

9   **LESSER SWAMP WARBLER** *Acrocephalus gracilirostris* L 15 cm. Note bright orange gape and black legs. Short-winged, white below, faint eyebrow. Warmer coloured than 8. Habitat: as 5. Voice: mid-high sustained thrush-like medleys of 'weet-weetweet-' with loud rapid melodious rattles, flutes and oriole-like warbles.

10   **LITTLE RUSH WARBLER** *Bradypterus baboecala*   L 12 cm. Breeds in colonies. Note short eyebrow, dark bill, rusty brown crown and mantle, freckled and striped breast. Habitat: dense vegetation in swamps and over water. Voice: very high, loud, accelerated, slightly descending 'trwit trwit trwit-trwit-trwit-trwittrwittrwittrwittrwit'. R

11   **GRAUER'S SWAMP (or Rush) WARBLER** *Bradypterus graueri*   L 13 cm. From 10 by longer eyebrow and slightly paler colouring. Not in same range as similar throat-spotted 12 and 14. Habitat: mountain forest swamps. R

12   **JA RIVER SCRUB WARBLER** *Bradypterus grandis*   L 13 cm. No similar *bradypterus*-warblers in its range and habitat, except maybe 10, which is warmer-coloured. Habitat: marshes at the edge of forests. R

13   **WHITE-WINGED SWAMP WARBLER** *Bradypterus carpalis*   L 13 cm. From all other warblers on this plate by all-white or creamy wing shoulder and white tips to wing coverts; white underparts heavily streaked dark brown on throat and breast. Habitat: reed beds. Voice: descending chirping whistle concluded with some explosive wing beats.

14   **BAMBOO WARBLER** *Bradypterus alfredi*   L 14 cm. Note white chin and grey breast and flanks. From 17 in same habitat by less warm colouring, faint throat spots and song. Habitat: undergrowth of bamboo, montane forest and adjacent areas. Voice: monotonous 'tsjuu-kuh tsjuu-kuh tsjuu-kuh-- - -'. R

15   **BANGWA FOREST WARBLER** *Bradypterus lopezi bangwaensis*   L 14 cm. A race of 16, characterised by reddish colour. Habitat: as 16.

▶

16 **EVERGREEN-FOREST (or Cameroon Scrub) WARBLER** *Bradypterus lopezi* L 14 cm. Several races occur in the region, of these nominate (a, from Bioco) shown and races *barakae* (b, more reddish brown) and *bangwaensis* (c, with whitish underparts). Note overall dark appearance without or with little white. Normally no other *bradypterus*-warbler in its habitat. Habitat: forest interior. Voice: high hurried rattled sharp '*tjutjutjutjutjut-*' and crescendoing camaroptera-like '*titju-titju-titju-titju*'.

17 **CINNAMON BRACKEN WARBLER** *Bradypterus cinnamomeus* L 15 cm. Crown darker than mantle, eyebrow well-defined. Habitat: undergrowth of montane forests, bamboo, plantations, moist thickets. Voice: very high powerful melodious rapid rattles '*fjuut-rrrrr*' or '*tjuut-weetweetweet*'.

18 **BROAD-TAILED WARBLER** *Schoenicola platyura* L 15 cm. Note small head and broad, brushy tail. Habitat: tall grass and shrubbery, often near water. Voice: extra high, unstructured, piercing '*sweeh sweeh sweeh -*'.

Plate 80

1 **GRASSHOPPER WARBLER** *Locustella naevia* L 13 cm. Note very long under tail-coverts. From 2 and 3 by more or less spotted and striped upperparts. Creeps mouse-like through low vegetation. Habitat: swamp edges. Voice: extra high, shrill, cicada-like, sustained trill, like a very fast electric sewing machine. NM.R

2 **EURASIAN RIVER WARBLER** *Locustella fluviatilis* L 13 cm. Note striped chin and very long chequered undertail coverts. Habitat: keeps low to the ground in dense tangled weedy vegetation. Voice: very high level sizzled almost-trill with phrases of up to 8–9 sec. (?)

3 **SAVI'S WARBLER** *Locustella luscinioides* L 14 cm. From 2 by cleaner throat and almost unmarked undertail coverts. Habitat: reedy habitats, often near streams and marches. Voice: extra high buzz. AM.NM.R

4 **OLIVACEOUS WARBLER** *Hippolais pallida* L 12 cm. From marsh and reed warblers by much paler lore. Note absence of any yellow or green tinge to plumage, short wings and faint wing panel. During the northern winter the local breeding races are augmented by migrating races from Europe. Range of breeding race *laeneni* (a, shorter-winged, otherwise not safely separable from migrants) indicated on map. Habitat: as 7 but often in drier areas. Voice: high rasping warble, sounding like a slightly speeded-up reed warbler. NM.RESa

5 **OLIVE-TREE WARBLER** *Hippolais olivetorum* L 16 cm. Note long sloping forehead, long bill, white edges to secondaries, long primary projection. Habitat: more or less wooded areas. Voice: mid-high pleasant but harsh reed warbler-like unhurried chattering. V

6 **MELODIOUS WARBLER** *Hippolais polyglotta* L 13 cm. From 7 by brownish legs, short primary projection, plain wings. Habitat: all types of woodland, parks, gardens, mangrove, but normally avoids acacia. NM

7 **ICTERINE WARBLER** *Hippolais icterina* L 13 cm. From 6 by blue-grey legs, more upright stance and more peaked crown, especially when excited. Habitat: open woodland, bush, gardens. Voice: high sustained unhurried varied phrases full of sharp powerful rattles and chuckles. NM

8 **LAURA'S WOODLAND WARBLER** *Phylloscopus laurae* L 10 cm. Note bright green and yellow colouring. From 16 by whitish undertail-coverts. Habitat: canopies of dense montane forests.

9 **RED-FACED WOODLAND WARBLER** *Phylloscopus laetus* L 9 cm. Note green upperparts and buff face and breast. Habitat: mountain forests and bamboo.

10 **UGANDA WOODLAND WARBLER** *Phylloscopus budongoensis* L 10 cm. Note darkish green colouring, slightly yellow-streaked breast, short primary projection. Habitat: mainly midstrata of dense mountain forests. R

11 **BROWN WOODLAND WARBLER** *Phylloscopus umbrovirens* L 10 cm. Note greenish wings and outer tail-feathers. Habitat: mountain forest undergrowth, bamboo and giant heath. R

12 **COMMON CHIFFCHAFF** *Phylloscopus collybita* L 11 cm. From 13 by (normally) dark legs, from other *phylloscopus*-warblers by all-white underparts. Habitat: forests and bamboo. Voice: low, soft '*tru-tru-tru*', followed by rhythmic, unstructured '*tri tru tri tri tru*'. NM

▶

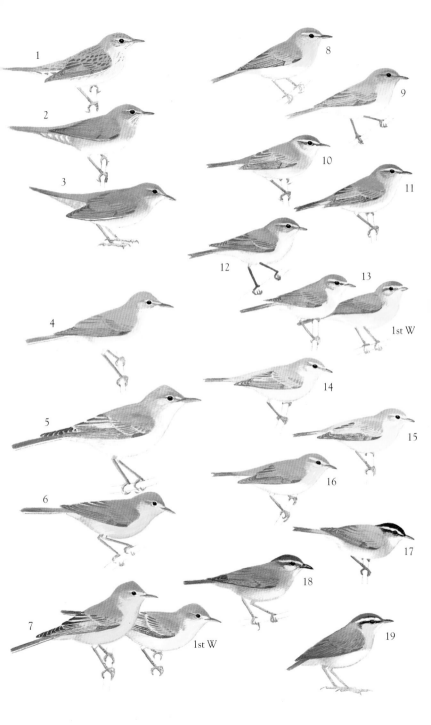

13 **WILLOW WARBLER** *Phylloscopus trochilus*   L 11 cm. Variable, but normally with faint-yellow eyebrow, throat and breast. Note long primary projection. Habitat: any type of wooded and bushed habitat. Voice: rich warbling whistle starting very high and jubilant, descending 5 notes to a melancholic end. NM

14 **EASTERN BONELLI'S WARBLER** *Phylloscopus orientalis*   L 12 cm. From 15 by more pure grey (not slightly green) upperparts. As 15 with greenish rump. Habitat: as 15. (?)

15 **(Western) BONELLI'S WARBLER** *Phylloscopus bonelli*   L 11 cm. Note general grey-pale green colouring and yellow edges of wing and tail feathers. Habitat: arid sparsely wooded areas and coastal bush. Voice: very high '*pjeeh pjeeh pjeeh trititititititee*' and very high short trill '*tseetsitsitsitsi*'. NM

16 **WOOD WARBLER** *Phylloscopus sibilatrix*   L 12 cm. Note white undertail coverts and yellow to head and breast. Habitat: mountain forests and woodland. Voice: extra high, rather short, fast, accelerated trill. NM

17 **BLACK-CAPPED WOODLAND WARBLER** *Phylloscopus herberti*   L 11 cm. From 18 and 19 by more contrasting head pattern and different bill. Not in same range as 19. Habitat: montane forest.

18 **GREEN HYLIA** *Hylia prasina*   L 12 cm. Darker than 13 and with more pronounced eyebrow. From 19 by longer tail . Often in flocks or in mixed bird waves. Habitat: undergrowth and midstrata of forest and bush.

19 **NEUMANN'S (or Short-Tailed) WARBLER** *Hemitesia neumanni*   L 13 cm. Note large head and short tail. Forages mainly near or on the ground, while 18 lives in higher strata of the forest. Habitat: undergrowth of mountain forests.

Plate 81

1 **RED-FACED CISTICOLA** *Cisticola erythrops*   L 13 cm. Note rufous face and uniform brown wing. Habitat: rank undergrowth near water. Voice: e.g. extreme high rapid lashing '*weepweepweepweep*' or '*weetje-weetje-weetje-weetje*'.

2 **SINGING CISTICOLA** *Cisticola cantans*   L 13 cm. From 1 by red wing panel and black loral spot. Habitat: undergrowth in highland areas. Voice: high loud strong irregular '*twit twit treetwit-treet tree twittriet tuweet*'.

3 **WHISTLING CISTICOLA** *Cisticola lateralis*   L 13 cm. Uniform dark brown, short tail, large bill, all tail feathers with dark spot near tip. Habitat: herbage in woodland and bush often along streams. Voice: high jubilant '*pju- pjup- pu-pju-wu-wihih*' or mid-high loud scolding '*pjneeh pjneeh –*'.

4 **TRILLING CISTICOLA** *Cisticola woosnami*   L 13 cm. Crown and wing panel rusty, contrasting slightly with rest of plumage. Rather heavy bill. Habitat: tall grass in woodland often on rocky hill sides. Voice: extreme high crescendoing fast trill.

5 **CHATTERING CISTICOLA** *Cisticola anonymus*   L 14 cm. Dark plumage, black bill, rusty forehead; tail steeply graduated with faint pattern above. Habitat: grassy places with some bush near forest, plantations, cultivation. Voice: mid-high rather harsh '*tsji-tsji-pwwwrrrrrr*'

6 **BUBBLING CISTICOLA** *Cisticola bulliens*   L 13 cm. As 5, but paler, 'faded-out'. Habitat: coastal and inland areas with high grass and some bush. Note: race *discolour* (Cameroon highlands, not depicted) has almost plain tail without terminal spots. R

7 **CHUBB'S CISTICOLA** *Cisticola chubbi*   L 14 cm. Note plain mantle and dark area between eye and bill. Habitat: dense undergrowth at well-wooded streams. Voice: high, undulating, chirping, fast '*tseetsee-wee-oh-tseewee-oh-tseetsee- -*' (actually an inseparable duet). Note: sometimes this species is split; in that case the western population (which lacks the dark tail spots and is coloured warmer buff than the eastern population) is split of and raised to species level as Brown-backed Cisticola *Cisticola discolor*.

8 **RATTLING CISTICOLA** *Cisticola chiniana*   L 14 cm. Rather plain. Crown and tail slightly more rusty than rest of plumage. Habitat: dry bush with tall grass, sometimes in wetter areas. Voice: basically a fast low fluted rattle '*tjak-tjak-tja*' together with high '*tieutieu-tieu*', '*prrreet*' or '*tjèh tjèh tjèh tjèh*' all with sparrow-like quality.

▶

Plate 81 (continued)

9   **ROCK-LOVING (or Lazy) CISTICOLA** *Cisticola aberrans*   L 13 cm. N-br plumage with brighter cap and deeper buff underparts. Only cisticola in rocky places, foraging mainly on the ground or in low vegetation. Habitat: bare rocky areas, often with some grass or scrub, but also in gardens. In West-Africa often found round 'inselbergs'. Voice: extra high, tit-like tinkling '*teet-teet*' followed by mid-high, nasal '*tèèhtèèhtèèh*'.

10   **RED-PATE CISTICOLA** *Cisticola ruficeps*   L 14 cm. In br plumage with warm brown upperparts and buff-rufous crown. In n-br plumage with grey-streaked mantle. Only cisticola within its habitat with reddish head, contrasting with grey-brown mantle. Habitat: bushed and wooded areas. Voice: extra high '*feeee-ferresh*' ('*feee*' slurred up).

11   **DORST'S CISTICOLA** *Cisticola dorsti*   L 11 cm. From 10 by buff vent and tail. Habitat: open country with some thickets or shrub, also in cassava plantations. Voice: short, metallic trill. R

12   **TINKLING CISTICOLA** *Cisticola rufilatus*   L 14 cm. Striking long eyebrow between rusty cheek and cap. Habitat: areas with mosaics of woodland, bush, thickets grass, bare ground. Voice: dry '*tjuktjuksreeeeh*' followed by high, hurried '*pweeepweeepweeepwee*' or extreme high rattling '*srrrrrreeh*'. R

13   **WINDING CISTICOLA** *Cisticola galactotes*   L 15 cm. From 14 and 15 by brighter colouring, from 16 by unstreaked rump and more red to wing coverts. Habitat: high weeds near lakes and marshes. Voice: e.g. dry rattle (like fast winding of a clock) '*tritritri-*' (0,5 sec). See note under 82.9.

14   **CARRUTHER'S CISTICOLA** *Cisticola carruthersi*   L 13 cm. Note bright buff head and greyish upperparts. Habitat: interior of papyrus swamps. Voice: rapid trill.

15   **CHIRPING CISTICOLA** *Cisticola pipiens*   L 14 cm. Br plumage shown, n-br plumage less grey and with black subdued. Back browner than 13 and 16 and underparts buffier. Note wide tail. Habitat: swamps, moist herbage along streams. Voice: loud decisive '*tit tit-threeee*'.

16   **LEVAILLANT'S CISTICOLA** *Cisticola tinniens*   L 13 cm. Grey wing coverts, red edges to tail feathers, broadly black-streaked rump. Habitat: highlands. Voice: rather compressed '*juju-thrill*' (last part lashed-up). Alternative name 'Tinkling Cisticola' should be reserved for 12. R

17   **STOUT CISTICOLA** *Cisticola robustus*   L 16 cm (♂), 13 cm (♀). Note smaller size of ♀ (as 18). Chestnut collar, black-striped crown, buff wing panel. Habitat: montane bush and woodland with moist places. Voice: high dry rapid rattled '*tit-tit-thrrree*'.

18   **CROAKING CISTICOLA** *Cisticola natalensis*   L 16 cm (♂), 14 cm (♀). Short tail, slightly rusty (not rufous) crown. Habitat: rank-grassed areas in bush and woodland. Voice: e.g. mid-high sustained hurried '*wreeeeep-wreeeep-wreeeep-*' or '*frjuu-wheep*' ('*-wheep*' lashed up high).

Plate 82 (continued)

SIERRA LEONE PRINIA *Schistolais leontica* L 12 cm. Note very striking pale eye. Habitat: forest edge and other places with thick cover. Voice: a soft, unstructured duet. R

BANDED PRINIA *Prinia bairdii* L 12 cm. Note white tips to tail feathers, tertials and wing coverts. Habitat: forest edges, often along streams. Voice: high hurried sharp staccato *'witwitwit- - - - -'* (sustained for up to 30 sec).

Plate 82

1   **NEDDICKY** *Cisticola fulvicapillus*   L 11 cm. Note small, plain-backed, rather short-tailed and large-billed jizz. Crown slightly more rusty than mantle. Habitat: low down in grass and scrub of woodland. Voice: very high '*fuu-fuu-fiu*'. R

2   **LONG-TAILED CISTICOLA** *Cisticola angusticaudus*   L 11 cm. Very similar to 1, but longer- and darker-tailed and with greyer back. Very small area of overlapping ranges. Habitat: Open places with long grass in woodland. Voice: as 1. R

3   **BLACK-TAILED CISTICOLA** *Cisticola melanurus*   L 11 cm. Note black, white-sided tail, tipped grey below. Habitat: miombo. R

4   **SHORT-WINGED (or Siffling) CISTICOLA** *Cisticola brachypterus*   L 10 cm. Very dull and uniform coloured, especially in not-striped breeding plumage. Habitat: more or less wooded and bushed habitats. Voice: extra high '*fifiwich-fifiwich-fifiwich*' and many other whistles.

5   **RUFOUS CISTICOLA** *Cisticola rufus*   L 10 cm. Brown with rusty tone, especially to rump. Very similar to 4, but little overlap of ranges. Habitat: open bush and scrub with single trees or other high posts for singing.

6   **FOXY CISTICOLA** *Cisticola troglodytes*   L 10 cm. From 4 by uniform reddish upperparts and mainly different range. Habitat: wooded grassland. R

7   **DESERT CISTICOLA** *Cisticola aridulus*   L 11 cm. Unstreaked rump, tail (which is very short in br plumage, but always longer than that of following 8-12) without any black. Less contrasting patterned above than 8–12. Habitat: arid grassy areas. Voice: very high sharp '*fifififififi*' in upward flight followed by a variety of extreme high twitters, '*seep's*' or '*tic's*' interspersed with short series of wing claps.

8   **DAMBO CISTICOLA** *Cisticola dambo*   L 12 cm. Note black-striped upperparts. Habitat: floodplains. R

9   **BLACK-BACKED (or –necked) CISTICOLA** *Cisticola eximius*   L 9 cm. Note bright colours of breeding plumage. N-br bird as 11, but not in same range. Habitat: wet grassland, recently burnt ground. Voice: very high '*tret-snap-tret-snap-*' (snap made by wings). Note: in South Africa it is 81.13, which is called Black-backed Cisticola.

10   **PECTORAL-PATCH CISTICOLA** *Cisticola brunnescens*   L 9 cm. Looks rather pale, 'washed-out'. The ♂ has tawny, faintly striped crown, ♀ with more striped crown. Breast-patches often not visible. Habitat: dry (in Cameroon) or moist (elsewhere) grass- and moorland. Voice: '*zip-zip-zip- - - - -zeep-zeep-zeep*', interspersed with clicking sounds, given in descending flight.

11   **WING-SNAPPING (or Ayres's) CISTICOLA** *Cisticola ayresii*   L 9 cm. May be confused with 10 and 12 in same range; best distinguished by song and display. Habitat: short grassland, also in marshes. Voice: song, given in flight, very variable: set of repeated phrases, interspersed with small variations; also (when diving) by wing snaps, given in ones or two's or in rapid volleys.

12   **FAN-TAILED (or Zitting) CISTICOLA** *Cisticola juncidis*   L 11 cm. Bright tawny rump, tail with subterminal black band, visible when spread. Habitat: dry rank grass often near marshes and inundations. Voice: extreme high '*zeet zeet zeet –*', coinciding with dips in high cruising display flight.

13   **SÃO TOMÉ PRINIA** *Prinia molleri*   L 12 cm. Dark upperparts with bright tawny cheeks. Habitat: all natural and cultivated habitats on São Tomé, except true forest. E, São Tomé.

14   **RIVER PRINIA** *Prinia fluviatilis*   L 12 cm. From 15 by greyer upperparts and less tawny flanks. Where occurring alongside 15 in wetter habitats. Habitat: swamps, rank vegetation along streams. R

15   **TAWNY-FLANKED PRINIA** *Prinia subflava*   L 12 cm. From cisticolas and other warblers by slim build and sideways tail waving. Note eyebrow and rusty edges of wing and tail feathers. Habitat: bush, open areas in forest, woodland, bush, swamp edges. Voice: extreme high staccato hurried '*weet-weet-weet-weet- -*' or a series of rapid '*tjiep-tjiep-tjiep- -*' of irregular length.

16   **WHITE-CHINNED PRINIA** *Schistolais leucopogon*   L 14 cm. Note all-grey plumage with black cheek, sharply demarcated from white chin and throat. Habitat: tall herbage and shrubbery in forest glades and cultivation. Voice: extra high, sharp, fast warbling '*fifi-weep-weep-fi*' and '*frifrifrifrifri -*'.

◀

Plate 83

1 **BUFF-BELLIED WARBLER** *Phyllolais pulchella* L 9 cm. Note pale grey upperparts, white outer tail feathers and absence of eye-stripe. Habitat: open acacia woodland. Voice: extra high, dry, short trills 'srrrrr'.

2 **CRICKET WARBLER** *Spiloptila clamans* L 13 cm. Unmistakable. Very small. Habitat: bare desert, often with some scrub. Voice: extra high, irregular mechanical rattle 'weetweetweetweetweetweet-' and extra high, level, piercing 'weet-weet-weet-weet- -'.

3 **RED-FRONTED WARBLER** *Urorhipis rufifrons* L 12 cm. Note black, often cocked tail, white wing bars, rufous-buff crown. Often in parties of 10–14. Habitat: dry bush and acacia. R

4 **STREAKED SCRUB WARBLER** *Scotocerca inquieta* L 12cm. Rather large-headed. Note cocked, often spread, mainly black tail. Normally on or near the ground. Habitat: desert scrub. R

5 **BLACK-COLLARED APALIS** *Apalis pulchra* L 11 cm. Unmistakable. In small flocks, normally not together with other species. Habitat: undergrowth at forest edges and around clearings. Voice: very high, rapid, complaining 'weet-weet-weet-weet' or 'witwitwitwitwitwit'.

6 **BLACK-CAPPED APALIS** *Apalis nigriceps* L 10 cm. Nominate (a) shown and race *collaris* (b, with all-white outertail feathers). Habitat: canopies of montane forest. Voice: extra high, dry trill 'srrrrrr srrrrr srrrrr – ' (each one 1 1/2 sec).

7 **BLACK-THROATED APALIS** *Apalis jacksoni* L 12 cm. Nominate (a) shown and race *bambuluensis* (b, with black crown). From 9 and 10 by yellow-green underparts, including breast. Habitat: montane forest edges. Voice: duets 'tuuttuut-tuuttuut-tuuttet' often just out of synchrony. R

8 **RWENZORI APALIS** *Apalis ruwenzorii* L 10 cm. Note all-grey upperparts including tail and pale salmon throat and belly. Habitat: undergrowth of montane forests and bamboo. Voice: very high, squeaking 'weeweeweeweeweewee'.

9 **MASKED APALIS** *Apalis binotata* L 10 cm. From 7 by all-green wings and (short) tail. Habitat: riverine belts. Voice: very high sharp rapid 'fiufiufiu-', high sustained 'fru-fru-fru- - -' or high fast 'krrrk krrrk keeler-keeler'.

10 **MOUNTAIN MASKED APALIS** *Apalis personata* L 10 cm. From 9 by black area, running further down from throat to belly and white spot (not stripe) on side of neck. Habitat: montane forest. Voice: as 9 (which normally occurs in lowlands).

11 **YELLOW-BREASTED APALIS** *Apalis flavida caniceps* L 11 cm. From other apalises by yellow breast. Habitat: wood-, bush- and scrubland. Voice: high dry 'tju-tju-tju - - -', 'terrut-terrut-terrut- - -' or sustained rapid 'tjuuptjuuptjuup-'.

12 **BUFF-THROATED APALIS** *Apalis rufogularis* L 11 cm. Western races have dark throats (a), while races in eastern parts of the D. R. of Congo have white throats (b); ♂♂ of latter races from 18 by uniform brown upperparts, ♀ by buff-orange tinge from chin down (♂ and ♀ of 18 are alike). Habitat: forests. Voice: high rapid rattling 'wrreet-wrreet-wrreet- -' (each 'wrreet' lashed up).

13 **SHARPE'S APALIS** *Apalis sharpii* L 11 cm. The ♂ overall dark sooty grey, ♀ from ♀ 12 by grey not brown upperparts. Note also absence of white in tail. Habitat: lowland forest and riverine belts. Voice: very high, rapid, staccato 'trittrittrit - - - -' (7x).

14 **GOSLING'S APALIS** *Apalis goslingi* L 11 cm. Note short tail and pale eye. Habitat: along forest streams. Voice: high sharp rapid tinkling 'tingk-tingk-tingk-' (6x).

15 **BAMENDA APALIS** *Apalis bamendae* L 11 cm. Only apalis with all-rufous head. Habitat: montane forest. Voice: very high, rapid 'weet-witwitweet-witwitweet- -', ('weet' higher). E, Cameroon.

16 **CHESTNUT-THROATED APALIS** *Apalis porphyrolaema* L 13 cm. From ♀♀ 12 and 13 by white tips to tail feathers. Habitat: montane forest interiors and edges. Voice: extra high, insect-like double-buzz 'turrrree-turrree'.

17 **GREY APALIS** *Apalis cinerea* L 13 cm. Note white outer tail-feathers. Habitat: dense montane forests. Voice: mid-high, rapid 'raprapraprapraprap' and extra high, insect-like 'trrrrrrt-tit' sometimes decelerated to a rapid 'tit-tit-tit-tit- -'.

18 **BROWN-HEADED APALIS** *Apalis alticola* L 12 cm. From other similar apalises by white tips to tail feathers. Habitat: forest and forest remains. Voice: as 12.

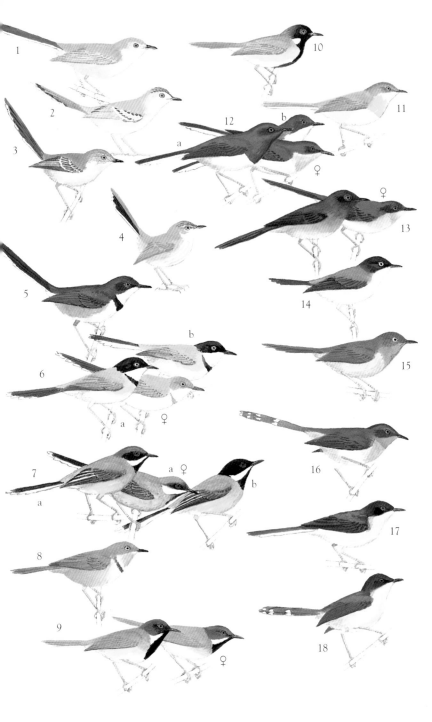

Plate 84

1   **GREEN-CAPPED EREMOMELA** *Eremomela scotops* L 10 cm. Note pale red-rimmed eye, green-grey cap and bright yellow breast band. Habitat: open woodland, riverine belts. Voice: high sustained rather staccato '*trrit-trrit-trrit-*'.

2   **SENEGAL EREMOMELA** *Eremomela pusilla* L 8 cm. Rather similar to 7, but with green, not grey back, yellow undertail coverts and pale eye. Hybridises with 3, where ranges meet. Habitat: more or less wooded areas, including gardens and mangrove. Also at forest edges.

3   **GREEN-BACKED EREMOMELA** *Eremomela canescens* L 10 cm. Note black streak through eye. Habitat: hilly, wooded and bushed habitats often near streams.

4   **RUFOUS-CROWNED EREMOMELA** *Eremomela badiceps* L 10 cm. From 5 by rufous extending to crown. Habitat: canopy at forest edges, riverine belts. Voice: extreme high hurried siffled '*sisisisi- -*' or very high soft fluted warbling very varied in pitch.

5   **TURNER'S EREMOMELA** *Eremomela turneri* L 10 cm. Rufous restricted to forehead. Habitat: canopies of montane forest edges. Voice: extra high, complex, unmusical siffling. R

6   **BLACK-NECKED EREMOMELA** *Eremomela atricollis* L 11 cm. Unmistakable. Habitat: miombo, bush.

7   **YELLOW-BELLIED EREMOMELA** *Eremomela icteropygialis* L 9 cm. From 8 by grey, not greenish rump. Habitat: desert, woodland, bush. Voice: very high '*titi-weeh titi-weeh*' or sharp descending hurried warbled '*si-si-ri-ti-ti-ti-tu wee*'. (AM)

8   **SALVADORI'S EREMOMELA** *Eremomela salvadorii* L 11 cm. See 7. Bright yellow underparts sharply demarcated from grey breast. Habitat: open areas with some bush.

9   **BLEATING WARBLER (or Grey-backed Camaroptera)** *Camaroptera brachyura* L 10 cm. Characterised by combination of grey upperparts and green wings. Easily recognised by call. Habitat: dense thickets, coastal bush, forest edges. Voice: mid-high very dry loud staccato '*treettreettreet*' (3–5x) and mid-high miaowing '*mèh mèh-mèh*'.

10 **MIOMBO WREN (or Stierling's Barred) WARBLER** *Calamonastes undosus* L 14 cm. All grey with slight barring to throat. Habitat: bush. Voice: extreme high '*tweet-tweet-tweet-*'. R

11 **YELLOW-BROWED CAMAROPTERA** *Camaroptera superciliaris* L 9 cm. From 80.8 by pale eye, white chin and throat, longer bill, shorter tail. Habitat: undergrowth at forest edges, old cultivation, riverine belts. Voice: mid-high loud miaowing e.g. '*piauw-piauw piauw-piauw*' or '*ee-wèh-wèh ee-wèh-wèh*'.

12 **OLIVE-GREEN CAMAROPTERA** *Camaroptera chloronota* L 10 cm. Of several races nominate (a, with grey underparts) and race *toroensis* (b, with buff-tawny underparts) shown. Habitat: dense undergrowth of forest and riverine belts. Voice: very long, rapid sequences of very high, penetrating '*weetweetweet---*' or '*wjeetwjeetwjeet----*' or '*wuutwuutwuut---*', often very slowly descending, lasting several seconds.

13 **GREEN CROMBEC** *Sylvietta virens* L 9 cm. Nominate (a) shown and race *flaviventris* (b, with yellowish underparts). Note dull colouring with pale tawny eyebrow, cheek and throat. Habitat: undergrowth of forest, riverine belts. Voice: extreme high descending sharp fast twitter '*si-see-sree-si-si-wee*', often followed by softer and lower syllables.

14 **LEMON-BELLIED CROMBEC** *Sylvietta denti* L 9 cm. Note mottled cheeks, buffy throat and pale rufous stripe down breast. Habitat: canopy at forest edge, deserted cultivation. Voice: extreme high siffled decelerated '*seeseeseeseesee-see-see see*'.

15 **WHITE-BROWED CROMBEC** *Sylvietta leucophrys* L 8 cm. Note striking white eyebrow and rufous-brown upperparts. Habitat: undergrowth of montane forests and bamboo.

16 **NORTHERN CROMBEC** *Sylvietta brachyura* L 7 cm. From 18 by pure grey upperparts, all-white eyebrow and white belly. Habitat: dry woodland, bush. Voice: very high, descending, short, hurried twitter '*tu-tjeet-ter-tsjee-tu-wee*'.

17 **RED-CAPPED CROMBEC** *Sylvietta ruficapilla* L 12 cm. Race *rufigenis* (a, more yellowish below) shown and race *schoutedeni* (b, with olive crown and nape). Note rufous ear coverts. Habitat: miombo. Voice: very high hurried warbling '*titi-tuwree-tuwree-three*' ('*-three*' characteristically 4 notes higher).

18 **LONG-BILLED CROMBEC** *Sylvietta rufescens* L 12 cm. See 16. Habitat: dry bush, semi-desert with some shrub. Voice: very high short soft yet shrill '*tuwee-threewee-threewee-three*'. R

Plate 85

1   **GREY-CAPPED WARBLER** *Eminia lepida*   L 15 cm. Unmistakable, but rather secretive; more often heard than seen. Habitat: undergrowth, tall herbage near water and suburban gardens. Voice: extra high, fast, rattling trill '*tirrrrrrr*', high song phrases like '*tutu-tu tu*' and other trills.

2   **ORIOLE WARBLER (or Moho)** *Hypergerus atriceps*   L 20 cm. Unmistakable, but shy and secretive. Habitat: undergrowth at forest edge, thickets, mangrove. Voice: very high, sharp, whistled '*puweeweeh pwik pwik*' or '*puwee pwik*', going up and down.

3   **RED-WINGED WARBLER** *Heliolais erythroptera*   L 13 cm. Note long bill. From prinia's and apalises by red wings. Habitat: tall-grassed places in woodland. Voice: high rapid '*fiufiufiufiu- - -*' (or '*fitfitfit- - -*') from ♂ with toneless twitter '*trtrtr---*' from ♀ in duet.

4   **WHITE-TAILED WARBLER** *Poliolais lopesi*   L 12 cm. Race *manengubae* (a) shown and nominate from Bioco (b, dark greyish-brown). Race *alexanderi* (not shown) is bluish grey with green wash to flanks. Habitat: undergrowth of montane forests. Voice: 2-syllabled, extra high '*tju tjeeh*', second part lower and slurred down or long series of '*tjeeh-tjeeh-tjeeh- - - -*' or '*tjuh-tjuh-tjuh- - - -*'

5   **MOUNTAIN YELLOW WARBLER** *Chloropeta similis*   L 13 cm. Crown and mantle uniform green. Song richer than 6. Habitat: more in mountains than 6, but habitats overlap. Voice: high crescendoing '*tjuu-tjuu-tjuu-tjuu-tjuu-tjuu- - -*' and other high fluted strophes with inbuilt tremolo's and differences in pitch.

6   **AFRICAN YELLOW WARBLER** *Chloropeta natalensis*   L 14 cm. From 5 by darker cap, from 80.7 and 80.13 by brighter yellow underparts and longer-tailed upright profile. As 5 with very wide bill base. Habitat: rather skulking in dense undergrowth. Voice: very high melodious staccato trills and rollers, connected by low dry '*tektek tek*'.

7   **PAPYRUS YELLOW WARBLER** *Chloropeta gracilirostris*   L 13 cm. Nominate (a, with dark eye and orange tinge to flanks) shown and race *bensoni* (b). Eyebrow ill-defined. From 5 and 6 also by very narrow bill. Habitat: papyrus, reeds. R

8   **MOUSTACHED GRASS WARBLER** *Melocichla mentalis*   L 19 cm. Large and reddish. Skulking. Habitat: tall herbage along streams in wooded landscapes. Voice: very high unhurried basically staccato phrases with sudden accelerations '*tjup tjup priweetweetweet tjup tjuwèh* '.

9   **GREEN LONGTAIL** *Urolais epichlora*   L 15 cm. Long tail diagnostic. No similar warbler in its restricted range and habitat. Habitat: montane forest. Voice: said to resemble that of chiffchaff (80.12).

10   **GRAUER'S WARBLER** *Graueria vittata*   L 15 cm. Jizz as a oversized, long-billed camaroptera (84.9). Habitat: dense montane forest undergrowth. R

11   **BLACK-HEADED RUFOUS WARBLER** *Bathmocercus cerviniventris*   L 13 cm. Unmistakable. Habitat: forest undergrowth, especially along streams. Voice: loud, whistled '*weeh-oh deee*' or similar variations, often repeated. R

12   **BLACK-FACED RUFOUS WARBLER** *Bathmocercus rufus*   L 13 cm. Unmistakable. Habitat: forest undergrowth. Voice: extra high, sharp '*tjeeeéé-tjeeeéé-tjeeeéé-*'.

13   **KEMP'S LONGBILL** *Macrosphenus kempi*   L 13 cm. Warm brown above, rusty red on flanks. Belly greyish in western race (not shown). Voice: partly as 14. Also '*dee-dee-dee - - -*' (8-12 times), starting rapidly, but slowed and slurred down.

14   **YELLOW LONGBILL** *Macrosphenus flavicans*   L 13 cm. Note white chin, throat and upperbreast. Habitat: dense forest undergrowth. Voice: rapidly descending slow fluted '*fjuu fjuu fjuu fjuu fjuu fjuu-fjuu*' (starting very high).

15   **GREY LONGBILL** *Macrosphenus concolor*   L 13 cm. Underparts only slightly paler than upperparts. Not unlike 91.15, but without latter's eye ring and with pale legs. Habitat: dense forest undergrowth. Voice: very high hurried crescendoing twitter, descending or with repeated phrases like '*-weet-turu-weet-*'.

16   **BOCAGE'S LONGBILL** *Amaurocichla bocagei*   L 13 cm. No other similar bird in its range and habitat. Habitat: on the ground along forest streams. Note: might be a babbler (Plate 77 and 78), not a warbler. E, São Tomé.

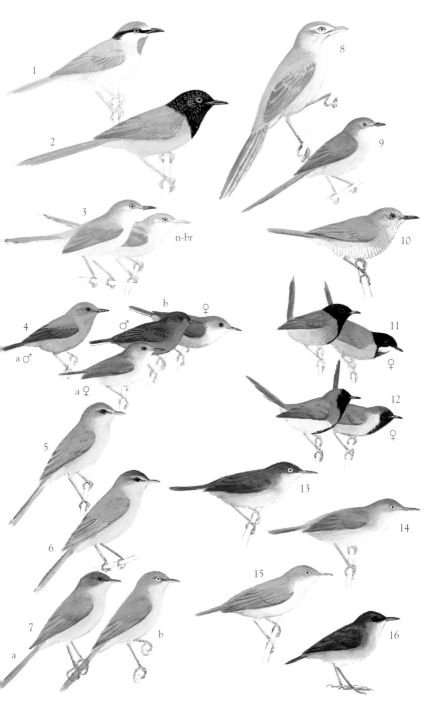

Plate 86

1   **BROWN PARISOMA** *Parisoma lugens*   L 13 cm. Rather sylvia warbler-like in jizz with peaked head. Note black chin, fine spotting to throat and especially the white tail edges. Habitat: thornbush. R

2   **YELLOW-BELLIED (or -breasted) HYLIOTA** *Hyliota flavigaster*   L 12 cm. From 3 by buff (not white) rear underparts, short white edges to tertials, stronger overall gloss. Habitat: miombo. Voice: unstructured sequence of well-separated very high scratchy notes '*treetreet twitreetreet wietwiet wit wit treetreet*'.

3   **SOUTHERN (or Mashona) HYLIOTA** *Hyliota australis*   L 11 cm. See 2. Rather dull black above. Habitat: woodland. Voice: very high short slightly scratchy phrases: '*tutree-tutree-twee-twee-treet*'. R

4   **VIOLET-BACKED HYLIOTA** *Hyliota violacea*   L 13 cm. White in wing absent in western part of range. Active gleaning insects from foliage and bark. Often in mixed bird parties. Habitat: canopy of forest especially at edges; not in miombo and less in woodland.

5   **RED-WINGED GREY WARBLER** *Drymocichla incana*   L 13 cm. From 85.3 by less extensive red in wing. Active and restless, gleaning insects in shrubs and lower parts of trees. Habitat: open woodland, often in thickets and near water. R

6   **FLOWERPECKER WEAVER FINCH** *Parmoptila woodhousei*   L 9 cm. Note: warbler-like in jizz and behaviour, but as 7 systematically a finch. Very secretive. Feeds on ants. Habitat: ground and understorey at forest edge.

7   **RED-FRONTED FLOWERPECKER WEAVER FINCH** *Parmoptila rubrifrons*   L 9 cm. Similar to 6 in behaviour, but note uniform buff underparts of ♂ and brown, speckled white cheeks of ♀. Habitat: midstrata and undergrowth of forest edges.

8   **BLACKCAP** *Sylvia atricapilla*   L 14 cm. Unmistakable. Habitat: forest, bamboo, bush, suburbs. Voice: high rich scratchy unhurried warbling starting with some squeaky notes. Starts to sing in Africa, shortly before return to Europe in spring. NM

9   **LESSER WHITETHROAT** *Sylvia curruca*   L 14 cm. Note black (not hazel) eye, small size and dark (not black) cheek. Habitat: open bush- and scrubland. Voice: very high, level, melodious rattle and very high, fast rattling warble. NM.R

10   **GARDEN WARBLER** *Sylvia borin*   L 14 cm. Note stubby bill and faint grey neck sides. Habitat: forest edges, woodland, bush, cultivation, suburbs. Voice: very long rapid sequence of jumbling mellow sharp and harsh notes.

11   **COMMON WHITETHROAT** *Sylvia communis*   L 14 cm. Most ♂♂ have less grey to sides of face than shown. Larger and with less intense buff to flanks than 16 and 17 which have similar wing pattern, but very restricted ranges. Habitat: scrubland, undergrowth of woodland and bush. Voice: modest hurried song with phrases of any length, higher sharper and faster than 12. NM

12   **BARRED WARBLER** *Sylvia nisoria*   L 16 cm. In flight with white tips to all tail feathers. The ♀ as 1stW (shown) but with paler eye: 1stW nondescript, but with white tail sides and slightly paler edges to wing coverts and tertials. Habitat: low scrub and undergrowth of woodland. V

13   **ORPHEAN WARBLER** *Sylvia hortensis*   L 15 cm. Note black legs and yellowish eye-colour (of ♂, pale brown in ♀). Habitat: open wood-, bush- and scrubland. Voice: high, unstructured, loud, melodious medleys of flutes, rattles and chuckles. NM.R

14   **SARDINIAN WARBLER** *Sylvia melanocephala*   L 13 cm. From 13 by smaller size, red rim to eye and pale legs. Habitat: woodland with dense scrub and thickly foliaged trees. NM.R

15   **SUBALPINE WARBLER** *Sylvia cantillans*   L 13 cm. Note white moustache. From other grey-headed sylvia warblers by red eye ring. The ♀ (not shown) as ♂, but with only a trace of red to underparts and a faint pink glow to throat. Habitat: open wood-, bush- and scrubland. Voice: unstructured medleys of dry, loud 'chuck' phrases repeated up to 8 times and very high, rapid, melodious warbling. NM

16   **TRISTRAM'S WARBLER** *Sylvia deserticola*   L 12 cm. Shown is n-br ♂/ ♀; br ♂ with full red-rusty throat. From 15 also by different wing patterning and colouring. Habitat: scrub and trees in desert. R

▶

Plate 86 (continued)

17 **SPECTACLED WARBLER** *Sylvia conspicillata* L 13 cm. Darker-eyed than 16. From 11 by white restricted to upper throat; 1stW from 10 by pink, not grey-yellow legs. Habitat: low bush along sea coast. NM.R

18 **MENETRIES'S WARBLER** *Sylvia mystacea* L 14 cm. Note combination of white eye ring in black face sides, grey-brownish wings and strong pink tinge to underparts, leaving faint white moustachial stripe. Habitat: wooded bush- and scrubland, cultivation and gardens. V

19 **RUEPPELL'S WARBLER** *Sylvia rueppelli* L 14 cm. The ♀ and wintering ♂♂ may have some black to chin and throat. Habitat: bush- and scrubland. NM.R

20 **DESERT WARBLER** *Sylvia nana* L 12 cm. Note pale eye and small size. Forages mostly on the ground. Habitat: dry coastal scrub. Voice: extra high, short, hurried warble '*trreee-tree-tri-ti-ti-tjee*'. R

Plate 87 (continued)

7 **YELLOW-FOOTED FLYCATCHER** *Muscicapa sethsmithi*   L 9 cm. Note yellow feet, white chin and pale grey breast. Habitat: forests.

8 **DUSKY-BLUE FLYCATCHER** *Muscicapa comitata*   L 12 cm. Note dark colouring, thin eyebrow, striking white throat, pale brown undertail coverts. Habitat: forest edges and glades.

9 **TESSMANN'S FLYCATCHER** *Muscicapa tessmanni*   L 12 cm. Very similar to 18, with which it shares its range, but whiter below, especially undertail coverts and without white eyebrow. Habitat: forest, plantations, overgrown plantations. R

0 **BOEHM'S FLYCATCHER** *Muscicapa boehmi*   L 12 cm. Note very upright stance and triangular spots below. Unobtrusive percher. Habitat: miombo. R

Plate 87

1 **BEDFORD'S PARADISE FLYCATCHER** *Terpsiphone bedfordi* L 18 cm. All-grey with black head. Note blue eyelid wattle. Habitat: forest undergrowth. Note: all paradise flycatchers are known to hybridise easily within their genus, which makes identification not always easy. E, D. R. of Congo.

2 **AFRICAN PARADISE FLYCATCHER** *Terpsiphone viridis* L 18 (+8) cm. Very variable (a, b and c), some extreme forms shown (even one of the two central tail feathers might be white, the other orange). Note white undertail coverts and large crest. Habitat: forest, woodland, bush, gardens.

3 **SÃO TOMÉ PARADISE FLYCATCHER** *Terpsiphone atrochalybeia* L 18 (+5) cm. Only paradise flycatcher on São Tomé. Habitat: all types of habitat, wherever there are trees or shrubs. E, São Tomé.

4 **RUFOUS-VENTED PARADISE FLYCATCHER** *Terpsiphone rufocinerea* L 18 (+5) cm. The ♀ (not shown) without tail streamers. From 2 by rufous undertail coverts, smaller crest and less conspicuous eye wattle. Habitat: forests and riverine belts. Note: two races of this species, *batesi* and *bannermanni*, are often split off together from this species to form an independent species: Bates's Paradise Flycatcher *Terpsiphone batesi* (a), distinguishable from nominate *rufocinerea* (b) by crestless blue-grey (not crested, blackish) head, lack of tail streamers (except some populations in Cameroon) and by different range.

5 **RED-BELLIED PARADISE FLYCATCHER** *Terpsiphone rufiventer* L 20 cm (except tail streamers of a). Many races occur, all with rufous underparts, of these nominate (a) shown, *neumanni* (b, with blue-black upperparts), *fagani* (c, with dark tail and flight feathers and without tail streamers) and *smithii* on Annobón (d, with brown upperparts). Habitat: forest interiors.

6 **CASSIN'S FLYCATCHER** *Muscicapa cassini* L 13 cm. Rather long-tailed, no eyebrow, faint breast band. Only grey flycatcher feeding along forest streams. Habitat: hawks from perch over forest streams.

7 **SWAMP FLYCATCHER** *Muscicapa aquatica* L 13 cm. Several races, of these plain nominate (a) and more contrasting race *infulata* (b) shown. Often with striking white chin. Habitat: only at lake shores and in swamps.

8 **SPOTTED FLYCATCHER** *Muscicapa striata* L 14 cm. Note faint streaking on forehead and slightly peaked crown. Hunts from low perch. Habitat: woodland, bush, gardens. Voice: extreme high '*tsjeeh-tjeh*' or thin '*tjièeh*'. NM

9 **GAMBAGA FLYCATCHER** *Muscicapa gambagae* L 10 cm. From 8 by not or less striped plumage, shorter wings and less upright stance. Habitat: dry, more or less wooded and bushed habitats. R

10 **(African) SOOTY FLYCATCHER** *Muscicapa infuscata* L 12 cm. Very dark with mottled underparts. Hunts from high exposed position. Habitat: forest edges and nearby areas.

11 **USSHER'S FLYCATCHER** *Muscicapa ussheri* L 12 cm. Very similar to 10, but blackish not dark brown. Habitat: normally high in the canopy, perching on a bare branch, often several together.

12 **ASHY (or Blue-grey) FLYCATCHER** *Muscicapa caerulescens* L 14 cm. Note pale plumage, white lore and eye ring, strong bill with paler lower mandible, uniform upperparts (including tail). Hawks from mid-stratum perch. Habitat: woodland, riverine belts, coastal bush. Voice: high '*peepeepeepu-peeweh*' sometimes changing to twittering song.

13 **OLIVACEOUS FLYCATCHER** *Muscicapa olivascens* L 13 cm. Rather featureless, but normally the only flycatcher living in the forest canopy. Habitat: forest interior.

14 **CHAPIN'S FLYCATCHER** *Muscicapa lendu* L 10 cm. Note yellowish gape, stumpy bill, brown eye and plain upperparts. Habitat: montane forests. R

15 **AFRICAN DUSKY FLYCATCHER** *Muscicapa adusta* L 12 cm. Race *obscura* (a) shown and *pumila* (b, darker and browner). Thickset, short-tailed, with narrow eye ring. Hunts from low perch. Habitat: highland, also in coastal regions. Forest edges, riverine belts, dense woodland, suburbs. Voice: call is extreme high '*sieeèh*'. R

16 **LITTLE GREY FLYCATCHER** *Muscicapa epulata* L 10 cm. Very small with blotched breast. Habitat: forest, deserted plantations, cultivation with trees.

◀

Plate 88

1   **SHRIKE FLYCATCHER** *Megabyas flammulatus*   L 15 cm. Quiet with tail characteristically swinging side to side. Note upright posture. Habitat: more or less open forests with dense undergrowth. Voice: extra high, very sharp '*srit-sru-wit-sweet-sweet*'.

2   **BLACK-AND-WHITE (or Vanga) FLYCATCHER** *Bias musicus*   L 15 cm. Active and conspicuous. Habitat: open forest and woodland. Voice: sequence of mid-high to very high, short to very short phrases '*tju-tjip-tjut-jip weet weet tjip-tju-weet*'.

3   **WHITE-EYED SLATY FLYCATCHER** *Melaenornis fischeri*   L 16 cm. Several races, of these *toruensis* (a, with faint eye ring) and *semicinctus* (b, darker with narrow eye ring) shown. Habitat: montane forest edges, woodland, gardens.

4   **SOUTHERN BLACK FLYCATCHER** *Melaenornis pammelaina*   L 20 cm. Glossy black with only slightly forked tail (see also 99.1-3). Habitat: wooded and bushed natural and cultivated areas. Voice: high loud melodious fluted '*feeh-tjuutjuu*' ('*feeh-*' extreme high).

5   **NORTHERN BLACK FLYCATCHER** *Melaenornis edolioides*   L 20 cm. Note sooty black colouring. Habitat: woodland, bush and gardens.

6   **PALE (, Pallid or Mouse-coloured) FLYCATCHER** *Melaenornis pallidus*   L 16 cm. From 87.8 by faint eye ring, flat crown and lack of any striking. Perches on low branch. Habitat: woodland, bush.

7   **YELLOW-EYED BLACK FLYCATCHER** *Melaenornis ardesiacus*   L 20 cm. Note striking yellow eye. Habitat: dense undergrowth at montane forest edges.

8   **NIMBA FLYCATCHER** *Melaenornis annamarulae*   L 18 cm. From very similar 5 by more bluish, less dull black plumage and very restricted, different range. Habitat: high up in trees around forest clearings. R

9   **FRASER'S FOREST FLYCATCHER** *Fraseria ocreata*   L 14 cm. Found in flocks of up to 20. Active and noisy. Habitat: forest interiors.

10   **WHITE-BROWED FOREST FLYCATCHER** *Fraseria cinerascens*   L 14 cm. Solitary, behaviour as other flycatchers. Note white eyebrow and scalloped, blotched breast and flanks. Habitat: at riversides in forests.

11   **SEMICOLLARED FLYCATCHER** *Ficedula semitorquata*   L 13 cm. In all plumages (except ♂) normally with double white wing bar and much white in tail. Habitat: all more or less wooded, natural and cultivated areas, including forest edges. Note: 1stW birds of 11, 12 and 13 have brown, not whitish (as ♀♀) breasts; identification of n-br ♂♂, ♀♀ and 1stW birds is very difficult in the field; note grey rump of ♀ 13 (less so in ♀ 11), ♀ 12 browner than ♀♀ 11 and 13; 1stW 13 often with only one wing bar (as 1stW 12). NM.R

12   **EUROPEAN PIED FLYCATCHER** *Ficedula hypoleuca*   L 13 cm. The ♂ has restricted white in wings, especially at base of primaries. May have (pale) partial second wing-bar. (This species has a form in which black of ♂ br plumage is replaced by dark brown.) Habitat: more or less wooded habitats including gardens. NM

13   **COLLARED FLYCATCHER** *Ficedula albicollis*   L 13 cm. Note white neck collar of ♂ and extension of white in primaries. Habitat: miombo and other woodland. NM.R

14   **GREY TIT FLYCATCHER** *Myioparus plumbeus*   L 14 cm. From 15 by paler underparts and constant fanning (not only wagging like 15) of tail. Active insect-hunter. Habitat: open woodland, riverine belts. Very high '*srrieeeèh*' (last part descending).

15   **GREY-THROATED TIT FLYCATCHER** *Myioparus griseigularis*   L 11 cm. Note uniform grey colouring below. Not a 'percher' but in behaviour very much like a warbler, active moving through the foliage gleaning insects, while constantly wagging its tail. Habitat: lower strata of swamp forest and nearby areas. Voice: very high 2-toned fluted '*preee-prrrruuurr*'.

16   **RED-BREASTED FLYCATCHER** *Ficedula parva*   L 11 cm. Note frequently flirted tail with distinctive pattern. The 1stW bird may have pale wing bar as shown. Habitat: all more or less wooded habitats, including desert oases. V

Plate 89

1 **BROWN-THROATED (or Scarlet-spectacled) WATTLE-EYE** *Platysteira cyanea* L 13 cm. Note red eye wattle, white wing bar and (in ♀) deep-brown throat. Habitat: mangrove, forest edges, woodland, bush. Voice: very high simple melody of sharp well-separated notes '*fee-fee-fee-wee-wee-fee*'.

2 **WHITE-FRONTED WATTLE-EYE** *Platysteira albifrons* L 11 cm. From all batis species by red eye wattle. Habitat: thickets, riverine belts. R

3 **BLACK-THROATED WATTLE-EYE** *Platysteira peltata* L 13 cm. Congo race *mentalis* (a) shown and Cameroon race *laticincta* (b, with broader breast band of ♂). From 1 by all black wings. Habitat: more or less wooded and bushed areas including gardens. Voice: high sharp lashing tit-like '*tsja-tsja-weet-o-weet-o-weet-o-*'. R

4 **WHITE-SPOTTED WATTLE-EYE** *Dyaphorophyia tonsa* L 9 cm. Note white rump and short tail. From 5 by full white collar (♂ only), higher eye wattle with white spot behind eye. Habitat: forest canopy. R

5 **CHESTNUT WATTLE-EYE** *Dyaphorophyia castanea* L 10 cm. See 4. Habitat: forest undergrowth.

6 **RED-CHEEKED WATTLE-EYE** *Dyaphorophyia b. blissetti* L 9 cm. The ♂ more glossy and bottle-green, not brown as ♀. From 8 by wider brighter chestnut throat sides. Habitat: forest understorey. Note: 6, 7 and 8 are races of one species.

7 **BLACK-NECKED WATTLE-EYE** *Dyaphorophyia blissetti chalybea* L 9 cm. As 6 and 8 with striking blue eye wattle, but without chestnut to face sides (♂) or throat (♀). Habitat: as 6.

8 **JAMESON'S WATTLE-EYE** *Dyaphorophyia blissetti jamesoni* L 9 cm. See 6 and 7. Habitat: as 6.

9 **YELLOW-BELLIED WATTLE-EYE** *Dyaphorophyia concreta* L 9 cm. Race *graueri* (a) and nominate (b, with different colour pattern to underparts) shown. The ♂ may have black breast spot. Habitat: forest. Voice: high fluted '*whit-whit tjuu-tjuu whip*' (descending to lashed-up '*whip*').

10 **RWENZORI BATIS** *Batis diops* L 12 cm. No (or little) white in neck. Note white spot at lore, appearing as a sort of 'second' eye. Most similar to sympatric 16, but larger and normally at higher altitudes. Habitat: montane forests and bamboo.

11 **CHINSPOT BATIS** *Batis molitor* L 12 cm. The ♂ with white eyebrow, well extending behind eye. Note striking rufous breast and throat patch (diagnostic!) of ♀. Habitat: woodland. Voice: very high penetrating sharp slow descending '*it's so sad*'.

12 **SENEGAL BATIS** *Batis senegalensis* L 10 cm. Only batis in much of its range; from other batises by different coloured ♀. Habitat: all types of more or less wooded, and bushed, natural and cultivated areas.

13 **GREY-HEADED BATIS** *Batis orientalis* L 10 cm. Very similar to 14, but with slightly greyer crown and mantle. Habitat: dry, more or less wooded areas.

14 **BLACK-HEADED BATIS** *Batis minor* L 10 cm. From most other batises in its range by black crown and mantle. Habitat: forest patches, woodland, riverine belts.

15 **ANGOLA BATIS** *Batis minulla* L 8 cm. From other batises in its range by tiny size and little white above lores. Habitat: forest edges. R

16 **ITURI BATIS** *Batis ituriensis* L 9 cm. Note absence of grey colouring. The ♀ has black chest collar. Only batis in its habitat and range. Habitat: forest canopies. R

17 **VERREAUX'S BATIS** *Batis minima* L 8 cm. Similar to 18, but ♀ with grey, not chestnut breast band. Habitat: forest edges and - remains. R

18 **BIOCO (or Fernando Po) BATIS** *Batis poensis* L 9 cm. Nominate (a, from Bioco, ♀ with diffuse lower edge of breast band) shown and race *occulta* (b, often treated as an independent species: West African Batis). Only batis within its range, except 17, which see. Habitat: all habitats with high trees.

19 **MARGARET'S BATIS** *Batis margaritae* L 12 cm. Note diagnostic rufous wing bar of ♀. Habitat: midstrata of dry dense forest and forest patches. R

Plate 90

1 **WHITE-TAILED BLUE FLYCATCHER** *Elminia albicauda* L 14 cm. Note tail pattern and darkish face. Habitat: montane open forest, riverine belts. R

2 **AFRICAN BLUE FLYCATCHER** *Elminia longicauda* L 14 cm. From 1 by bluer colouring and lack of white in tail. Habitat: mangrove, lower storeys of forest, moist woodland, bush, gardens, cultivation.

3 **WHITE-TAILED CRESTED FLYCATCHER** *Elminia albonotata* L 13 cm. Note tail pattern. Habitat: montane forests and forest remains. Voice: very high hesitating wagtail-like '*tweet treet treetoweet*' with high fluted '*weet tsio-weet*'.

4 **DUSKY CRESTED FLYCATCHER** *Elminia nigromitrata* L 9 cm. Underparts not paler than upperparts. Habitat: forest undergrowth and moist bush.

5 **WHITE-BELLIED CRESTED FLYCATCHER** *Elminia albiventris* L 9 cm. Note white belly centre and all-black tail. Habitat: montane forest undergrowth.

6 **CHESTNUT-CAPPED FLYCATCHER** *Erythrocercus mccallii* L 10 cm. Unmistakable. Active and with much tail flirting. In flocks and in bird waves. Habitat: forests.

7 **BLUE-MANTLED CRESTED FLYCATCHER** *Trochocercus cyanomelas* L 12 cm. Unmistakable. Note row(s) of white wing spots in ♀. Habitat: dense undergrowth and midstrata of forests. Voice: very varied medley of instrumental sounds like high, nasal '*wheet-whit wheet-whit*'; low, rapid, liquid '*weetweetweetweet*' and fluted trill '*wuruwuwuwuwu*'. R

8 **BLUE-HEADED CRESTED FLYCATCHER** *Trochocercus nitens* L 12 cm. Not unlike other small tail-fanning flycatchers, but note sharp demarcation of white and black on breast. Habitat: dense forest undergrowth.

9 **YELLOW (West African or Western) PENDULINE TIT** *Anthoscopus parvulus* L 7 cm. Smaller than any other yellow bird and with different bill form. Note black frontal spots. Habitat: dry acacia steppe.

10 **GREY PENDULINE TIT** *Anthoscopus caroli* L 8 cm. Very variable, of several races *roccatii* (a) shown and race *ansorgei* (b, with white underparts). No black frontal spots. Habitat: open forest, woodland. Voice: extreme high '*wit wit wit witterdewitterdewitterdewit*'. R

11 **FOREST (or Yellow-fronted) PENDULINE TIT** *Anthoscopus flavifrons* L 7 cm. Not unlike greenish sunbird, but smaller and with different bill form. Note yellow-orange spot at forehead. Habitat: canopy and mid-levels of forest.

12 **SENNAR (or Sudan) PENDULINE TIT** *Anthoscopus punctifrons* L 7 cm. From 9 by whitish belly. Habitat: open bush. Voice: extra high, thin, piercing '*fie fie fie fie –*' alternated with a low, dry trill.

13 **TIT-HYLIA** *Pholidornis rushiae* L 8 cm. Note tiny size and yellow rear part of body. Habitat: forest canopies.

14 **SPOTTED CREEPER** *Salpornis spilonotus* L 15 cm. No other similar bird in this part of Africa. Habitat: miombo and forest edges.

15 **MIOMBO (or Northern) GREY TIT** *Parus griseiventris* L 15 cm. Note white cheeks. Habitat: miombo.

16 **WHITE-WINGED BLACK TIT** *Parus leucomelas* L 15 cm. Race *insignis* (a) shown and race *guineensis* (b, with white eye). Unmistakable; imm b however has also black eyes. Habitat: open woodland, thornbush. Note: the two races often treated as two separate species, *insignis* as White-winged Tit (a) and *guineensis* as White-shouldered Tit (b).

17 **WHITE-BELLIED TIT** *Parus albiventris* L 14 cm. Unmistakable. Habitat: montane forest edges and more or less wooded and bushed grassland, including gardens.

18 **RUFOUS-BELLIED TIT** *Parus rufiventris* L 14 cm. Imm's have dark eyes! Habitat: miombo and other woodland.

19 **STRIPE-BREASTED TIT** *Parus fasciiventer* L 12 cm. Note long stripe down breast. No other similar tit within its range and habitat. Habitat: montane forests and giant heath.

20 **DUSKY TIT** *Parus funereus* L14cm. Note conspicuous red eye. Habitat: forest, riverine belts, plantations. Voice: loud lowered sometimes hoarse '*viouuuh*' or questioning '*vreeeeh?*'.

Plate 91

1 **YELLOW WHITE-EYE** *Zosterops senegalensis* L 10 cm. Unmistakable. Habitat: forest edges and interiors, giant heath, all types of woodland and suburban gardens.

2 **PRÍNCIPE WHITE-EYE** *Zosterops ficedulinus* L 10 cm. Only white-eye on São Tomé and Príncipe. Habitat: all areas with trees away from settlement. E, São Tomé and Príncipe.

3 **ANNOBÓN WHITE -EYE** *Zosterops griseovirescens* L 12 cm. Only white-eye on Annobón. Habitat: all areas with trees. E Annobón.

4 **FERNANDO PO SPEIROPS** *Speirops brunneus* L 12 cm. Unmistakable. Habitat: forest clearings, heathland scrub, open woodland. E, Bioco.

5 **BLACK-CAPPED SPEIROPS** *Speirops lugubris* L 13 cm. Race *melanocephalus* (a, from Mt Cameroon) and nominate (b, from São Tomé) shown. Note: these races often treated as 2 separate species. Note dark cap and white at base of bill. In all areas with trees.

6 **PRÍNCIPE SPEIROPS** *Speirops leucophaeus* L 13 cm. Unmistakable. Habitat: forest, bush, plantations. E, Príncipe.

7 **(Southern) PYGMY SUNBIRD** *Hedydipna platura* L 8 cm (+ 5 cm). In n-br plumage (without tail streamers) from 8 and 20 by all-green (not purple-banded) chest and purple, not blue or green rump. Habitat: dry, bushed and wooded areas. AM

8 **VARIABLE (Yellow-Bellied) SUNBIRD** *Cinnyris venusta* L 10 cm. The ♂ from 20 by blue rump and longer bill. Note blue-black tail of ♂ and ♀. Habitat: forest edges, riverine belts, bush, gardens. Voice: very high descending very fast warbler-like chatter and very high level fast twittering.

9 **WHITE-BELLIED SUNBIRD** *Cinnyris talatala* L 11 cm. Unmistakable. Note absence of eye stripe in ♀. Habitat: woodland, bush, gardens. Voice: combination of very high '*uweet-uweet*', a fast wren-like trill and other short twitters. R

10 **COPPER SUNBIRD** *Cinnyris cuprea* L 11 cm. Note black tail with pale sides of ♀. Habitat: forest edges, open woodland, bush, cultivation, gardens. Voice: song is combination of its sparrow-like call '*dutdutdutdut-*' and slow high nasal twittering.

11 **WESTERN OLIVE SUNBIRD** *Cyanomitra obscura* L 14 cm. The ♂ (not the ♀) may show yellow tufts. From 12 and 13 by much longer bill. Habitat: forest, woodland, riverine belts, gardens.

12 **BATES'S SUNBIRD** *Cinnyris batesi* L 11 cm. Very similar to 13, but with shorter tail, narrower bill and darker underparts. No tufts. Habitat: upper forest strata, cultivation.

13 **LITTLE GREEN SUNBIRD** *Anthreptes seimundi* L 9 cm. From 12 by paler underparts. Note narrow yellowish eye ring. Habitat: open forest.

14 **BROWN SUNBIRD** *Anthreptes gabonicus* L 10 cm. Note white in face. Habitat: mangroves, tree belts along rivers, swamp thickets.

15 **FRASER'S (or Scarlet-tufted) SUNBIRD** *Deleornis fraseri* L 11 cm. Green-headed race *cameroonensis* (a) and grey-headed race *axillaris* (b) shown. Other races in West Africa as a. Note narrow eye ring. The ♂ from all other greenish ♂ and ♀ sunbirds by (often concealed) scarlet tufts. Habitat: forest canopy.

16 **ANCHIETA'S (or Red-and-blue) SUNBIRD** *Anthreptes anchietae* L 10 cm. Unmistakable. Habitat: miombo. R

17 **WESTERN VIOLET-BACKED SUNBIRD** *Anthreptes longuemarei* L 13 cm. Unmistakable. Note white eyebrow of ♀. Habitat: miombo and other woodland. Voice: high unstructured reed warbler-like twittering. AM

18 **VIOLET-TAILED SUNBIRD** *Anthreptes aurantium* L 11 cm. Note green wings. Habitat: wooded and overgrown streams.

19 **GREEN (or Yellow-chinned) SUNBIRD** *Anthreptes rectirostris* L 9 cm. From 20 by whitish chin and paler belly. Habitat: forest canopy.

20 **COLLARED SUNBIRD** *Hedydipna collaris* L 10 cm. Unmistakable, but see 7. Note green rump and short bill. Habitat: forest, riverine belts, coastal bush, suburbs. Voice: very high fast '*tu-ju-ti-ju-ti-ju-ti-ju-*' and other unstructured siffles and twitters.

Plate 92

1 **PRÍNCIPE SUNBIRD** *Anabathmis hartlaubii*   L 14 cm. Only sunbird on Príncipe. Habitat: forest, woodland, plantations, gardens. E, Príncipe

2 **NEWTON'S (Yellow-breasted) SUNBIRD** *Anabathmis newtonii*   L 9 cm. Only small sunbird on São Tomé. Habitat: forest, woodland, plantations, gardens. E, São Tomé.

3 **CAMEROON (Blue-headed) SUNBIRD** *Cyanomitra orates*   L 12 cm. From other similar sunbirds in its range by yellowish, not grey underparts. Habitat: forest, especially along streams.

4 **BUFF-THROATED SUNBIRD** *Chalcomitra adelberti*   L 11 cm. Unmistakable. Habitat: forest and adjacent areas. Also in cultivated areas with trees. R

5 **MIOMBO DOUBLE-COLLARED SUNBIRD** *Cinnyris manoensis*   L10 cm. From most other double-collared sunbirds by olivaceous rump and by different range, except 17, which has darker belly and green rump. Habitat: miombo. R

6 **RWENZORI (or Stuhlmann's) DOUBLE-COLLARED SUNBIRD** *Cinnyris stuhlmanni* L 12 cm. From 7 in same range by paler belly, longer bill and preference for higher altitudes. Habitat: normally at high altitudes in mountains.

7 **NORTHERN DOUBLE-COLLARED SUNBIRD** *Cinnyris reichenowi preussi*   L 10 cm. From similar 9 in same range by purple breast band and uppertail coverts. See also 6. Habitat: montane forest, bamboo and gardens.

8 **EASTERN DOUBLE-COLLARED SUNBIRD** *Cinnyris mediocris*   L 10 cm. Only (and incidentally) seen in eastern parts of the D. R. of Congo, outside range of other double-collared sunbirds. Note green rump, orange (not red) breast and yellowish underparts of ♂. Habitat: forest edges, bamboo, gardens. R

9 **OLIVE-BELLIED SUNBIRD** *Cinnyris chloropygia*   L 10 cm. Note green rump and dusky underparts of ♂. The ♀ has streaked underparts and distinct eyebrow. Habitat: forest edges, moist bush, cultivation.

10 **TINY SUNBIRD** *Cinnyris minulla*   L 8 cm. Similar to 9, but much smaller. Note narrow red chest band and dark brown wings. Habitat: forests.

11 **REGAL SUNBIRD** *Cinnyris regia*   L 11 cm. From 12 by yellow belly. Habitat: montane forest and bamboo.

12 **ROCKEFELLER'S SUNBIRD** *Cinnyris rockefelleri*   L 11 cm. Very restricted range. Note red undertail coverts. Habitat: montane forest and bamboo. R

13 **URSULA'S (Mouse-Coloured) SUNBIRD** *Cinnyris ursulae*   L 9 cm. No similar bird in its range and habitat. Habitat: forest. R

14 **REICHENBACH'S SUNBIRD** *Anabathmis reichenbachii*   L 11 cm. Note yellow undertail coverts. Tail graduated, each feather with pale tips. May show yellow tufts. Habitat: forest edges, cultivation, gardens. Prefers habitats along rivers.

15 **ORANGE-TUFTED SUNBIRD** *Cinnyris bouvieri*   L 10 cm. Note long bill and purple front of ♂. May show yellow-orange tufts. Habitat: open woodland.

16 **PALESTINE (or Northern Orange-tufted) SUNBIRD** *Cinnyris osea*   L 10 cm. Restricted range. From similar 15 by shorter bill. Habitat: woodland, places with some vegetation in deserts. RES.AM.R

17 **SHELLEY'S SUNBIRD** *Cinnyris reichenowi shelleyi*   L 12 cm. Note red (not maroon) breast band in combination with dark belly. Habitat: miombo, woodland, and bush, gardens. Voice: high rapid unstructured twittering around high slightly thrush-like rattle '*tututututututut*'. Note: race of 7. R

18 **PURPLE-BANDED SUNBIRD** *Cinnyris bifasciata*   L 11 cm. Note black belly, maroon (not red) breast band and rather short bill. Habitat: dense riverine belts, forest, coastal scrub, mangroves. Voice: very high '*tit-tit-trrriritrrr*'. R

19 **SPLENDID SUNBIRD** *Cinnyris coccinigastra*   L 14 cm. Note purple head and breast. Some pure red feathers in chest-band. Habitat: forest edges and other wooded areas including gardens.

▶

20 **JOHANNA'S SUNBIRD** *Cinnyris johannae* L 14 cm. From 21 by green chin, striking short tail and yellow pectoral tufts. Note striped underparts of ♀. Habitat: forest, plantations, suburbs.

21 **SUPERB SUNBIRD** *Cinnyris superba* L 14 cm. Note long bill of ♂ and ♀, black wing of ♂ and orange and yellow tinges to underparts of ♀. Habitat: forest canopy.

Plate 93

1 **(Yellow-tufted) MALACHITE SUNBIRD** *Nectarinia famosa* L 15 (+9) cm. More shining than reflecting green. The ♀ from most other ♀♀ sunbirds by rather yellow-greenish underparts with rather well-defined moustachial stripe. Habitat: more or less open wooded and scrubbed areas, gardens and any place with large flowers at any altitude. Voice: very high, unstructured slow tinkling, build around high '*tink-tink*'.

2 **BRONZY SUNBIRD** *Nectarinia kilimensis* L 15 (+7) cm. Very dark with bronze and green reflections. The ♀ has diffuse streaks below. No n-br plumage and no tufts. Habitat: montane forest edges, wooded and bushed areas. Voice: very high excited rapid sustained twittering '*ritiritititiririti---*'.

3 **BOCAGE'S SUNBIRD** *Nectarinia bocagei* L 15 (+5) cm. Overall black with weak bluish reflections. Central tail feathers long and wide. The ♀ is bright yellowish below. No n-br plumage and no tufts. Habitat: woodland.

4 **SCARLET-TUFTED MALACHITE SUNBIRD** *Nectarinia johnstoni* L 16 (+12) cm. Reflecting (not shining as 1) green with black undertail coverts, the ♀ dusky with faintly, finely barred throat. Habitat: montane and alpine areas.

5 **GOLDEN-WINGED SUNBIRD** *Nectarinia reichenowi* L 15 cm (+ 5 cm). Unmistakable. Habitat: montane forests, bamboo, bushed areas, gardens, cultivation, grassland with flowers. R

6 **PURPLE-BREASTED SUNBIRD** *Nectarinia purpureiventris* L 13 cm (+ 7 cm). Unmistakable. Habitat: open, montane forests. R

7 **RED-CHESTED SUNBIRD** *Cinnyris erythrocerca* L 12 cm (+ 3 cm). Only black-bellied, green sunbird with elongated central tail feathers except larger and green-rumped 13. Breast band maroon, not scarlet. Habitat: shrubbery and undergrowth near water, swamps and gardens.

8 **(São Tomé) GIANT SUNBIRD** *Dreptes thomensis* L 18 cm. Unmistakable. Forest and immediate surroundings. E, São Tomé.

9 **BLUE-THROATED BROWN SUNBIRD** *Cyanomitra cyanolaema* L 14 cm. Note brown upperparts and restricted blue to forehead and throat. The ♂ may show yellow tufts. The ♀ shows diagnostic white lines above and below eye. Habitat: forest canopy.

10 **BLUE-HEADED SUNBIRD** *Cyanomitra alinae* L 14 cm. Note saffron mantle of ♂ and ♀ and dark underparts of ♂. Habitat: montane forest canopies.

11 **BANNERMAN'S SUNBIRD** *Cyanomitra bannermani* L 14 cm. Very much like 12, but ranges just don't overlap and has shorter bill. Habitat: forest and forest remains especially along streams. R

12 **GREEN-HEADED SUNBIRD** *Cyanomitra verticalis* L 14 cm. The ♂ from ♂ 11 by more brilliant reflections especially on throat and chin. Habitat: forest, bamboo, bush, gardens, cultivation.

13 **CONGO (Black-bellied) SUNBIRD** *Cinnyris congensis* L 12 (+8) cm. Unmistakable, bluish green with long tail. Habitat: forest edges, especially along rivers or at clearings. R

14 **BEAUTIFUL SUNBIRD** *Cinnyris pulchella* L 12 (+8) cm. Unmistakable. Habitat: more or less wooded, natural and cultivated areas.

15 **CARMELITE SUNBIRD** *Chalcomitra fuliginosa* L 13 cm. The ♂ looks all-black in the field, except in worn plumage (a). Note reflecting uppertail coverts. The ♀ from ♀ 17 by lack of visible eyebrow. Habitat: open wooded country, cultivation, gardens.

16 **SCARLET-CHESTED SUNBIRD** *Chalcomitra senegalensis* L 14 cm. The ♂ is unmistakable; ♀ is heavily marked below. Habitat: woodland, bush, suburbs. Voice: mid-high slow '*tuut twit-tuut twuut*'.

17 **AMETHYST (or Black) SUNBIRD** *Chalcomitra amethystina* L 14 cm. Looks all-black in the field with occasionally a small reflecting spot. The ♀ from ♀ 15 by distinct eyebrow. Habitat: forest edges, woodland, mangroves, suburbs. Voice: mid-high sustained rather slow '*tuut puwiet-puwiet tututut fuwie*'.

18 **GREEN-THROATED SUNBIRD** *Chalcomitra rubescens* L 13 cm. Widespread nominate (a, with green moustache and beard) and race *crossensis* (b, restricted to western Cameroon and Nigeria) shown. Habitat: tall woodland.

Plate 94

1 **WHITE HELMET SHRIKE** *Prionops plumatus* L 21 cm. Several races occur, mainly differing in size of crest and extend of white in wing. Parties of up to 20. Habitat: miombo, bush, thornbush.

2 **(Northern) RED-BILLED HELMET SHRIKE** *Prionops caniceps* L 20 cm. Nominate (a, with black cheek) shown; similar race *harterti* (with white cheek as next race) not shown. Race *rufiventris* (b) is more extensive and deeper rufous below. Note: in the past a and b were often described as separate species . Habitat: forest canopy.

3 **YELLOW-CRESTED HELMET SHRIKE** *Prionops alberti* L 20 cm. Unmistakable. Habitat: montane woodland, bamboo and forest.

4 **RETZ'S (Red-billed) HELMET SHRIKE** *Prionops retzii* L 20 cm. In flight with striking white tail corners. In parties of up to 20. Habitat: woodland, riverine belts.

5 **BRUBRU** *Nilaus afer* L 13 cm. Nominate (a) shown, race *nigrotemporalis* (b, without white eyebrow and with rufous striping on flanks) and race *affinis* (c, only black and white). Habitat: miombo, thornbush. Voice: very high inquiring short trill '*prrrrriii?*'.

6 **BLACK-COLLARED BULBUL SHRIKE** *Neolestes torquatus* L 16 cm. In flocks feeding on fruits. (Might be a bulbul, plate 70–72). Habitat: wooded country. Voice: high hurried nasal miaowing '*weetu-wee-tree-tree-tu-weet tree-treet*'.

7 **BLACKCAP (Marsh) TCHAGRA** *Tchagra minutus* L 17 cm. Note black cap of ♂, broken by eyebrow in ♀. From black-crowned 9 by buff, not grey underparts and red eye. Habitat: tall grass and herbage near streams and in swamps. Voice: e.g. high very loud rapid '*weetweetweet*'.

8 **BROWN-CROWNED (or Three-streaked) TCHAGRA** *Tchagra australis* L 18 cm. Note grey-brown crown bordered by black. Pale eye not always visible. Normally forages on the ground. Habitat: open bush with dense thickets. Voice: e.g. loud resounding descending Chaffinch-like '*weeweetree-tree-tree tree*'.

9 **BLACK-CROWNED TCHAGRA** *Tchagra senegala* L 20 cm. Note black crown, striking whitish eyebrows and grey underparts. Habitat: dry bushed and wooded areas with dense weedy and thorny cover. Voice: mid-high loud unhurried human-like whistles (♂), interrupted by cackling laughter of ♀.

10 **NORTHERN PUFFBACK** *Dryoscopus gambensis* L 20 cm. The ♂ from 11 by grey shoulders and rump. Note red eye and white edges to flight feathers of ♀. Note: the ♂♂ 10–14 may display (in flight and perched) as shown (a).

11 **BLACK-BACKED (or Southern) PUFFBACK** *Dryoscopus cubla* L 16 cm. From 5c by larger size, red eye and all-black mantle. Habitat: forest, riverine belts, woodland. Voice: e.g. loud lashing whistles like rapid '*weet-tee-weet-tee-weet-tee-*' ('*tee*' low and almost toneless).

12 **RED-EYED (or Black-shouldered) PUFFBACK** *Dryoscopus senegalensis* L 16 cm. Note red eye of ♂ and almost white underparts of ♀. Habitat: open forest.

13 **PINK-FOOTED PUFFBACK** *Dryoscopus angolensis* L 15 cm. Unmistakable (pink legs!): the ♀ from ♀ 14 also by less heavy bill. Habitat: forest. R

14 **SABINE'S PUFFBACK** *Dryoscopus sabini* L 16 cm. Note dark eye; also the heavy bill of ♀. Habitat: forest edge and other areas with tall trees.

15 **SOOTY BOUBOU** *Laniarius leucorhynchus* L 21 cm. Deep pure black. Often fluffs up its rump feathers. Imm shows white bill, partly retained in ad plumage. Habitat: forest undergrowth.

▶

16 **MOUNTAIN SOOTY BOUBOU** *Laniarius poensis* L 19 cm. Deep slaty black. From 15 by more bluish plumage and different range. Habitat: forest undergrowth, bamboo. Voice: duet of high fluid '*shit-whit trrrril*' (♂), directly answered by high lashing '*puwheet*' (F). R

17 **BOCAGE'S (or Grey-green) BUSH SHRIKE** *Malaconotus bocagei* L 15 cm. Note pied plumage, not unlike that of puffbacks, but with different head shape. Habitat: areas with tall trees, including forest and gardens.

18 **YELLOW-THROATED NICATOR** *Nicator vireo* L 14 cm. From 19 by smaller size, thinner bill, yellow throat patch. Habitat: canopy and middle strata of forest.

19 **WESTERN NICATOR** *Nicator chloris* L 21 cm. Note large bill. Solitary and secretive. Habitat: thickets, understorey of woodland, riverine belts. Voice: high hurried '*weet-weet-weet-weet-weet kisch kisch*' (last part loud and explosive).

Plate 95

1 **TURATI'S BOUBOU** *Laniarius turatii* L 18 cm. Note white mantle spots and pink wash to underparts. Habitat: high dense bush, woodland and forest edge. R

2 **TROPICAL BOUBOU** *Laniarius aethiopicus* L 24 cm. From 3 by pale pinkish wash to underparts and different habitat. Habitat: forest edges, riverine belts, thickets, gardens. Voice: varied duets e.g. raucous introduction of ♂, answered by piping flutes from F, together: '*graagraagraa-wutwut*'. Note: *L. ferrugineus* (Southern Boubou), of which this species might be a race, occurs only in southern Africa.

3 **SWAMP BOUBOU** *Laniarius bicolor* L 24 cm. Pure white below. Habitat: papyrus, reedbeds, riverine thickets. Voice: magpie-like rattle '*tjetjetjetjit*', immediately answered by a hollow pressed-out '*fiuu*'.

4 **MOUNT KUPÉ BUSH SHRIKE** *Malaconotus kupeensis* L 18 cm. No similar bird in its restricted range and habitat. Habitat: montane forest. E, Cameroon.

5 **GORGEOUS (or Perrin's) BUSH SHRIKE** *Telephorus viridis* L 18 cm. The ♀ (not shown) from ♂ by narrower black breast band and greener tail. Habitat: dense forest undergrowth near streams. Voice: duet sounding as low fluid fast '*pupupuwee*' ('-*wee*' is lashed-up higher answer of F).

6 **DOHERTY'S BUSH SHRIKE** *Telephorus dohertyi* L 18 cm. From 5 by uniform yellow lower breast and belly. Habitat: Thick undergrowth at forest edge. Note: not shown is rare morph, in which red at head is replaced by yellow.

7 **LUEHDER'S BUSH SHRIKE** *Laniarius luehderi* L 19 cm. Unmistakable. Habitat: dense undergrowth at forest edges, often near streams.

8 **YELLOW-CROWNED GONOLEK** *Laniarius barbarus* L 18 cm. Unmistakable. Habitat: dense undergrowth in woodland and riverine bush, gardens.

9 **BLACK-HEADED GONOLEK** *Laniarius erythrogaster* L 20 cm. Note pale eye and black crown. Habitat: dense parts of bush. Voice: very high, pure, fluted '*fee-fju-fee-ju*'. R

10 **YELLOW-BREASTED BOUBOU** *Laniarius atroflavus* L 18 cm. No other similar bird in its range. Habitat: dense undergrowth at forest edge in mountains.

11 **PAPYRUS GONOLEK (or Bush Shrike)** *Laniarius mufumbiri* L 20 cm. From 11 by white eye, wingbar and undertail coverts. Habitat: papyrus swamp. R

12 **ORANGE-BREASTED BUSH SHRIKE** *Malaconotus sulfureopectus* L 17 cm. Note yellow eye stripe. Habitat: dense canopy and midstrata at forest edges, dense parts of wooded and bushed areas. Voice: fluted '*futututèèh*' varied in pitch and speed.

13 **BLACK-FRONTED BUSH SHRIKE** *Malaconotus nigrifrons* L 18 cm. From 14 by lack of white above eye. Habitat: canopy and midstrata of forest. Voice: duets, e.g. low, mellow '*prooh*' of ♂, followed directly by lashed-up '*tweeet*', together '*prooh tweeet*'. R

▶

14 **MANY-COLOURED BUSH SHRIKE** *Malaconotus multicolor* L 18 cm. Occurs in different colour forms (a, throughout, b, throughout, c, eastern parts of the D. C. of Congo and d, Sierra Leone-Togo). Note white above eye except in d. Habitat: as 13.

15 **FIERY-BREASTED BUSH SHRIKE** *Malaconotus cruentus* L 25 cm. Note white around eye. No wing-bars visible in folded wing. Birds in SW Cameroon may have yellow underparts (a). Habitat: canopies and midstrata of forests.

16 **LAGDEN'S BUSH SHRIKE** *Malaconotus lagdeni* L 20 cm. Note black, yellow and green wing pattern. Habitat: montane forests. R

17 **GREEN-BREASTED BUSH SHRIKE** *Malaconotus gladiator* L 23 cm. Overall dark grey and olive green. Habitat: montane forest. R

18 **GREY-HEADED BUSH SHRIKE** *Malaconotus blanchoti* L 23 cm. From 19 by white further restricted to lore and yellow eye. Habitat: riverine belts in woodland. Voice: mid-high fluted '*fweeee fweeee fweeeep*' (each '*fweeee*' slightly crescendoing).

19 **MONTEIRO'S BUSH SHRIKE** *Malaconotus monteiri* L 22 cm. From 18 by white circling eye, larger bill and pale blue (not yellow) eyes, from 15 by wing bars. Habitat: dense foliage of woodland. R

Plate 96

1 **YELLOW-BILLED (or Long-tailed) SHRIKE** *Corvinella corvina* L 30 cm. Very large with long tail. Habitat: bushed and wooded areas.

2 **EMIN'S SHRIKE** *Lanius gubernator* L 15 cm. Note chestnut (not grey) rump and brown, tail feathers narrowly edged white (not black-and-white). Habitat: lightly wooded and bushed areas.

3 **SOUZA'S SHRIKE** *Lanius souzae* L 18 cm. White edge to dull-brown mantle (absent in imm) diagnostic. Habitat: miombo and other woodland. R

4 **RED-BACKED SHRIKE** *Lanius collurio* L 18 cm. The ♂ from 2 by lack of white eyebrow and wing spot, grey, not reddish rump and by more white in tail.; note reddish mantle of 1stW and grey hindcrown of ♀. Habitat: woodland, grassland with bush and thickets, forest edges. NM

5 **ISABELLINE (or Red-tailed) SHRIKE** *Lanius isabellinus* L 17 cm. All-'red' tail in all plumages diagnostic. Habitat: dry open scrubland, bush, woodland, farmland. EM

6 **MASKED (or Nubian) SHRIKE** *Lanius nubicus* L 20 cm. Broad white eyebrow and large shoulder patch diagnostic. Habitat: wooded, natural and cultivated areas. EM

7 **WOODCHAT SHRIKE** *Lanius senator* L 18 cm. Race *badius* (a) shown and nominate (b, with partly white primaries and white along edges of wing feathers). Only shrike with contrasting rusty-rufous crown and neck. Note whitish rump of imm. Habitat: bushed areas. NM

8 **MACKINNON'S SHRIKE** *Lanius mackinnoni* L 20 cm. From 9 by white eyebrow and scapulars. No or only very little white to closed wings. Habitat: more or less bushed natural and cultivated areas.

9 **LESSER GREY SHRIKE** *Lanius minor* L 21 cm. Ad ♂ has black forehead, which is spotted black in ♀. Note pinkish underparts, paler in ♀. Habitat: more or less bushed natural and cultivated areas. NM

10 **GREY-BACKED FISCAL** *Lanius excubitoroides* L 25 cm. Gregarious. Note black forehead and very long tail. Habitat: wooded and bushed natural and cultivated areas, including gardens. R

11 **SOUTHERN GREY SHRIKE** *Lanius meridionalis* L 25 cm. Very pale, almost all-white (except wings and tail). Habitat: dry, more or less wooded and bushed areas. NM

12 **FISCAL SHRIKE** *Lanius collaris* L 22 cm. Unmistakable. Note whitish shoulders and dark rump of imm. Habitat: any type of country with possibilities to perch (dead branches, telephone wires etc), from where to catch small prey and insects.

13 **SÃO TOMÉ (or Newton's) FISCAL** *Lanius newtoni* L 19 cm. Only shrike on São Tomé. Habitat: open forest. E, São Tomé.

Plate 97

1   **EURASIAN GOLDEN ORIOLE** *Oriolus oriolus*   L 24 cm. From 2 by uniform black (♂) wings; ♀ by green-edged (not yellow-edged) wing feathers. Habitat: forest edges, woodland, open forest with large trees. Voice: normally silent in Africa. Mid-high liquid very melodious rapid 'weet-weet-worio' and descending miaowing cry. NM.R

2   **AFRICAN GOLDEN ORIOLE** *Oriolus auratus*   L 25 cm. Note yellow-edged wing feathers of ♂ and ♀. Habitat: forest edges, woodland and open areas with large trees. Voice: high, melodious, fluted 'weet-weet-oh-wee-o-weer'. RES.AM

3   **BLACK-WINGED ORIOLE** *Oriolus nigripennis*   L 24 cm. From 5–7 by absence of white in wing. Black central tail feathers. Habitat: forest.

4   **SÃO TOMÉ ORIOLE** *Oriolus crassirostris*   L 24 cm. Only oriole on São Tomé. No similar bird within its range. Habitat: mainly in forests. E, São Tomé.

5   **WESTERN BLACK-HEADED ORIOLE** *Oriolus brachyrhynchus*   L 22 cm. From 7 by more grey wing coverts, green- (not yellow-)edged tertials, paler (less green) middle tail feathers. Habitat: more restricted to true forest than 7.

6   **MOUNTAIN ORIOLE** *Oriolus percivali*   L 24 cm. Extensive black in wing. No green in tail and wing feathers edged yellow, not white or green. Habitat: forest, plantations, cultivation with high trees.

7   **EASTERN BLACK-HEADED ORIOLE** *Oriolus larvatus*   L 24 cm. As 5 but central tail feathers greener and edges of wing feathers paler grey. Tail from below all yellow, without black at base as 5 and 6. Only restricted overlap with range of 5 and less a forest bird than 6. Habitat: woodland, plantations, suburbs.

8   **WESTERN JACKDAW** *Corvus monedula*   L 36 cm. Note pale eye and grey neck. Habitat: mountains with cliffs and gorges and some wood. V

9   **CAPE (or Black) CROW** *Corvus capensis*   L 45 cm. Note long slender bill. Usually in flocks. Habitat: grassland with some trees. V

10   **PIED CROW** *Corvus albus*   L 45 cm. Unmistakable. Habitat: town and villages, wooded grassland, areas near rivers, lakes, swamps.

11   **BROWN-NECKED RAVEN** *Corvus ruficollis*   L 45 cm. Often also with brown wings and mantle. Habitat: desert and semi-desert.

12   **PIAPIAC** *Ptilostomus afer*   L 35 cm. Note red eye and long tail. Associated with cattle. Habitat: lightly wooded grassland with palms.

13   **HOUSE CROW** *Corvus splendens*   L 45 cm. Note hooded jizz and greyish-brown neck. Originally coming from Asia. Habitat: elsewhere in Africa in towns at the coast, from where spreading inland; might occur in Nigeria. (I).(?)

14   **FAN-TAILED RAVEN** *Corvus rhipidurus*   L 45 cm. Note short tail. May be as brown as 11. Habitat: dry rocky areas.

15   **WHITE-NECKED RAVEN** *Corvus albicollis*   L 55 cm. Very large with huge bill. Habitat: rocky, bushed and wooded mountainous areas. R

Plate 98

1 **RED-WINGED STARLING** *Onychognathus morio*   L 30 cm. The ♂ from 2, 3 and 4 by blue (not green) gloss to head. Note dark eye of ♀. Habitat: any more or less wooded area near rocky outcrops or buildings (including town centres). Note: only the population in the D. C. of Congo might be this species; the other populations in West Africa might form a different species: Neumann's Starling *Onychognathus neumanni*.

2 **CHESTNUT-WINGED STARLING** *Onychognathus fulgidus*   L 30 cm. Note greenish gloss to head of ♂. Larger and longer tailed than 4. Habitat: lowland forests.

3 **SLENDER-BILLED STARLING** *Onychognathus tenuirostris*   L 5 cm. Note slender bill, greenish gloss to head of ♂ and (in ♀) scalloped feathering. Habitat: montane forests, moorland and cultivation. Voice: mid-high, somewhat rasping, rapid '*pju pjee-pjeepji*'. R

4 **WALLER'S STARLING** *Onychognathus walleri*   L 20 cm. Note relative small size and short bill. Habitat: montane forest. Voice: very high whistling '*fju-fjee-fjee-fjee*'.

5 **PRÍNCIPE GLOSSY STARLING** *Lamprotornis ornatus*   L 26 cm. Looks blackish; less colourful than 7, which occurs also on Príncipe Island. Habitat: wooded areas. E, Príncipe.

6 **EMERALD STARLING** *Lamprotornis iris*   L 18 cm. Note absence of blue colouring; no black wing spots. Habitat: any area with bush or trees, except forest. R

7 **SPLENDID GLOSSY STARLING** *Lamprotornis splendidus*   L 30 cm. Arboreal species with diagnostic coppery patch on neck sides and black bar across secondaries. Habitat: forest, cultivation, gardens. Voice: low miaowing '*kiauw-kjew*'. AM.RES

8 **RUEPPELL'S GLOSSY STARLING** *Lamprotornis purpuropterus*   L 35 cm. No green colouring, no wing spots; large wings and long tail. Habitat: more or less wooded and bushed areas, normally near settlement.

9 **PURPLE GLOSSY STARLING** *Lamprotornis purpureus*   L 25 cm. Green gloss restricted to wings and back. Habitat: more or less wooded and bushed natural and cultivated habitats, including gardens.

10 **BRONZE-TAILED GLOSSY STARLING** *Lamprotornis chalcurus*   L 20 cm. Note purple (not greenish) middle tail-feathers. Shorter-tailed than 14. Imm brownish black with green gloss above. Habitat: bushed areas.

11 **COPPER-TAILED GLOSSY STARLING** *Lamprotornis cupreocaudus*   L 20 cm. No green in plumage and with coppery tail. From 17 by pale eye. Often together with 7. Habitat: canopy of lowland forest.

12 **SHARP-TAILED STARLING** *Lamprotornis acuticaudus*   L 23 cm. Note red (♂) or orange (♀) eye, pale underwing and pointed tail. Habitat: dry woodland. Voice: high lashing '*sreep-sreep tjisreep mewi-sreep*'.

13 **LESSER BLUE-EARED STARLING** *Lamprotornis chloropterus*   L 19 cm. Note short ear coverts (longer in 14). Imm of race *elisabeth* (SE parts of the D. R. of Congo, not shown) is rufous below (good field mark in flocks). Gregarious in loose flocks often together with other glossy starlings. Habitat: as 14. Voice: high, miaowing, throaty, rather staccato '*reh piu tu tju pri tju tui*'.

14 **GREATER BLUE-EARED STARLING** *Lamprotornis chalybaeus*   L 22 cm. From 15 by extensive blue (not bluish-green) belly, larger wing spots, longer tail, more slender, brighter, bluer appearance. Habitat: woodland, bush, suburbs. Voice: very high miaowing reed warbler-like '*mew-u-mewe prrrrtju tjup puti-tutjeh*'.

15 **CAPE GLOSSY STARLING** *Lamprotornis nitens*   L 22 cm. Darker, less green than 13 and 14. Habitat: as 14. Voice: high miaowing yet fluting '*meh-ju-wee meh-meh-ju-wee tju-pu-ruh -*'. R

16 **LONG-TAILED GLOSSY STARLING** *Lamprotornis caudatus*   L 25 (+ 30) cm. Only long-tailed glossy starling in its range. Habitat: woodland, suburbans, cultivation, mangrove.

17 **PURPLE-HEADED GLOSSY STARLING** *Lamprotornis purpureiceps*   L 20 cm. From 7, with which its shares its range and habitat, by compact size, dark plumage and dark eye. Habitat: lowland forest.

Plate 99

1   **SHINING DRONGO** *Dicrurus atripennis*   L 22 cm. From 3 by black, not whitish underwing, stronger gloss and different habitat. Noisy, in flocks, often together with other bird species. Habitat: lowland forest.

2   **SQUARE-TAILED DRONGO** *Dicrurus ludwigii*   L 18 cm. Small with dull purplish gloss and undeep forked tail. Perches less exposed than 3. Habitat: forest, riverine belts.

3   **FORK-TAILED DRONGO** *Dicrurus adsimilis*   L 24 cm. From 2 by larger size and deeply forked tail, from 1 by different habitat. Noisy. Hawks insects from an exposed position. Habitat: forest edges, dry woodland, farmland with some trees. Note: The similar drongo from the rainforest belt Nigeria-Congo's is often treated as an independent species: Velvet-mantled Drongo *Dicrurus modeste*.

4   **YELLOW-BILLED OXPECKER** *Buphagus africanus*   L 22 cm. Unmistakable. Habitat: game reserves and other places with game or cattle.

5   **RED-BILLED OXPECKER** *Buphagus erythrorhynchus*   L 21 cm. From 4 by all-red bill, yellow eye ring and uniform upperparts. Habitat: mainly found in game reserves. R

6   **WATTLED STARLING** *Creatophora cinerea*   L 21 cm. Striking white rump in flight. Highly nomadic in very large flocks. Habitat: open woodland, and bush. AM.R

7   **COMMON STARLING** *Sturnus vulgaris*   L 20 cm. Occasionally seen in Mauritania. Habitat: man-made habitats like farmyards, play-fields, orchards. V

8   **GREY-NECKED PICATHARTES** *Picathartes oreas*   L 32 cm. Unmistakable. Habitat: near large rocks, caves and cliffs in rain forest. Keeps to the undergrowth. Note: as 9 a babbler, not a starling. R

9   **WHITE-NECKED PICATHARTES** *Picathartes gymnocephalus*   L 32 cm. Unmistakable. Habitat: as 8.

10   **STUHLMANN'S STARLING** *Poeoptera stuhlmanni*   L 17 cm. From 11 by shorter tail, less gloss, darker wing and narrow yellow eye ring. Habitat: forest. Note: only ♀♀, not ♂♂ of 10 and 11 have chestnut in wings.

11   **NARROW-TAILED STARLING** *Poeoptera lugubris*   L 18 cm. Note pale wing of ♂, strong gloss and long, pointed tail. Sparrow-sized. Habitat: forest.

12   **SHARPE'S STARLING** *Pholia sharpii*   L 15 cm. Note buff belly and undertail coverts, and pale eye. Habitat: montane forest canopies.

13   **VIOLET-BACKED (Amethyst or Plum-coloured) STARLING** *Cinnyricinclus leucogaster* L 18 cm. Note characteristic yellow gape of ♀. Habitat: attracted to fruiting trees at forest edges, woodland, gardens. AM

14   **CHESTNUT-BELLIED STARLING** *Lamprotornis pulcher*   L 20 cm. Unmistakable. Shows pale wing patch in flight. Habitat: wooded and bushed areas often near settlement.

15   **WHITE-COLLARED STARLING** *Grafisia torquata*   L 20 cm. The ♂ is unmistakable; note pale eye of all-brown, slightly pale-scaled ♀. Habitat: from woodland to dry areas with sparse trees. Not on the ground. R

Plate 100

1 **WHITE-BILLED BUFFALO WEAVER** *Bubalornis albirostris* L 25 cm. Unmistakable. White bill of ♂ turns to black in n-br plumage. Habitat: wooded and bushed areas.

2 **CHESTNUT-MANTLED SPARROW WEAVER** *Plocepasser rufoscapulatus* L 18 cm. Note grey (♂, pale brown in ♀) streak over crown. Habitat: miombo. R

3 **CHESTNUT-CROWNED SPARROW WEAVER** *Plocepasser superciliosus* L 17 cm. Note rufous rump. Habitat: dry wooded and bushed areas.

4 **IAGO SPARROW** *Passer iagoensis* L 15 cm. Note black forehead and crown of ♂. The ♀ is greyer than ♀♀ 5 and 6 and has black bill. Habitat: towns, villages, dry terrain with sparse trees. E, Cape Verde.

5 **SPANISH SPARROW** *Passer hispaniolensis* L 15 cm. Breeding ♂ (not shown) with black bill, more black in mantle and solid black breast. The ♀ from ♀ 6 by faint striping to breast. Habitat: towns, villages, cultivated areas. R

6 **HOUSE SPARROW** *Passer domesticus* L 15 cm. Note grey rump and pale tawny mantle of ♂; ♀ almost impossible to separate from ♀ 5. Habitat: confined to human settlement. (I).

7 **TREE SPARROW** *Passer montanus* L 14 cm. Note rufous crown and black cheek patch. Habitat: sparsely wooded country, cultivation, edges of towns and villages. (?)

8 **GREY-HEADED SPARROW** Passer griseus L 15 cm. Note rufous rump. Habitat: bushed and wooded areas, including cultivation and suburbs.

9 **RUFOUS (or Great) SPARROW** *Passer motitensis* L 15 cm. The ♂ and ♀ more brightly coloured than 6. Note striking rufous rump in flight. Black chin spot reduced in n-br plumage (not shown). Habitat: dry areas away from settlement.

10 **DESERT SPARROW** *Passer simplex* L 13 cm. The ♂ as an uncoloured, very pale House Sparrow, ♀ very different, almost uniform orange-tawny. Habitat: oases in desert.

11 **YELLOW-SPOTTED PETRONIA** *Petronia pyrgita* L 13 cm. Note white chin and overall grey tone. Habitat: more or less wooded and bushed natural and cultivated areas. Note: ♂♂ and some ♀♀ of 11–13 have a small concealed yellow throat patch.

12 **BUSH PETRONIA** *Petronia dentata* L 13 cm. The ♂ is faint rufous around cheek. Note tawny wash to mantle of ♂ and ♀. Habitat: forest edges and woodland, often near water. AM

13 **SOUTHERN YELLOW-THROATED PETRONIA** *Petronia superciliaris* L 15 cm. Long conspicuous white eyebrow diagnostic. Yellow throat patch normally concealed. Habitat: woodland, thornbush, riverine belts. Voice: high fast '*tsjee-tsjee-tsjee*'. R

14 **SUDAN GOLDEN SPARROW** *Passer luteus* L 11 cm. Unmistakable. (Note that bill of ♂ is pale in n-br plumage). Habitat: open areas with some bush, scrub and grass cover. Also near settlement. RES.AM

15 **SPECKLE-FRONTED WEAVER** *Sporopipes frontalis* L 13 cm. Small. Always in flocks and in colonies. Habitat: bushed (and wooded) areas, often near water.

16 **GROSBEAK WEAVER** *Amblyospiza albifrons* L 18 cm. Pairs or loose colonies in tall reeds and elephant grass. Habitat: marshes, swamps, wet places in forest and woodland.

17 **BRAMBLING** *Fringilla montifringilla* L 16 cm. Note white rump in flight. Habitat: forest edges, woodland, cultivation. V

18 **CHAFFINCH** *Fringilla coelebs* L 16 cm. Note conspicuous wing bars. Habitat: suburbs, plantations. . Voice: pleasant short melodious chatter gradually lowered between start and finish '*tsi-tsi-wee-wirre-wirre-wee-wir*'. (?)

19 **CUT-THROAT FINCH** *Amadina fasciata* L 12 cm. Note zigzag barring of underparts (♂ and ♀). Forages often on the ground. Pairs-groups. Habitat: dry woodland, bush, cultivation, near waterholes.

Plate 101

1 **LARGE GOLDEN WEAVER** *Ploceus xanthops*   L 16 cm. Note large size, creamy eye, uniform colouring. Not colonial. Habitat: reeds, moist bushed areas. Sometimes in suburbs.

2 **PRÍNCIPE GOLDEN WEAVER** *Ploceus princeps*   L 15 cm. Note orange head. One of the commonest bird on Príncipe. Habitat: forest edge, bush, villages. E, Príncipe

3 **ORANGE WEAVER** *Ploceus aurantius*   L 13 cm. Social. Note thin, pale bill. Habitat: forest edges, swamps and reedbeds.

4 **SPECTACLED WEAVER** *Ploceus ocularis*   L 14 cm. The ♂ from ♂ 3 by black bib and lack of black in wing. Skulking. Not colonial. Habitat: dense vegetation at forest edge, riverine belts, suburbs. Voice: very high lowered fast wader-like '*fwee-fwee-fwee-fwee-fwee*'.

5 **BAGLAFECHT WEAVER** *Ploceus baglafecht*   L 14 cm. From several races *stuhlmanni* (a) and *eremobius* (b, with black forehead and crown) shown. Only black-cheeked weaver with yellow chin and throat. Habitat: montane forest edges.

6 **BANNERMAN'S WEAVER** *Ploceus bannermani*   L 14 cm. From 4 by black cheek and all-yellow breast. The ♀ is similar to the ♂. Habitat: montane forest. R

7 **HEUGLIN'S MASKED WEAVER** *Ploceus heuglini*   L 14 cm. Less social. Note pale yellow eye and yellow-orange forehead. Habitat: dry woodland.

8 **SLENDER-BILLED WEAVER** *Ploceus pelzelni*   L 12 cm. Note small size and thin bill. The ♀ has uniform yellow face sides and black bill. Small colonies. Habitat: marshes, swamps, damp woodland.

9 **LITTLE WEAVER** *Ploceus luteolus*   L 12 cm. Small and with short bill; lacks orange tones. Habitat: woodland, thornbush, gardens.

10 **VILLAGE (or Black-headed) WEAVER** *Ploceus cucullatus*   L 20 cm. Not all races depicted, *collaris* (a) and *nigriceps* (b) shown. Social (breeds in colonies). Habitat: more or less wooded and bushed areas, including farmland and gardens.

11 **NORTHERN BROWN-THROATED WEAVER** *Ploceus castanops*   L 14 cm. Social. Note heavy bill, small rufous mask and plain mantle. Habitat: breeds in papyrus and reedbeds, but wanders to forest edges and other wooded areas when not breeding.

12 **BOCAGE'S WEAVER** *Ploceus temporalis*   L 13 cm. Note pale eye, olive-green cheeks and narrow olive-rufous bib. Small colonies. Habitat: riverine belts, reed beds, high grass. R

13 **BATES'S WEAVER** *Ploceus batesi*   L 14 cm. The ♂ with unique cherry-red mask. Note dark eye of ♂ and ♀. Habitat: forest. E, Cameroon

14 **VITELLINE (or Southern) MASKED WEAVER** *Ploceus velatus*   L 12 cm. Note red eye. From 18 by all-yellow breast, from 18 and 19 by different habitat and extensive range. Small to large colonies. Habitat: more or less wooded areas often away from water, suburbs.

15 **LESSER MASKED WEAVER** *Ploceus intermedius*   L 12 cm. Note absence of orange tones and diagnostic pale eye, this feature shared with ♀ which is more yellow than most other ♀♀ weavers. Pairs, large colonies often together with 10. Habitat: nests in trees over water or in reed beds. Open thornbush, woodlands. R

16 **NORTHERN MASKED WEAVER** *Ploceus taeniopterus*   L 15 cm. Very social. Black mask merging gradually in rufous of crown and breast. Habitat: reedbeds and nearby bushes.

17 **YELLOW-BACKED WEAVER** *Ploceus melanocephalus*   L 14 cm. Nominate (a) shown and race *capitalis* (b, with deep chestnut below black throat). Note yellow neck and plain mantle. Habitat: riverine belts, lake edges, swamps.

18 **RUWET'S MASKED WEAVER** *Ploceus ruweti*   L 14 cm. From 14 by habitat, restricted range and orange-rufous breast. Habitat: swamp. R

19 **KATANGA'S MASKED WEAVER** *Ploceus katangae*   L 14 cm. Very similar to 14, but not in same range and with different habitat. Habitat: swamps. R

20 **STRANGE WEAVER** *Ploceus alienus*   L 14 cm. Combines rufous bib with black (not dark brown) head and olive-green mantle. Habitat: montane forest edges and bamboo.

Plate 102

1   **BROWN-CAPPED WEAVER** *Ploceus insignis*   L 13 cm. From 2 and 4 (with similar patterned upperparts) by brown or black crown. Habitat: forests. R

2   **YELLOW-CAPPED WEAVER** *Ploceus dorsomaculatus*   L 14 cm. From similar black-chinned 4 by yellow throat Habitat: forests. R

3   **BLACK-CHINNED WEAVER** *Ploceus nigrimentum*   L 15 cm. Note unique combination of pale eye and black mantle. Habitat: woodland.

4   **PREUSS'S GOLDEN-BACKED WEAVER** *Ploceus preussi*   L 15 cm. Note black chin and throat. Woodpecker-like feeding behaviour. Habitat: forests.

5   **WEYN'S WEAVER** *Ploceus weynsi*   L 15 cm. From 101.10 by dark brown back and pale eye. Habitat: forests. R

6   **YELLOW-MANTLED WEAVER** *Ploceus tricolor*   L 14 cm. Unmistakable. Habitat: canopy of forests.

7   **BLACK-NECKED (or Western Spectacled) WEAVER** *Ploceus nigricollis*   L 13 cm. Race *brachypterus* (a, bright yellowish olive above, not black or black-necked) and nominate (b, with black upperparts and narrowly yellow-edged flight feathers) shown. Not social. Habitat: forests.

8   **DARK-BACKED WEAVER** *Ploceus bicolor*   L 13 cm. Head darker than mantle. Throat may be all black, not speckled black as shown. Not social. Habitat: forests, moist woodland. R

9   **BLACK-BILLED WEAVER** *Ploceus melanogaster*   L 13 cm. Unmistakable. Habitat: forest, near the ground.

10   **MAXWELL'S BLACK WEAVER** *Ploceus albinucha*   L 13 cm. Nominate (a, normally with greyish or even white neck patch) and race *holomelas* (b, without grey neck patch) shown. Race *maxwelli* (from Fernando Po, not shown) also without white neck patch, but browner below as b. Social. Habitat: forests.

11   **VIEILLOT'S BLACK WEAVER** *Ploceus nigerrimus*   L 14 cm. Nominate (a) shown and race *castaneofuscus* (b). Unmistakable. The ♀♀ greenish, not black as ♀♀ 10 and 12. Very social. Habitat: forest edges, woodland.

12   **YELLOW-LEGGED WEAVER** *Ploceus flavipes*   L 15 cm. Faintly green-scaled. Yellowish legs diagnostic. Pairs or small groups. Habitat: forests. E, D. R. of Congo.

13   **BAR-WINGED WEAVER** *Ploceus angolensis*   L 12 cm. Not colonial. Often in mixed bird parties. Habitat: woodland. R

14   **SÃO TOMÉ WEAVER** *Ploceus sanctithomae*   L 14 cm. Nuthatch-like feeding behaviour. Habitat: moist wooded and bushed grassland. E, São Tomé.

15   **LOANGO SLENDER-BILLED WEAVER** *Ploceus subpersonatus*   L 13 cm. Overall golden yellow with black head and uniform green mantle and wings. Habitat: open forest near water. R

16   **COMPACT WEAVER** *Ploceus superciliosus*   L 12 cm. Note solid-brown upperparts. Pairs-woodland, cultivation. E, Nigeria.

17   **GOLDEN-NAPED WEAVER** *Ploceus aureonucha*   L 16 cm. From 4 by greenish underparts. No yellow stripe through mantle of F. Habitat: forests.

18   **GIANT WEAVER** *Ploceus grandis*   L 21 cm. Ressembling a unusual large Village Weaver (101.10). Habitat: forest, woodland.

Plate 103

1   **RED-CROWNED MALIMBE** *Malimbus coronatus*   L 16 cm. Red of M restricted to crown. Habitat: forests.

2   **CASSIN'S MALIMBE** *Malimbus cassini*   L 16 cm. From 5 and 7 by narrower red-orange breast band , black undertail coverts and all-black F. Habitat: wet parts of forests.

3   **RACHEL'S MALIMBE** *Malimbus racheliae*   L 16 cm. From 102.17 by yellow undertail coverts. The F from F 4 by more orange to breast. Habitat: forest.

4   **GOLA MALIMBE** *Malimbus ballmanni*   L 16 cm. No other bird with yellow ruff at neck. Note yellow undertail coverts. Habitat: forests.

5   **RED-VENTED MALIMBE** *Malimbus scutatus*   L 16 cm. As 7 but with more extensively red undertail coverts. The F from 6 by red undertail coverts and different bill colour. Habitat: forests.

6   **GRAY'S (or Blue-billed) MALIMBE** *Malimbus nitens*   L 16 cm. Note pale bill. See also F 5. Habitat: moist forest often along streams.

7   **IBADAN MALIMBE** *Malimbus ibadensis*   L 17 cm. From 5 (with more extensive range and different habitat) by less or no red to undertail coverts. Note narrow red girdle over breast of F. Habitat: open woodland, cultivation.

8   **RED-HEADED MALIMBE** *Malimbus rubricollis*   L 17 cm. Note absence of red to breast. Habitat: forest, woodland, dense bush.

9   **RED-BELLIED MALIMBE** *Malimbus erythrogaster*   L 16 cm. Unmistakable. Habitat: forest. R

10   **CRESTED MALIMBE** *Malimbus malimbicus*   L 16 cm. Only ♂ has a small crest. From other malimbs by black neck. Habitat: forest and dense thickets.

11   **RED-HEADED WEAVER** *Anaplectes rubriceps*   L 14 cm. Race *leuconotus* (a) shown, nominate (b, with all-red head) and race *gurneyi* (c, as a, but with yellow edges to flight feathers). N-br ♂ as ♀. In br season small groups of one ♂ with several ♀♀. Nomadic outside br season. Habitat: woodland, thornbush.

12   **RED-HEADED QUELEA** *Quelea erythrops*   L 11 cm. Note sharply defined red of ♂ mask and in ♀ dark mark near base of bill, yellow eyebrow and white (not yellow) chin. Small flocks. Habitat: marsh shrubbery and moist grassland. Note: 'queleas' (12–14) are sometimes called 'diochs' in western Africa.

13   **RED-BILLED QUELEA** *Quelea quelea*   L 12 cm. Colour forms a, b and most common c shown. Red bill diagnostic in both sexes and in all colour forms. Very gregarious (flocks of far more than 10.000 may occur). Habitat: dry bushed natural and cultivated areas. AM

14   **CARDINAL QUELEA** *Quelea cardinalis*   L 10 cm. The ♂ from 12 by gradual transition of red from head to rest of body, ♀ by yellowish chin. Gregarious (but less so than 13). Habitat: grass- and farmland. R

15   **PARASITIC WEAVER (or Cuckoo Finch)** *Anomalospiza imberbis*   L 12 cm. From other weavers and canaries by short conical bill and combination of clean yellow head and green streaked upperparts. N-br ♂ less bright. Br ♀ (not shown) with streaked breast sides and flanks. Pairs-small flocks. Brood parasite, using cisticolas as host. Habitat: moist open and bushed natural and cultivated areas (or in all habitats where cisticolas occur). Voice: high soft chattering without the siffling inhaling and nasal quality of true weavers.

16   **BOB-TAILED WEAVER** *Brachycope anomala*   L 10cm. Note very short tail and loose, fluffy feathering. From 102.16 by golden-brown neck and nape. Habitat: open parts along rivers in forests.

Plate 104

1   **LONG-TAILED WHYDAH** *Euplectes progne*   L 57 cm (♂), 18 cm (♀). Note large wings and plain colouring of ♀; n-br ♂ retains colourful wing. Habitat: damp open grassland. Note: 1–6 are often called 'widows', which name in this book is reserved for 106.8–12.

2   **YELLOW-SHOULDERED WHYDAH** *Euplectes macrourus*   L 20 cm (♂), 13 cm (♀). Note yellow shoulders of ♀ and n-br ♂. Habitat: moist open grassland at mid-high altitudes.

3   **MARSH WHYDAH** *Euplectes hartlaubi*   L 20 cm (♂), 15 cm (♀). The ♂ is longer-tailed than 6; ♀ nondescript. Habitat: marshes, swamp edges, moist grassland.

4   **RED-COLLARED WHYDAH** *Euplectes ardens*   L 27 cm (♂), 12 cm (♀). Nominate (a) shown and race *concolor* (b, all black). The ♀ is nondescript, n-br ♂ with blackish wings and more or less elongated tail. Habitat: marshy open grassland with some shrub. R

5   **WHITE-WINGED WHYDAH** *Euplectes albonotatus*   L 16 cm (♂), 12 cm (♀). Nominate (a) shown and race *eques* (b, with brown, not yellow wing shoulder). The ♀ has some (often concealed) rufous at wing bend and shows more or less a white wing flash in flight. Habitat: bushed areas with tall grass.

6   **RED-SHOULDERED WHYDAH** *Euplectes axillaris*   L 17 cm (♂), 13 cm (♀). The ♂ from 5 by absence of white in wing. The ♀ and n-br ♂ shows some rufous at wing shoulder. Habitat: swamp edges, long-grassed places, sugarcane.

7   **BLACK-WINGED RED (or Fire-crowned) BISHOP** *Euplectes hordeaceus*   L 14 cm. The ♀ from ♀ 11 by rich tawny face sides and breast band. N-br ♂ has much darker wing than ♂ 8 and 11. Often in flocks together with 12. Habitat: reed beds, elephant grass, sugarcane.

8   **NORTHERN RED BISHOP** *Euplectes franciscanus*   L 10 cm. Note black (not red) crown. Brown tail concealed between red tail coverts. Habitat: open and bushed tall grass areas.

9   **BLACK BISHOP** *Euplectes gierowii*   L 12 cm. The ♀ shows dark-mottled moustachial area and buff-coloured breast. N-br ♂ is rather dark with blackish wing. Habitat: bushed tall grassland, sugarcane. R

10   **YELLOW-CROWNED (or Golden) BISHOP** *Euplectes afer*   L 12 cm. Nominate (a) shown and race *ladoensis* (b, with yellow breast collar and flanks). Nondescript ♀ is only faintly striped below; n-br ♂ more heavily streaked above. Habitat: swamps, moist grassland.

11   **RED BISHOP** *Euplectes orix*   L 12 cm. The ♂ from ♂ 8 by black forehead (not extending to crown) and from ♂ 7 by red, not whitish undertail coverts, ♀ by rich tawny breast band. Habitat: reed beds, elephant grass, sugarcane.

12   **GOLDEN-BACKED BISHOP** *Euplectes aureus*   L 14 cm. From 13 by more extensive yellow upperparts and white undertail coverts. Habitat: reed beds, tall grass. R

13   **YELLOW(-rumped) BISHOP** *Euplectes capensis*   L 14 cm (♂), 12 cm (♀). Note (in flight) yellowish rump of ♀ and n-br ♂. Habitat: montane tall grassland with some bush, forest edges.

Plate 105

1   CRIMSON- (or Red-)WINGED PYTILIA *Pytilia phoenicoptera*   L 13 cm. Note red tail, red wings and barred underparts. Habitat: tall grass of bushed and wooded areas.

2   RED-FACED (or Yellow-winged) PYTILIA *Pytilia hypogrammica*   L 13 cm. Note combination of grey upperparts and yellow (or orange-yellow) wings. Outer tail feathers black. Habitat: open woodland, bush, cultivation.

3   ORANGE-WINGED (or Golden-backed) PYTILIA *Pytilia afra*   L 11 cm. Note deep orange-yellow in wings. Habitat: forest, miombo and other woodland, thornbush. Voice: mid-high '*trip trip trip -*' or extreme high '*tseep tseep tseep -*'.

4   GREEN-WINGED PYTILIA (or Melba Finch) *Pytilia melba*   L 12 cm. Not all races depicted, race *citerior* (a, face all-red and breast yellow) and nominate (b) shown. From 1-3 by all-green wings. Forages near or on the ground. Habitat: dry woodland, thornbush, thickets, grassland, cultivation. Voice: quiet unstructured sequence of well-separated notes '*fjuw prri sreeh juut-tjuw-tjih*'. Call is lowered '*fieeuw*'.

5   WHITE-BREASTED BLACKFINCH *Nigrita fusconota*   L 10 cm. *Sylvia* warbler-like but not hooded and much smaller. Habitat: forest edges and clearings, riverine belts.

6   CHESTNUT-BREASTED BLACKFINCH *Nigrita bicolor*   L 10 cm. Very dark. Skulking. Note fine warbler-like bill of this and last species. Habitat: forest edges and clearings.

7   PALE-FRONTED BLACKFINCH *Nigrita luteifrons*   L 10 cm. The ♂ from ♀ by more yellow to crown, red eye, black underparts. Habitat: forest, lower in canopy than 8.

8   GREY-HEADED (or -Crowned) BLACKFINCH *Nigrita canicapilla*   L 15 cm. Race *emiliae* (a) and nominate (b, with rows of white wing spots) shown. Habitat: forest, riverine tree belts, plantations.

9   FERNANDO PO (or Little) OLIVEBACK *Nesocharis shelleyi*   L 9 cm. From 11 by different range. Habitat: montane areas; forest clearings, plantations.

10   GREY-HEADED (or White-cheeked) OLIVEBACK *Nesocharis capistrata*   L 12 cm. Note yellow flanks. Habitat: undergrowth of forest edges and wet, wooded and bushed areas.

11   WHITE-COLLARED OLIVEBACK *Nesocharis ansorgei*   L 10 cm. See 9, which has shorter tail. Habitat: wet, wooded and bushed areas with thick grass and shrubbery at higher elevations.

12   BLACK-BELLIED FIREFINCH *Lagonosticta rara*   L 13 cm. Mantle of ♂ is concolorous with head and breast. Habitat: tall grass and herbage in wooded and bushed areas.

13   BAR-BREASTED FIREFINCH *Lagonosticta rufopicta*   L 10 cm. Very similar to 15, but upperparts uniform brown not tinged red. White spots form irregular bars. Rump and upper tail-coverts more crimson-red than breast and head. Habitat: herbaceous places in wooded and bushed habitats, often near water.

14   BROWN FIREFINCH *Lagonosticta nitidula*   L 10 cm. From all other firefinches by brown (not pink) rump. Habitat: thick vegetation near water.

15   RED-BILLED FIREFINCH *Lagonosticta senegala*   L 10 cm. Not all races depicted, nominate (a) shown and race *ruberrima* (b, deeper red above, including crown). The ♂ from other firefinches by pink legs, pale brown flanks and lower belly and ♀ from several other ♀♀ firefinches by the pink spot in front of eye. Habitat: open thornbush, cultivation, suburbs. May enter houses. Voice: unstructured soft song of slightly hoarse notes and trills round basic '*-tit-weet-*'.

16   AFRICAN (or Blue-billed) FIREFINCH *Lagonosticta rubricata*   L 11 cm. Not all races depicted, *polionota* (a) shown and *congica* (b, overall paler with browner upperparts). Bill partly pink. Habitat: forest edges, woodland, bush, thornbush. Voice: extreme high (or very high) shrill, warbling or silvery-rattling trills.

17   ROCK FIREFINCH *Lagonosticta sanguinodorsalis*   L 11 cm. Very restricted range, where it is the only firefinch with a red back. Note also the grey crown. Habitat: open woodland. E, Nigeria.

18   KULIKORO (or Mali) FIREFINCH *Lagonosticta virata*   L 10 cm. From 19 by different range, from 16 by different colour of lower mandible, fewer white spots and brownish, not red forehead. Habitat: rocky hillsides with sparse grass and scrub. R

▶

Plate 105 (continued)

19   **PALE-BILLED FIREFINCH** *Lagonosticta landanae*   L 11 cm. The ♂ from 16 by red crown, ♂ and ♀ from 16 and 20 by partly pink upper mandible, from 14 and 15 by black lower belly and tail. Habitat: dry grassy areas, thornbush.

20   **JAMESON'S FIREFINCH** *Lagonosticta rhodopareia*   L 11 cm. Race *ansorgei* (a) shown and race *umbrodorsalis* (b, sometimes treated as an independent species: Chad Firefinch). No or only very few white spots. From similar firefinches by all-grey or blue bill (except 18, which has different range). Habitat: tall grass, herbage and shrubbery in bush and woodland. Voice: mid-high warbled loud (or soft) rapid (or very fast) trills. R

21   **BLACK-FACED FIREFINCH** *Lagonosticta larvata*   L 11 cm. Not all races depicted, *vinacea* (a) and *nigricollis* (b) shown. Note dark mask; race *nigricollis* from 107.8–10 by green-grey back. Habitat: areas with tall grass, thickets, open woodland.

Plate 106 (continued)

BAKA (or Black-faced Firefinch) INDIGOBIRD *Vidua larvaticola*   L 11 cm. See 14.
Parasitises 105.21. Habitat: open woodland with tall grass. R

QUAIL FINCH INDIGOBIRD *Vidua nigeriae*   L 11 cm. See 14. Parasitises 108.1.
Habitat: wet grassland. R

WILSON'S (or Bar-breasted Firefinch) INDIGOBIRD *Vidua wilsoni*   L 11 cm. See 14.
Parasitises 105.13. Habitat: woodland, bush.

Plate 106

1   **CRIMSON SEEDCRACKER** *Pyrenestes sanguineus*   L 14 cm. From 2 by different range. Habitat: wet bush, marshes, dense scrub. R

2   **BLACK-BELLIED SEEDCRACKER** *Pyrenestes ostrinus*   L 15 cm. The ♂ from ♂ 5 by uniform dark grey bill and more red to tail. Habitat: tall grass and shrubbery at forest edge, gardens. Note: bill size of 1 and 2 very variable, independent of race or sex; often birds with different bill sizes paired (as shown).

3   **(Western) BLUEBILL** *Spermophaga haematina*   L 15 cm. Several races, of these nominate (a, ♂ with black rump) shown and race *pustulata* (b, with less black to cheek). Note black crown and forehead. Habitat: forest edge, thickets, scrub.

4   **GRANT'S BLUEBILL** *Spermophaga poliogenys*   L 14 cm. The ♂ as 5 but with black nape and smaller bill: note scaled grey plumage of ♀. Habitat: forest undergrowth. R

5   **RED-HEADED BLUEBILL** *Spermophaga ruficapilla*   L 15 cm. Note bright blue-and-red bill and all-black tail. Habitat: tall grass and shrubbery, normally away from settlement. R

6   **DYBOWSKI'S DUSKY TWINSPOT** *Euschistospiza dybowskii*   L 13 cm. From 107.6–7 by purple-red mantle and all grey head and breast. Habitat: open woodland, forest edge, cultivation.

7   **DUSKY TWINSPOT** *Euschistospiza cinereovinacea*   L 12 cm. Generally very dark with grey mantle. Habitat: tall grassy glades of montane forests. R

8   **PIN-TAILED WIDOW** *Vidua macroura*   L 30 cm (♂), 12 cm (♀). The ♀ as ♀♀ 9–14, but smaller. N-br ♂ as ♀. Parasites e.g. 107.14. Habitat: forest edges, open woodland, and scrubland, suburbs.

9   **LONG-TAILED PARADISE WIDOW** *Vidua paradisaea*   L 15 cm except tail streamers. Note: 9–15 can be separated by range, length and form of longest tail streamers and intensity of neck colouring. They are brood parasites, from which the ♂♂ incorporate parts of the song of their hosts in their own repertoire. This species parasites mainly 105.4. Habitat: open woodland, bush (as for the 10–13). E, São Tomé.

10   **TOGO'S PARADISE WIDOW** *Vidua togoensis*   L 15 cm except tail streamers. See 9. Parasites mainly 105.3. R

11   **UELLE'S (or Exclamatory) PARADISE WIDOW** *Vidua interjecta*   L 15 cm except tail streamers. See 9. Parasites mainly 105.1.

12   **SAHEL PARADISE WIDOW** *Vidua orientalis*   L 15 cm except tail streamers. See 9. Parasites mainly 105.4.

13   **BROAD-TAILED PARADISE WIDOW** *Vidua obtusa*   L 30 cm (♂), 15 cm (♀). N-br ♂ as ♀. See 9. Parasites 105.3. Note: in this book the long-tailed species of the genus *vidua* are called 'widows', to separate them from the long-tailed *euplectes* weavers (104.1–5), which are called 'whydahs'.

14   **JOS PLATEAU INDIGOBIRD** *Vidua maryae*   L 11 cm. Note: 14-22 are almost impossible to separate in the field, but note bill and leg colour and basic colour to gloss. Compare also their ranges. All are brood parasites, who incorporate parts of their host's song in their own voice. Parasites mainly 105.16. Habitat: forest edges, woodland. E, Nigeria.

15   **VILLAGE INDIGOBIRD** *Vidua chalybeata*   L 11 cm. Parasites 105.15. See 14. Habitat: woodland, thornbush, cultivation.

16   **VARIABLE INDIGOBIRD** *Vidua funerea*   L 12 cm. See 14. Parasitises 105.16. Habitat: forest edge, thornbush, riverine belts, gardens. R

17   **GOLDBREAST (or Jambandu) INDIGOBIRD** *Vidua raricola*   L 11 cm. See 14. Parasitises 105.12 and 108.8. Habitat: woodland and bush with tall grass. Note: 17 and 21 are named after the bird, they parasitise , in this case 108.8 the Zebra Finch (or Goldbreast).

18   **DUSKY (or Black) INDIGOBIRD** *Vidua purpurascens*   L 11 cm. See 14. Parasitises 105.20. Habitat: thornbush. R

19   **CAMEROON INDIGOBIRD** *Vidua camerunensis*   L 11 cm. See 14. Parasitises 105.12, 105.16, 106.6 and 107.6. Habitat: forst edge, woodland, cultivation.

◀

Plate 107

1 **GREEN-BACKED TWINSPOT** *Mandingoa nitidula* L 10 cm. Nominate (a, resembling several other races) and race from Bioco *virginiae* (b, with red bill) shown. Note tiny size. Often on the ground. Habitat: undergrowth of forest edges, moist thickets. Voice: extreme high cicada-like trill 'trrrrr'. R

2 **RED-FACED CRIMSONWING** *Cryptospiza reichenovii* L 12 cm. Generally browner, less grey than 3, the ♂ with red sides to face. Check also ranges. Habitat: undergrowth of montane forest, often near streams. Voice: extreme high siffled 'srrreeeeh'.

3 **ABYSSINIAN CRIMSONWING** *Cryptospiza salvadorii* L 12 cm. Rather pale. Note narrow red eye ring of ♂. Habitat: montane forest edges and bamboo. R

4 **DUSKY CRIMSONWING** *Cryptospiza jacksoni* L 12 cm. Much darker than 2, where in same range. Habitat: dense montane forest undergrowth. R

5 **SHELLEY'S CRIMSONWING** *Cryptospiza shelleyi* L 13 cm. Note pink bill of ♂ and mainly pink bill of ♀. Habitat: dense undergrowth of montane forest edges. R

6 **BROWN TWINSPOT** *Clytospiza monteiri* L 13 cm. Underparts rufous (not black), spotted white. White spots on belly arranged in bars. Habitat: tall grass and shrubbery in montane forest glades and moist bush.

7 **PETER'S (or Red-throated) TWINSPOT** *Hypargos niveoguttatus* L 13 cm. From ♀♀ 106.3-5 by rufous-brown mantle, from 106.6–7 by red head. Habitat: tall-grassy places, forest edges, bush. Voice: extreme high descending to mid high 'fififififi-tjeh-tjeh sreeeh' (last part extreme high again).

8 **LAVENDER WAXBILL** *Estrilda caerulescens* L 10 cm. From 9 and 10 by red undertail coverts. Note red bill. Habitat: dry, more or less wooded areas.

9 **BLACK-TAILED GREY WAXBILL** *Estrilda perreini* L 11 cm. From 10 by grey (not pink) bill, black undertail coverts, different range. Habitat: dense undergrowth at forest edge, woodland with thick tangled grass. R

10 **CINDERELLA WAXBILL** *Estrilda thomensis* L 11 cm. Note partly pink bill base and partly red (not all-black) tail feathers. Habitat: dry miombo, bush, thorn scrub, riverine belts. Note: This species occurs outside the area in Angola, not on São Tomé (where it erroneously was supposed to live) or elsewhere in the area.

11 **YELLOW-BELLIED (or Swee) WAXBILL** *Estrilda melanotis* L 9 cm. Note that ♀ is placed in front of ♂ for easy comparison with 13. The ♀ (with white chin!) from 13 by black upper mandible, paler eye and no pink girdle around lower belly. Habitat: mainly in tall grass at edges of montane forest, wooded streams.

12 **ANAMBRA WAXBILL** *Estrilda poliopareia* L 12 cm. Pale eye diagnostic. Habitat: long grass in swamps or at the edge of forest. E, Nigeria.

13 **FAWN-BREASTED WAXBILL** *Estrilda paludicola* L 12 cm. Longer-tailed than 11 with red upper and lower mandible. Habitat: wet grassland, swamps, forest edges, cultivation.

14 **ORANGE-CHEEKED WAXBILL** *Estrilda melpoda* L 10 cm. From all red-rumped waxbills by orange face sides. Habitat: forest edges, open woodland, swamps, cultivation, gardens.

15 **CRIMSON-RUMPED WAXBILL** *Estrilda rhodopyga* L 10 cm. Note bi-coloured bill, red in wings and red rump. Habitat: tall grass and shrubbery in woodland, bush.

16 **BLACK-RUMPED WAXBILL** *Estrilda troglodytes* L 9 cm. Note black rump and white sides to tail. Habitat: dry, natural and cultivated areas with scattered scrub, often along streams. Also at swamp edges.

17 **COMMON WAXBILL** *Estrilda astrild* L 11 cm. The ♂ from ♀ by more extensive black to underparts. Imm (not shown) has blackish bill but differs from 15 by lack of red on rump and in wings. Flocks of up to 30. Habitat: tall grass and shrubbery in woodland, bush, often near water or settlement. Voice: mid-high soft nasal song 'tju-tu-tu-wee-teesj'.

18 **BLACK-FACED WAXBILL** *Estrilda nigriloris* L 11 cm. Black lores diagnostic. Habitat: grassland with some trees or bush. E, D. R. of Congo.

▶

Plate 107 (continued)

19   **BLACK-CROWNED WAXBILL** *Estrilda nonnula*   L 10 cm. Note white undertail coverts and creamy white underparts. Habitat: moist tall grass near forest edges, woodland, and bush, cultivation and gardens.

20   **BLACK-HEADED WAXBILL** *Estrilda atricapilla*   L 10 cm. Not all races depicted, nominate (a) and *avakubi* (b, with white belly) shown. Note black undertail coverts. Habitat: montane forest, bamboo.

Plate 108 (continued)

8   **CORN BUNTING** *Miliaria calandra*   L 18 cm. Rather plain, differing from ♀♀ sparrows by typical bunting bill. Habitat: open woodland and cultivation, often on the ground or on telephone wires. V

9   **ORTOLAN BUNTING** *Emberiza hortulana* · L 15 cm. Note pale eye-ring and olive-yellow head and rump. Habitat: short-grassed areas with some trees and bush. NM.R

0   **CRETZSCHMAR'S BUNTING** *Emberiza caesia*   L 15 cm. Note pale eye-ring, blue-grey head and rusty colouring. Habitat: dry wooded and bushed areas, often near settlement. V

Plate 108

1   **AFRICAN QUAIL FINCH** *Ortygospiza atricollis*   L 10 cm. Nominate (a) and race *ansorgei* (b, with black head and upperparts) shown. *Race muelleri* (c, not shown) as a. Skulking; does not perch but lives exclusively on the ground. Habitat: wet grassland, occasionally in drier areas. Voice: high '*ti-tjeeterik-tjeeterik- - -*' when flushed.

2   **BLACK-CHINNED QUAIL FINCH** *Ortygospiza gabonensis*   L 9 cm. Nominate (a) and race *fuscata* (b) shown. Black b very similar to 1 b, but bill all-red and no white in chin. Habitat: moist grassland. Voice: very high soft '*tiktiktik tjek tiktik-*' when flushed.

3   **LOCUST FINCH** *Ortygospiza locustella*   L 9 cm. As 1 and 2 a ground dweller. Note red wings and pale eyes. Habitat: wet grassland, swamps, open woodland. R

4   **AFRICAN (or Warbling) SILVERBILL** *Lonchura cantans*   L 10 cm. Note creamy colouring and black rump and tail. Habitat: dry open areas, often near settlement.

5   **BRONZE MANNIKIN** *Lonchura cucullata*   L 9 cm. Note plain bill. Imm from imm 6 by buff-brown breast (and upperparts) and dark-grey bill. Flies in small swarms as small, dancing black dots. Habitat: long grass in woodland, bush, cultivation, marshes, suburbs.

6   **BI-COLOURED (Black-and-white or Red-backed) MANNIKIN** *Lonchura bicolor*   L 9 cm. Not all races depicted, nominate (a), *poensis* (b, with rump and flight feathers spotted white) and *nigriceps* (c, with rufous back) shown. Note dark upperparts of imm with pale-grey bill. Habitat: forest edges, woodland, bush, grassland, cultivation, suburbs.

7   **MAGPIE MANNIKIN** *Lonchura fringilloides*   L 11 cm. Some pale rufous to flanks. Imm from imm 6 by larger size and darker bill. Often together with other mannikins. Habitat: forest edges, moist shrubby woodland, gardens.

8   **ZEBRA WAXBILL (or Goldbreast)** *Amandava subflava*   L 9 cm. Unmistakable. Habitat: wet tall grassland, reedbeds, herbage at forest edge.

9   **CORDON-BLEU (or Blue Waxbill)** *Uraeginthus angolensis*   L 12 cm. The ♂ from ♀ (and from ♀ 10) by blue colouring extending onto lower flanks. The ♀ not safely separable from ♀ 10, but ♂ and ♀ of both species are normally seen together, making confusion unlikely. Habitat: thickets in woodland, bush.

10   **RED-CHEEKED CORDON-BLEU** *Uraeginthus bengalus*   L 13 cm. See 9. Habitat: woodland, bush, often near settlement.

11   **GOLDEN-BREASTED BUNTING** *Emberiza flaviventris*   L 15 cm. White streak below eye and broad white wing bars diagnostic. Habitat: woodland, thornbush, plantations, gardens. Voice: very high siffled '*tueeh-tueeh-tueeh*'.

12   **CABANIS'S BUNTING** *Emberiza cabanisi*   L 16 cm. Nominate (a) and race *orientalis* (b, with buffish-and-grey upperparts) shown. From 11 by absence of white stripe direct under eye. Habitat: miombo and other types of woodland, and bush. Voice: extreme high tit-like fast '*fijuut-fijuut-fijuut-fijuut-tuder-jeet-tuder-jeet-*' ('*-tude-*' very short and soft).

13   **HOUSE BUNTING** *Emberiza striolata*   L 13 cm. Only bunting with streaked chin and throat Upperparts, except head, uniform buff-rufous, without red wing flash as 16 or wing bars as 17. Habitat: arid stony areas. R

14   **LARK-LIKE BUNTING** *Emberiza impetuani*   L 13 cm. From (most) true larks by longer tail, smaller bill and more horizontal stance. Note typical bunting form of bill with lower mandible seemingly larger than upper mandible. Habitat: dry rocky areas with scarce scrub cover. Voice: mid-high Chaffinch-like '*tjuder-weeet-weet*'. R

15   **BROWN-RUMPED (or Nigerian) BUNTING** *Emberiza affinis* (formerly *forbesi*)   L 14 cm. From 11 by lack of white in wings. Habitat: dry open woodland.

16   **CINNAMON-BREASTED (Rock) BUNTING** *Emberiza tahapisi*   L 15 cm. Conspicuous orange-red wing panel in flight. Habitat: dry wooded and bushed areas with rocky slopes. Often at road sides. Voice: very high short '*tuder-fiu-weet*' ('*-fiu-*' as a sort of much higher overtone). AM

17   **ROCK BUNTING** *Emberiza cia*   L 16 cm. Note white wing bars and rufous underparts. Habitat: open rocky areas. (?)

◀

Plate 109

1   **ORIOLE FINCH** *Linurgus olivaceus*   L 13 cm. From all other small yellow birds by orange bill and black nape. Habitat: undergrowth at montane forest edges.

2   **LINNET** *Carduelis cannabina*   L 13 cm. Note diagnostic combination of grey head with buff (orange) mantle. Characteristic '*twit-twit twit-twit-twit -*' on rising. Habitat: places with grass, trees, hedges, scrub, including cultivation, orchards, plantations. V

3   **GREENFINCH** *Carduelis chloris*   L 15 cm. Greenish with much yellow in wings and tail, especially in flight. Habitat: woodland, hedges, gardens, cultivation. Note: Goldfinch *Carduelis carduelis* (not shown) with striking red-white-and-black head colouring and yellow wing bar probably died out on Santiago (Cape Verde), where it was introduced. V

4   **TRUMPETER FINCH** *Rhodopechys githanginea*   L 14 cm. Note orange bill and pure grey to head in all dresses. Habitat: rocky and stony deserts and semi-deserts.

5   **SÃO TOMÉ GROSBEAK** *Neospiza concolor*   L 19 cm. One of the rarest existing birds, seen only a few times (about 1890 and 1991). Only on São Tomé, where no similar bird occurs in its habitat: Habitat: tall forest trees. E, São Tomé.

6   **YELLOW-RUMPED (or Black-throated) SEEDEATER (or Canary)** *Serinus atrogularis*   L 11 cm. Blackish throat patch very variable, sometimes absent. Note diagnostic yellow rump in flight. Habitat: woodland, thornbush, farmland. Voice: very high mumbled continuous flow of warbles, flutes, trills and rolls.

7   **WHITE-RUMPED SEEDEATER (or Canary)** *Serinus leucopygius*   L 10 cm. Note white rump and pale colouring. Habitat: wooded and bushed, natural and cultivated areas, including gardens.

8   **STRIPE-BREASTED SEEDEATER** *Serinus reichardi*   L 15 cm. From 9 by whitish, lightly striped breast and by different range. Often treated as race of 9. Habitat: as 9.

9   **STREAKY-HEADED SEEDEATER** *Serinus gularis*   L 15 cm. Ad from 8 by unmarked underparts. Imm (not shown) from 8 by warmer-brown plumage with slightly heavier striping above and by less prominent eyebrow. Habitat: miombo, bush, cultivation, gardens. Voice: sequence of high short up-and-down rattles, flutes and trills.

10   **YELLOW-CROWNED CANARY** *Serinus canicollis*   L 13 cm. Note striking double wing bars. Habitat: from montane grassland to coastal scrub, including gardens. Voice: very high very rapid sustained fluted warbling with basic '-fiu-' sound.

11   **AFRICAN CITRIL** *Serinus citrinelloides*   L 12 cm. With longer, sharper bill than 13, and with more striped flanks. Small area of overlapping ranges. Habitat: forest edges, bamboo, woodland, lake sides, cultivation, gardens.

12   **PAPYRUS CANARY** *Serinus koliensis*   L 12 cm. Note stubby bill and rather ill-defined wing bars. Restricted range and habitat. Habitat: papyrus swamps. R

13   **BLACK-FACED CANARY** *Serinus capistratus*   L 12 cm. From 11 by stubbier bill, less streaked underparts and different, just overlapping range. Habitat: forest edges and clearings, swamps.

14   **YELLOW-FRONTED (or -eyed) CANARY** *Serinus mozambicus*   L 12 cm. Note sharply demarcated eyebrow and cheek, black moustachial stripe, small pointed bill, yellow rump. Habitat: open forest, woodland, bush, suburbs. Voice: very high hurried fluted variations on a short strophe '*prt-preep-irre-pieeh-weeh*'.

15   **BRIMSTONE (or Bully) CANARY** *Serinus sulphuratus*   L 15 cm. From 14 by larger size, large bill and green (not yellow) rump. Habitat: open woodland, bush, forest edges. Voice: very high short warbled medleys of up-and-down flutes, trills and rolls.

16   **BLACK-EARED SEEDEATER** *Serinus mennelli*   L 13 cm. The ♀ (not shown) from ♂ by dark brown (not black) face sides. Habitat: miombo and other types of woodland. Voice: basically a sustained flow of three short phrases together sounding as '-*wuhwuh-feeh-tjèh-*'.

17   **THICK-BILLED SEEDEATER** *Serinus burtoni*   L 15 cm. Race *tanganjicae* (a) shown and nominate (b, white on forehead). Large with very heavy bill. Habitat: undergrowth of montane forest, bamboo. R

▶

Plate 109 (continued)

18   **STREAKY SEEDEATER** *Serinus striolatus*   L 15 cm. Heavily streaked; note characteristic face pattern. Often shows a greenish panel in closed wing. Habitat: montane forest edges.

19   **PRÍNCIPE SEEDEATER** *Serinus rufobrunneus*   L 12 cm. Strikingly short-tailed. No similar bird in its range. Nominate (a, Príncipe) and race *thomensis* (b, São Tomé) shown. Habitat: forest edge, woodland, plantations gardens. E, São Tomé and Príncipe.

DISTRIBUTION MAPS

The first and most important step when trying to identify an unknown species is by comparing it with the plates. Confirmation of an identification is possible when the bird is seen in its habitat as described in the captions opposite the plates.

The chances of seeing a particular bird refer to the likelihood of its being seen in its habitat and range.

The information about range and status, provided in the distribution maps for all species described and illustrated in the book, can support or weaken your identification.

Look for instance at maps 106.15 and 106.16, which give the ranges of the only two red-legged indigobirds; it is very unlikely, that you will have seen the Variable Indigobird (105.16) in Ghana or elsewhere in West Africa, because according to the maps this species is restricted to Gabon and the Congo's.

The English bird names are given below the maps: each map is further referenced to its species by the plate number and species number (e.g. species number 4 on plate 20 is 20.4).

The shaded areas on the maps give a rough impression of the known range of the species. The status is indicated by the intensity of the shading, an asterix or a thin cross.

An **asterix** in a map indicates the place of a small population of a species cut-off from its main range by the border of our area (e.g. see map 46.6 of the Red-backed Mousebird, who has its main range in southern Africa) or points to a small isolated population of a species (e.g. see map 12.14 of Hartlaub's Duck, which has a small isolated population in the wetlands of Mali, but is frequent to common in the more southern forested areas).

A **small cross** refers to a the place where only incidentally a certain species was sighted.

STATUS KEY

STATUS	CHANCE OF SEEING SPECIES	MAPS	INDICATION IN THE TEXT
Common	60-100%	Dark shading	
Frequent	10-60%	Mid-grey shading	
Uncommon	Very small	Pale grey shading	
Small or cut off population	10-100%	Asterix	
Rare or vagrant	Negligible	Small cross	R or V
Uncertain	?	?	(?)
Introduced		(I)	(I)

If no other information within the framework of a map is given the particular species is a breeding resident in the indicated area. If there is a code in the bottom left corner of a map, the species is at least partly a migrant (see migration key).

DISTRIBUTION MAPS

MIGRATION KEY

RES   Resident (only applied, when needed in combination with another symbol)

AM   African Migrant, migrating from other parts within the area or from elsewhere in Africa

NM   Northern Migrant, migrating from Europe, North Africa and the Middle East

EM   Eastern Migrant, migrating from the Far East

WM   Western Migrant, migrating from the Americas

( )   Brackets around a symbol are applied in combinations with other symbols to indicate an insubordinate role. E.g. RES/(NM) indicates a resident species, which numbers are slightly augmented in the period of the northern winter

- - - - -   An interrupted line indicates a breeding visitor north or south of that line

↓ ↓ ↓   Arrows are put in areas, that are only/mainly overflown by migrants

OTHER SYMBOLS USED IN THE MAPS

V   Vagrant
R   Rare
E   Endemic

RACES

Races within the range of a species are indicated by letters (**a, b, c**) on the maps as mentioned in the plate captions. See for instance map 7.4 (Purple Heron) or 27.3 (Plumed Guineafowl).

EXAMPLE

This is the map of the Abdim's Stork. It is frequent in a zone from East Senegal to the Sudan, uncommon in the southern parts of Gabon and both the Congo's, while small populations exist in Sierra Leone and Liberia; it has incidentally been reported from The Gambia and the South of Ghana and Nigeria, while it might occur in the centre of the D. R. of Congo. The birds seen south of the interrupted line are breeding migrants from the North.

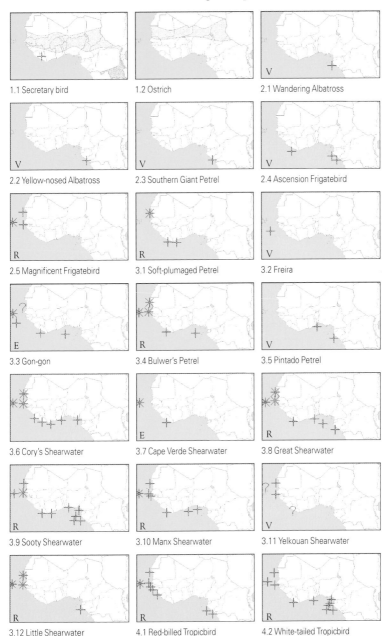

1.1 Secretary bird

1.2 Ostrich

2.1 Wandering Albatross

2.2 Yellow-nosed Albatross

2.3 Southern Giant Petrel

2.4 Ascension Frigatebird

2.5 Magnificent Frigatebird

3.1 Soft-plumaged Petrel

3.2 Freira

3.3 Gon-gon

3.4 Bulwer's Petrel

3.5 Pintado Petrel

3.6 Cory's Shearwater

3.7 Cape Verde Shearwater

3.8 Great Shearwater

3.9 Sooty Shearwater

3.10 Manx Shearwater

3.11 Yelkouan Shearwater

3.12 Little Shearwater

4.1 Red-billed Tropicbird

4.2 White-tailed Tropicbird

Maps for species numbers 4.3 to 7.2

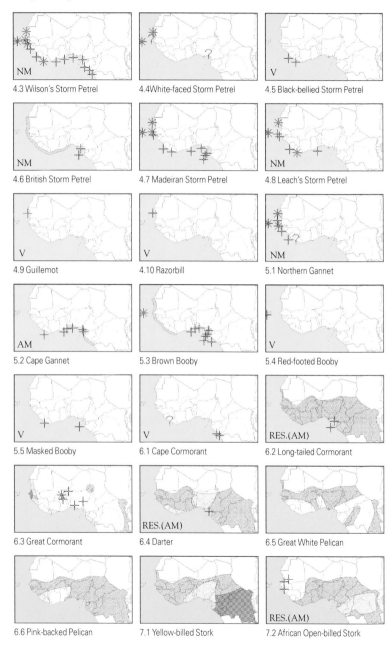

4.3 Wilson's Storm Petrel

4.4 White-faced Storm Petrel

4.5 Black-bellied Storm Petrel

4.6 British Storm Petrel

4.7 Madeiran Storm Petrel

4.8 Leach's Storm Petrel

4.9 Guillemot

4.10 Razorbill

5.1 Northern Gannet

5.2 Cape Gannet

5.3 Brown Booby

5.4 Red-footed Booby

5.5 Masked Booby

6.1 Cape Cormorant

6.2 Long-tailed Cormorant

6.3 Great Cormorant

6.4 Darter

6.5 Great White Pelican

6.6 Pink-backed Pelican

7.1 Yellow-billed Stork

7.2 African Open-billed Stork

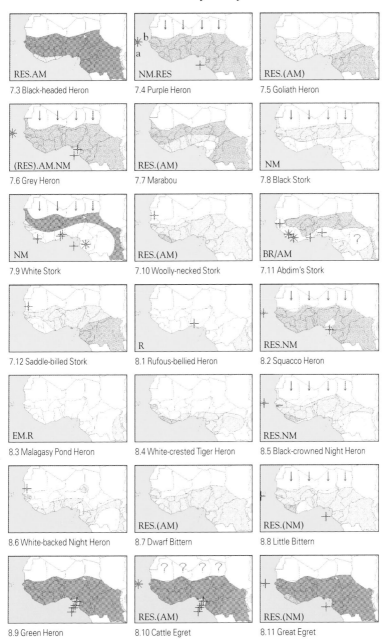

7.3 Black-headed Heron

7.4 Purple Heron

7.5 Goliath Heron

7.6 Grey Heron

7.7 Marabou

7.8 Black Stork

7.9 White Stork

7.10 Woolly-necked Stork

7.11 Abdim's Stork

7.12 Saddle-billed Stork

8.1 Rufous-bellied Heron

8.2 Squacco Heron

8.3 Malagasy Pond Heron

8.4 White-crested Tiger Heron

8.5 Black-crowned Night Heron

8.6 White-backed Night Heron

8.7 Dwarf Bittern

8.8 Little Bittern

8.9 Green Heron

8.10 Cattle Egret

8.11 Great Egret

Maps for species numbers 8.12 to 10.4

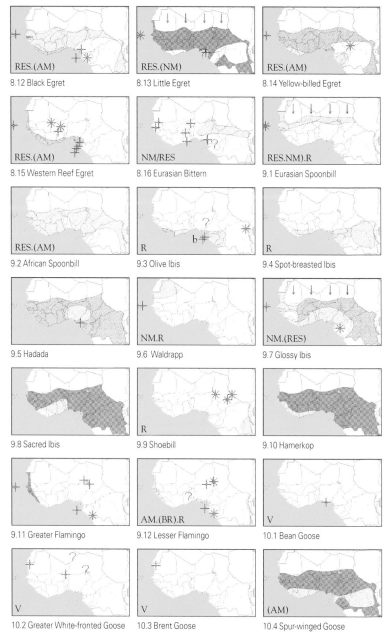

8.12 Black Egret

8.13 Little Egret

8.14 Yellow-billed Egret

8.15 Western Reef Egret

8.16 Eurasian Bittern

9.1 Eurasian Spoonbill

9.2 African Spoonbill

9.3 Olive Ibis

9.4 Spot-breasted Ibis

9.5 Hadada

9.6 Waldrapp

9.7 Glossy Ibis

9.8 Sacred Ibis

9.9 Shoebill

9.10 Hamerkop

9.11 Greater Flamingo

9.12 Lesser Flamingo

10.1 Bean Goose

10.2 Greater White-fronted Goose

10.3 Brent Goose

10.4 Spur-winged Goose

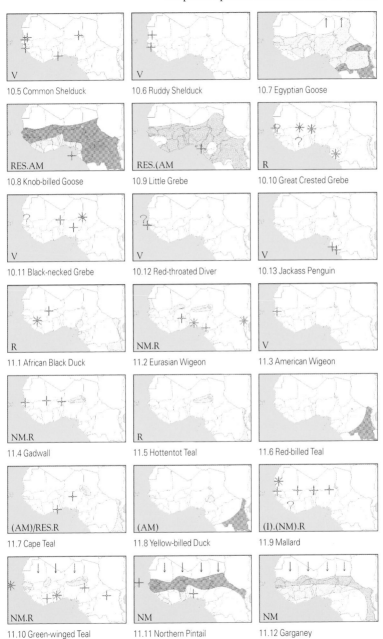

10.5 Common Shelduck

10.6 Ruddy Shelduck

10.7 Egyptian Goose

10.8 Knob-billed Goose

10.9 Little Grebe

10.10 Great Crested Grebe

10.11 Black-necked Grebe

10.12 Red-throated Diver

10.13 Jackass Penguin

11.1 African Black Duck

11.2 Eurasian Wigeon

11.3 American Wigeon

11.4 Gadwall

11.5 Hottentot Teal

11.6 Red-billed Teal

11.7 Cape Teal

11.8 Yellow-billed Duck

11.9 Mallard

11.10 Green-winged Teal

11.11 Northern Pintail

11.12 Garganey

Maps for species numbers 11.13 to 13.5b

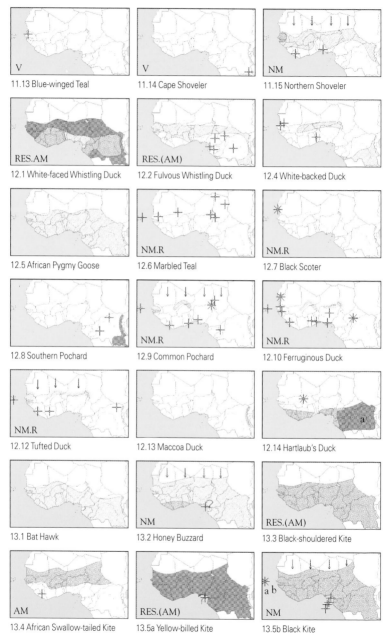

11.13 Blue-winged Teal

11.14 Cape Shoveler

11.15 Northern Shoveler

12.1 White-faced Whistling Duck

12.2 Fulvous Whistling Duck

12.4 White-backed Duck

12.5 African Pygmy Goose

12.6 Marbled Teal

12.7 Black Scoter

12.8 Southern Pochard

12.9 Common Pochard

12.10 Ferruginous Duck

12.12 Tufted Duck

12.13 Maccoa Duck

12.14 Hartlaub's Duck

13.1 Bat Hawk

13.2 Honey Buzzard

13.3 Black-shouldered Kite

13.4 African Swallow-tailed Kite

13.5a Yellow-billed Kite

13.5b Black Kite

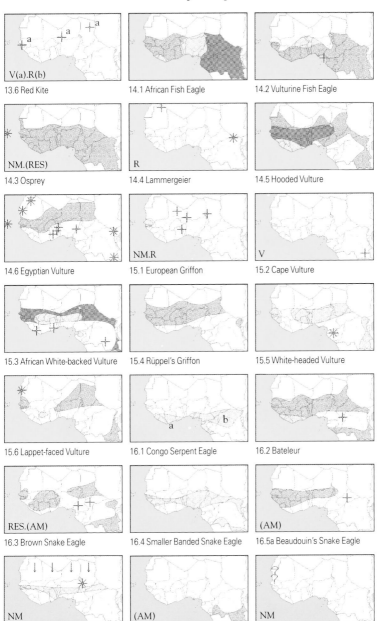

13.6 Red Kite

14.1 African Fish Eagle

14.2 Vulturine Fish Eagle

14.3 Osprey

14.4 Lammergeier

14.5 Hooded Vulture

14.6 Egyptian Vulture

15.1 European Griffon

15.2 Cape Vulture

15.3 African White-backed Vulture

15.4 Rüppel's Griffon

15.5 White-headed Vulture

15.6 Lappet-faced Vulture

16.1 Congo Serpent Eagle

16.2 Bateleur

16.3 Brown Snake Eagle

16.4 Smaller Banded Snake Eagle

16.5a Beaudouin's Snake Eagle

16.5b European Snake Eagle

16.5c Black-breasted Snake Eagle

17.1 Northern Harrier

267

Maps for species numbers 17.2 to 20.6

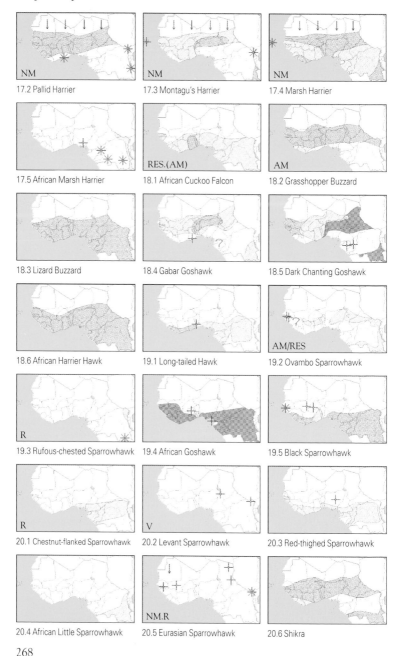

17.2 Pallid Harrier

17.3 Montagu's Harrier

17.4 Marsh Harrier

17.5 African Marsh Harrier

18.1 African Cuckoo Falcon

18.2 Grasshopper Buzzard

18.3 Lizard Buzzard

18.4 Gabar Goshawk

18.5 Dark Chanting Goshawk

18.6 African Harrier Hawk

19.1 Long-tailed Hawk

19.2 Ovambo Sparrowhawk

19.3 Rufous-chested Sparrowhawk

19.4 African Goshawk

19.5 Black Sparrowhawk

20.1 Chestnut-flanked Sparrowhawk

20.2 Levant Sparrowhawk

20.3 Red-thighed Sparrowhawk

20.4 African Little Sparrowhawk

20.5 Eurasian Sparrowhawk

20.6 Shikra

Maps for species numbers 21.1 to 24.6

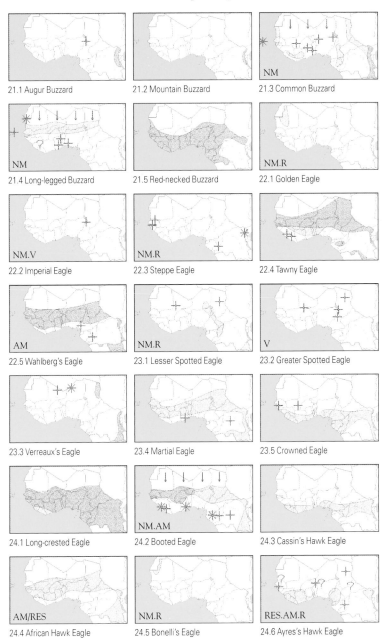

21.1 Augur Buzzard

21.2 Mountain Buzzard

21.3 Common Buzzard

21.4 Long-legged Buzzard

21.5 Red-necked Buzzard

22.1 Golden Eagle

22.2 Imperial Eagle

22.3 Steppe Eagle

22.4 Tawny Eagle

22.5 Wahlberg's Eagle

23.1 Lesser Spotted Eagle

23.2 Greater Spotted Eagle

23.3 Verreaux's Eagle

23.4 Martial Eagle

23.5 Crowned Eagle

24.1 Long-crested Eagle

24.2 Booted Eagle

24.3 Cassin's Hawk Eagle

24.4 African Hawk Eagle

24.5 Bonelli's Eagle

24.6 Ayres's Hawk Eagle

Maps for species numbers 25.1 to 27.3

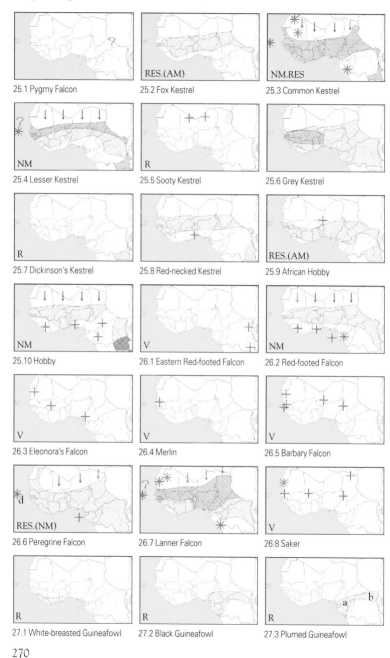

25.1 Pygmy Falcon

25.2 Fox Kestrel

25.3 Common Kestrel

25.4 Lesser Kestrel

25.5 Sooty Kestrel

25.6 Grey Kestrel

25.7 Dickinson's Kestrel

25.8 Red-necked Kestrel

25.9 African Hobby

25.10 Hobby

26.1 Eastern Red-footed Falcon

26.2 Red-footed Falcon

26.3 Eleonora's Falcon

26.4 Merlin

26.5 Barbary Falcon

26.6 Peregrine Falcon

26.7 Lanner Falcon

26.8 Saker

27.1 White-breasted Guineafowl

27.2 Black Guineafowl

27.3 Plumed Guineafowl

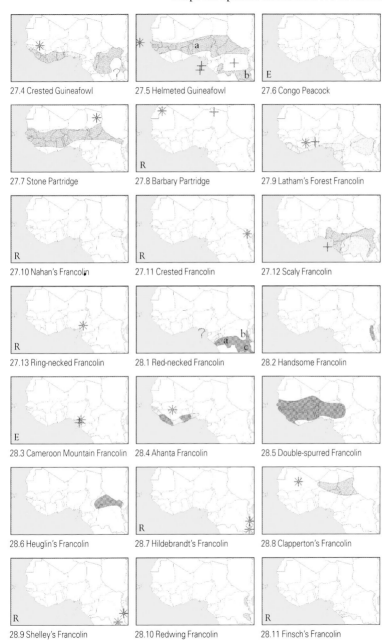

27.4 Crested Guineafowl

27.5 Helmeted Guineafowl

27.6 Congo Peacock

27.7 Stone Partridge

27.8 Barbary Partridge

27.9 Latham's Forest Francolin

27.10 Nahan's Francolin

27.11 Crested Francolin

27.12 Scaly Francolin

27.13 Ring-necked Francolin

28.1 Red-necked Francolin

28.2 Handsome Francolin

28.3 Cameroon Mountain Francolin

28.4 Ahanta Francolin

28.5 Double-spurred Francolin

28.6 Heuglin's Francolin

28.7 Hildebrandt's Francolin

28.8 Clapperton's Francolin

28.9 Shelley's Francolin

28.10 Redwing Francolin

28.11 Finsch's Francolin

271

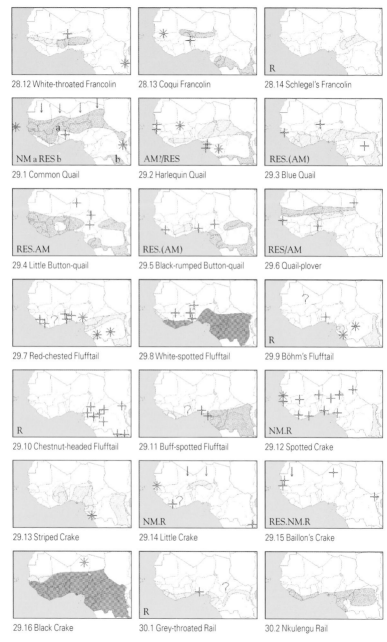

28.12 White-throated Francolin

28.13 Coqui Francolin

28.14 Schlegel's Francolin

29.1 Common Quail

29.2 Harlequin Quail

29.3 Blue Quail

29.4 Little Button-quail

29.5 Black-rumped Button-quail

29.6 Quail-plover

29.7 Red-chested Flufftail

29.8 White-spotted Flufftail

29.9 Böhm's Flufftail

29.10 Chestnut-headed Flufftail

29.11 Buff-spotted Flufftail

29.12 Spotted Crake

29.13 Striped Crake

29.14 Little Crake

29.15 Baillon's Crake

29.16 Black Crake

30.1 Grey-throated Rail

30.2 Nkulengu Rail

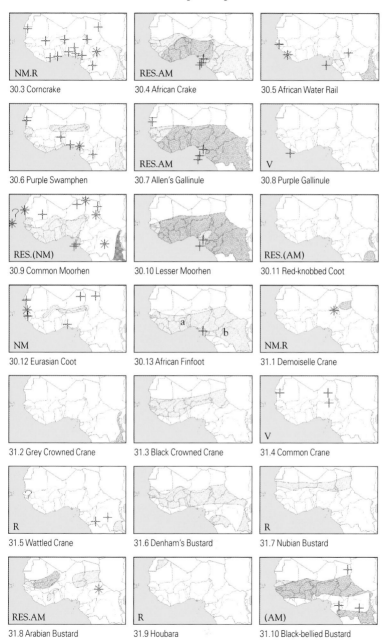

30.3 Corncrake

30.4 African Crake

30.5 African Water Rail

30.6 Purple Swamphen

30.7 Allen's Gallinule

30.8 Purple Gallinule

30.9 Common Moorhen

30.10 Lesser Moorhen

30.11 Red-knobbed Coot

30.12 Eurasian Coot

30.13 African Finfoot

31.1 Demoiselle Crane

31.2 Grey Crowned Crane

31.3 Black Crowned Crane

31.4 Common Crane

31.5 Wattled Crane

31.6 Denham's Bustard

31.7 Nubian Bustard

31.8 Arabian Bustard

31.9 Houbara

31.10 Black-bellied Bustard

273

Maps for species numbers 31.11 to 33.9

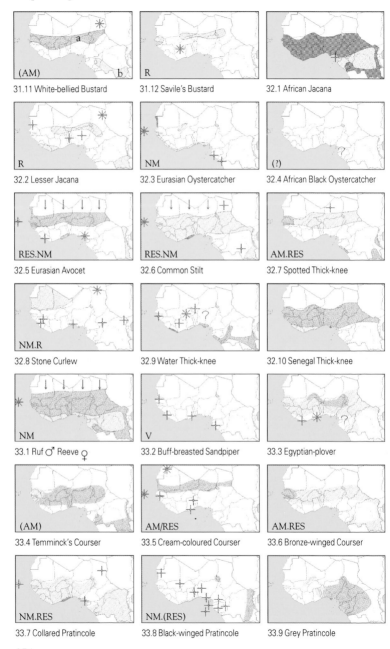

31.11 White-bellied Bustard

31.12 Savile's Bustard

32.1 African Jacana

32.2 Lesser Jacana

32.3 Eurasian Oystercatcher

32.4 African Black Oystercatcher

32.5 Eurasian Avocet

32.6 Common Stilt

32.7 Spotted Thick-knee

32.8 Stone Curlew

32.9 Water Thick-knee

32.10 Senegal Thick-knee

33.1 Ruf ♂ Reeve ♀

33.2 Buff-breasted Sandpiper

33.3 Egyptian-plover

33.4 Temminck's Courser

33.5 Cream-coloured Courser

33.6 Bronze-winged Courser

33.7 Collared Pratincole

33.8 Black-winged Pratincole

33.9 Grey Pratincole

274

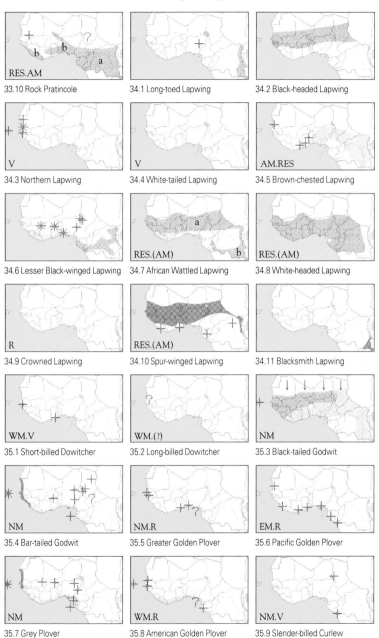

33.10 Rock Pratincole

34.1 Long-toed Lapwing

34.2 Black-headed Lapwing

34.3 Northern Lapwing

34.4 White-tailed Lapwing

34.5 Brown-chested Lapwing

34.6 Lesser Black-winged Lapwing

34.7 African Wattled Lapwing

34.8 White-headed Lapwing

34.9 Crowned Lapwing

34.10 Spur-winged Lapwing

34.11 Blacksmith Lapwing

35.1 Short-billed Dowitcher

35.2 Long-billed Dowitcher

35.3 Black-tailed Godwit

35.4 Bar-tailed Godwit

35.5 Greater Golden Plover

35.6 Pacific Golden Plover

35.7 Grey Plover

35.8 American Golden Plover

35.9 Slender-billed Curlew

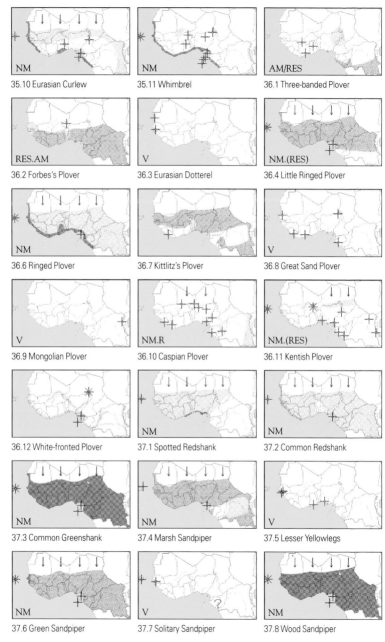

35.10 Eurasian Curlew

35.11 Whimbrel

36.1 Three-banded Plover

36.2 Forbes's Plover

36.3 Eurasian Dotterel

36.4 Little Ringed Plover

36.6 Ringed Plover

36.7 Kittlitz's Plover

36.8 Great Sand Plover

36.9 Mongolian Plover

36.10 Caspian Plover

36.11 Kentish Plover

36.12 White-fronted Plover

37.1 Spotted Redshank

37.2 Common Redshank

37.3 Common Greenshank

37.4 Marsh Sandpiper

37.5 Lesser Yellowlegs

37.6 Green Sandpiper

37.7 Solitary Sandpiper

37.8 Wood Sandpiper

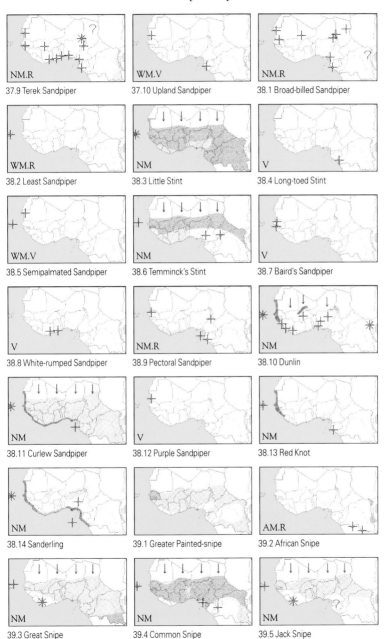

37.9 Terek Sandpiper

37.10 Upland Sandpiper

38.1 Broad-billed Sandpiper

38.2 Least Sandpiper

38.3 Little Stint

38.4 Long-toed Stint

38.5 Semipalmated Sandpiper

38.6 Temminck's Stint

38.7 Baird's Sandpiper

38.8 White-rumped Sandpiper

38.9 Pectoral Sandpiper

38.10 Dunlin

38.11 Curlew Sandpiper

38.12 Purple Sandpiper

38.13 Red Knot

38.14 Sanderling

39.1 Greater Painted-snipe

39.2 African Snipe

39.3 Great Snipe

39.4 Common Snipe

39.5 Jack Snipe

277

Maps for species numbers 39.6 to 41.7

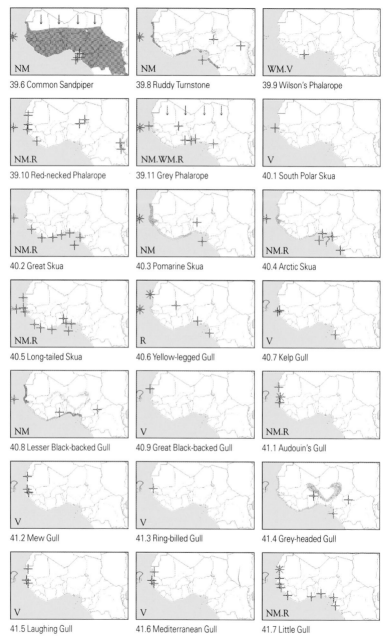

39.6 Common Sandpiper

39.8 Ruddy Turnstone

39.9 Wilson's Phalarope

39.10 Red-necked Phalarope

39.11 Grey Phalarope

40.1 South Polar Skua

40.2 Great Skua

40.3 Pomarine Skua

40.4 Arctic Skua

40.5 Long-tailed Skua

40.6 Yellow-legged Gull

40.7 Kelp Gull

40.8 Lesser Black-backed Gull

40.9 Great Black-backed Gull

41.1 Audouin's Gull

41.2 Mew Gull

41.3 Ring-billed Gull

41.4 Grey-headed Gull

41.5 Laughing Gull

41.6 Mediterranean Gull

41.7 Little Gull

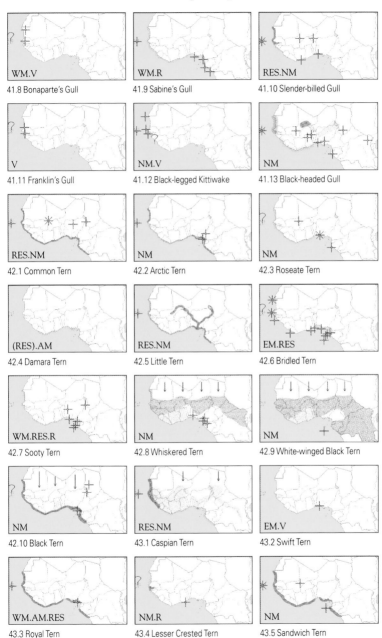

41.8 Bonaparte's Gull

41.9 Sabine's Gull

41.10 Slender-billed Gull

41.11 Franklin's Gull

41.12 Black-legged Kittiwake

41.13 Black-headed Gull

42.1 Common Tern

42.2 Arctic Tern

42.3 Roseate Tern

42.4 Damara Tern

42.5 Little Tern

42.6 Bridled Tern

42.7 Sooty Tern

42.8 Whiskered Tern

42.9 White-winged Black Tern

42.10 Black Tern

43.1 Caspian Tern

43.2 Swift Tern

43.3 Royal Tern

43.4 Lesser Crested Tern

43.5 Sandwich Tern

Maps for species numbers 43.6 to 44.16

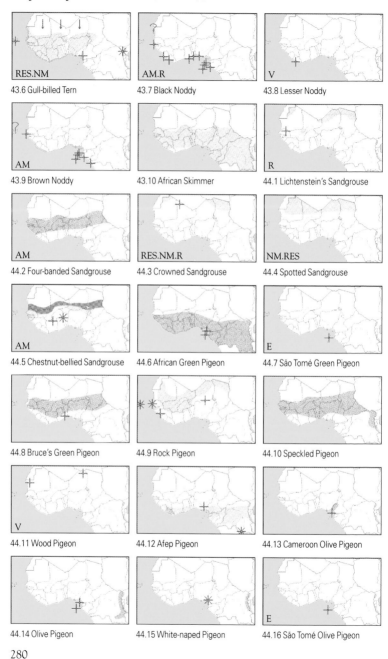

43.6 Gull-billed Tern

43.7 Black Noddy

43.8 Lesser Noddy

43.9 Brown Noddy

43.10 African Skimmer

44.1 Lichtenstein's Sandgrouse

44.2 Four-banded Sandgrouse

44.3 Crowned Sandgrouse

44.4 Spotted Sandgrouse

44.5 Chestnut-bellied Sandgrouse

44.6 African Green Pigeon

44.7 São Tomé Green Pigeon

44.8 Bruce's Green Pigeon

44.9 Rock Pigeon

44.10 Speckled Pigeon

44.11 Wood Pigeon

44.12 Afep Pigeon

44.13 Cameroon Olive Pigeon

44.14 Olive Pigeon

44.15 White-naped Pigeon

44.16 São Tomé Olive Pigeon

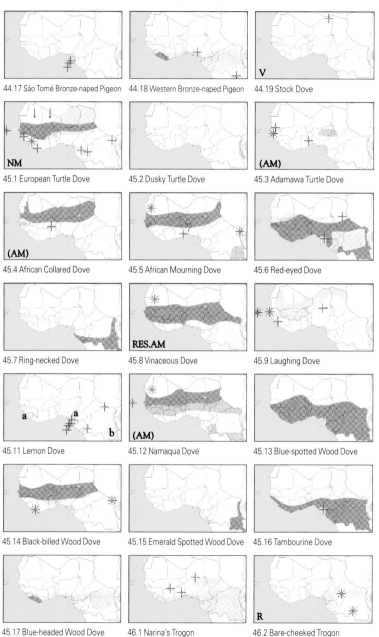

44.17 São Tomé Bronze-naped Pigeon

44.18 Western Bronze-naped Pigeon

44.19 Stock Dove

45.1 European Turtle Dove

45.2 Dusky Turtle Dove

45.3 Adamawa Turtle Dove

45.4 African Collared Dove

45.5 African Mourning Dove

45.6 Red-eyed Dove

45.7 Ring-necked Dove

45.8 Vinaceous Dove

45.9 Laughing Dove

45.11 Lemon Dove

45.12 Namaqua Dove

45.13 Blue-spotted Wood Dove

45.14 Black-billed Wood Dove

45.15 Emerald Spotted Wood Dove

45.16 Tambourine Dove

45.17 Blue-headed Wood Dove

46.1 Narina's Trogon

46.2 Bare-cheeked Trogon

281

Maps for species numbers 46.3 to 47.6

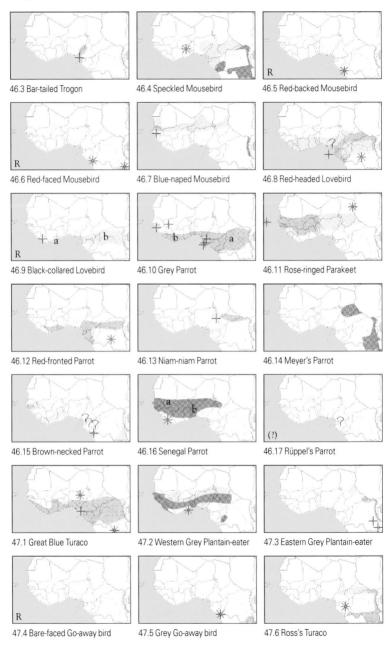

46.3 Bar-tailed Trogon

46.4 Speckled Mousebird

46.5 Red-backed Mousebird

46.6 Red-faced Mousebird

46.7 Blue-naped Mousebird

46.8 Red-headed Lovebird

46.9 Black-collared Lovebird

46.10 Grey Parrot

46.11 Rose-ringed Parakeet

46.12 Red-fronted Parrot

46.13 Niam-niam Parrot

46.14 Meyer's Parrot

46.15 Brown-necked Parrot

46.16 Senegal Parrot

46.17 Rüppel's Parrot

47.1 Great Blue Turaco

47.2 Western Grey Plantain-eater

47.3 Eastern Grey Plantain-eater

47.4 Bare-faced Go-away bird

47.5 Grey Go-away bird

47.6 Ross's Turaco

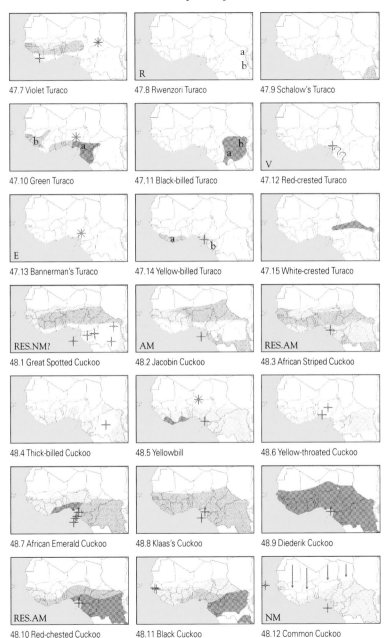

47.7 Violet Turaco

47.8 Rwenzori Turaco

47.9 Schalow's Turaco

47.10 Green Turaco

47.11 Black-billed Turaco

47.12 Red-crested Turaco

47.13 Bannerman's Turaco

47.14 Yellow-billed Turaco

47.15 White-crested Turaco

48.1 Great Spotted Cuckoo

48.2 Jacobin Cuckoo

48.3 African Striped Cuckoo

48.4 Thick-billed Cuckoo

48.5 Yellowbill

48.6 Yellow-throated Cuckoo

48.7 African Emerald Cuckoo

48.8 Klaas's Cuckoo

48.9 Diederik Cuckoo

48.10 Red-chested Cuckoo

48.11 Black Cuckoo

48.12 Common Cuckoo

283

Maps for species numbers 48.13 to 49.15

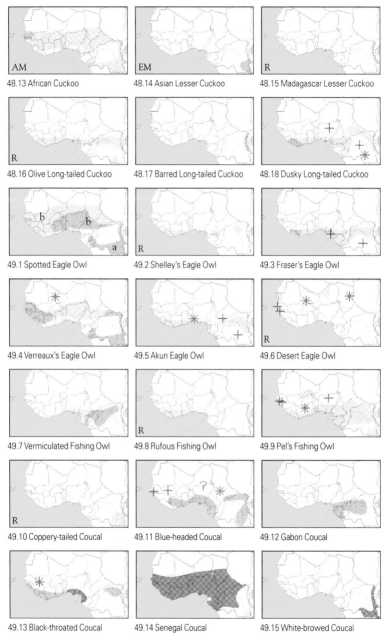

48.13 African Cuckoo

48.14 Asian Lesser Cuckoo

48.15 Madagascar Lesser Cuckoo

48.16 Olive Long-tailed Cuckoo

48.17 Barred Long-tailed Cuckoo

48.18 Dusky Long-tailed Cuckoo

49.1 Spotted Eagle Owl

49.2 Shelley's Eagle Owl

49.3 Fraser's Eagle Owl

49.4 Verreaux's Eagle Owl

49.5 Akun Eagle Owl

49.6 Desert Eagle Owl

49.7 Vermiculated Fishing Owl

49.8 Rufous Fishing Owl

49.9 Pel's Fishing Owl

49.10 Coppery-tailed Coucal

49.11 Blue-headed Coucal

49.12 Gabon Coucal

49.13 Black-throated Coucal

49.14 Senegal Coucal

49.15 White-browed Coucal

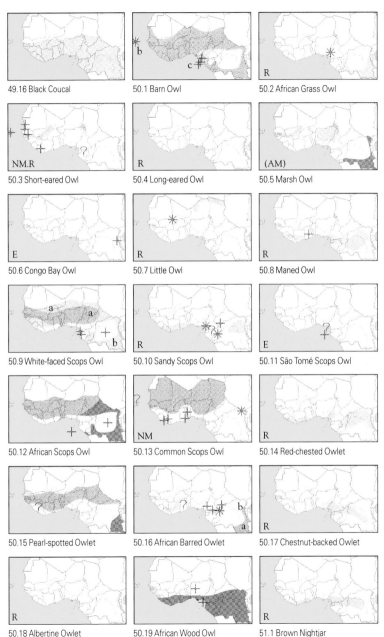

49.16 Black Coucal

50.1 Barn Owl

50.2 African Grass Owl

50.3 Short-eared Owl

50.4 Long-eared Owl

50.5 Marsh Owl

50.6 Congo Bay Owl

50.7 Little Owl

50.8 Maned Owl

50.9 White-faced Scops Owl

50.10 Sandy Scops Owl

50.11 São Tomé Scops Owl

50.12 African Scops Owl

50.13 Common Scops Owl

50.14 Red-chested Owlet

50.15 Pearl-spotted Owlet

50.16 African Barred Owlet

50.17 Chestnut-backed Owlet

50.18 Albertine Owlet

50.19 African Wood Owl

51.1 Brown Nightjar

Maps for species numbers 51.2 to 53.1

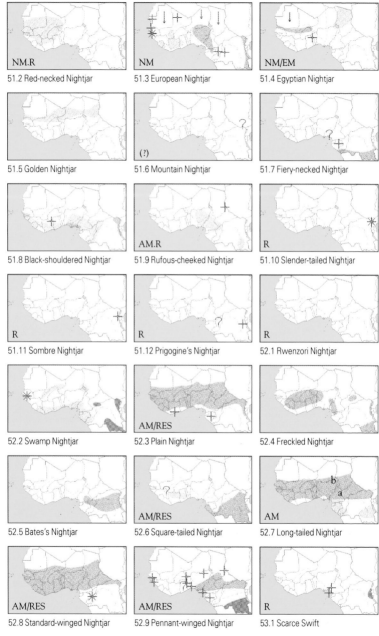

NM.R
51.2 Red-necked Nightjar

NM
51.3 European Nightjar

NM/EM
51.4 Egyptian Nightjar

51.5 Golden Nightjar

(?)
51.6 Mountain Nightjar

?
51.7 Fiery-necked Nightjar

51.8 Black-shouldered Nightjar

AM.R
51.9 Rufous-cheeked Nightjar

R
51.10 Slender-tailed Nightjar

R
51.11 Sombre Nightjar

R
51.12 Prigogine's Nightjar

R
52.1 Rwenzori Nightjar

52.2 Swamp Nightjar

AM/RES
52.3 Plain Nightjar

52.4 Freckled Nightjar

52.5 Bates's Nightjar

AM/RES
52.6 Square-tailed Nightjar

AM
52.7 Long-tailed Nightjar

AM/RES
52.8 Standard-winged Nightjar

AM/RES
52.9 Pennant-winged Nightjar

R
53.1 Scarce Swift

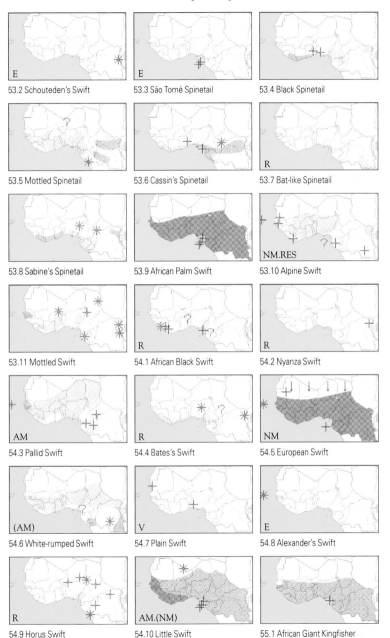

53.2 Schouteden's Swift

53.3 São Tomé Spinetail

53.4 Black Spinetail

53.5 Mottled Spinetail

53.6 Cassin's Spinetail

53.7 Bat-like Spinetail

53.8 Sabine's Spinetail

53.9 African Palm Swift

53.10 Alpine Swift

53.11 Mottled Swift

54.1 African Black Swift

54.2 Nyanza Swift

54.3 Pallid Swift

54.4 Bates's Swift

54.5 European Swift

54.6 White-rumped Swift

54.7 Plain Swift

54.8 Alexander's Swift

54.9 Horus Swift

54.10 Little Swift

55.1 African Giant Kingfisher

Maps for species numbers 55.2 to 56.8

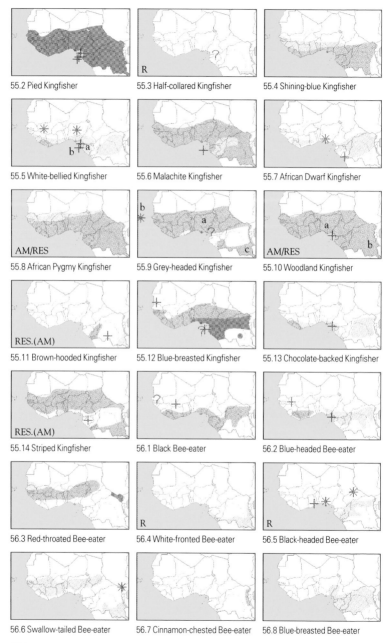

55.2 Pied Kingfisher

55.3 Half-collared Kingfisher

55.4 Shining-blue Kingfisher

55.5 White-bellied Kingfisher

55.6 Malachite Kingfisher

55.7 African Dwarf Kingfisher

55.8 African Pygmy Kingfisher

55.9 Grey-headed Kingfisher

55.10 Woodland Kingfisher

55.11 Brown-hooded Kingfisher

55.12 Blue-breasted Kingfisher

55.13 Chocolate-backed Kingfisher

55.14 Striped Kingfisher

56.1 Black Bee-eater

56.2 Blue-headed Bee-eater

56.3 Red-throated Bee-eater

56.4 White-fronted Bee-eater

56.5 Black-headed Bee-eater

56.6 Swallow-tailed Bee-eater

56.7 Cinnamon-chested Bee-eater

56.8 Blue-breasted Bee-eater

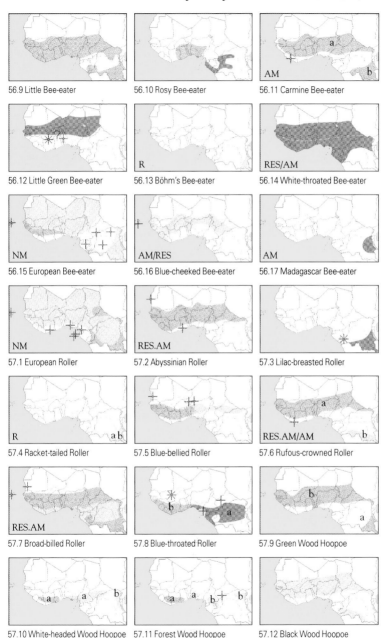

56.9 Little Bee-eater

56.10 Rosy Bee-eater

56.11 Carmine Bee-eater

56.12 Little Green Bee-eater

56.13 Böhm's Bee-eater

56.14 White-throated Bee-eater

56.15 European Bee-eater

56.16 Blue-cheeked Bee-eater

56.17 Madagascar Bee-eater

57.1 European Roller

57.2 Abyssinian Roller

57.3 Lilac-breasted Roller

57.4 Racket-tailed Roller

57.5 Blue-bellied Roller

57.6 Rufous-crowned Roller

57.7 Broad-billed Roller

57.8 Blue-throated Roller

57.9 Green Wood Hoopoe

57.10 White-headed Wood Hoopoe

57.11 Forest Wood Hoopoe

57.12 Black Wood Hoopoe

Maps for species numbers 57.13 to 59.3

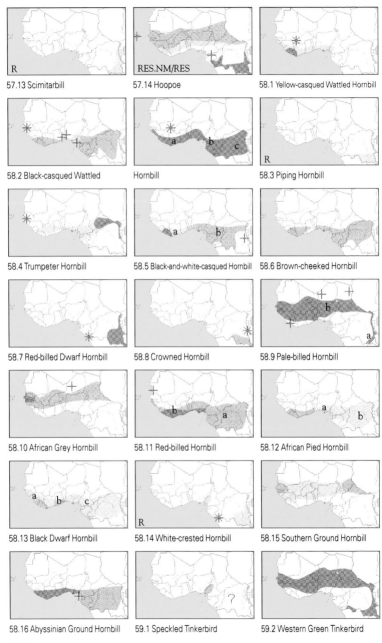

57.13 Scimitarbill

57.14 Hoopoe

58.1 Yellow-casqued Wattled Hornbill

58.2 Black-casqued Wattled Hornbill

58.3 Piping Hornbill

58.4 Trumpeter Hornbill

58.5 Black-and-white-casqued Hornbill

58.6 Brown-cheeked Hornbill

58.7 Red-billed Dwarf Hornbill

58.8 Crowned Hornbill

58.9 Pale-billed Hornbill

58.10 African Grey Hornbill

58.11 Red-billed Hornbill

58.12 African Pied Hornbill

58.13 Black Dwarf Hornbill

58.14 White-crested Hornbill

58.15 Southern Ground Hornbill

58.16 Abyssinian Ground Hornbill

59.1 Speckled Tinkerbird

59.2 Western Green Tinkerbird

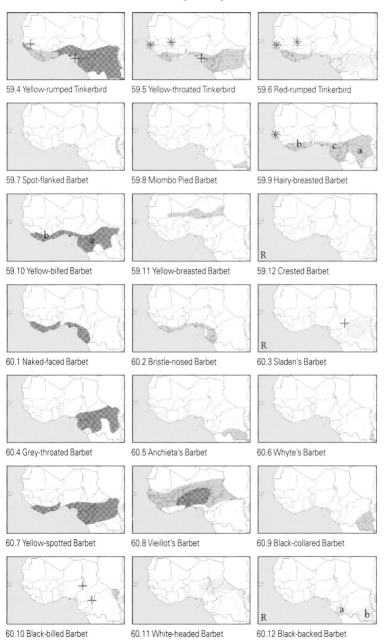

59.4 Yellow-rumped Tinkerbird

59.5 Yellow-throated Tinkerbird

59.6 Red-rumped Tinkerbird

59.7 Spot-flanked Barbet

59.8 Miombo Pied Barbet

59.9 Hairy-breasted Barbet

59.10 Yellow-billed Barbet

59.11 Yellow-breasted Barbet

59.12 Crested Barbet

60.1 Naked-faced Barbet

60.2 Bristle-nosed Barbet

60.3 Sladen's Barbet

60.4 Grey-throated Barbet

60.5 Anchieta's Barbet

60.6 Whyte's Barbet

60.7 Yellow-spotted Barbet

60.8 Vieillot's Barbet

60.9 Black-collared Barbet

60.10 Black-billed Barbet

60.11 White-headed Barbet

60.12 Black-backed Barbet

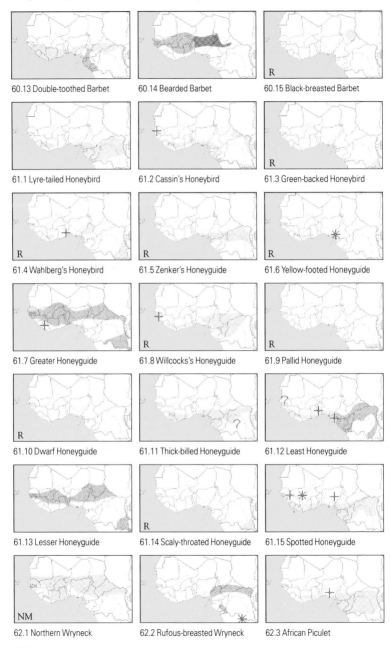

60.13 Double-toothed Barbet

60.14 Bearded Barbet

60.15 Black-breasted Barbet

61.1 Lyre-tailed Honeybird

61.2 Cassin's Honeybird

61.3 Green-backed Honeybird

61.4 Wahlberg's Honeybird

61.5 Zenker's Honeyguide

61.6 Yellow-footed Honeyguide

61.7 Greater Honeyguide

61.8 Willcocks's Honeyguide

61.9 Pallid Honeyguide

61.10 Dwarf Honeyguide

61.11 Thick-billed Honeyguide

61.12 Least Honeyguide

61.13 Lesser Honeyguide

61.14 Scaly-throated Honeyguide

61.15 Spotted Honeyguide

62.1 Northern Wryneck

62.2 Rufous-breasted Wryneck

62.3 African Piculet

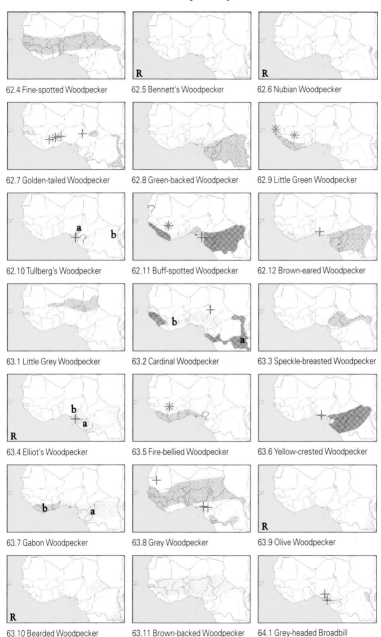

62.4 Fine-spotted Woodpecker

62.5 Bennett's Woodpecker

62.6 Nubian Woodpecker

62.7 Golden-tailed Woodpecker

62.8 Green-backed Woodpecker

62.9 Little Green Woodpecker

62.10 Tullberg's Woodpecker

62.11 Buff-spotted Woodpecker

62.12 Brown-eared Woodpecker

63.1 Little Grey Woodpecker

63.2 Cardinal Woodpecker

63.3 Speckle-breasted Woodpecker

63.4 Elliot's Woodpecker

63.5 Fire-bellied Woodpecker

63.6 Yellow-crested Woodpecker

63.7 Gabon Woodpecker

63.8 Grey Woodpecker

63.9 Olive Woodpecker

63.10 Bearded Woodpecker

63.11 Brown-backed Woodpecker

64.1 Grey-headed Broadbill

Maps for species numbers 64.2 to 65.5

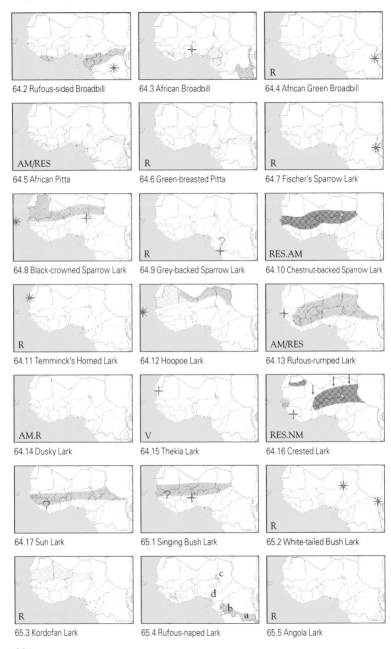

64.2 Rufous-sided Broadbill

64.3 African Broadbill

64.4 African Green Broadbill

64.5 African Pitta

64.6 Green-breasted Pitta

64.7 Fischer's Sparrow Lark

64.8 Black-crowned Sparrow Lark

64.9 Grey-backed Sparrow Lark

64.10 Chestnut-backed Sparrow Lark

64.11 Temminck's Horned Lark

64.12 Hoopoe Lark

64.13 Rufous-rumped Lark

64.14 Dusky Lark

64.15 Thekla Lark

64.16 Crested Lark

64.17 Sun Lark

65.1 Singing Bush Lark

65.2 White-tailed Bush Lark

65.3 Kordofan Lark

65.4 Rufous-naped Lark

65.5 Angola Lark

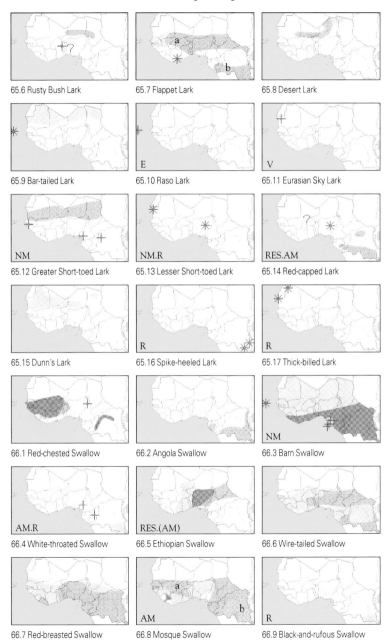

65.6 Rusty Bush Lark

65.7 Flappet Lark

65.8 Desert Lark

65.9 Bar-tailed Lark

65.10 Raso Lark

65.11 Eurasian Sky Lark

65.12 Greater Short-toed Lark

65.13 Lesser Short-toed Lark

65.14 Red-capped Lark

65.15 Dunn's Lark

65.16 Spike-heeled Lark

65.17 Thick-billed Lark

66.1 Red-chested Swallow

66.2 Angola Swallow

66.3 Barn Swallow

66.4 White-throated Swallow

66.5 Ethiopian Swallow

66.6 Wire-tailed Swallow

66.7 Red-breasted Swallow

66.8 Mosque Swallow

66.9 Black-and-rufous Swallow

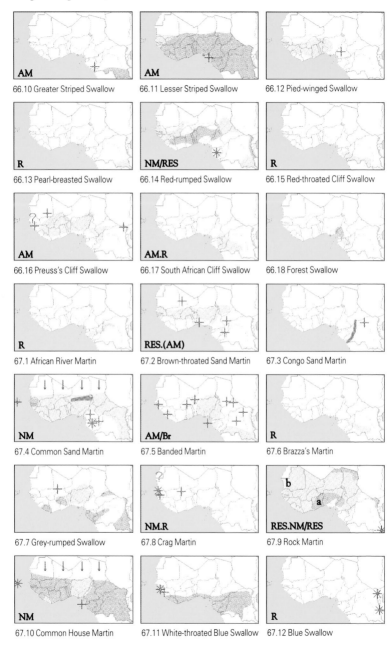

66.10 Greater Striped Swallow

66.11 Lesser Striped Swallow

66.12 Pied-winged Swallow

66.13 Pearl-breasted Swallow

66.14 Red-rumped Swallow

66.15 Red-throated Cliff Swallow

66.16 Preuss's Cliff Swallow

66.17 South African Cliff Swallow

66.18 Forest Swallow

67.1 African River Martin

67.2 Brown-throated Sand Martin

67.3 Congo Sand Martin

67.4 Common Sand Martin

67.5 Banded Martin

67.6 Brazza's Martin

67.7 Grey-rumped Swallow

67.8 Crag Martin

67.9 Rock Martin

67.10 Common House Martin

67.11 White-throated Blue Swallow

67.12 Blue Swallow

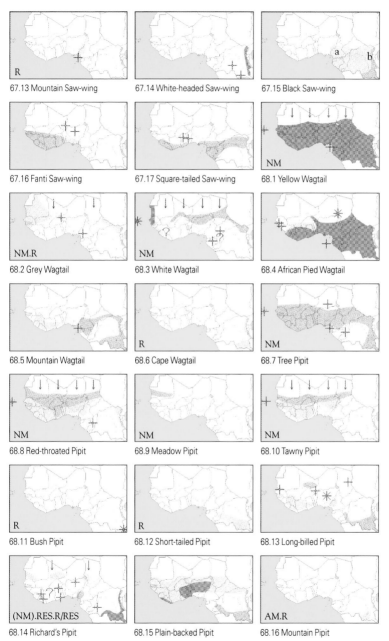

67.13 Mountain Saw-wing

67.14 White-headed Saw-wing

67.15 Black Saw-wing

67.16 Fanti Saw-wing

67.17 Square-tailed Saw-wing

68.1 Yellow Wagtail

68.2 Grey Wagtail

68.3 White Wagtail

68.4 African Pied Wagtail

68.5 Mountain Wagtail

68.6 Cape Wagtail

68.7 Tree Pipit

68.8 Red-throated Pipit

68.9 Meadow Pipit

68.10 Tawny Pipit

68.11 Bush Pipit

68.12 Short-tailed Pipit

68.13 Long-billed Pipit

68.14 Richard's Pipit

68.15 Plain-backed Pipit

68.16 Mountain Pipit

Maps for species numbers 68.17 to 70.4

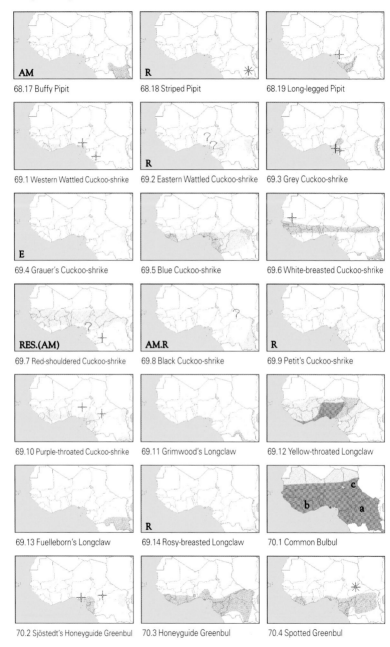

68.17 Buffy Pipit

68.18 Striped Pipit

68.19 Long-legged Pipit

69.1 Western Wattled Cuckoo-shrike

69.2 Eastern Wattled Cuckoo-shrike

69.3 Grey Cuckoo-shrike

69.4 Grauer's Cuckoo-shrike

69.5 Blue Cuckoo-shrike

69.6 White-breasted Cuckoo-shrike

69.7 Red-shouldered Cuckoo-shrike

69.8 Black Cuckoo-shrike

69.9 Petit's Cuckoo-shrike

69.10 Purple-throated Cuckoo-shrike

69.11 Grimwood's Longclaw

69.12 Yellow-throated Longclaw

69.13 Fuelleborn's Longclaw

69.14 Rosy-breasted Longclaw

70.1 Common Bulbul

70.2 Sjöstedt's Honeyguide Greenbul

70.3 Honeyguide Greenbul

70.4 Spotted Greenbul

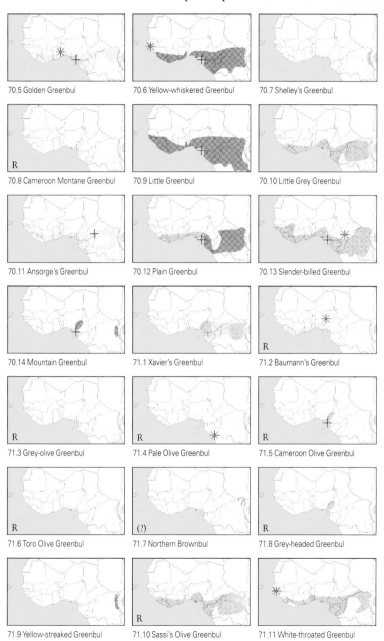

70.5 Golden Greenbul

70.6 Yellow-whiskered Greenbul

70.7 Shelley's Greenbul

70.8 Cameroon Montane Greenbul

70.9 Little Greenbul

70.10 Little Grey Greenbul

70.11 Ansorge's Greenbul

70.12 Plain Greenbul

70.13 Slender-billed Greenbul

70.14 Mountain Greenbul

71.1 Xavier's Greenbul

71.2 Baumann's Greenbul

71.3 Grey-olive Greenbul

71.4 Pale Olive Greenbul

71.5 Cameroon Olive Greenbul

71.6 Toro Olive Greenbul

71.7 Northern Brownbul

71.8 Grey-headed Greenbul

71.9 Yellow-streaked Greenbul

71.10 Sassi's Olive Greenbul

71.11 White-throated Greenbul

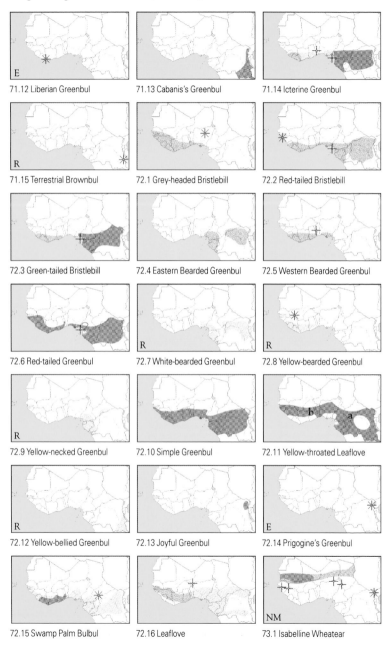

71.12 Liberian Greenbul

71.13 Cabanis's Greenbul

71.14 Icterine Greenbul

71.15 Terrestrial Brownbul

72.1 Grey-headed Bristlebill

72.2 Red-tailed Bristlebill

72.3 Green-tailed Bristlebill

72.4 Eastern Bearded Greenbul

72.5 Western Bearded Greenbul

72.6 Red-tailed Greenbul

72.7 White-bearded Greenbul

72.8 Yellow-bearded Greenbul

72.9 Yellow-necked Greenbul

72.10 Simple Greenbul

72.11 Yellow-throated Leaflove

72.12 Yellow-bellied Greenbul

72.13 Joyful Greenbul

72.14 Prigogine's Greenbul

72.15 Swamp Palm Bulbul

72.16 Leaflove

73.1 Isabelline Wheatear

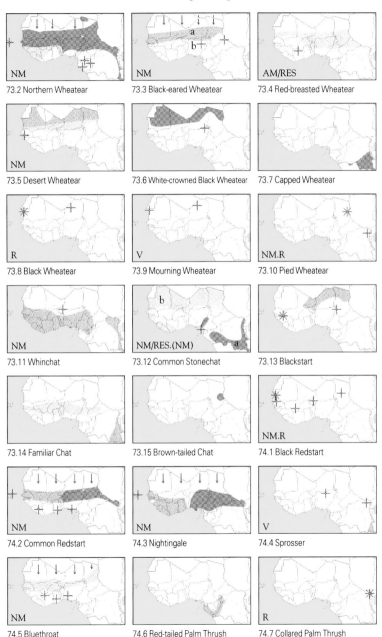

73.2 Northern Wheatear

73.3 Black-eared Wheatear

73.4 Red-breasted Wheatear

73.5 Desert Wheatear

73.6 White-crowned Black Wheatear

73.7 Capped Wheatear

73.8 Black Wheatear

73.9 Mourning Wheatear

73.10 Pied Wheatear

73.11 Whinchat

73.12 Common Stonechat

73.13 Blackstart

73.14 Familiar Chat

73.15 Brown-tailed Chat

74.1 Black Redstart

74.2 Common Redstart

74.3 Nightingale

74.4 Sprosser

74.5 Bluethroat

74.6 Red-tailed Palm Thrush

74.7 Collared Palm Thrush

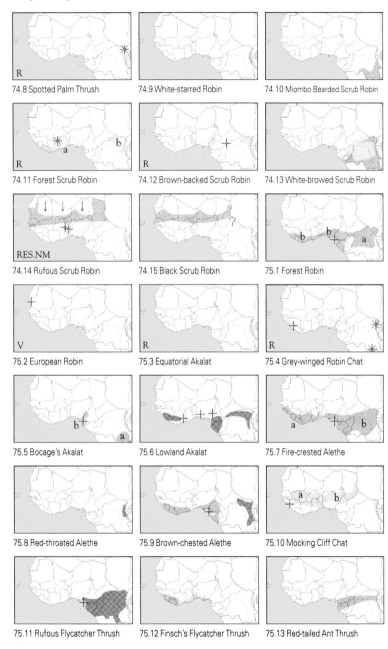

74.8 Spotted Palm Thrush

74.9 White-starred Robin

74.10 Miombo Bearded Scrub Robin

74.11 Forest Scrub Robin

74.12 Brown-backed Scrub Robin

74.13 White-browed Scrub Robin

74.14 Rufous Scrub Robin

74.15 Black Scrub Robin

75.1 Forest Robin

75.2 European Robin

75.3 Equatorial Akalat

75.4 Grey-winged Robin Chat

75.5 Bocage's Akalat

75.6 Lowland Akalat

75.7 Fire-crested Alethe

75.8 Red-throated Alethe

75.9 Brown-chested Alethe

75.10 Mocking Cliff Chat

75.11 Rufous Flycatcher Thrush

75.12 Finsch's Flycatcher Thrush

75.13 Red-tailed Ant Thrush

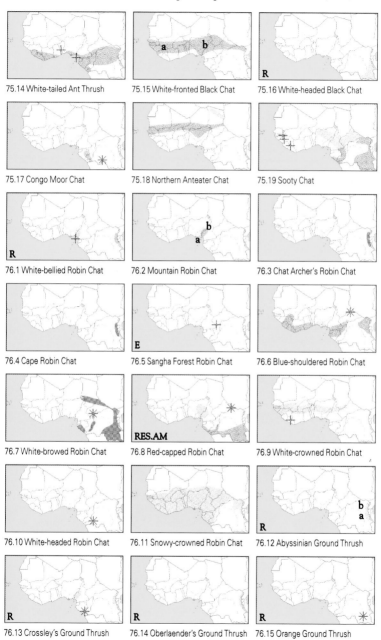

75.14 White-tailed Ant Thrush

75.15 White-fronted Black Chat

75.16 White-headed Black Chat

75.17 Congo Moor Chat

75.18 Northern Anteater Chat

75.19 Sooty Chat

76.1 White-bellied Robin Chat

76.2 Mountain Robin Chat

76.3 Chat Archer's Robin Chat

76.4 Cape Robin Chat

76.5 Sangha Forest Robin Chat

76.6 Blue-shouldered Robin Chat

76.7 White-browed Robin Chat

76.8 Red-capped Robin Chat

76.9 White-crowned Robin Chat

76.10 White-headed Robin Chat

76.11 Snowy-crowned Robin Chat

76.12 Abyssinian Ground Thrush

76.13 Crossley's Ground Thrush

76.14 Oberlaender's Ground Thrush

76.15 Orange Ground Thrush

Maps for species numbers 76.16 to 78.1

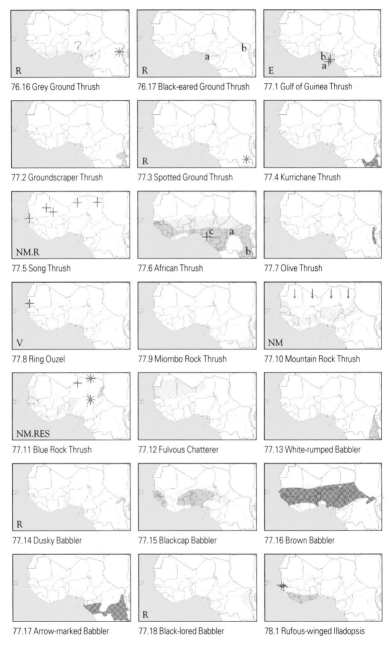

76.16 Grey Ground Thrush

76.17 Black-eared Ground Thrush

77.1 Gulf of Guinea Thrush

77.2 Groundscraper Thrush

77.3 Spotted Ground Thrush

77.4 Kurrichane Thrush

77.5 Song Thrush

77.6 African Thrush

77.7 Olive Thrush

77.8 Ring Ouzel

77.9 Miombo Rock Thrush

77.10 Mountain Rock Thrush

77.11 Blue Rock Thrush

77.12 Fulvous Chatterer

77.13 White-rumped Babbler

77.14 Dusky Babbler

77.15 Blackcap Babbler

77.16 Brown Babbler

77.17 Arrow-marked Babbler

77.18 Black-lored Babbler

78.1 Rufous-winged Illadopsis

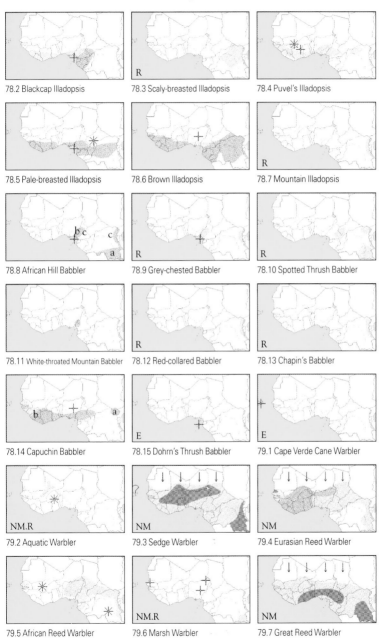

78.2 Blackcap Illadopsis

78.3 Scaly-breasted Illadopsis

78.4 Puvel's Illadopsis

78.5 Pale-breasted Illadopsis

78.6 Brown Illadopsis

78.7 Mountain Illadopsis

78.8 African Hill Babbler

78.9 Grey-chested Babbler

78.10 Spotted Thrush Babbler

78.11 White-throated Mountain Babbler

78.12 Red-collared Babbler

78.13 Chapin's Babbler

78.14 Capuchin Babbler

78.15 Dohrn's Thrush Babbler

79.1 Cape Verde Cane Warbler

79.2 Aquatic Warbler

79.3 Sedge Warbler

79.4 Eurasian Reed Warbler

79.5 African Reed Warbler

79.6 Marsh Warbler

79.7 Great Reed Warbler

305

Maps for species numbers 79.8 to 80.10

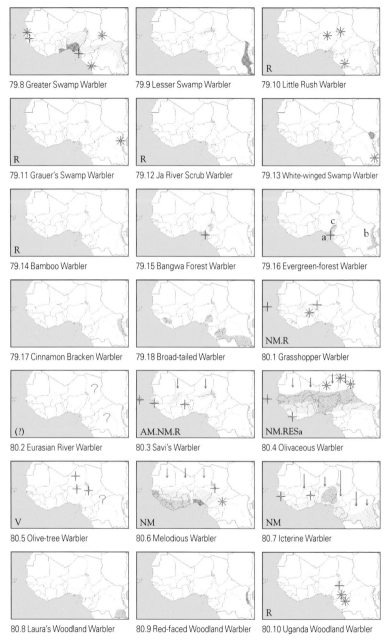

79.8 Greater Swamp Warbler

79.9 Lesser Swamp Warbler

79.10 Little Rush Warbler

79.11 Grauer's Swamp Warbler

79.12 Ja River Scrub Warbler

79.13 White-winged Swamp Warbler

79.14 Bamboo Warbler

79.15 Bangwa Forest Warbler

79.16 Evergreen-forest Warbler

79.17 Cinnamon Bracken Warbler

79.18 Broad-tailed Warbler

80.1 Grasshopper Warbler

80.2 Eurasian River Warbler

80.3 Savi's Warbler

80.4 Olivaceous Warbler

80.5 Olive-tree Warbler

80.6 Melodious Warbler

80.7 Icterine Warbler

80.8 Laura's Woodland Warbler

80.9 Red-faced Woodland Warbler

80.10 Uganda Woodland Warbler

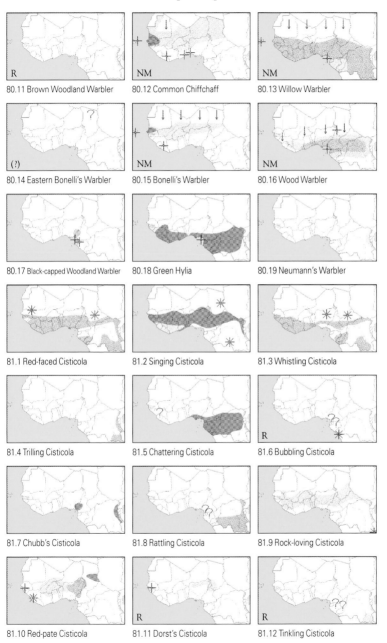

80.11 Brown Woodland Warbler

80.12 Common Chiffchaff

80.13 Willow Warbler

80.14 Eastern Bonelli's Warbler

80.15 Bonelli's Warbler

80.16 Wood Warbler

80.17 Black-capped Woodland Warbler

80.18 Green Hylia

80.19 Neumann's Warbler

81.1 Red-faced Cisticola

81.2 Singing Cisticola

81.3 Whistling Cisticola

81.4 Trilling Cisticola

81.5 Chattering Cisticola

81.6 Bubbling Cisticola

81.7 Chubb's Cisticola

81.8 Rattling Cisticola

81.9 Rock-loving Cisticola

81.10 Red-pate Cisticola

81.11 Dorst's Cisticola

81.12 Tinkling Cisticola

Maps for species numbers 81.13 to 82.15

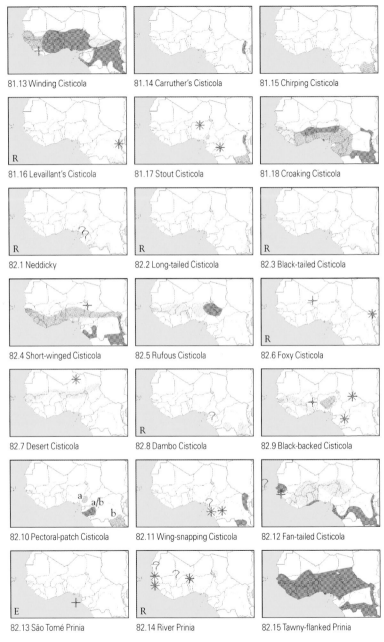

81.13 Winding Cisticola

81.14 Carruther's Cisticola

81.15 Chirping Cisticola

81.16 Levaillant's Cisticola

81.17 Stout Cisticola

81.18 Croaking Cisticola

82.1 Neddicky

82.2 Long-tailed Cisticola

82.3 Black-tailed Cisticola

82.4 Short-winged Cisticola

82.5 Rufous Cisticola

82.6 Foxy Cisticola

82.7 Desert Cisticola

82.8 Dambo Cisticola

82.9 Black-backed Cisticola

82.10 Pectoral-patch Cisticola

82.11 Wing-snapping Cisticola

82.12 Fan-tailed Cisticola

82.13 São Tomé Prinia

82.14 River Prinia

82.15 Tawny-flanked Prinia

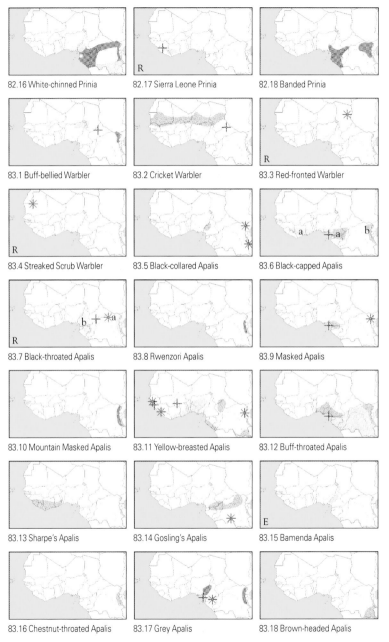

82.16 White-chinned Prinia

82.17 Sierra Leone Prinia

82.18 Banded Prinia

83.1 Buff-bellied Warbler

83.2 Cricket Warbler

83.3 Red-fronted Warbler

83.4 Streaked Scrub Warbler

83.5 Black-collared Apalis

83.6 Black-capped Apalis

83.7 Black-throated Apalis

83.8 Rwenzori Apalis

83.9 Masked Apalis

83.10 Mountain Masked Apalis

83.11 Yellow-breasted Apalis

83.12 Buff-throated Apalis

83.13 Sharpe's Apalis

83.14 Gosling's Apalis

83.15 Bamenda Apalis

83.16 Chestnut-throated Apalis

83.17 Grey Apalis

83.18 Brown-headed Apalis

Maps for species numbers 84.1 to 85.3

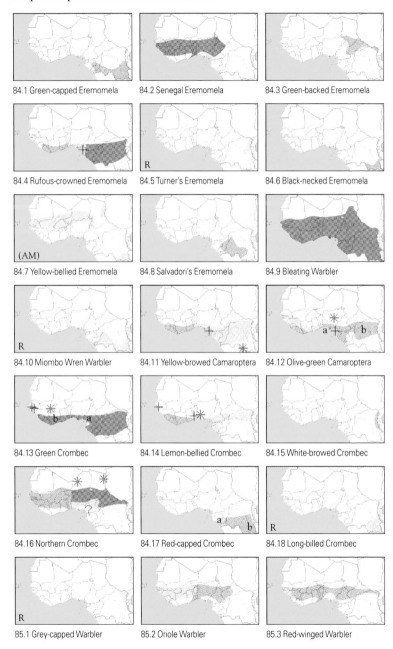

84.1 Green-capped Eremomela

84.2 Senegal Eremomela

84.3 Green-backed Eremomela

84.4 Rufous-crowned Eremomela

84.5 Turner's Eremomela

84.6 Black-necked Eremomela

84.7 Yellow-bellied Eremomela

84.8 Salvadori's Eremomela

84.9 Bleating Warbler

84.10 Miombo Wren Warbler

84.11 Yellow-browed Camaroptera

84.12 Olive-green Camaroptera

84.13 Green Crombec

84.14 Lemon-bellied Crombec

84.15 White-browed Crombec

84.16 Northern Crombec

84.17 Red-capped Crombec

84.18 Long-billed Crombec

85.1 Grey-capped Warbler

85.2 Oriole Warbler

85.3 Red-winged Warbler

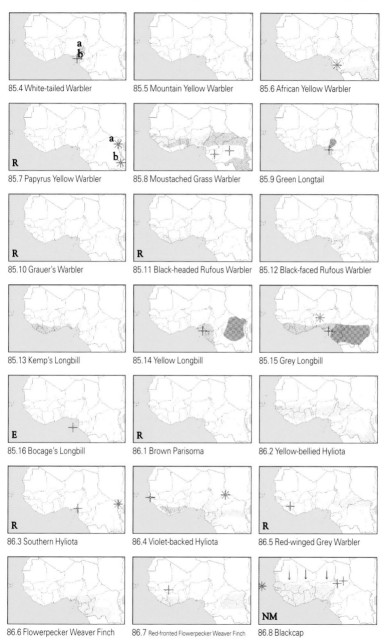

85.4 White-tailed Warbler

85.5 Mountain Yellow Warbler

85.6 African Yellow Warbler

85.7 Papyrus Yellow Warbler

85.8 Moustached Grass Warbler

85.9 Green Longtail

85.10 Grauer's Warbler

85.11 Black-headed Rufous Warbler

85.12 Black-faced Rufous Warbler

85.13 Kemp's Longbill

85.14 Yellow Longbill

85.15 Grey Longbill

85.16 Bocage's Longbill

86.1 Brown Parisoma

86.2 Yellow-bellied Hyliota

86.3 Southern Hyliota

86.4 Violet-backed Hyliota

86.5 Red-winged Grey Warbler

86.6 Flowerpecker Weaver Finch

86.7 Red-fronted Flowerpecker Weaver Finch

86.8 Blackcap

311

Maps for species numbers 86.9 to 87.9

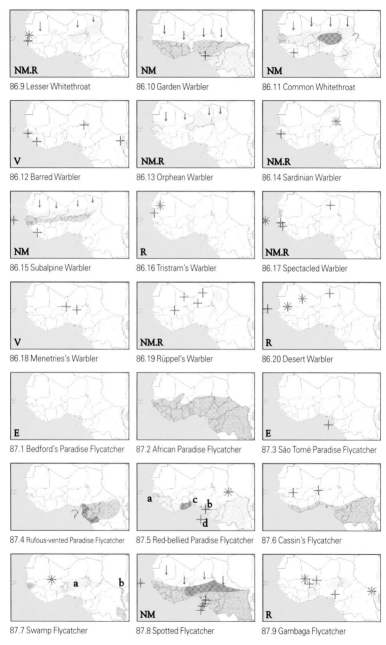

86.9 Lesser Whitethroat

86.10 Garden Warbler

86.11 Common Whitethroat

86.12 Barred Warbler

86.13 Orphean Warbler

86.14 Sardinian Warbler

86.15 Subalpine Warbler

86.16 Tristram's Warbler

86.17 Spectacled Warbler

86.18 Menetries's Warbler

86.19 Rüppel's Warbler

86.20 Desert Warbler

87.1 Bedford's Paradise Flycatcher

87.2 African Paradise Flycatcher

87.3 São Tomé Paradise Flycatcher

87.4 Rufous-vented Paradise Flycatcher

87.5 Red-bellied Paradise Flycatcher

87.6 Cassin's Flycatcher

87.7 Swamp Flycatcher

87.8 Spotted Flycatcher

87.9 Gambaga Flycatcher

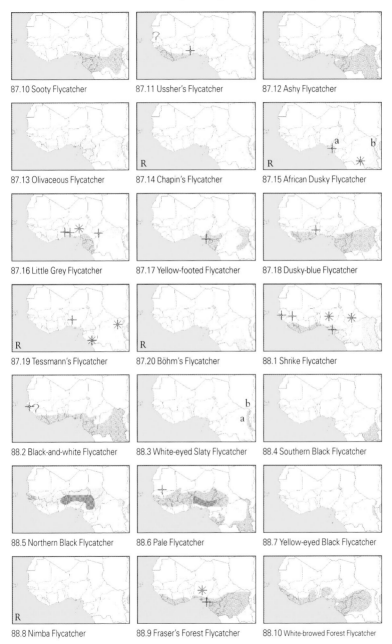

87.10 Sooty Flycatcher

87.11 Ussher's Flycatcher

87.12 Ashy Flycatcher

87.13 Olivaceous Flycatcher

87.14 Chapin's Flycatcher

87.15 African Dusky Flycatcher

87.16 Little Grey Flycatcher

87.17 Yellow-footed Flycatcher

87.18 Dusky-blue Flycatcher

87.19 Tessmann's Flycatcher

87.20 Böhm's Flycatcher

88.1 Shrike Flycatcher

88.2 Black-and-white Flycatcher

88.3 White-eyed Slaty Flycatcher

88.4 Southern Black Flycatcher

88.5 Northern Black Flycatcher

88.6 Pale Flycatcher

88.7 Yellow-eyed Black Flycatcher

88.8 Nimba Flycatcher

88.9 Fraser's Forest Flycatcher

88.10 White-browed Forest Flycatcher

Maps for species numbers 88.11 to 89.15

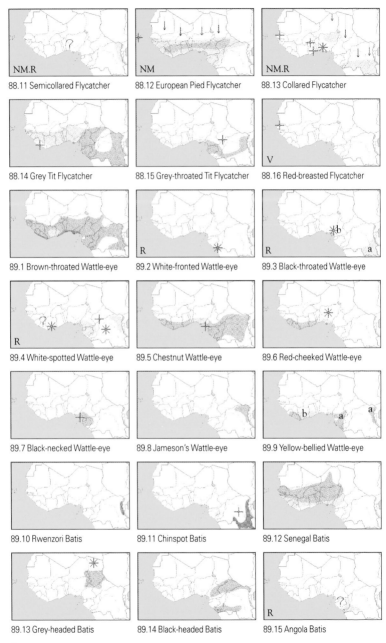

88.11 Semicollared Flycatcher

88.12 European Pied Flycatcher

88.13 Collared Flycatcher

88.14 Grey Tit Flycatcher

88.15 Grey-throated Tit Flycatcher

88.16 Red-breasted Flycatcher

89.1 Brown-throated Wattle-eye

89.2 White-fronted Wattle-eye

89.3 Black-throated Wattle-eye

89.4 White-spotted Wattle-eye

89.5 Chestnut Wattle-eye

89.6 Red-cheeked Wattle-eye

89.7 Black-necked Wattle-eye

89.8 Jameson's Wattle-eye

89.9 Yellow-bellied Wattle-eye

89.10 Rwenzori Batis

89.11 Chinspot Batis

89.12 Senegal Batis

89.13 Grey-headed Batis

89.14 Black-headed Batis

89.15 Angola Batis

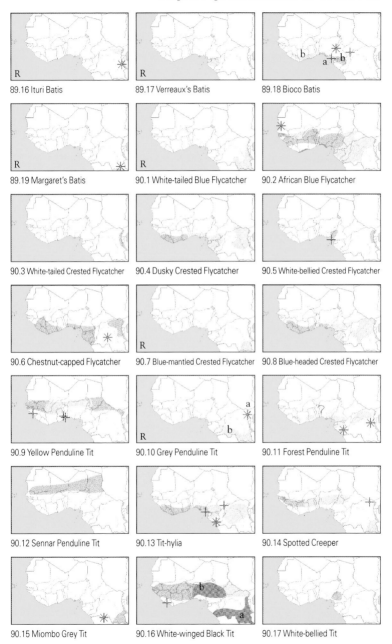

89.16 Ituri Batis

89.17 Verreaux's Batis

89.18 Bioco Batis

89.19 Margaret's Batis

90.1 White-tailed Blue Flycatcher

90.2 African Blue Flycatcher

90.3 White-tailed Crested Flycatcher

90.4 Dusky Crested Flycatcher

90.5 White-bellied Crested Flycatcher

90.6 Chestnut-capped Flycatcher

90.7 Blue-mantled Crested Flycatcher

90.8 Blue-headed Crested Flycatcher

90.9 Yellow Penduline Tit

90.10 Grey Penduline Tit

90.11 Forest Penduline Tit

90.12 Sennar Penduline Tit

90.13 Tit-hylia

90.14 Spotted Creeper

90.15 Miombo Grey Tit

90.16 White-winged Black Tit

90.17 White-bellied Tit

Maps for species numbers 90.18 to 91.18

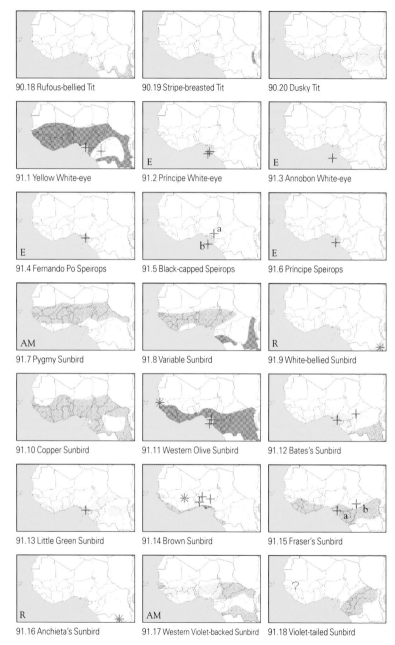

90.18 Rufous-bellied Tit

90.19 Stripe-breasted Tit

90.20 Dusky Tit

91.1 Yellow White-eye

91.2 Príncipe White-eye

91.3 Annobon White-eye

91.4 Fernando Po Speirops

91.5 Black-capped Speirops

91.6 Príncipe Speirops

91.7 Pygmy Sunbird

91.8 Variable Sunbird

91.9 White-bellied Sunbird

91.10 Copper Sunbird

91.11 Western Olive Sunbird

91.12 Bates's Sunbird

91.13 Little Green Sunbird

91.14 Brown Sunbird

91.15 Fraser's Sunbird

91.16 Anchieta's Sunbird

91.17 Western Violet-backed Sunbird

91.18 Violet-tailed Sunbird

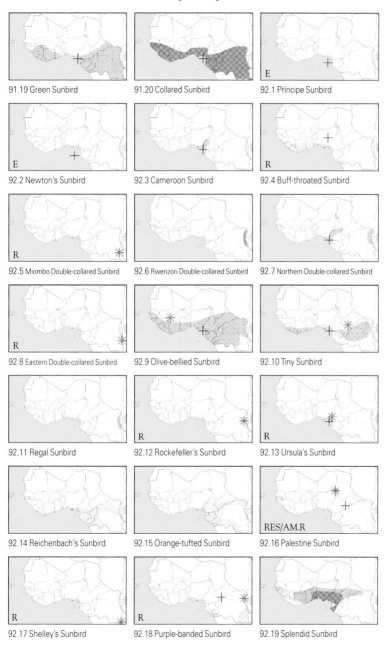

91.19 Green Sunbird

91.20 Collared Sunbird

92.1 Príncipe Sunbird

92.2 Newton's Sunbird

92.3 Cameroon Sunbird

92.4 Buff-throated Sunbird

92.5 Miombo Double-collared Sunbird

92.6 Rwenzori Double-collared Sunbird

92.7 Northern Double-collared Sunbird

92.8 Eastern Double-collared Sunbird

92.9 Olive-bellied Sunbird

92.10 Tiny Sunbird

92.11 Regal Sunbird

92.12 Rockefeller's Sunbird

92.13 Ursula's Sunbird

92.14 Reichenbach's Sunbird

92.15 Orange-tufted Sunbird

92.16 Palestine Sunbird

92.17 Shelley's Sunbird

92.18 Purple-banded Sunbird

92.19 Splendid Sunbird

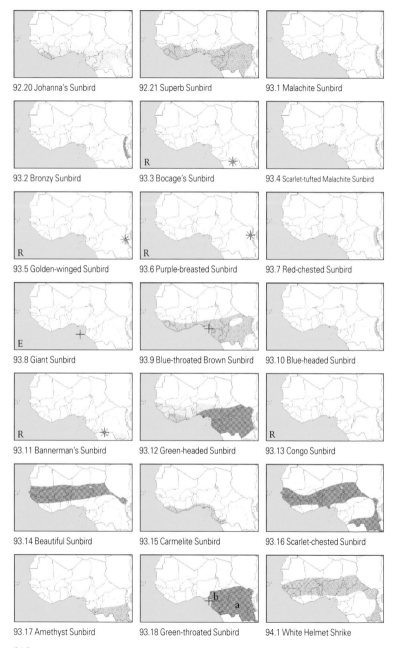

92.20 Johanna's Sunbird

92.21 Superb Sunbird

93.1 Malachite Sunbird

93.2 Bronzy Sunbird

93.3 Bocage's Sunbird

93.4 Scarlet-tufted Malachite Sunbird

93.5 Golden-winged Sunbird

93.6 Purple-breasted Sunbird

93.7 Red-chested Sunbird

93.8 Giant Sunbird

93.9 Blue-throated Brown Sunbird

93.10 Blue-headed Sunbird

93.11 Bannerman's Sunbird

93.12 Green-headed Sunbird

93.13 Congo Sunbird

93.14 Beautiful Sunbird

93.15 Carmelite Sunbird

93.16 Scarlet-chested Sunbird

93.17 Amethyst Sunbird

93.18 Green-throated Sunbird

94.1 White Helmet Shrike

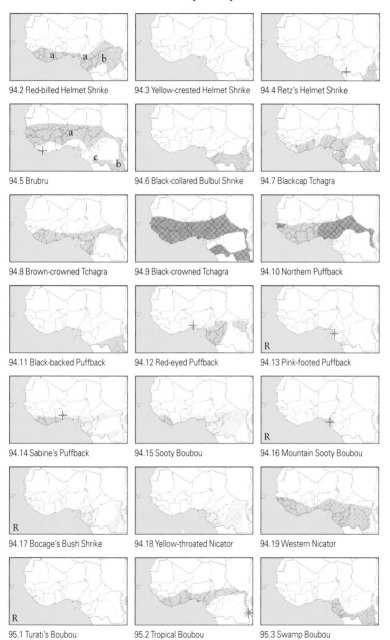

94.2 Red-billed Helmet Shrike

94.3 Yellow-crested Helmet Shrike

94.4 Retz's Helmet Shrike

94.5 Brubru

94.6 Black-collared Bulbul Shrike

94.7 Blackcap Tchagra

94.8 Brown-crowned Tchagra

94.9 Black-crowned Tchagra

94.10 Northern Puffback

94.11 Black-backed Puffback

94.12 Red-eyed Puffback

94.13 Pink-footed Puffback

94.14 Sabine's Puffback

94.15 Sooty Boubou

94.16 Mountain Sooty Boubou

94.17 Bocage's Bush Shrike

94.18 Yellow-throated Nicator

94.19 Western Nicator

95.1 Turati's Boubou

95.2 Tropical Boubou

95.3 Swamp Boubou

Maps for species numbers 95.4 to 96.5

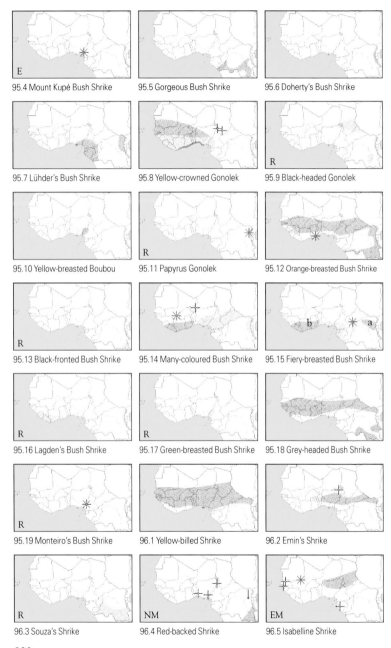

95.4 Mount Kupé Bush Shrike

95.5 Gorgeous Bush Shrike

95.6 Doherty's Bush Shrike

95.7 Lühder's Bush Shrike

95.8 Yellow-crowned Gonolek

95.9 Black-headed Gonolek

95.10 Yellow-breasted Boubou

95.11 Papyrus Gonolek

95.12 Orange-breasted Bush Shrike

95.13 Black-fronted Bush Shrike

95.14 Many-coloured Bush Shrike

95.15 Fiery-breasted Bush Shrike

95.16 Lagden's Bush Shrike

95.17 Green-breasted Bush Shrike

95.18 Grey-headed Bush Shrike

95.19 Monteiro's Bush Shrike

96.1 Yellow-billed Shrike

96.2 Emin's Shrike

96.3 Souza's Shrike

96.4 Red-backed Shrike

96.5 Isabelline Shrike

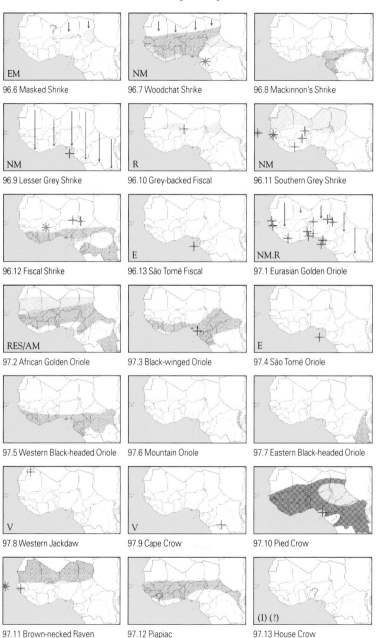

96.6 Masked Shrike

96.7 Woodchat Shrike

96.8 Mackinnon's Shrike

96.9 Lesser Grey Shrike

96.10 Grey-backed Fiscal

96.11 Southern Grey Shrike

96.12 Fiscal Shrike

96.13 São Tomé Fiscal

97.1 Eurasian Golden Oriole

97.2 African Golden Oriole

97.3 Black-winged Oriole

97.4 São Tomé Oriole

97.5 Western Black-headed Oriole

97.6 Mountain Oriole

97.7 Eastern Black-headed Oriole

97.8 Western Jackdaw

97.9 Cape Crow

97.10 Pied Crow

97.11 Brown-necked Raven

97.12 Piapiac

97.13 House Crow

321

Maps for species numbers 97.14 to 99.2

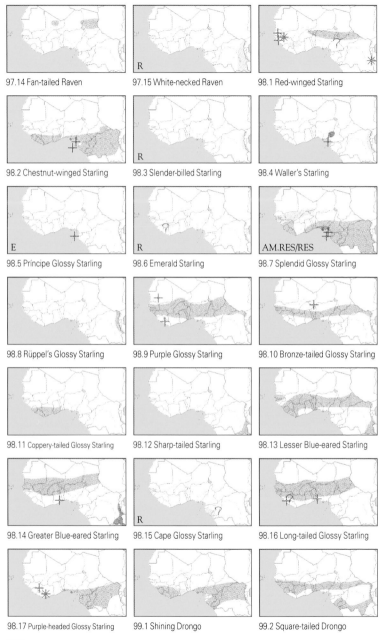

97.14 Fan-tailed Raven

97.15 White-necked Raven

98.1 Red-winged Starling

98.2 Chestnut-winged Starling

98.3 Slender-billed Starling

98.4 Waller's Starling

98.5 Principe Glossy Starling

98.6 Emerald Starling

98.7 Splendid Glossy Starling

98.8 Rüppel's Glossy Starling

98.9 Purple Glossy Starling

98.10 Bronze-tailed Glossy Starling

98.11 Coppery-tailed Glossy Starling

98.12 Sharp-tailed Starling

98.13 Lesser Blue-eared Starling

98.14 Greater Blue-eared Starling

98.15 Cape Glossy Starling

98.16 Long-tailed Glossy Starling

98.17 Purple-headed Glossy Starling

99.1 Shining Drongo

99.2 Square-tailed Drongo

322

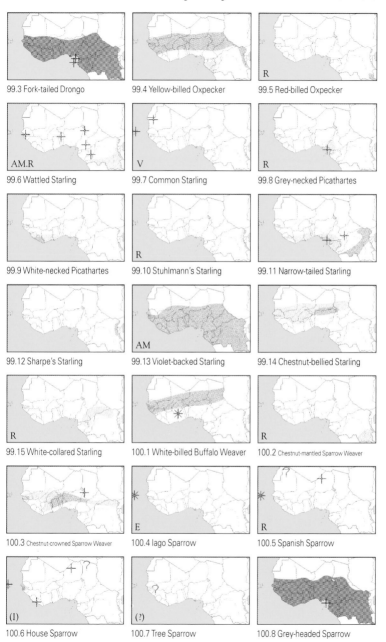

99.3 Fork-tailed Drongo

99.4 Yellow-billed Oxpecker

99.5 Red-billed Oxpecker

99.6 Wattled Starling

99.7 Common Starling

99.8 Grey-necked Picathartes

99.9 White-necked Picathartes

99.10 Stuhlmann's Starling

99.11 Narrow-tailed Starling

99.12 Sharpe's Starling

99.13 Violet-backed Starling

99.14 Chestnut-bellied Starling

99.15 White-collared Starling

100.1 White-billed Buffalo Weaver

100.2 Chestnut-mantled Sparrow Weaver

100.3 Chestnut-crowned Sparrow Weaver

100.4 Iago Sparrow

100.5 Spanish Sparrow

100.6 House Sparrow

100.7 Tree Sparrow

100.8 Grey-headed Sparrow

Maps for species numbers 100.9 to 101.10

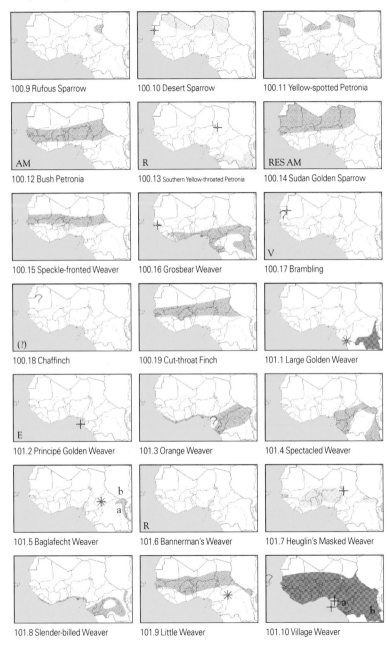

100.9 Rufous Sparrow

100.10 Desert Sparrow

100.11 Yellow-spotted Petronia

100.12 Bush Petronia — AM

100.13 Southern Yellow-throated Petronia — R

100.14 Sudan Golden Sparrow — RES AM

100.15 Speckle-fronted Weaver

100.16 Grosbear Weaver

100.17 Brambling — V

100.18 Chaffinch — (?)

100.19 Cut-throat Finch

101.1 Large Golden Weaver

101.2 Principé Golden Weaver — E

101.3 Orange Weaver

101.4 Spectacled Weaver

101.5 Baglafecht Weaver

101.6 Bannerman's Weaver — R

101.7 Heuglin's Masked Weaver

101.8 Slender-billed Weaver

101.9 Little Weaver

101.10 Village Weaver

324

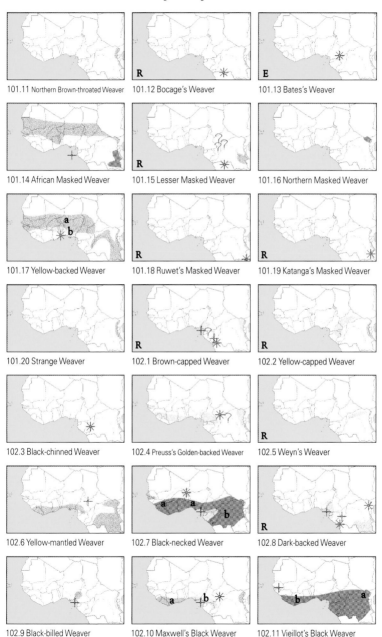

101.11 Northern Brown-throated Weaver

101.12 Bocage's Weaver

101.13 Bates's Weaver

101.14 African Masked Weaver

101.15 Lesser Masked Weaver

101.16 Northern Masked Weaver

101.17 Yellow-backed Weaver

101.18 Ruwet's Masked Weaver

101.19 Katanga's Masked Weaver

101.20 Strange Weaver

102.1 Brown-capped Weaver

102.2 Yellow-capped Weaver

102.3 Black-chinned Weaver

102.4 Preuss's Golden-backed Weaver

102.5 Weyn's Weaver

102.6 Yellow-mantled Weaver

102.7 Black-necked Weaver

102.8 Dark-backed Weaver

102.9 Black-billed Weaver

102.10 Maxwell's Black Weaver

102.11 Vieillot's Black Weaver

325

Maps for species numbers 102.12 to 103.14

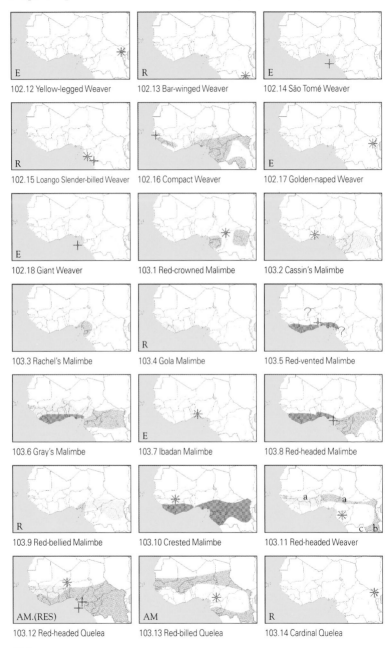

102.12 Yellow-legged Weaver

102.13 Bar-winged Weaver

102.14 São Tomé Weaver

102.15 Loango Slender-billed Weaver

102.16 Compact Weaver

102.17 Golden-naped Weaver

102.18 Giant Weaver

103.1 Red-crowned Malimbe

103.2 Cassin's Malimbe

103.3 Rachel's Malimbe

103.4 Gola Malimbe

103.5 Red-vented Malimbe

103.6 Gray's Malimbe

103.7 Ibadan Malimbe

103.8 Red-headed Malimbe

103.9 Red-bellied Malimbe

103.10 Crested Malimbe

103.11 Red-headed Weaver

103.12 Red-headed Quelea

103.13 Red-billed Quelea

103.14 Cardinal Quelea

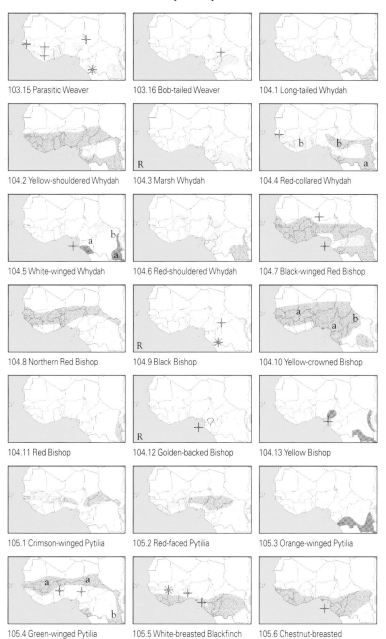

103.15 Parasitic Weaver

103.16 Bob-tailed Weaver

104.1 Long-tailed Whydah

104.2 Yellow-shouldered Whydah

104.3 Marsh Whydah

104.4 Red-collared Whydah

104.5 White-winged Whydah

104.6 Red-shouldered Whydah

104.7 Black-winged Red Bishop

104.8 Northern Red Bishop

104.9 Black Bishop

104.10 Yellow-crowned Bishop

104.11 Red Bishop

104.12 Golden-backed Bishop

104.13 Yellow Bishop

105.1 Crimson-winged Pytilia

105.2 Red-faced Pytilia

105.3 Orange-winged Pytilia

105.4 Green-winged Pytilia

105.5 White-breasted Blackfinch

105.6 Chestnut-breasted

Maps for species numbers 105.7 to 106.6

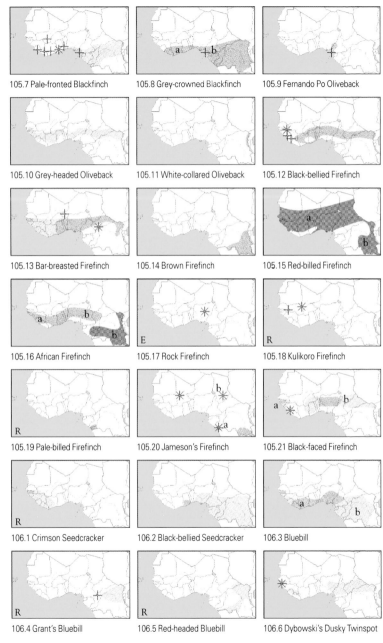

105.7 Pale-fronted Blackfinch

105.8 Grey-crowned Blackfinch

105.9 Fernando Po Oliveback

105.10 Grey-headed Oliveback

105.11 White-collared Oliveback

105.12 Black-bellied Firefinch

105.13 Bar-breasted Firefinch

105.14 Brown Firefinch

105.15 Red-billed Firefinch

105.16 African Firefinch

105.17 Rock Firefinch

105.18 Kulikoro Firefinch

105.19 Pale-billed Firefinch

105.20 Jameson's Firefinch

105.21 Black-faced Firefinch

106.1 Crimson Seedcracker

106.2 Black-bellied Seedcracker

106.3 Bluebill

106.4 Grant's Bluebill

106.5 Red-headed Bluebill

106.6 Dybowski's Dusky Twinspot

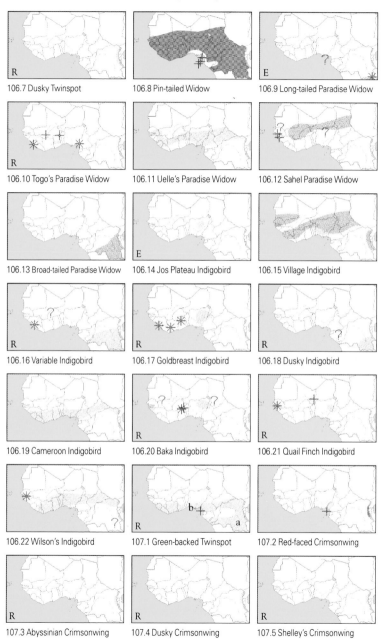

106.7 Dusky Twinspot

106.8 Pin-tailed Widow

106.9 Long-tailed Paradise Widow

106.10 Togo's Paradise Widow

106.11 Uelle's Paradise Widow

106.12 Sahel Paradise Widow

106.13 Broad-tailed Paradise Widow

106.14 Jos Plateau Indigobird

106.15 Village Indigobird

106.16 Variable Indigobird

106.17 Goldbreast Indigobird

106.18 Dusky Indigobird

106.19 Cameroon Indigobird

106.20 Baka Indigobird

106.21 Quail Finch Indigobird

106.22 Wilson's Indigobird

107.1 Green-backed Twinspot

107.2 Red-faced Crimsonwing

107.3 Abyssinian Crimsonwing

107.4 Dusky Crimsonwing

107.5 Shelley's Crimsonwing

Maps for species numbers 107.6 to 108.6

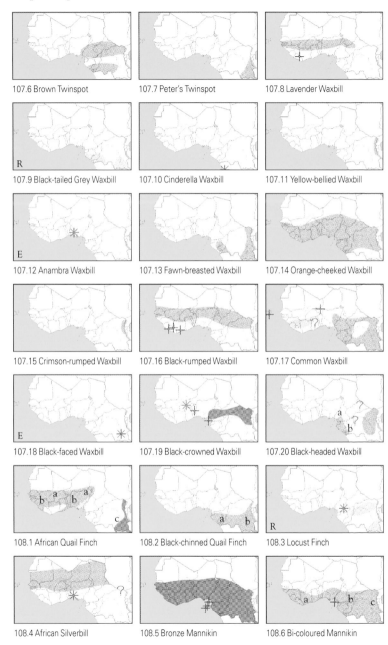

107.6 Brown Twinspot

107.7 Peter's Twinspot

107.8 Lavender Waxbill

107.9 Black-tailed Grey Waxbill

107.10 Cinderella Waxbill

107.11 Yellow-bellied Waxbill

107.12 Anambra Waxbill

107.13 Fawn-breasted Waxbill

107.14 Orange-cheeked Waxbill

107.15 Crimson-rumped Waxbill

107.16 Black-rumped Waxbill

107.17 Common Waxbill

107.18 Black-faced Waxbill

107.19 Black-crowned Waxbill

107.20 Black-headed Waxbill

108.1 African Quail Finch

108.2 Black-chinned Quail Finch

108.3 Locust Finch

108.4 African Silverbill

108.5 Bronze Mannikin

108.6 Bi-coloured Mannikin

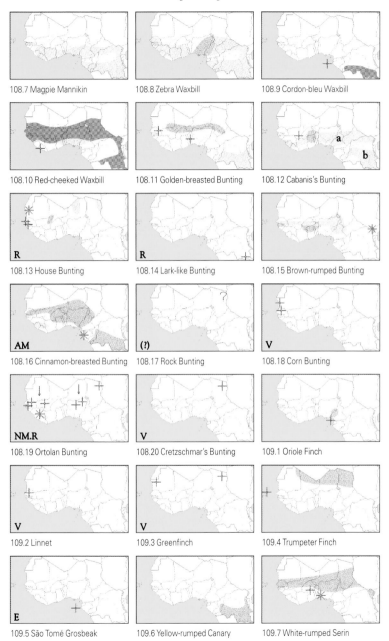

108.7 Magpie Mannikin

108.8 Zebra Waxbill

108.9 Cordon-bleu Waxbill

108.10 Red-cheeked Waxbill

108.11 Golden-breasted Bunting

108.12 Cabanis's Bunting

108.13 House Bunting

108.14 Lark-like Bunting

108.15 Brown-rumped Bunting

108.16 Cinnamon-breasted Bunting

108.17 Rock Bunting

108.18 Corn Bunting

108.19 Ortolan Bunting

108.20 Cretzschmar's Bunting

109.1 Oriole Finch

109.2 Linnet

109.3 Greenfinch

109.4 Trumpeter Finch

109.5 São Tomé Grosbeak

109.6 Yellow-rumped Canary

109.7 White-rumped Serin

Maps for species numbers 109.8 to 109.19

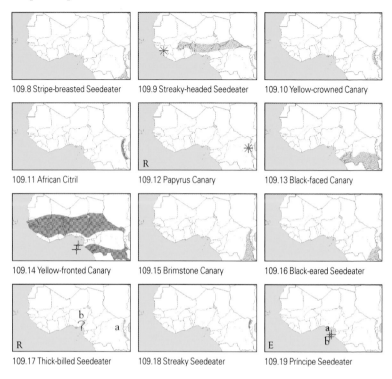

109.8 Stripe-breasted Seedeater

109.9 Streaky-headed Seedeater

109.10 Yellow-crowned Canary

109.11 African Citril

109.12 Papyrus Canary

109.13 Black-faced Canary

109.14 Yellow-fronted Canary

109.15 Brimstone Canary

109.16 Black-eared Seedeater

109.17 Thick-billed Seedeater

109.18 Streaky Seedeater

109.19 Principe Seedeater

APPENDIX

The following appendix gives the French and Portuguese names for every bird species mentioned in the plates. The French name is given as the second entry, and the Portuguese name is third. As in the main text the alternative English names, as used in other field guides, appear in brackets in lower-case type. Many birds that have not previously had an official name in Portuguese appear here for the first time in that language.

Plate 1
1 :SECRETARY BIRD :Messager serpentaire :Secretário
2 :OSTRICH :Autriche d'Afrique :Avestruz

Plate 2
1 :WANDERING ALBATROSS :Albatros hurleur :Albatroz-viageiro
2 :YELLOW-NOSED ALBATROSS :Albatros à bec jaune :Albatroz-de-bico-amarelo
3 :SOUTHERN GIANT PETREL :Fulmar géant :Fulmar-antárctico
4 :ASCENSION FRIGATEBIRD :Frégate aigle-de-mer :Fragata de Ascensão
5 :MAGNIFICENT FRIGATEBIRD :Frégate superbe :Rabiforcado

Plate 3
1 :SOFT-PLUMAGED PETREL :Pétrel soyeux :Freira-meridional
2 :FREIRA :Pterodroma de Madère :Freira
3 :GON-GON :Pterodroma gongon :Gon-gon
4 :BULWER'S PETREL :Pétrel de Bulwer :Alma-negra
5 :PINTADO PETREL :Pétrel damier :Pardela do Cabo
6 :CORY'S SHEARWATER :Puffin cendré :Cagarra
7 :CAPE VERDE SHEARWATER :Puffin de Cabo Verde :Cagarra de Cabo Verde
8 :GREAT SHEARWATER :Puffin majeur :Pardela-grande
9 :SOOTY SHEARWATER :Puffin fuligineux :Pardela-preta
10 :MANX SHEARWATER :Puffin des Anglais :Pardela-sombria
11 :YELKOUAN SHEARWATER :Puffin de Méditerranée :Pardela-mediterrânica
12 :LITTLE SHEARWATER :Puffin semblable :Pardela-pequena

Plate 4
1 :RED-BILLED TROPICBIRD :Grand Phaéton :Rabo-de-palha-de-bico-vermelho
2 :WHITE-TAILED TROPICBIRD :Petit Phaéton :Rabo-de-palha-de-bico-amarelo

3 :WILSON'S STORM PETREL :Océanite de Wilson :Painho-casquilho
4 :WHITE-FACED STORM PETREL :Océanite frégate :Painho-de-faces-brancas
5 :BLACK-BELLIED STORM PETREL :Océanite à ventre noir :Painho-de-ventre-preto
6 :BRITISH (or European) STORM PETREL :Océanite tempête :Painho-de-cauda-quadrada
7 :MADEIRAN STORM PETREL :Océanite de Castro :Painho da Madeira
8 :LEACH'S STORM PETREL :Océanite culblanc :Painho-de-cauda-forcada
9 :GUILLEMOT :Guillemot de Troïl :Airo
10 :RAZORBILL :Petit Pingouin :Torda-mergulheira

Plate 5
1 :NORTHERN GANNET :Fou de Bassan :Ganso-patola
2 :CAPE GANNET :Fou du Cap :Alcatraz do Cabo
3 :BROWN BOOBY :Fou brun :Alcatraz-pardo
4 :RED-FOOTED BOOBY :Fou á pieds rouges :Alcatraz-de-patas-vermelhas
5 :MASKED BOOBY :Fou masqué :Alcatraz-mascarado

Plate 6
1 :CAPE CORMORANT :Cormoran du Cap :Corvo-marinho do Cabo
2 :LONG-TAILED (or Reed) CORMORANT :Cormoran africain :Corvo-marinho-africano
3 :GREAT (or White-breasted) CORMORANT :Grand Cormoran :Corvo-marinho-de-faces-brancas
4 :DARTER :Anhinga :Mergulhão-serpente
5 :GREAT WHITE(-breasted) PELICAN :Pélican blanc :Pelicano-branco
6 :PINK-BACKED PELICAN :Pélican roussâtre :Pelicano-rosado

Plate 7
1 :YELLOW-BILLED STORK (or Wood Ibis) :Tantale ibis :Cegonha-de-bico-amarelo

2 :AFRICAN OPEN-BILLED STORK :Bec-ouvert africain :Cegonha-de-bico-aberto

3 :BLACK-HEADED HERON :Héron mélanocéphale :Garça-de-cabeça-preta

4 :PURPLE HERON :Héron pourpré :Garça-vermelha

5 :GOLIATH HERON :Héron goliath :Garça-gigante

6 :GREY HERON :Héron cendré :Garça-real

7 :MARABOU (Stork) :Marabout d'Afrique :Marabu

8 :BLACK STORK :Cigogne noire :Cegonha-preta

9 :WHITE STORK :Cigogne blanche :Cegonha-branca

10 :WOOLLY- (or White-)NECKED STORK :Cigogne épiscopale :Cegonha-de-pescoço-lanudo

11 :ABDIM'S STORK :Cigogne d'Abdim :Cegonha de Abdim

12 :SADDLE-BILLED STORK :Jabiru du Sénégal :Jabiru-africano

Plate 8

1 :RUFOUS-BELLIED HERON :Héron à ventre roux :Garça-de-barriga-vermelha

2 :SQUACCO HERON :Crabier chevelu :Papa-ratos-comum

3 :MALAGASY POND HERON :Crabier blanc :Papa-ratos-branco

4 :WHITE-CRESTED TIGER HERON (or Bittern) :Onoré à huppe blanche :Garça-tigre-africana

5 :BLACK-CROWNED NIGHT HERON :Bihoreau gris :Garça-nocturna

6 :WHITE-BACKED NIGHT HERON :Bihoreau à dos blanc :Garça-de-dorso-branco

7 :DWARF BITTERN :Blongios de Sturm :Garçote-anão

8 :LITTLE BITTERN :Blongios nain :Garçote-comum

9 :GREEN(-backed or Striated) HERON :Héron vert :Papa-ratos-africano

10 :CATTLE EGRET :Héron garde-boeufs :Garça-boieira

11 :GREAT (White) EGRET :Grande Aigrette :Garça-branca-grande

12 :BLACK EGRET (or Heron) :Aigrette ardoisée :Garça-ardósia

13 :LITTLE EGRET :Aigrette garzette :Garça-branca-pequena

14 :YELLOW-BILLED (or Intermediate) EGRET :Aigrette intermédiaire :Garça-de-bico-amarelo

15 :WESTERN REEF EGRET :Aigrette gorge blanche :Garça-negra

16 :EURASIAN BITTERN :Butor étoilé :Abetouro-comum

Plate 9

1 :EURASIAN SPOONBILL :Spatule blanche :Colhereiro-africano

2 :AFRICAN SPOONBILL :Spatule d'Afrique :Colhereiro-europeu

3 :OLIVE (or Green) IBIS :Ibis olive :Íbis-olivácea

4 :SPOT-BREASTED IBIS :Ibis vermiculé :Íbis-malhada

5 :HADADA :Ibis hagedash :Íbis Hadada

6 :WALDRAPP :Ibis chauve :Íbis-calva

7 :GLOSSY IBIS :Ibis falcinelle :Íbis-preta

8 :SACRED IBIS :Ibis sacré :Íbis-sagrada

9 :SHOEBILL :Bec-en-sabot du Nil :Bico-de-sapato

10 :HAMERKOP :Ombrette du Sénégal :Pássaro-martelo

11 :GREATER FLAMINGO :Grand Flamant :Flamingo-comum

12 :LESSER FLAMINGO :Petit Flamant :Flamingo-pequeno

Plate 10

1 :BEAN GOOSE :Oie des moissons :Ganso-campestre

2 :GREATER WHITE-FRONTED GOOSE :Oie rieuse :Ganso-grande-de-testa-branca

3 :BRENT GOOSE :Bernache cravant :Ganso-de-faces-negras

4 :SPUR-WINGED GOOSE :Plectroptère de Gambia :Ganso-esporado

5 :COMMON SHELDUCK :Tadorne de Belon :Pato-branco

6 :RUDDY SHELDUCK :Tadorne casarca :Pato-ferrugíneo

7 :EGYPTIAN GOOSE :Oie d'Egypte :Ganso do Egipto

8 :KNOB-BILLED DUCK (or Goose) :Canard casqué :Pato-de-casquete

9 :LITTLE GREBE (or Dabchick) :Grèbe castagneux :Mergulhão-pequeno

10 :GREAT CRESTED GREBE :Grèbe huppé :Mergulhão-de-crista

11 :BLACK-NECKED GREBE. :Grèbe à cou noir :Mergulhão-de-pescoço-preto

12 :RED-THROATED DIVER :Plongeon catmarin :Mobelha-pequena

13 :JACKASS PENGUIN :Manchot du Cap :Pinguim do Cabo

Plate 11

1 :AFRICAN BLACK DUCK :Canard noir :Pato-preto-africano

2 :EURASIAN WIGEON :Canard siffleur :Piadeira

3 :AMERICAN WIGEON :Canard siffleur d'Amerique :Piadeira-americana

4 :GADWALL :Canard chipeau :Frisada

5 :HOTTENTOT TEAL :Sarcelle

hottentote :Marrequinho-hotentote
6 :RED-BILLED TEAL :Canard à bec rouge :Marrequinho-de-bico-vermelho
7 :CAPE TEAL (or Cape Wigeon) :Sarcelle du Cap :Marrequinho do Cabo
8 :YELLOW-BILLED DUCK :Canard à bec jaune :Pato-de-bico-amarelo
9 :MALLARD :Canard colvert :Pato-real
10 :GREEN-WINGED (,Common or European) TEAL :Sarcelle d'hiver :Marrequinha
11 :NORTHERN PINTAIL :Canard pilet :Arrabio
12 :GARGANEY :Sarcelle d'été :Marreco
13 :BLUE-WINGED TEAL :Sarcelle soucrourou :Pato-de-asa-azul
14 :CAPE SHOVELER :Canard du Cap :Pato-trombeteiro do Cabo
15 :NORTHERN SHOVELER :Canard souchet :Pato-trombeteiro-europeu

Plate 12
1 :WHITE-FACED WHISTLING (or Tree) DUCK :Dendrocygne veuf :Pato-assobiador-de-faces-brancas
2 :FULVOUS WHISTLING (or Tree) DUCK :Dendrocygne fauve :Pato-assobiador-de-peito-amarelo
3 :BLACK-BELLIED WHISTLING (or Tree) DUCK :Dendrocygne à bec rouge :Pato-assobiador-de-barriga-preta
4 :WHITE-BACKED DUCK :Erismature à dos blanc :Pato-de-dorso-branco
5 :AFRICAN PYGMY GOOSE :Sarcelle à Oreillons :Ganso-anão-africano
6 :MARBLED TEAL :Sarcelle marbrée :Pardilheira
7 :BLACK SCOTER :Macreuse noire :Pato-preto
8 :SOUTHERN POCHARD :Nette brune :Zarro-africano
9 :COMMON POCHARD :Fuligule milouin :Zarro-comum
10 :FERRUGINOUS DUCK :Fuligule nyroca :Zarro-castanho
11 :LESSER SCAUP :Fuligule à tête noire :Zarro-americano
12 :TUFTED DUCK :Fuligule morillon :Zarro-negrinha
13 :MACCOA DUCK :Erismature maccoa :Pato-de-rabo-alçado-africano
14 :HARTLAUB'S DUCK :Ptéronette de Hartlaub :Pato de Hartlaub

Plate 13
1 :BAT HAWK :Milan des chauves-souris :Papa-morcegos
2 :HONEY BUZZARD :Bondrée apivore :Bútio-vespeiro
3 :BLACK-SHOULDERED KITE :Elanion blanc :Peneireiro-cinzento
4 :AFRICAN SWALLOW- (or Scissor-)TAILED KITE :Milan de Riocour :Peneireiro-cauda-de-andorinha
5a :BLACK KITE :Milan noir :Milhafre-preto
5b :YELLOW-BILLED KITE :Milan à bec jaune :Milhafre-de-bico-amarelo
6 :RED KITE :Milan royal :Milhano

Plate 14
1 :AFRICAN FISH EAGLE (or West African River Eagle) :Pygargue vocifer :Águia-pesqueira-africana
2 :VULTURINE FISH EAGLE (or Palm-Nut Vulture) :Palmiste d'Angola :Abutre-das-palmeiras
3 :OSPREY :Balbuzard pêcheur :Águia-pesqueira
4 :LAMMERGEIER :Gypaète barbu :Quebra-ossos
5 :HOODED VULTURE :Vauteur charognard :Abutre-de-capuz
6 :EGYPTIAN VULTURE :Percnoptère d'Egypte :Abutre do Egipto

Plate 15
1 :EUROPEAN GRIFFON :Vauteur fauve :Grifo-europeu
2 :CAPE VULTURE :Vauteur chassefiente :Grifo do Cabo
3 :AFRICAN WHITE-BACKED VULTURE :Vauteur africain :Grifo-de-dorso-branco
4 :RUEPPELL'S GRIFFON :Vauteur de Rüppell :Grifo de Rüppell
5 :WHITE-HEADED VULTURE :Vauteur à tête blanche :Abutre-de-cabeça-branca
6 :LAPPET-FACED VULTURE :Vauteur oricou :Abutre-real

Plate 16
1 :CONGO SERPENT EAGLE :Serpentaire du Congo :Águia-cobreira-congolesa
2 :BATELEUR :Bateleur à queue courte :Águia-bailarina
3 :BROWN SNAKE EAGLE :Circaète brun :Águia-cobreira-escura
4 :SMALLER (or Western) BANDED SNAKE EAGLE :Circaète cendré :Águia-cobreira-de-cauda-branca
5a :BEAUDOUIN'S SNAKE EAGLE :Circaète Beaudouin :Águia-cobreira de Beaudouin
5b :EUROPEAN (or Short-toed) SNAKE EAGLE :Circaète Jean-le-Blanc :Águia-cobreira-europeia

5c :BLACK-BREASTED SNAKE EAGLE
:Circaète à poitrine noire :Águia-
cobreira-de-peito-preto

Plate 17
1 :NORTHERN (or Hen) HARRIER :Busard
Saint-Martin :Tartaranhão-azulado
2 :PALLID HARRIER :Busard pâle
:Tartaranhão-pálido
3 :MONTAGU'S HARRIER :Busard cendré
:Tartaranhão-caçador
4 :MARSH HARRIER :Busard des roseaux
:Tartaranhão-ruivo-dos-pauis
5 :AFRICAN MARSH HARRIER :Busard
grenouillard :Tartaranhão-dos-pauis-
africano

Plate 18
1 :AFRICAN CUCKOO FALCON (or
Hawk) :Baza coucou :Falcão-cuco
2 :GRASSHOPPER BUZZARD :Buse des
sauterelles :Bútio-dos-gafanhotos
3 :LIZARD BUZZARD :Buse unibande
:Mioto-papa-lagartos
4 :GABAR GOSHAWK :Autour gabar
:Gavião-gabar
5 :DARK CHANTING GOSHAWK
:Autour-chanteur sombre :Açor-cantor-
escuro
6 :AFRICAN HARRIER HAWK (or
Gymnogene) :Serpentaire gymnogène
:Serpentário-pequeno

Plate 19
1 :LONG-TAILED HAWK :Autour à longue
queue :Açor-rabilongo
2 :OVAMBO SPARROWHAWK :Epervier
de l'Ovambo :Gavião de Ovambo
3 :RUFOUS-CHESTED SPARROWHAWK
:Epervier menu :Gavião-de-peito-
vermelho
4 :AFRICAN GOSHAWK :Autour tachiro
:Açor-africano
5 :BLACK (or Great) SPARROWHAWK
:Autour noir :Açor-preto

Plate 20
1 :CHESTNUT-FLANKED
SPARROWHAWK (or Goshawk)
:Autour à flancs roux :Gavião-de-flancos-
vermelhos
2 :LEVANT SPARROWHAWK :Epervier à
pieds courts :Gavião-de-pé-curto
3 :RED-THIGHED (or Western Little)
SPARROWHAWK :Epervier de Hartlaub
:Gavião de Hartlaub
4 :AFRICAN LITTLE SPARROWHAWK
:Epervier minulle :Gavião-pequeno

5 :EURASIAN SPARROWHAWK :Epervier
d'Europe :Gavião da Europa
6 :SHIKRA :Epervier shikra :Gavião-shikra

Plate 21
1 :AUGUR BUZZARD :Buse augure :Bútio-
augur
2 :MOUNTAIN BUZZARD :Buse
montagnarde :Bútio-da-montanha
3 :COMMON BUZZARD :Buse variable
:Águia-de-asa-redonda
4 :LONG-LEGGED BUZZARD :Buse féroce
:Bútio-mouro
5 :RED-NECKED (or -tailed) BUZZARD
:Buse d'Afrique :Bútio-africano

Plate 22
1 :GOLDEN EAGLE :Aigle royal :Águia-real
2 :IMPERIAL EAGLE :Aigle impérial
:Águia-imperial
3 :STEPPE EAGLE :Aigle des steppes
:Águia-das-estepes
4 :TAWNY EAGLE :Aigle ravisseur :Águia-
rapace
5 :WAHLBERG'S EAGLE :Aigle de
Wahlberg :Águia de Wahlberg

Plate 23
1 :LESSER SPOTTED EAGLE :Aigle
pomarin :Águia-pomarina
2 :GREATER SPOTTED EAGLE :Aigle
criard :Águia-gritadeira
3 :VERREAUX'S EAGLE :Aigle de Verreaux
:Águia de Verreaux
4 :MARTIAL EAGLE :Aigle martial :Águia-
marcial
5 :CROWNED (Hawk) EAGLE :Aigle
blanchard :Águia-coroada

Plate 24
1 :LONG-CRESTED (Hawk) EAGLE
:Lophaetus occipitalis :Águia-de-poupa
2 :BOOTED EAGLE :Aigle botté :Águia-
calçada
3 :CASSIN'S HAWK EAGLE :Spizaète de
Cassin :Águia de Cassin
4 :AFRICAN HAWK EAGLE :Aigle autour
Fascié :Águia-açor-africana
5 :BONELLI'S EAGLE :Aigle de Bonelli
:Águia de Bonelli
6 :AYRES'S HAWK EAGLE :Aigle d'Ayres
:Águia de Ayres

Plate 25
1 :PYGMY FALCON :Fauconnet d'Afrique
:Falcão-pigmeu
2 :FOX KESTREL :Faucon renard :Falcão-

raposino
3 :COMMON (or Rock) KESTREL
:Crécerelle des clochers :Peneireiro-
vulgar
4 :LESSER KESTREL :Faucon crécerellette
:Peneireiro-das-torres
5 :SOOTY FALCON :Faucon concolore
:Falcão-sombrio
6 :GREY KESTREL :Faucon ardoisé :Falcão-
cinzento
7 :DICKINSON'S KESTREL :Faucon de
Dickinson :Falcão de Dickinson
8 :RED-NECKED FALCON (or Kestrel)
:Faucon chicquera :Falcão-de-nuca-
vermelha
9 :AFRICAN HOBBY :Faucon de Cuvier
:Ógea-africano
10 :HOBBY, (European) :Faucon hobereau
:Ógea-europeu

Plate 26
1 :EASTERN RED-FOOTED FALCON
:Faucon de l'Amour :Falcão de Amur
2 :RED-FOOTED FALCON :Faucon kobez
:Falcão-de-pés-vermelhos
3 :ELEONORA'S FALCON :Faucon
d'Eléonore :Falcão-da-rainha
4 :MERLIN :Faucon émerillon :Esmerilhão
5 :BARBARY FALCON :Faucon barbarique
:Falcão-tagarote
6 :PEREGRINE FALCON :Faucon pèlerin
:Falcão-peregrino
7 :LANNER FALCON :Faucon lanier
:Alfaneque
8 :SAKER :Faucon sacre :Falcão-sacre

Plate 27
1 :WHITE-BREASTED GUINEAFOWL
:Pintade à poitrine :Pintada-de-peito-
branco
2 :BLACK GUINEAFOWL :Pintade noire
:Pintada-preta
3 :PLUMED GUINEAFOWL :Pintade
plumifère :Pintada-plumífera
4 :CRESTED GUINEAFOWL :Pintade de
Pucheran :Fraca-de-crista
5 :HELMETED GUINEAFOWL, (Grey-
breasted) :Pintade sauvage :Fraca da
Guiné
6 :CONGO PEACOCK :Paon du Congo
:Pavão-congolês
7 :STONE PARTRIDGE :Poule de rocher
:Galinha-do-mato
8 :BARBARY PARTRIDGE :Perdrix gambra
:Perdiz-mourisca
9 :LATHAM'S FOREST FRANCOLIN
:Francolin de Latham :Francolim de
Latham
10 :NAHAN'S FRANCOLIN :Francolin de
Nahan :Francolim de Nahan

11 :CRESTED FRANCOLIN :Francolin
huppé :Francolim-de-poupa
12 :SCALY FRANCOLIN :Francolin écaillé
:Francolim-escamado
13 :RING-NECKED FRANCOLIN
:Francolin à collier :Francolim-de-colar

Plate 28
1 :RED-NECKED FRANCOLIN :Francolin
à gourge rouge :Francolim-de-garganta-
vermelha
2 :HANDSOME FRANCOLIN :Francolin
noble :Francolim-nobre
3 :CAMEROON MOUNTAIN
FRANCOLIN :Francolin du Mount
Cameroun :Francolim-camaronês
4 :AHANTA FRANCOLIN :Francolin
d'Ahanta :Francolim de Ahanta
5 :DOUBLE-SPURRED FRANCOLIN
:Francolin à double éperon :Francolim-
biesporado
6 :HEUGLIN'S FRANCOLIN :Francolin à
bec jaune :Francolim-de-bico-amarelo
7 :HILDEBRANDT'S FRANCOLIN
:Francolin de Hildebrandt :Francolim de
Hildebrandt
8 :CLAPPERTON'S FRANCOLIN
:Francolin de Clapperton :Francolim de
Clapperton
9 :SHELLEY'S FRANCOLIN :Francolin de
Shelley :Francolim de Shelley
10 :REDWING FRANCOLIN :Francolin de
Levaillant :Francolim-de-asas-vermelhas
11 :FINSCH'S FRANCOLIN :Francolin de
Finsch :Francolim de Finsch
12 :WHITE-THROATED FRANCOLIN
:Francolin à gorge blanche :Francolim-de-
garganta-branca
13 :COQUI FRANCOLIN :Francolin coqui
:Francolim-coqui
14 :SCHLEGEL'S FRANCOLIN :Francolin
de Schlegel :Francolim de Schlegel

Plate 29
1 :COMMON QUAIL :Caille des blés
:Codorniz-comum
2 :HARLEQUIN QUAIL :Caille arlequine
:Codorniz-arlequim
3 :BLUE QUAIL, (African) :Caille bleue
:Codorniz-azul
4 :LITTLE (,African or Kurrichane)
BUTTON-QUAIL :Turnix d'Afrique
:Toirão-comum
5 :BLACK-RUMPED BUTTON-QUAIL
:Turnix nain :Toirão-hotentote
6 :QUAIL-PLOVER :Turnix de Meiffren
:Toirão-de-asa-branca
7 :RED-CHESTED FLUFFTAIL :Râle à
camail :Frango-de-água-de-peito-
vermelho

8 :WHITE-SPOTTED FLUFFTAIL :Râle
perlé :Frango-de-água-mosqueado
9 :BOEHM'S (or Streaky-breasted)
FLUFFTAIL :Râle de Böhm :Frango-de-
água de Böhm
10 :CHESTNUT-HEADED FLUFFTAIL
:Râle à tête rousse :Frango-de-água-de-
cabeça-vermelha
11 :BUFF-SPOTTED FLUFFTAIL :Râle
ponctué :Frango-de-água-elegante
12 :SPOTTED CRAKE :Marouette ponctuée
:Franga-de-água-grande
13 :STRIPED CRAKE :Marouette rayée
:Franga-de-água-estriada
14 :LITTLE CRAKE :Marouette poussin
:Franga-de-água-bastarda
15 :BAILLON'S CRAKE :Marouette de
Baillon :Franga-de-água-pequena
16 :BLACK CRAKE :Marouette noire
:Franga-de-água-preta

Plate 30

1 :GREY-THROATED RAIL :Râle à gorge
grise :Frango-de-água-de-garganta-
cinzenta
2 :NKULENGU RAIL :Râle à pieds rouges
:Frango-de-água-de-pés-vermelhos
3 :CORNCRAKE, (European) :Râle des
genets :Codornizão-europeu
4 :AFRICAN CRAKE :Râle des prés
:Codornizão-africano
5 :AFRICAN WATER RAIL :Râle bleuâtre
:Frango-de-água-azul
6 :PURPLE SWAMPHEN :Talève poule-
sultane :Caimão-comum
7 :ALLEN'S GALLINULE (or Reed-Hen)
:Talève d'Allen :Caimão de Allen
8 :PURPLE GALLINULE (or King Reed-
Hen) :Talève pourprée
:Caimão-americano
9 :COMMON MOORHEN :Gallinule poule
d'eau :Galinha-de-água-comum
10 :LESSER MOORHEN :Gallinule africaine
:Galinha-de-água-pequena
11 :RED-KNOBBED COOT :Foulque à crête
:Galeirão-de-crista
12 :EURASIAN COOT :Foulque macroule
:Galeirão-europeu
13 :AFRICAN FINFOOT :Grébifoulque du
Sénégal :Pés-de-barbatana

Plate 31

1 :DEMOISELLE CRANE :Grue demoiselle
:Grou-pequeno
2 :GREY CROWNED CRANE :Grue royal
:Grou-coroado-austral
3 :BLACK CROWNED CRANE :Grue
couronnée :Grou-coroado-negro
4 :COMMON CRANE :Grue cendrée
:Grou-comum

5 :WATTLED CRANE :Grue caronculée
:Grou-carunculado
6 :DENHAM'S (or Stanley's) BUSTARD
:Outarde de Denham :Abetarda de
Denham
7 :NUBIAN BUSTARD :Outarde nubienne
:Abetarda-nubiana
8 :ARABIAN (or Sudan) BUSTARD
:Outarde arabe :Abetarda-árabe
9 :HOUBARA :Outarde houbara :Hubara
10 :BLACK-BELLIED BUSTARD :Outarde à
ventre noir :Sisão-de-barriga-preta
11 :WHITE-BELLIED (or Senegal)
BUSTARD :Outarde du Sénégal :Sisão do
Senegal
12 :SAVILE'S BUSTARD :Outarde de Saville
:Sisão de Savile

Plate 32

1 :AFRICAN JACANA (or Lily-Trotter)
:Jacana à oitrine dorée :Jacana-africana
2 :LESSER JACANA :Jacana nain :Jacana-
pequena
3 :EURASIAN OYSTERCATCHER
:Huîtrier pie :Ostraceiro-europeu
4 :AFRICAN BLACK OYSTERCATCHER
:Huîtrier de Moquin :Ostraceiro-preto-
africano
5 :EURASIAN AVOCET :Avocette
élégante :Alfaiate
6 :COMMON (or Black-winged) STILT
:Échasse blanche :Perna-longa
7 :SPOTTED THICK-KNEE :Oedicnème du
tachard :Alcaravão do Cabo
8 :STONE CURLEW :Oedicnème criard
:Alcaravão-europeu
9 :WATER THICK-KNEE :Oedicnème
vermiculé :Alcaravão-aquático
10 :SENEGAL THICK-KNEE :Oedicnème du
Sénégal :Alcaravão do Senegal

Plate 33

1 :RUFF (M), REEVE (F) :Chevalier
combattant :Combatente
2 :BUFF-BREASTED SANDPIPER
:Bécasseau rousset :Pilrito-canela
3 :EGYPTIAN-PLOVER :Pluvian d'Egypte
:Ave-crocodilo
4 :TEMMINCK'S COURSER :Courvite de
Temminck :Corredor de Temminck
5 :CREAM-COLOURED COURSER
:Courvite isabelle :Corredor
6 :BRONZE-WINGED (or Violet-tipped)
COURSER :Courvite à ailes violettes
:Corredor-de-patas-vermelhas
7 :COLLARED (or Common)
PRATINCOLE :Glaréole à collier
:Perdiz-do-mar-europeia
8 :BLACK-WINGED PRATINCOLE
:Glaréole à ailes noires :Perdiz-do-mar-de-

asa-preta
9 :GREY PRATINCOLE :Glaréole grise
:Perdiz-do-mar-cinzenta
10 :ROCK PRATINCOLE :Glaréole aureolée
:Perdiz-do-mar-escura

Plate 34

1 :LONG-TOED (or White-faced)
LAPWING :Vanneau à ailes blanches
:Abibe-de-faces-brancas
2 :BLACK-HEADED LAPWING :Vanneau
coiffé :Abibe-de-cabeça-preta
3 :NORTHERN LAPWING :Vanneau
huppé :Abibe-comum
4 :WHITE-TAILED LAPWING :Vanneau à
queue blanche :Abibe-de-cauda-branca
5 :BROWN-CHESTED (Wattled)
LAPWING :Vanneau caronculé :Abibe-
de-peito-ruivo
6 :LESSER BLACK-WINGED LAPWING
:Vanneau demi-deuil :Abibe-lúgubre
7 :AFRICAN WATTLED LAPWING
:Vanneau du Sénégal :Abibe do Senegal
8 :WHITE-HEADED (or -crowned)
LAPWING :Vanneau à tête blanche
:Abibe-de-coroa-branca
9 :CROWNED LAPWING :Vanneau
couronné :Abibe-coroado
10 :SPUR-WINGED LAPWING :Vanneau
éperonné :Abibe-esporado
11 :BLACKSMITH LAPWING :Vanneau
armé :Abibe-armado

Plate 35

1 :SHORT-BILLED DOWITCHER :Bécassin
roux :Maçarico-de-bico-curto
2 :LONG-BILLED DOWITCHER :Bécassin
à long bec :Maçarico-de-bico-comprido
3 :BLACK-TAILED GODWIT :Barge à
queue noire :Maçarico-de-bico-direito
4 :BAR-TAILED GODWIT :Barge rousse
:Fuselo
5 :GREATER GOLDEN PLOVER :Pluvier
doré :Tarambola-dourada
6 :PACIFIC GOLDEN PLOVER :Pluvier
fauvem :Tarambola-dourada-siberiana
7 :GREY PLOVER :Pluvier argenté
:Tarambola-cinzenta
8 :AMERICAN GOLDEN PLOVER :Pluvier
bronzé :Tarambola-dourada-americana
9 :SLENDER-BILLED CURLEW :Courlis à
bec grêle :Maçarico-de-bico-fino
10 :EURASIAN CURLEW :Courlis cendré
:Maçarico-real
11 :WHIMBREL :Courlis corlieu :Maçarico-
galego

Plate 36

1 :THREE-BANDED PLOVER :Pluvier à

triple collier :Borrelho-de-tripla-coleira
2 :FORBES'S (Banded) PLOVER :Pluvier de
Forbes :Borrelho de Forbes
3 :EURASIAN DOTTEREL :Pluvier
guignard :Tarambola-carambola
4 :LITTLE RINGED PLOVER :Petit
Gravelot :Borrelho-pequeno-de-coleira
5 :SEMIPALMATED PLOVER :Pluvier
semipalmé :Borrelho-semipalmado
6 :RINGED PLOVER :Grand Gravelot
:Borrelho-grande-de-coleira
7 :KITTLITZ'S (Sand) PLOVER :Pluvier
pâtre :Borrelho de Kittlitz
8 :GREAT SAND PLOVER :Pluvier de
Leschenault :Borrelho-do-deserto
9 :MONGOLIAN PLOVER :Pluvier mongol
:Borrelho-mongol
10 :CASPIAN PLOVER :Pluvier asiatique
:Borrelho-asiático
11 :KENTISH PLOVER :Pluvier à collier
interrompu :Borrelho-de-coleira-
interrompida
12 :WHITE-FRONTED (Sand) PLOVER
:Pluvier à front blanc :Borrelho-de-testa-
branca

Plate 37

1 :SPOTTED REDSHANK :Chevalier
arlequin :Perna-vermelha-escuro
2 :COMMON REDSHANK :Chevalier
gambette :Perna-vermelha-comum
3 :COMMON GREENSHANK :Chevalier
aboyeur :Perna-verde-comum
4 :MARSH SANDPIPER :Chevalier
stagnatile :Perna-verde-fino
5 :LESSER YELLOWLEGS :Petit chevalier à
pattes jaunes :Perna-amarela-pequeno
6 :GREEN SANDPIPER :Chevalier culblanc :Pássaro-bique-bique
7 :SOLITARY SANDPIPER :Chevalier
solitaire :Maçarico-solitário
8 :WOOD SANDPIPER :Chevalier sylvain
:Maçarico-bastardo
9 :TEREK SANDPIPER :Bargette de Terek
:Maçarico-sovela
10 :UPLAND SANDPIPER :Maubèche des
camps :Maçarico-dos-campos

Plate 38

1 :BROAD-BILLED SANDPIPER
:Bécasseau falcinelle :Pilrito-de-bico-
largo
2 :LEAST SANDPIPER :Bécasseau
minuscule :Pilrito-minúsculo
3 :LITTLE STINT :Bécasseau minute
:Pilrito-pequeno
4 :LONG-TOED STINT :Bécasseau à longs
doigts :Pilrito-de-dedos-compridos
5 :SEMIPALMATED SANDPIPER
:Bécasseau semipalmé :Pilrito-

semipalmado

6 :TEMMINCK'S STINT :Bécasseau de
Temminck :Pilrito de Temminck

7 :BAIRD'S SANDPIPER :Bécasseau de
Baird :Pilrito de Baird

8 :WHITE-RUMPED SANDPIPER
:Bécasseau de Bonaparte :Pilrito de
Bonaparte

9 :PECTORAL SANDPIPER :Bécasseau
tachète :Pilrito-peitoral

10 :DUNLIN :Bécasseau variable :Pilrito-
comum

11 :CURLEW SANDPIPER :Bécasseau
cocorli :Pilrito-de-bico-comprido

12 :PURPLE SANDPIPER :Bécasseau violet
:Pilrito-escuro

13 :RED KNOT :Bécasseau maubèche
:Seixoeira

14 :SANDERLING :Bécasseau sanderling
:Pilrito-sanderlingo

Plate 39

1 :GREATER PAINTED-SNIPE :Rhynchée
peinte :Narceja-pintada

2 :AFRICAN SNIPE :Bécassine africaine
:Narceja-africana

3 :GREAT SNIPE :Bécassine double
:Narceja-real

4 :COMMON SNIPE :Bécassine des marais
:Narceja-comum

5 :JACK SNIPE :Bécassine sourde :Narceja-
galega

6 :COMMON SANDPIPER :Chevalier
guignetta :Maçarico-das-rochas

7 :SPOTTED SANDPIPER :Chevalier
grivelé :Maçarico-maculado

8 :RUDDY TURNSTONE :Tournepierre à
collier :Rola-do-mar

9 :WILSON'S PHALAROPE :Phalarope de
Wilson :Falaropo de Wilson

10 :RED-NECKED PHALAROPE :Phalarope
à bec étroit :Falaropo-de-bico-fino

11 :GREY PHALAROPE :Phalarope á bec
large :Falaropo-de-bico-grosso

Plate 40

1 :SOUTH POLAR SKUA :Skua de
McCormick :Moleiro-antárctico

2 :GREAT SKUA :Grande Labbe :Moleiro-
grande

3 :POMARINE SKUA :Labbe pomarine
:Moleiro-pomarino

4 :ARCTIC SKUA :Labbe parasite :Moleiro-
parasítico

5 :LONG-TAILED SKUA :Labbe à longue
queue :Moleiro-de-cauda-comprida

6 :YELLOW-LEGGED GULL :Goéland
leucophée :Gaivota-argêntea

7 :KELP GULL :Goéland dominicain
:Gaivota-dominicana

8 :LESSER BLACK-BACKED GULL
:Goéland brun :Gaivota-de-asa-escura

9 :GREAT BLACK-BACKED GULL
:Goéland marin :Alcatraz

Plate 41

1 :AUDOUIN'S GULL :Goéland de
Audouin :Gaivota de Audouin

2 :MEW (or Common) GULL :Goéland
cendré :Gaivota-parda

3 :RING-BILLED GULL :Goéland à bec
cerclé :Gaivota do Delaware

4 :GREY-HEADED GULL :Mouette à tête
grise :Gaivota-de-cabeça-cinzenta

5 :LAUGHING GULL :Goéland atricille
:Gaivota-risonha

6 :MEDITERRANEAN GULL :Mouette
mélanocéphale :Gaivota-de-cabeça-preta

7 :LITTLE GULL :Mouette pygmée
:Gaivota-pequena

8 :BONAPARTE'S GULL :Mouette de
Bonaparte :Gaivota de Bonaparte

9 :SABINE'S GULL :Mouette de Sabine
:Gaivota de Sabine

10 :SLENDER-BILLED GULL :Goéland
railleur :Gaivota-de-bico-fino

11 :FRANKLIN'S GULL :Mouette de
Franklin :Gaivota de Franklin

12 :BLACK-LEGGED KITTIWAKE :Mouette
tridactyle :Gaivota-tridáctila

13 :BLACK-HEADED GULL :Mouette rieuse
:Guincho-comum

Plate 42

1 :COMMON TERN :Sterne pierregarin
:Gaivina-comum

2 :ARCTIC TERN :Sterne arctique
:Gaivina-árctica

3 :ROSEATE TERN :Sterne de Dougall
:Gaivina-rósea

4 :DAMARA TERN :Sterne des baleiniers
:Gaivina da Damaralândia

5 :LITTLE TERN :Sterne naine :Gaivina-
pequena

6 :BRIDLED TERN :Sterne bridée :Gaivina-
de-dorso-castanho

7 :SOOTY TERN :Sterne fuligineuse
:Gaivina-sombria

8 :WHISKERED TERN :Guifette moustac
:Gaivina-dos-pauis

9 :WHITE-WINGED BLACK TERN
:Guifette leucoptère :Gaivina-de-asa-
branca

10 :BLACK TERN :Guifette noire :Gaivina-
preta

Plate 43

1 :CASPIAN TERN :Sterne caspienne
:Gaivina-de-bico-vermelho

2 :SWIFT (or Greater Crested) TERN
:Sterne huppée :Gaivina-de-bico-amarelo
3 :ROYAL TERN :Sterne royal :Gaivina-real
4 :LESSER CRESTED TERN :Sterne
voyageuse :Gaivina-de-bico-laranja
5 :SANDWICH TERN :Sterne caugek
:Garajau-comum
6 :GULL-BILLED TERN :Sterne hansel
:Gaivina-de-bico-preto
7 :BLACK NODDY :Noddi noir :Nodi-preto
8 :LESSER NODDY :Noddi marianne :Nodi-
pequeno
9 :BROWN NODDY :Noddi brun :Nodi-
castanho
10 :AFRICAN SKIMMER :Bec-en-ciseaux
d'Afrique :Bico-de-tesoura-africano

Plate 44

1 :LICHTENSTEIN'S SANDGROUSE
:Ganga de Lichtenstein :Cortiçol de
Lichtenstein
2 :FOUR-BANDED SANDGROUSE
:Ganga quadribande :Cortiçol-de-quatro-
bandas
3 :CROWNED SANDGROUSE :Ganga
couronné :Cortiçol-coroado
4 :SPOTTED SANDGROUSE :Ganga
tacheté :Cortiçol-malhado
5 :CHESTNUT-BELLIED SANDGROUSE
:Ganga à ventre brun :Cortiçol-de-
barriga-castanha
6 :AFRICAN GREEN PIGEON :Pigeon vert
à front nu :Pombo-verde-africano
7 :SÃO TOMÉ GREEN PIGEON :Pigeon
vert de São Tomé :Pombo-verde de São
Tomé
8 :BRUCE'S GREEN PIGEON :Treron
waalia :Pombo-verde-de-ventre-amarelo
9 :ROCK PIGEON :Pigeon biset :Pombo-
doméstico
10 :SPECKLED (or Rock) PIGEON :Pigeon
de Guinée :Pombo da Guiné
11 :WOOD PIGEON :Pigeon ramier :Pombo-
torcaz
12 :AFEP PIGEON :Pigeon gris :Pombo-
congolês
13 :CAMEROON OLIVE PIGEON :Pigeon
du Cameroun :Pombo-camaronês
14 :OLIVE (or Rameron) PIGEON :Pigeon
rameron :Pombo-de-olho-amarelo
15 :WHITE-NAPED PIGEON :Pigeon à
nuque blanche :Pombo-de-nuca-branca
16 :SÃO TOMÉ OLIVE PIGEON :Pigeon de
São Tomé :Pombo de São Tomé
17 :SÃO TOMÉ BRONZE-NAPED PIGEON
:Pigeon de Malherbe :Pombo de Malherbe
18 :WESTERN BRONZE-NAPED PIGEON
:Pigeon à nuque bronzée :Pombo-de-
nuca-bronzeada
19 :STOCK DOVE :Pigeon colombin :Pombo-
bravo

Plate 45

1 :EUROPEAN TURTLE DOVE
:Tourterelle des bois :Rola-europeia
2 :DUSKY (or Pink-breasted) TURTLE
DOVE :Tourterelle cendrée :Rola-escura
3 :ADAMAWA TURTLE DOVE
:Tourterelle à poitrine rose :Rola-
camaronesa
4 :AFRICAN COLLARED (or Rose-grey)
DOVE :Tourterelle rieuse :Rola-de-
cabeça-rosada
5 :AFRICAN MOURNING DOVE
:Tourterelle pleureuse :Rola-chorosa
6 :RED-EYED DOVE :Tourterelle à collier
:Rola-de-olhos-vermelhos
7 :RING-NECKED (or Cape Turtle) DOVE
:Tourterelle du Cap :Rola do Cabo
8 :VINACEOUS DOVE :Tourterelle vineuse
:Rola-de-peito-vináceo
9 :LAUGHING DOVE :Tourterelle maillée
:Rola-das-palmeiras
10 :EURASIAN COLLARED DOVE
:Tourterelle turque :Rola-turca
11 :LEMON (or Cinnamon) DOVE
:Tourterelle à masque blanc :Rola-de-
faces-brancas
12 :NAMAQUA DOVE :Tourtelette à
masque de fer :Rola-rabilonga
13 :BLUE-SPOTTED (or Red-billed) WOOD
DOVE :Tourtelette améthystine :Rola-de-
manchas-azuis
14 :BLACK-BILLED WOOD DOVE
:Tourtelette d'Abyssinie :Rola da
Abissínia
15 :EMERALD- (or Green-)SPOTTED
WOOD DOVE :Tourtelette émeraudine
:Rola-esmeraldina
16 :TAMBOURINE DOVE :Tourtelette
tambourette :Rola-tamborina
17 :BLUE-HEADED WOOD DOVE
:Tourtelette demoiselle :Rola-de-cabeça-
azul

Plate 46

1 :NARINA'S TROGON :Couroucou narina
:Republicano
2 :BARE-CHEEKED TROGON :Couroucou
à joues jaunes :Republicano-de-faces-
amarelas
3 :BAR-TAILED TROGON :Couroucou à
queue barrée :Republicano-de-cauda-
barrada
4 :SPECKLED MOUSEBIRD :Coliou strié
:Rabo-de-junco-estriado
5 :RED-BACKED MOUSEBIRD :Coliou à
dos roux :Rabo-de-junco-de-dorso-
vermelho
6 :RED-FACED MOUSEBIRD :Coliou à
face rouge :Rabo-de-junco-de-faces-
vermelhas
7 :BLUE-NAPED MOUSEBIRD :Coliou à

nuque bleue :Rabo-de-junco-de-nuca-azul

8 :RED-HEADED LOVEBIRD :Inséparable à tête rouge :Inseparável-de-cabeça-vermelha

9 :BLACK-COLLARED LOVEBIRD :Inséparable à collier noir :Inseparável-de-colar

10 :GREY PARROT :Perroquet gris :Papagaio-cinzento

11 :ROSE-RINGED PARAKEET :Perruche à collier :Periquito-de-colar

12 :RED-FRONTED (or -headed) PARROT :Perroquet à front rouge :Papagaio-de-testa-vermelha

13 :NIAM-NIAM PARROT :Perroquet des niam-niam :Papagaio de Niam-niam

14 :MEYER'S PARROT :Perroquet de Meyer :Papagaio de Meyer

15 :BROWN-NECKED (or Cape) PARROT :Perroquet robuste :Papagaio-de-pescoço-castanho

16 :SENEGAL (or Yellow-bellied) PARROT :Perroquet youyou :Papagaio-senegalês

17 :RUEPPELL'S PARROT :Perroquet de Rüppell :Papagaio de Rüppell

Plate 47

1 :GREAT BLUE TURACO :Touraco géant :Andua-gigante

2 :WESTERN GREY PLANTAIN-EATER :Touraco gris :Andua-cinzento-ocidental

3 :EASTERN GREY PLANTAIN-EATER :Touraco à queue barrée :Andua-cinzento-oriental

4 :BARE-FACED GO-AWAY BIRD :Touraco masqué :Andua-mascarado

5 :GREY GO-AWAY BIRD :Touraco concolor :Andua-unicolor

6 :ROSS'S TURACO :Touraco de Lady Ross :Andua de Ross

7 :VIOLET TURACO :Touraco violet :Andua-violeta

8 :RWENZORI TURACO :Touraco du Rwenzori :Andua das Ruwenzori

9 :SCHALOW'S TURACO :Touraco de Schalow :Andua de Schalow

10 :GREEN TURACO :Touraco vert :Andua da Guiné

11 :BLACK-BILLED TURACO :Touraco à bec noir :Andua-de-bico-preto

12 :RED-CRESTED TURACO :Touraco pauline :Andua-de-crista-vermelha

13 :BANNERMAN'S TURACO :Touraco de Bannerman :Andua de Bannerman

14 :YELLOW-BILLED (or Verreaux's) TURACO :Touraco à gros bec :Andua de Verreaux

15 :WHITE-CRESTED TURACO :Touraco à huppe blanche :Andua-de-poupa-branca

Plate 48

1 :GREAT SPOTTED CUCKOO :Coucou geai :Cuco-rabilongo

2 :JACOBIN (or Black-and-white) CUCKOO :Coucou jacobin :Cuco-jacobino

3 :AFRICAN STRIPED CUCKOO :Coucou de Levaillant :Cuco de Levaillant

4 :THICK-BILLED CUCKOO :Coucou d'Audebert :Cuco-de-bico-grosso

5 :YELLOWBILL (or Green Coucal) :Malcoha à bec jaune :Cuco-verde

6 :YELLOW-THROATED CUCKOO :Coucou à gorge jaune :Cuco-de-garganta-amarela

7 :AFRICAN EMERALD CUCKOO :Coucou foliotocol :Cuco-esmeraldino

8 :KLAAS'S CUCKOO :Coucou de Klaas :Cuco de Klaas

9 :DIEDERIK (or Didric) CUCKOO :Coucou didric :Cuco-didrique

10 :RED-CHESTED CUCKOO :Coucou solitaire :Cuco-de-peito-vermelho

11 :BLACK CUCKOO :Coucou criard :Cuco-preto

12 :COMMON (or European) CUCKOO :Coucou gris :Cuco-canoro

13 :AFRICAN CUCKOO :Coucou africain :Cuco-africano

14 :ASIAN LESSER CUCKOO :Petit coucou d'Asie :Cuco-pequeno

15 :MADAGASCAR LESSER CUCKOO :Petit coucou malgache :Cuco-malgaxe

16 :OLIVE LONG-TAILED CUCKOO :Coucou olivâtre :Cuco-oliváceo

17 :BARRED LONG-TAILED CUCKOO :Coucou montagnard :Cuco-da-montanha

18 :DUSKY LONG-TAILED CUCKOO :Coucou de Mechow :Cuco-escuro

Plate 49

1 :SPOTTED EAGLE OWL :Grand-Duc africain :Bufo-africano

2 :SHELLEY'S EAGLE OWL :Grand-Duc bandé :Bufo-barrado

3 :FRASER'S EAGLE OWL :Grand-Duc à aigrettes :Bufo de Fraser

4 :VERREAUX'S (or Giant) EAGLE OWL :Grand-Duc de Verreaux :Bufo de Verreaux

5 :AKUN EAGLE OWL :Grand-Duc tacheté :Bufo-malhado

6 :DESERT EAGLE OWL :Grand-Duc du désert :Bufo-real

7 :VERMICULATED (or Bouvier's) FISHING OWL :Chouette-pêcheur de Bouvier :Corujão-pesqueiro de Bouvier

8 :RUFOUS FISHING OWL :Chouette-pêcheur à dos roux :Corujão-pesqueiro-ruivo

9 :PEL'S FISHING OWL :Chouette-
  pêcheuse de Pel :Corujão-pesqueiro de Pel
10 :COPPERY-TAILED COUCAL :Coucal
  des papyrus :Cuco-cauda-de-cobre
11 :BLUE-HEADED COUCAL :Coucal
  moine :Cuco-de-nuca-azul
12 :GABON COUCAL :Coucal du Gabon
  :Cuco do Gabão
13 :BLACK-THROATED COUCAL :Coucal
  à ventre blanc :Cuco-de-ventre-branco
14 :SENEGAL COUCAL :Coucal du Sénégal
  :Cuco-senegalês
15 :WHITE-BROWED COUCAL :oucal à
  sourcils blancs :Cuco-de-sobrancelhas-
  brancas
16 :BLACK COUCAL :Coucal de Grill
  :Cuco-variável

Plate 50

1 :BARN OWL :Chouette effraie :Coruja-
  das-torres
2 :AFRICAN GRASS OWL :Effraie du Cap
  :Coruja-dos-campos
3 :SHORT-EARED OWL :Hibou des marais
  :Coruja-do-nabal
4 :LONG-EARED OWL :Hibou moyen-duc
  :Bufo-pequeno
5 :MARSH OWL :Hibou du Cap :Coruja-
  dos-pauis
6 :CONGO BAY OWL :Chouette de
  Prigogine :Coruja-congolesa
7 :LITTLE OWL :Chouette chevêche
  :Mocho-galego
8 :MANED (or Akun Scops) OWL :Hibou à
  crinière :Mocho-de-crina
9 :WHITE-FACED SCOPS OWL :Petit-Duc
  à face blanche :Mocho-de-faces-brancas
10 :SANDY SCOPS OWL :Petit-Duc à bec
  jaune :Mocho-de-bico-amarelo
11 :SÃO TOMÉ SCOPS OWL :Petit-Duc de
  São Tomé :Mocho de São Tomé
12 :AFRICAN SCOPS OWL :Petit-Duc
  africain :Mocho do Senegal
13 :COMMON SCOPS OWL :Petit-Duc
  scops :Mocho-de-orelhas
14 :RED-CHESTED OWLET :Chevêchette à
  pieds jaunes :Mocho-de-peito-ruivo
15 :PEARL-SPOTTED OWLET
  :Chevêchette perlée :Mocho-pigmeu-
  africano
16 :AFRICAN BARRED OWLET
  :Chevêchette à poitrine barrée :Mocho-
  barrado
17 :CHESTNUT-BACKED (or Sjöstedt's)
  OWLET :Chevêchette à queue barrée
  :Mocho-de-dorso-ruivo
18 :ALBERTINE OWLET :Chevêchette du
  Graben :Mocho de Alberto
19 :AFRICAN WOOD OWL :Chouette
  africaine :Coruja-da-floresta

Plate 51

1 :BROWN NIGHTJAR :Engoulevent à
  deux taches :Noitibó-bimaculado
2 :RED-NECKED NIGHTJAR :Engoulevent
  à collier roux :Noitibó-de-nuca-vermelha
3 :EUROPEAN NIGHTJAR :Engoulevent
  d'Europe :Noitibó da Europa
4 :EGYPTIAN NIGHTJAR :Engoulevent du
  Sahara :Noitibó-do-deserto
5 :GOLDEN NIGHTJAR :Engoulevent doré
  :Noitibó-dourado
6 :MOUNTAIN NIGHTJAR :Engoulevent
  d'Abyssinie :Noitibó-montês
7 :FIERY-NECKED NIGHTJAR
  :Engoulevent musicien :Noitibó-musical
8 :BLACK-SHOULDERED NIGHTJAR
  :Engoulevent à épaulettes noires
  :Noitibó-de-ombros-negros
9 :RUFOUS-CHEEKED NIGHTJAR
  :Engoulevent à joues rousses :Noitibó-de-
  faces-vermelhas
10 :SLENDER-TAILED NIGHTJAR
  :Engoulevent de Reichenow :Noitibó de
  Reichenow
11 :SOMBRE (or Dusky) NIGHTJAR
  :Engoulevent sombre :Noitibó-escuro
12 :PRIGOGINE'S NIGHTJAR :Engoulevent
  de prigogine :Noitibó de Prigogine

Plate 52

1 :RWENZORI NIGHTJAR :Engoulevent de
  Rwenzori :Noitibó das Ruwenzori
2 :SWAMP (or Natal) NIGHTJAR
  :Engoulevent de Natal :Noitibó de Natal
3 :PLAIN NIGHTJAR :Engoulevent terne
  :Noitibó-claro
4 :FRECKLED (or Rock) NIGHTJAR
  :Engoulevent pointillé :Noitibó-das-
  rochas
5 :BATES'S NIGHTJAR :Engoulevent de
  Bates :Noitibó de Bates
6 :SQUARE-TAILED (,Gabon or
  Mozambique) NIGHTJAR :Engoulevent
  de Mozambique :Noitibó de Moçambique
7 :LONG-TAILED NIGHTJAR
  :Engoulevent à longue queue :Noitibó-
  rabilongo
8 :STANDARD-WINGED NIGHTJAR
  :Engoulevent à balanciers :Noitibó-porta-
  estandarte
9 :PENNANT-WINGED NIGHTJAR
  :Engoulevent porte-étendard :Noitibó-de-
  balanceiros

Plate 53

1 :SCARCE SWIFT :Martinet de Shoa
  :Andorinhão de Shoa
2 :SCHOUTEDEN'S SWIFT :Martinet de
  Schouteden :Andorinhão-congolês
3 :SÃO TOMÉ SPINETAIL :Martinet de

São Tomé :Rabo-espinhoso de São Tomé e Príncipe

4 :BLACK (or Chapin's) SPINETAIL :Martinet de Chapin :Rabo-espinhoso de Chapin

5 :MOTTLED(-throated) SPINETAIL :Martinet d'Ussher :Rabo-espinhoso de Ussher

6 :CASSIN'S SPINETAIL :Martinet de Cassin :Rabo-espinhoso de Cassin

7 :BAT-LIKE (or Böhm's) SPINETAIL. :Martinet de Böhm :Rabo-espinhoso de Böhm

8 :SABINE'S SPINETAIL :Martinet de Sabine :Rabo-espinhoso de Sabine

9 :AFRICAN PALM SWIFT :Martinet des palmes :Andorinhão-das-palmeiras

10 :ALPINE SWIFT :Martinet alpin :Andorinhão-real

11 :MOTTLED SWIFT :Martinet marbré :Andorinhão-malhado

Plate 54

1 :AFRICAN BLACK SWIFT :Martinet du Cap :Andorinhão-preto-africano

2 :NYANZA SWIFT :Martinet du Nyanza :Andorinhão de Nyanza

3 :PALLID SWIFT :Martinet Pâle :Andorinhão-pálido

4 :BATES'S SWIFT :Martinet de Bates :Andorinhão-camaronês

5 :EUROPEAN SWIFT :Martinet noir :Andorinhão-preto-europeu

6 :WHITE-RUMPED SWIFT :Martinet cafre :Andorinhão-cafre

7 :PLAIN SWIFT :Martinet unicolore :Andorinhão-da-serra

8 :ALEXANDER'S SWIFT :Martinet du Cap-Vert :Andorinhão de Cabo Verde

9 :HORUS SWIFT :Martinet horus :Andorinhão-horus

10 :LITTLE SWIFT :Martinet des maisons :Andorinhão-pequeno

Plate 55

1 :AFRICAN GIANT KINGFISHER :Alcyon géant :Guarda-rios-gigante

2 :PIED KINGFISHER :Alcyon pie :Guarda-rios-malhado

3 :HALF-COLLARED KINGFISHER :Martin-pêcheur à demi-collier :Guarda-rios-de-colar

4 :SHINING-BLUE KINGFISHER :Martin-pêcheur azuré :Guarda-rios-resplandecente

5 :WHITE-BELLIED KINGFISHER :Martin-pêcheur à vent blanc :Guarda-rios-de-ventre-branco

6 :MALACHITE KINGFISHER :Martin-pêcheur huppé :Guarda-rios-de-poupa

7 :AFRICAN DWARF KINGFISHER :Martin-pêcheur à tête rousse :Guarda-rios-anão

8 :AFRICAN PYGMY KINGFISHER :Martin-pêcheur pygmée :Guarda-rios-pigmeu

9 :GREY-HEADED (, -hooded or Chestnut-bellied) KINGFISHER :Martin-chasseur à tête grise :Guarda-rios-de-cabeça-cinzenta

10 :WOODLAND (or Senegal) KINGFISHER :Martin-chasseur du Sénégal :Guarda-rios-dos-bosques

11 :BLUE-BREASTED KINGFISHER :Martin-chasseur à poitrine bleue :Guarda-rios-de-peito-azul

12 :BROWN-HOODED KINGFISHER :Martin-chasseur à tête brune :Guarda-rios-de-cabeça-castanha

13 :CHOCOLATE-BACKED KINGFISHER :Martin-chasseur marron :Guarda-rios-de-dorso-castanho

14 :STRIPED KINGFISHER :Martin-chasseur strié :Guarda-rios-estriado

Plate 56

1 :BLACK BEE-EATER :Guêpier noir :Abelharuco-preto

2 :BLUE-HEADED BEE-EATER :Guêpier à tête bleue :Abelharuco-de-cabeça-azul

3 :RED-THROATED BEE-EATER :Guêpier à gorge rouge :Abelharuco-de-garganta-vermelha

4 :WHITE-FRONTED BEE-EATER :Guêpier à front blanc :Abelharuco-de-testa-branca

5 :BLACK-HEADED BEE-EATER :Guêpier à tête noire :Abelharuco-de-cabeça-preta

6 :SWALLOW-TAILED BEE-EATER :Guêpier à queue d'aronde :Abelharuco-de-cauda-forcada

7 :CINNAMON-CHESTED (or -breasted) BEE-EATER :Guêpier montagnard :Abelharuco-montês

8 :BLUE-BREASTED BEE-EATER :Guêpier à collier bleu :Abelharuco-de-peito-azul

9 :LITTLE BEE-EATER :Guêpier nain :Abelharuco-pequeno

10 :ROSY BEE-EATER :Guêpier gris-rose :Abelharuco-rosado

11 :CARMINE BEE-EATER :Guêpier écarlate :Abelharuco-carmim

12 :LITTLE GREEN BEE-EATER :Guêpier d'Orient :Abelharuco-verde-pequeno

13 :BOEHM'S BEE-EATER :Guêpier de Böhm :Abelharuco de Böhm

14 :WHITE-THROATED BEE-EATER :Guêpier à gorge blanche :Abelharuco-de-garganta-branca

15 :EUROPEAN BEE-EATER :Guêpier d'Europe :Abelharuco-europeu

16 :BLUE-CHEEKED BEE-EATER :Guêpier de Perse :Abelharuco-verde

17 :MADAGASCAR (or Olive) BEE-EATER :Guêpier malgache :Abelharuco-malgaxe

Plate 57

1 :EUROPEAN ROLLER :Rollier d'Europe :Rolieiro-europeu

2 :ABYSSINIAN ROLLER :Rollier d'Abyssinie :Rolieiro da Abissínia

3 :LILAC-BREASTED ROLLER :Rollier à longs brins :Rolieiro-de-peito-lilás

4 :RACKET-TAILED ROLLER :Rollier à raquettes :Rolieiro-de-cauda-espalmada

5 :BLUE-BELLIED ROLLER :Rollier à ventre bleu :Rolieiro-de-barriga-azul

6 :RUFOUS-CROWNED (or Purple) ROLLER :Rollier varié :Rolieiro-de-coroa-vermelha

7 :BROAD-BILLED ROLLER :Rolle violet :Rolieiro-de-bico-amarelo

8 :BLUE-THROATED ROLLER :Rolle à gorge bleue :Rolieiro-de-garganta-azul

9 :GREEN (or Red-billed) WOOD HOOPOE :Irrisor moqueur :Zombeteiro-de-bico-vermelho

10 :WHITE-HEADED WOOD HOOPOE :Irrisor à tête blanche :Zombeteiro-de-cabeça-branca

11 :FOREST WOOD HOOPOE :Irrisor à tête brune :Zombeteiro-de-cabeça-castanha

12 :BLACK WOOD HOOPOE :Irrisor noir :Zombeteiro-negro

13 :SCIMITARBILL, (Greater) :Irrisor namaquois :Bico-de-cimitarra

14 :HOOPOE :Huppe fasciée :Poupa

Plate 58

1 :YELLOW-CASQUED WATTLED HORNBILL :Grand calao à casque jaune :Calau-de-casquete-amarelo

2 :BLACK-CASQUED WATTLED HORNBILL :Grand calao à casque noir :Calau-grande

3 :PIPING HORNBILL :Calao siffleur :Calau-assobiador

4 :TRUMPETER HORNBILL :Calao trompette :Calau-trombeteiro

5 :BLACK-AND-WHITE-CASQUED HORNBILL :Calao à joues grises :Calau-de-faces-cinzentas

6 :BROWN-CHEEKED (or White-thighed) HORNBILL :Calao à joues brunes :Calau-de-faces-castanhas

7 :RED-BILLED DWARF HORNBILL :Calao pygmée :Calau-pigmeu-de-bico-vermelho

8 :CROWNED HORNBILL :Calao couronné :Calau-coroado

9 :PALE-BILLED HORNBILL :Calao à bec pâle :Calau-de-bico-pálido

10 :AFRICAN GREY HORNBILL :Petit calao à bec noir :Calau-cinzento

11 :RED-BILLED HORNBILL :Calao à bec rouge :Calau-de-bico-vermelho

12 :AFRICAN PIED HORNBILL :Calao longibande :Calau-preto

13 :BLACK DWARF HORNBILL :Calao pygmée à bec noir :Calau-pigmeu-de-bico-preto

14 :WHITE-CRESTED HORNBILL :Calao à huppe blanche :Calau-de-crista-branca

15 :SOUTHERN GROUND HORNBILL :Calao terrestre du sud :Calau-gigante

16 :ABYSSINIAN GROUND HORNBILL :Calao terrestre d'Abyssinie :Calau-gigante da Abissínia

Plate 59

1 :SPECKLED TINKERBIRD :Barbion grivelé :Barbadinho-malhado

2 :WESTERN GREEN TINKERBIRD :Barbion montagnard :Barbadinho-da-montanha

3 :YELLOW-FRONTED TINKERBIRD :Barbion à front jaune :Barbadinho-de-testa-amarela

4 :YELLOW- (, Lemon- or Golden-)RUMPED TINKERBIRD :Barbion à croupion jaune :Barbadinho-de-uropígio-amarelo

5 :YELLOW-THROATED TINKERBIRD :Barbion à gorge jaune :Barbadinho-de-garganta-amarela

6 :RED-RUMPED TINKERBIRD :Barbion à croupion rouge :Barbadinho-de-uropígio-vermelho

7 :SPOT-FLANKED BARBET :Barbican funèbre :Barbaças-fúnebre

8 :MIOMBO PIED BARBET :Barbican du Miombo :Barbaças-do-miombo

9 :HAIRY-BREASTED BARBET :Barbican hérissé :Barbaças-hirsuto

10 :YELLOW-BILLED BARBET :Barbican pourpre :Barbaças-de-bico-amarelo

11 :YELLOW-BREASTED BARBET :Barbican perlé :Barbaças-de-peito-amarelo

12 :CRESTED BARBET :Barbican promépic :Barbaças-de-poupa

Plate 60

1 :NAKED-FACED BARBET :Barbican chauve :Barbaças-calvo

2 :BRISTLE-NOSED BARBET :Barbican à narines emplumées :Barbaças-de-narinas-emplumadas

3 :SLADEN' BARBET :Barbican de Sladen :Barbaças de Sladen

4 :GREY-THROATED BARBET :Barbican

APPENDIX

de Bonaparte :Barbaças-de-garganta-
cinzenta
5 :ANCHIETA'S BARBET :Barbican à tête
jaune :Barbaças de Anchieta
6 :WHYTE'S BARBET :Barbican de Whyte
:Barbaças de Whyte
7 :YELLOW-SPOTTED BARBET :Barbican
à taches jaunes :Barbaças-de-malhas-
amarelas
8 :VIEILLOT'S BARBET :Barbican de
Vieillot :Barbaças de Vieillot
9 :BLACK-COLLARED BARBET :Barbican
à collier :Barbaças-de-colar
10 :BLACK-BILLED BARBET :Barbican
guifsobalito :Barbaças-de-bico-preto
11 :WHITE-HEADED BARBET :Barbican à
tête blanche :Barbaças-de-cabeça-branca
12 :BLACK-BACKED BARBET :Barbican de
Levaillant :Barbaças-pequeno
13 :DOUBLE-TOOTHED BARBET
:Barbican bidenté :Barbaças-bidentado
14 :BEARDED BARBET :Barbican à poitrine
rouge :Barbaças-de-peito-vermelho
15 :BLACK-BREASTED BARBET :Barbican
à poitrine noire :Barbaças-de-peito-preto

Plate 61

1 :LYRE-TAILED HONEYGUIDE
:Indicateur à queue-en-lyre :Indicador-de-
cauda-lira
2 :CASSIN'S HONEYBIRD :Indicateur
pygmée :Indicador de Cassin
3 :GREEN-BACKED (or Slender-billed)
HONEYBIRD :Indicateur gris :Indicador-
cinzento
4 :WAHLBERG'S (or Sharp-billed)
HONEYBIRD :Indicateur de Wahlberg
:Indicador de Wahlberg
5 :ZENKER'S HONEYGUIDE :Indicateur de
Zenker :Indicador de Zenker
6 :YELLOW-FOOTED (or Serle's)
HONEYGUIDE :Indicateur de Eisentraut
:Indicador-de-patas-amarelas
7 :GREATER (or Black-throated)
HONEYGUIDE :Grand indicateur
:Indicador-grande
8 :WILLCOCKS'S HONEYGUIDE
:Indicateur de Willcocks :Indicador de
Willcocks
9 :PALLID (or Eastern) HONEYGUIDE
:Indicateur pâle :Indicador-oriental
10 :DWARF HONEYGUIDE :Indicateur nain
:Indicador-anão
11 :THICK-BILLED HONEYGUIDE
:Indicateur à gros bec :Indicador-de-bico-
grosso
12 :LEAST HONEYGUIDE :Indicateur
minule :Indicador-pigmeu
13 :LESSER HONEYGUIDE :Petit indicateur
:Indicador-pequeno
14 :SCALY-THROATED HONEYGUIDE

:Indicateur varié :Indicador-de-garganta-
malhada
15 :SPOTTED HONEYGUIDE :Indicateur
tacheté :Indicador-malhado

Plate 62

1 :NORTHERN (or Eurasian) WRYNECK
:Torcol fourmilier :Torcicolo-europeu
2 :RUFOUS-BREASTED (or Red-throated)
WRYNECK :Torcol à gorge rousse
:Torcicolo-de-garganta-vermelha
3 :AFRICAN PICULET :Picule :Pica-pau-
pigmeu
4 :FINE-SPOTTED WOODPECKER :Pic
punctué :Pica-pau-ponteado
5 :BENNETT'S WOODPECKER :Pic de
Bennett :Pica-pau de Bennett
6 :NUBIAN WOODPECKER :Pic de Nubie
:Pica-pau-nubiano
7 :GOLDEN-TAILED WOODPECKER :Pic
à queue dorée :Pica-pau-de-cauda-
dourada
8 :GREEN-BACKED (or Little Spotted)
WOODPECKER :Pic à dos vert :Pica-
pau-de-dorso-verde
9 :LITTLE GREEN (or Golden-backed)
WOODPECKER :Pic barré :Pica-pau-
barrado
10 :TULLBERG'S (or Fine-banded)
WOODPECKER :Pic de Tullberg :Pica-
pau de Tullberg
11 :BUFF-SPOTTED WOODPECKER :Pic
tacheté :Pica-pau-malhado
12 :BROWN-EARED WOODPECKER :Pic à
oreillons bruns :Pica-pau-de-orelhas-
castanhas

Plate 63

1 :LITTLE GREY WOODPECKER :Petit pic
gris :Pica-pau-cinzento-pequeno
2 :CARDINAL WOODPECKER :Pic
cardinal :Pica-pau-cardeal
3 :SPECKLE-BREASTED WOODPECKER
:Pic à poitrine tachetée :Pica-pau-de-
peito-malhado
4 :ELLIOT'S WOODPECKER :Pic d'Elliot
:Pica-pau de Elliott
5 :FIRE-BELLIED WOODPECKER :Pic à
ventre de feu :Pica-pau-ventre-de-fogo
6 :YELLOW-CRESTED WOODPECKER
:Pic à couronne d'or :Pica-pau-de-crista-
amarela
7 :GABON WOODPECKER :Pic du Gabon
:Pica-pau do Gabão
8 :GREY WOODPECKER :Pic gris :Pica-
pau-cinzento-africano
9 :OLIVE WOODPECKER :Pic olive :Pica-
pau-esverdeado
10 :BEARDED WOODPECKER :Pic barbu
:Pica-pau-de-bigode

346

11 :BROWN-BACKED WOODPECKER :Pic
à dos brun :Pica-pau-de-dorso-castanho

Plate 64
1 :GREY-HEADED BROADBILL :Eurylame
à tête grise :Bico-largo-de-cabeça-
cinzenta
2 :RUFOUS-SIDED BROADBILL
:Eurylame à flancs roux :Bico-largo-de-
flancos-vermelhos
3 :AFRICAN BROADBILL :Eurylame du
Cap :Bico-largo-africano
4 :AFRICAN GREEN BROADBILL
:Eurylame de Grauer :Bico-largo de
Grauer
5 :AFRICAN PITTA :Brève d'Angola
:Tordo-formigueiro-angolano
6 :GREEN-BREASTED PITTA :Brève à
poitrine verte :Tordo-formigueiro-de-
peito-verde
7 :FISCHER'S SPARROW LARK :Alouette-
moineau de Fischer :Cotovia-pardal de
Fischer
8 :BLACK-CROWNED SPARROW LARK
:Alouette-moineau à front blanc
:Cotovia-pardal-de-testa-branca
9 :GREY-BACKED SPARROW LARK
:Alouette-moineau à dos gris :Cotovia-
pardal-de-dorso-cinzento
10 :CHESTNUT-BACKED SPARROW
LARK :Alouette-moineau à oreillons
blancs :Cotovia-pardal-de-dorso-
castanho
11 :TEMMINCK'S HORNED LARK
:Alouette bilophe :Cotovia de Temminck
12 :HOOPOE LARK :Sirli du désert
:Calhandra-de-bico-curvo
13 :RUFOUS-RUMPED LARK :Alouette à
queue rousse :Cotovia-de-uropígio-ruivo
14 :DUSKY LARK :Alouette brune
:Calhandra-sombria
15 :THEKLA LARK :Cochevis de Thékla
:Cotovia-montesina
16 :CRESTED LARK :Cochevis huppé
:Cotovia-de-poupa
17 :SUN LARK :Cochevis modeste :Cotovia-
modesta

Plate 65
1 :SINGING BUSH LARK :Alouette
chanteuse :Cotovia-cantora
2 :WHITE-TAILED BUSH LARK :Alouette
à queue blanche :Cotovia-de-cauda-
branca
3 :KORDOFAN LARK :Alouette du
Kordofan :Cotovia do Cordofão
4 :RUFOUS-NAPED LARK :Alouette à
nuque rousse :Cotovia-de-nuca-vermelha
5 :ANGOLA LARK :Alouette d'Angola
:Cotovia de Angola

6 :RUSTY BUSH LARK :Alouette rousse
:Cotovia-ruiva
7 :FLAPPET LARK :Alouette bourdonnante
:Cotovia-zumbidora
8 :DESERT LARK :Ammomane isabelline
:Cotovia-do-deserto
9 :BAR-TAILED LARK :Ammomane
élégante :Cotovia-das-dunas
10 :RASO LARK :Alouette de Raso :Laverca
do Razo
11 :EURASIAN SKY LARK :Alouette des
champs :Laverca
12 :GREATER SHORT-TOED LARK
:Alouette calandrelle :Calhandrinha-
comum
13 :LESSER SHORT-TOED LARK :Alouette
pispolette :Calhandrinha-das-marismas
14 :RED-CAPPED (or African Short-toed)
LARK :Alouette cendrille
:Calhandrinha-de-barrete-vermelho
15 :DUNN 'S LARK :Alouette de Dunn
:Cotovia de Dunn
16 :SPIKE-HEELED LARK :Alouette
éperonée :Cotovia-esporada
17 :THICK- BILLED LARK :Alouette de
Clotbey :Cotovia-de-bico-grosso

Plate 66
1 :RED-CHESTED SWALLOW :Hirondelle
à gorge rousse :Andorinha da Guiné
2 :ANGOLA SWALLOW :Hirondelle
d'Angola :Andorinha de Angola
3 :BARN (or European) SWALLOW
:Hirondelle de cheminée :Andorinha-das-
chaminés
4 :WHITE-THROATED SWALLOW
:Hirondelle à gorge blanche :Andorinha-
de-garganta-branca
5 :ETHIOPIAN SWALLOW :Hirondelle
d'Ethiopie :Andorinha da Etiópia
6 :WIRE-TAILED SWALLOW :Hirondelle à
longs brins :Andorinha-de-cauda-longa
7 :RED-BREASTED SWALLOW
:Hirondelle à ventre roux :Andorinha-de-
ventre-vermelho
8 :MOSQUE SWALLOW :Hirondelle des
mosquées :Andorinha do Senegal
9 :BLACK-AND-RUFOUS SWALLOW
:Hirondelle rousse-et-noire :Andorinha-
vermelha-e-preta
10 :GREATER STRIPED SWALLOW
:Hirondelle à tête rousse :Andorinha-de-
cabeça-vermelha
11 :LESSER STRIPED SWALLOW
:Hirondelle striée :Andorinha-estriada
12 :PIED-WINGED SWALLOW :Hirondelle
à ailes tachetés :Andorinha-de-asas-
malhadas
13 :PEARL-BREASTED SWALLOW
:Hirondelle à gorge perlée :Andorinha-
de-pérolas

14 :RED-RUMPED SWALLOW :Hirondelle rousseline :Andorinha-dáurica

15 :RED-THROATED CLIFF SWALLOW :Hirondelle à gorge fauve :Andorinha-de-garganta-amarela

16 :PREUSS'S CLIFF SWALLOW :Hirondelle de Preuss :Andorinha de Preuss

17 :SOUTH AFRICAN CLIFF SWALLOW :Hirondelle sud-africaine :Andorinha-sul-africana

18 :FOREST SWALLOW :Hirondelle de forêt :Andorinha-das-florestas

Plate 67

1 :AFRICAN RIVER MARTIN :Hirondelle de rivière :Andorinha-dos-rios

2 :BROWN-THROATED SAND MARTIN :Hirondelle paludicole :Andorinha-das-barreiras-africana

3 :CONGO SAND MARTIN :Hirondelle de rivage du Congo :Andorinha-congolesa

4 :COMMON SAND MARTIN :Hirondelle de rivage :Andorinha-das-barreiras

5 :BANDED MARTIN :Hirondelle à collier :Andorinha-de-colar

6 :BRAZZA'S MARTIN :Hirondelle de Brazza :Andorinha de Brazza

7 :GREY-RUMPED SWALLOW :Hirondelle à croupion gris :Andorinha-de-uropígio-cinzento

8 :CRAG MARTIN :Hirondelle de rochers :Andorinha-das-rochas

9 :ROCK MARTIN :Hirondelle isabelline :Andorinha-isabel

10 :COMMON HOUSE MARTIN :Hirondelle de fenêtre :Andorinha-dos-beirais

11 :WHITE-THROATED BLUE SWALLOW :Hirondelle noire :Andorinha-azul-de-garganta-branca

12 :BLUE SWALLOW :Hirondelle bleue :Andorinha-azul

13 :MOUNTAIN SAW-WING :Hirondelle brune :Andorinha-da-montanha

14 :WHITE-HEADED SAW-WING :Hirondelle à tête blanche :Andorinha-de-cabeça-branca

15 :BLACK SAW-WING :Hirondelle hérissée :Andorinha-preta

16 :FANTI SAW-WING :Hirondelle fanti :Andorinha-fuliginosa

17 :SQUARE-TAILED SAW-WING :Hirondelle à queue courte :Andorinha-de-cauda-curta

Plate 68

1 :YELLOW WAGTAIL :Bergeronnette printanière :Alvéola-amarela

2 :GREY WAGTAIL :Bergeronnette des ruisseaux :Alvéola-cinzenta

3 :WHITE WAGTAIL :Bergeronnette grise :Alvéola-branca

4 :AFRICAN PIED WAGTAIL :Bergeronnette pie :Alvéola-africana

5 :MOUNTAIN (or Long-tailed) WAGTAIL :Bergeronnette à longue queue :Alvéola-de-cauda-comprida

6 :CAPE WAGTAIL :Bergeronnette du Cap :Alvéola do Cabo

7 :TREE PIPIT :Pipit des arbres :Petinha-das-árvores

8 :RED-THROATED PIPIT :Pipit à gorge rousse :Petinha-de-garganta-ruiva

9 :MEADOW PIPIT :Pipit des prés :Petinha-dos-prados

10 :TAWNY PIPIT :Pipit rousseline :Petinha-dos-campos

11 :BUSH(-veld) PIPIT :Pipit cafre :Petinha-dos-arbustos

12 :SHORT-TAILED PIPIT :Pipit à queue courte :Petinha-de-cauda-curta

13 :LONG-BILLED PIPIT :Pipit à long bec :Petinha-de-bico-comprido

14 :RICHARD'S PIPIT :Pipit de Richard :Petinha de Richard

15 :PLAIN-BACKED PIPIT :Pipit à dos roux :Petinha-de-dorso-liso

16 :MOUNTAIN PIPIT :Pipit du Drakensberg :Petinha-da-montanha

17 :BUFFY PIPIT :Pipit du Vaal :Petinha de Vaal

18 :STRIPED PIPIT :Pipit strié de Sundevall :Petinha-estriada

19 :LONG-LEGGED PIPIT :Pipit à longes pattes :Petinha-de-ventre-pálido

Plate 69

1 :WESTERN WATTLED CUCKOO-SHRIKE :Echenilleur à barbillons :Picanço-cuco-carunculado-ocidental

2 :EASTERN WATTLED CUCKOO-SHRIKE :Echenilleur loriot :Picanço-cuco-carunculado-oriental

3 :GREY CUCKOO-SHRIKE :Echenilleur gris :Picanço-cuco-cinzento

4 :GRAUER'S CUCKOO-SHRIKE :Echenilleur de Grauer :Picanço-cuco de Grauer

5 :BLUE CUCKOO-SHRIKE :Echenilleur bleu :Picanço-cuco-azul

6 :WHITE-BREASTED CUCKOO-SHRIKE :Echenilleur à gorge blanche :Picanço-cuco-de-peito-branco

7 :RED-SHOULDERED CUCKOO-SHRIKE :Echenilleur à épaulettes rouges :Picanço-cuco-de-ombros-vermelhos

8 :BLACK CUCKOO-SHRIKE :Echenilleur noir :Picanço-cuco-preto

9 :PETIT'S CUCKOO-SHRIKE :Echenilleur de Petit :Picanço-cuco de Petit

10 :PURPLE-THROATED CUCKOO-
SHRIKE :Echenilleur pourpré
:Picanço-cuco-de-garganta-púrpura
11 :GRIMWOOD'S LONGCLAW
:Sentinelle de Grimwood :Sentinela de
Grimwood
12 :YELLOW-THROATED LONGCLAW
:Sentinelle à gorge jaune :Sentinela-de-
garganta-amarela
13 :FUELLEBORN'S LONGCLAW
:Sentinelle de Fülleborn :Sentinela de
Fülleborn
14 :ROSY-BREASTED (or Pink-throated)
LONGCLAW :Sentinelle à gorge rose
:Sentinela-de-garganta-rosada

Plate 70
1 :COMMON (or Black-eyed) BULBUL
:Bulbul commun :Bulbul-comum
2 :SJÖSTEDT'S HONEYGUIDE
GREENBUL :Bulbul bruyant :Bulbul de
Sjöstedt
3 :HONEYGUIDE GREENBUL :Bulbul à
queue blanche :Bulbul-de-cauda-branca
4 :SPOTTED GREENBUL :Bulbul tâcheté
:Bulbul-malhado
5 :GOLDEN GREENBUL :Bulbul doré
:Bulbul-dourado
6 :YELLOW-WHISKERED GREENBUL
:Bulbul à moustaches jaunes :Bulbul-de-
bigodes-amarelos
7 :SHELLEY'S GREENBUL :Bulbul de
Masuku :Bulbul de Masuku
8 :CAMEROON MONTANE GREENBUL
:Bulbul concolore :Bulbul-montês
9 :LITTLE GREENBUL :Bulbul verdâtre
:Bulbul-pequeno
10 :LITTLE GREY GREENBUL :Bulbul
gracile :Bulbul-cinzento-pequeno
11 :ANSORGE'S GREENBUL :Bulbul
d'Ansorge :Bolbul de Ansorge
12 :PLAIN (or Cameroon Sombre)
GREENBUL :Bulbul curvirostre :Bulbul-
sombrio
13 :SLENDER-BILLED GREENBUL :Bulbul
à bec grêle :Bulbul-de-bico-fino
14 :MOUNTAIN GREENBUL, (Western)
:Bulbul à gorge grise :Bulbul-de-garganta-
cinzenta

Plate 71
1 :XAVIER'S GREENBUL :Bulbul ictérin
tâcheté :Bulbul de Xavier
2 :BAUMANN'S GREENBUL :Bulbul de
Baumann :Bulbul de Baumann
3 :GREY-OLIVE GREENBUL :Bulbul vert-
olive :Bulbul-de-ventre-ruivo
4 :PALE OLIVE GREENBUL :Bulbul à
ventre roux :Bulbul-de-ventre-fulvo
5 :CAMEROON OLIVE GREENBUL

:Bulbul olivâtre :Bulbul-camaronês
6 :TORO OLIVE GREENBUL :Bulbul du
Toro :Bulbul de Toro
7 :NORTHERN BROWNBUL :Bulbul brun
:Bulbul-castanho
8 :GREY-HEADED GREENBUL :Bulbul à
ventre jaune :Bulbul-de-cabeça-cinzenta
9 :YELLOW-STREAKED GREENBUL
:Bulbul à stries jaunes :Bulbul-de-estrias-
amarelas
10 :SASSI'S OLIVE GREENBUL :Bulbul de
Lorenz :Bulbul de Lorenz
11 :WHITE-THROATED GREENBUL
:Bulbul à gorge blanche :Bulbul-de-
garganta-branca
12 :LIBERIAN GREENBUL :Bulbul ictérin
tâcheté :Bulbul da Libéria
13 :CABANIS'S GREENBUL :Bulbul de
Canabis :Bulbul de Cabanis
14 :ICTERINE GREENBUL :Bulbul ictérin
:Bulbul-icterino
15 :TERRESTRIAL BROWNBUL :Bulbul
jaboteur :Bulbul-terrestre

Plate 72
1 :GREY-HEADED BRISTLEBILL :Bulbul
fourmilier :Bulbul-formigueiro
2 :RED-TAILED BRISTLEBILL :Bulbul
moustac :Bulbul-de-cauda-ruiva
3 :GREEN-TAILED BRISTLEBILL :Bulbul à
queue verte :Bulbul-de-cauda-verde
4 :EASTERN BEARDED BULBUL :Bulbul
crinon oriental :Bulbul-barbudo-oriental
5 :WESTERN BEARDED GREENBUL
:Bulbul crinon occidental :Bulbul-
barbudo-ocidental
6 :RED-TAILED GREENBUL :Bulbul à
barbe blanche :Bulbul-de-cauda-vermelha
7 :WHITE-BEARDED GREENBUL :Bulbul
de Reichenow :Bulbul de Reichenow
8 :YELLOW-BEARDED GREENBUL
:Bulbul à barbe jaune :Bulbul-de-barba-
amarela
9 :YELLOW-NECKED GREENBUL :Bulbul
de Falkenstein :Bulbul de Falkenstein
10 :SIMPLE GREENBUL :Bulbul modeste
:Bulbul-modesto
11 :YELLOW-THROATED LEAFLOVE
:Bulbul à gorge claire :Bulbul-de-
garganta-amarela
12 :YELLOW-BELLIED GREENBUL :Bulbul
à poitrine jaune :Bulbul-de-ventre-
amarelo
13 :JOYFUL GREENBUL :Bulbul joyeux
:Bulbul-alegre
14 :PRIGOGINE'S GREENBUL :Bulbul de
Pripogine :Bulbul de Prigogine
15 :SWAMP (or White-tailed) PALM
GREENBUL :Bulbul des raphias :Bulbul-
de-cauda-branca

16 :LEAFLOVE :Bulbul à queue rousse :Bulbul-de-cauda-castanha

Plate 73

1 :ISABELLINE WHEATEAR :Traquet isabelle :Chasco-isabel
2 :NORTHERN (or European) WHEATEAR :Traquet motteux :Chasco-cinzento
3 :BLACK-EARED (or Spanish) WHEATEAR :Traquet oreillard :Chasco-ruivo
4 :RED-BREASTED WHEATEAR :Traquet à poitrine rousse :Chasco-de-peito-ruivo
5 :DESERT WHEATEAR :Traquet du désert :Chasco-do-deserto
6 :WHITE-CROWNED BLACK WHEATEAR :Traquet à tête blanche :Chasco-de-coroa-branca
7 :CAPPED WHEATEAR :Traquet du Cap :Chasco-de-barrete
8 :BLACK WHEATEAR :Traquet rieur :Chasco-preto
9 :MOURNING WHEATEAR :Traquet deuil :Chasco-fúnebre
10 :PIED WHEATEAR :Traquet pie :Chasco-dominó
11 :WHINCHAT :Traquet tarier :Cartaxo-nortenho
12 :COMMON STONECHAT :Traquet pâtre :Cartaxo-comum
13 :BLACKSTART :Traquet de roche à queue noire :Cartaxo-de-cauda-preta
14 :FAMILIAR (or Red-tailed) CHAT :Traquet de roche à queue rousse :Cartaxo-de-cauda-vermelha
15 :BROWN-TAILED CHAT :Traquet de roche à queue brune :Cartaxo-de-cauda-castanha

Plate 74

1 :BLACK REDSTART :Rougequeue noir :Rabirruivo-preto
2 :COMMON (or European) REDSTART :Rougequeue à front blanc :Rabirruivo-de-testa-branca
3 :NIGHTINGALE :Rossignol philomèle :Rouxinol-comum
4 :SPROSSER (or Thrush Nightingale) :Rossignol progné :Rouxinol-grande
5 :BLUETHROAT :Gorgebleu à miroir :Pisco-de-peito-azul
6 :RED-TAILED PALM THRUSH :Cichladuse à queue rousse :Tordo-das-palmeiras-de-cauda-vermelha
7 :COLLARED PALM THRUSH :Cichladuse de Peters :Tordo-das-palmeiras-de-colar
8 :SPOTTED PALM (or Morning) THRUSH :Cichladuse à poitrine tachetée :Tordo-das-palmeiras-malhado
9 :WHITE-STARRED ROBIN :Akalat étoilé :Pisco-de-ventre-amarelo
10 :MIOMBO BEARDED SCRUB ROBIN :Robin-agrobate barbu du Miombo :Rouxinol-do-miombo
11 :FOREST SCRUB ROBIN :Robin-agrobate de Ghana :Rouxinol-da-floresta
12 :BROWN-BACKED SCRUB ROBIN :Robin-agrobate à dos brun :Rouxinol-de-dorso-castanho
13 :WHITE-BROWED SCRUB ROBIN :Robin-agrobate à dos roux :Rouxinol-de-dorso-vermelho
14 :RUFOUS SCRUB ROBIN :Agrobate roux :Rouxinol-do-mato
15 :BLACK SCRUB ROBIN :Merle podobe :Rouxinol-negro

Plate 75

1 :FOREST-ROBIN :Rougegorge de fôret :Pisco-das-florestas
2 :EUROPEAN ROBIN :Rougegorge familier :Pisco-de-peito-ruivo
3 :EQUATORIAL AKALAT :Merle rougegorge équatorial :Pisco-equatorial
4 :GREY-WINGED ROBIN CHAT :Cossyphe à sourcils blancs :Pisco-de-asa-cinzenta
5 :BOCAGE'S AKALAT :Akalat à joues rousses :Pisco de Bocage
6 :LOWLAND (or Common) AKALAT :Merle rougegorge :Pisco-de-peito-laranja
7 :FIRE-CRESTED (or White-tailed) ALETHE :Alèthe à gorge rousse :Pisco-de-poupa-vermelha
8 :RED-THROATED ALETHE :Alethe poliophrys :Pisco-de-garganta-ruiva
9 :BROWN-CHESTED ALETHE :Alèthe à poitrine brune :Pisco-de-peito-castanho
10 :MOCKING CLIFF CHAT :Traquet de roche à ventre roux :Cartaxo-das-rochas-de-ventre-vermelho
11 :RUFOUS FLYCATCHER THRUSH :Grive fourmilière rousse :Pisco-formigueiro-ruivo
12 :FINSCH'S FLYCATCHER THRUSH :Grive fourmilière de Finsch :Pisco-formigueiro de Finsch
13 :RED-TAILED ANT THRUSH :Grive fourmilière à queue rousse :Pisco-formigueiro-de-cauda-ruiva
14 :WHITE-TAILED ANT THRUSH :Grive fourmilière à queue blanche :Pisco-formigueiro-de-cauda-branca
15 :WHITE-FRONTED BLACK CHAT :Traquet noir à front blanc :Cartaxo-formigueiro-de-testa-branca
16 :WHITE-HEADED BLACK (or Arnott's) CHAT :Traquet d'Arnott :Cartaxo de Arnott

17 :CONGO MOOR CHAT :Traquet-fourmilier du Congo :Cartaxo-formigueiro-congolês
18 :NORTHERN ANTEATER CHAT :Traquet-fourmilier brun du nord :Cartaxo-formigueiro-setentrional
19 :SOOTY CHAT :Traquet-fourmilier noir :Cartaxo-formigueiro-preto

Plate 76
1 :WHITE-BELLIED ROBIN CHAT :Cossyphe à ventre blanc :Pisco-de-ventre-branco
2 :MOUNTAIN ROBIN CHAT :Cossyphe d'Isabelle :Pisco-montês
3 :ARCHER'S ROBIN CHAT :Cossyphe d'Archer :Pisco de Archer
4 :CAPE (or Common) ROBIN CHAT :Cossyphe du Cap :Pisco do Cabo
5 :SANGHA FOREST ROBIN :Rougegorge de fôret de Sanghra :Pisco de Sangha
6 :BLUE-SHOULDERED ROBIN CHAT :Cossyphe à ailes bleues :Pisco-de-ombro-azul
7 :WHITE-BROWED (or Heuglin's) ROBIN CHAT :Cossyphe d'Heuglin :Pisco de Heuglin
8 :RED-CAPPED (or Natal) ROBIN CHAT :Cossyphe à calotte rousse :Pisco-de-barrete-vermelho
9 :WHITE-CROWNED ROBIN CHAT :Grand Cossyphe à tête blanche :Pisco-de-coroa-branca
10 :WHITE-HEADED ROBIN CHAT :Cossyphe à tête blanche d'Angola :Pisco-de-cabeça-branca
11 :SNOWY-CROWNED ROBIN CHAT :Petit Cossyphe à tête blanche :Pisco-de-queixo-preto
12 :ABYSSINIAN GROUND THRUSH :Grive de Piaggia :Tordo de Piaggia
13 :CROSSLEY'S GROUND THRUSH :Grive de Crossley :Tordo de Crossley
14 :OBERLAENDER'S GROUND THRUSH :Grive d'Oberlaender :Tordo de Oberländer
15 :ORANGE GROUND THRUSH :Grive de Gurney :Tordo de Gurney
16 :GREY GROUND THRUSH :Grive olivâtre :Tordo-cinzento
17 :BLACK-EARED GROUND THRUSH :Grive du Cameroun :Tordo-camaronês

Plate 77
1 :GULF OF GUINEA THRUSH :Merle de São Tomé :Melro de São Tomé
2 :GROUNDSCRAPER THRUSH :Merle litsitsirupa :Tordo-litsitsirupa
3 :SPOTTED GROUND THRUSH :Grive tachetée :Tordo-malhado

4 :KURRICHANE THRUSH :Merle kurrichane :Tordo de Kurrichane
5 :SONG THRUSH :Grive musicienne :Tordo-comum
6 :AFRICAN THRUSH, (West) :Merle africain :Melro-africano
7 :OLIVE THRUSH :Merle olivâtre :Melro-olatáceo
8 :RING OUZEL :Grive à plastron :Melro-de-peito-branco
9 :MIOMBO ROCK THRUSH :Monticole angolais :Melro-das-rochas-do-miombo
10 :MOUNTAIN (,Common or European) ROCK THRUSH :Monticole merle-de-roche :Melro-das-rochas-europeu
11 :BLUE ROCK THRUSH :Monticole merle-bleu :Melro-azul
12 :FULVOUS CHATTERER :Cratérope fauve :Zaragateiro-fulvo
13 :WHITE-RUMPED BABBLER :Cratérope de Hartlaub :Zaragateiro-de-uropígio-branco
14 :DUSKY BABBLER :Cratérope ombré (,ou fuligineux) :Zaragateiro-escuro
15 :BLACKCAP BABBLER :Cratérope à tête noire :Zaragateiro-de-cabeça-preta
16 :BROWN BABBLER :Cratérope brun :Zaragateiro-castanho
17 :ARROW-MARKED BABBLER :Cratérope fléché :Zaragateiro de Jardine
18 :BLACK-LORED BABBLER :Cratérope masqué :Zaragateiro-de-mascarilha

Plate 78
1 :RUFOUS-WINGED ILLADOPSIS :Akalat à ailes rousses :Zaragateiro-de-asa-ruiva
2 :BLACKCAP ILLADOPSIS :Akalat à tête noire :Zaragateiro-de-barrete-preto
3 :SCALY-BREASTED ILLADOPSIS :Akalat àpoitrine écaillée :Zaragateiro-de-peito-escamoso
4 :PUVEL'S ILLADOPSIS :Akalat de Puvel :Zaragateiro de Puvel
5 :PALE-BREASTED ILLADOPSIS :Akalat à poitrine blanche :Zaragateiro-de-peito-pálido
6 :BROWN ILLADOPSIS :Akalat brun :Zaragateiro-de-colar
7 :MOUNTAIN ILLADOPSIS :Akalat montagnard :Zaragateiro-da-montanha
8 :AFRICAN HILL BABBLER :Akalat à tête sombre :Zaragateiro-de-cabeça-cinzenta
9 :GREY-CHESTED ILLADOPSIS :Akalat à poitrine grise :Zaragateiro-de-peito-cinzento
10 :SPOTTED THRUSH BABBLER :Akalat a dos roux :Zaragateiro-tordo
11 :WHITE-THROATED MOUNTAIN BABBLER :Phyllanthe à gorge blanche :Zaragateiro-de-garganta-branca

APPENDIX

12 :RED-COLLARED BABBLER :Phyllanthe
à collier roux :Zaragateiro-de-colar-
vermelho
13 :CHAPIN'S BABBLER :Phyllanthe de
Chapin :Zaragateiro de Chapin
14 :CAPUCHIN BABBLER :Cratérope
capucin :Zaragateiro-capuchinho
15 :DOHRN'S THRUSH BABBLER
:Cratérope de Principé :Zaragateiro de
Dohrn

Plate 79
1 :CAPE VERDE CANE WARBLER
:Rousserolle de Chapin :Rouxinol-dos-
caniços de Cabo Verde
2 :AQUATIC WARBLER :Phragmite
aquatique :Felosa-aquática
3 :SEDGE WARBLER :Phragmite des joncs
:Felosa-dos-juncos
4 :EURASIAN REED WARBLER
:Rousserolle effarvate :Rouxinol-
pequeno-dos-caniços
5 :AFRICAN REED WARBLER :Rousserolle
africaine :Rouxinol-dos-caniços-africano
6 :MARSH WARBLER :Rousserolle
verderolle :Felosa-palustre
7 :GREAT REED WARBLER :Rousserolle
turdoïde :Rouxinol-grande-dos-caniços
8 :GREATER SWAMP WARBLER
:Rousserolle de cannes :Rouxinol-grande-
dos-pântanos
9 :LESSER SWAMP WARBLER
:Rousserolle à bec fin :Rouxinol-pequeno-
dos-pântanos
10 :LITTLE RUSH WARBLER :Bouscarle
caqueteuse :Felosa-dos-juncos-africana
11 :GRAUER'S SWAMP (or Rush)
WARBLER :Bouscarle de Grauer :Felosa
de Grauer
12 :JA RIVER SCRUB WARBLER :Bouscarle
géante :Felosa-camaronesa
13 :WHITE-WINGED SWAMP WARBLER
:Bouscarle à ailes blanches :Felosa-de-asa-
branca
14 :BAMBOO WARBLER :Bouscarle des
bambous :Felosa-dos-bambus
15 :BANGWA FOREST WARBLER
:Bouscarle de bois de Bangwa :Felosa de
Bangwa
16 :EVERGREEN-FOREST (or Cameroon
Scrub) WARBLER :Bouscarle de Lopes
:Felosa de Lopes
17 :CINNAMON BRACKEN WARBLER
:Bouscarle cannelle :Felosa-canela
18 :BROAD-TAILED WARBLER
:Graminicole à queue large :Felosa-de-
cauda-larga

Plate 80
1 :GRASSHOPPER WARBLER :Locustelle

tachetée :Felosa-malhada
2 :EURASIAN RIVER WARBLER
:Locustelle fluviatile :Felosa-fluvial
3 :SAVI'S WARBLER :Locustelle luscinioïde
:Felosa-unicolor
4 :OLIVACEOUS WARBLER :Hypolaïs pâle
:Felosa-pálida
5 :OLIVE-TREE WARBLER :Hypolaïs des
oliviers :Felosa-das-oliveiras
6 :MELODIOUS WARBLER :Hypolaïs
polyglotte :Felosa-poliglota
7 :ICTERINE WARBLER :Hypolaïs ictérine
:Felosa-icterina
8 :LAURA'S WOODLAND WARBLER
:Pouillot de Laura :Felosa de Laura
9 :RED-FACED WOODLAND WARBLER
:Pouillot à face rousse :Felosa-de-faces-
ruivas
10 :UGANDA WOODLAND WARBLER
:Pouillot de l'Ouganda :Felosa do Uganda
11 :BROWN WOODLAND WARBLER
:Pouillot ombré :Felosa-castanha
12 :COMMON CHIFFCHAFF :Pouillot
véloce :Felosa-comum
13 :WILLOW WARBLER :Pouillot fitis
:Felosa-musical
14 :EASTERN BONELLI'S WARBLER
:Pouillot d'est de Bonelli :Felosa-oriental
15 :BONELLI'S WARBLER, (Western)
:Pouillot de Bonelli :Felosa de Bonelli
16 :WOOD WARBLER :Pouillot siffleur
:Felosa-assobiadeira
17 :BLACK-CAPPED WOODLAND
WARBLER :Pouillot à tête noire :Felosa-
de-barrete-preto
18 :GREEN HYLIA :Hylia verte :Felosa-
verdinha
19 :NEUMANN'S (or Short-Tailed)
WARBLER :Crombec de Neumann
:Felosa de Neumann

Plate 81
1 :RED-FACED CISTICOLA :Cisticole à
face rousse :Fuinha-de-faces-vermelhas
2 :SINGING CISTICOLA :Cisticole
chanteuse :Fuinha-cantora
3 :WHISTLING CISTICOLA :Cisticole
siffleuse :Fuinha-assobiadeira
4 :TRILLING CISTICOLA :Cisticole de
Woosnam :Fuinha de Woosnam
5 :CHATTERING CISTICOLA :Cisticole
babillarde :Fuinha-tagarela
6 :BUBBLING CISTICOLA :Cisticole
murmure :Fuinha-sussurrante
7 :CHUBB'S CISTICOLA :Cisticole de
Chubb :Fuinha de Chubb
8 :RATTLING CISTICOLA :Cisticole
grinçante :Fuinha-chocalheira
9 :ROCK-LOVING (or Lazy) CISTICOLA
:Cisticole paresseuse :Fuinha-preguiçosa
10 :RED-PATE CISTICOLA :Cisticole à tête

rousse :Fuinha-de-cabeça-vermelha

11 :DORST'S CISTICOLA :Cisticole de Dorst :Fuinha de Dorst

12 :TINKLING CISTICOLA :Cisticole grise :Fuinha-cinzenta

13 :WINDING CISTICOLA :Cisticole roussâtre :Fuinha-de-dorso-cinzento

14 :CARRUTHER'S CISTICOLA :Cisticole de Carruthers :Fuinha de Carruthers

15 :CHIRPING CISTICOLA :Cisticole pépiante :Fuinha-chilreante

16 :LEVAILLANT'S CISTICOLA :Cisticole à sonnette :Fuinha de Levaillant

17 :STOUT CISTICOLA :Cisticole robuste :Fuinha-grande

18 :CROAKING CISTICOLA :Cisticole striée :Fuinha de Natal

Plate 82

1 :NEDDICKY :Cisticole à couronne rousse :Fuinha-de-barrete-vermelho

2 :LONG-TAILED CISTICOLA :Cisticole à queue fine :Fuinha-rabilonga

3 :BLACK-TAILED CISTICOLA :Cisticole à queue noire :Fuinha-de-cauda-preta

4 :SHORT-WINGED (or Siffling) CISTICOLA :Cisticole à ailes courtes :Fuinha-de-asa-curta

5 :RUFOUS CISTICOLA :Cisticole rousse :Fuinha-ruiva

6 :FOXY CISTICOLA :Cisticole russule :Fuinha-de-dorso-ruivo

7 :DESERT CISTICOLA :Cisticole du désert :Fuinha-do-deserto

8 :DAMBO CISTICOLA :Cisticole dambo :Fuinha-dambo

9 :BLACK-BACKED (or -necked) CISTICOLA :Cisticole à dos noir :Fuinha-de-cabeça-castanha

10 :PECTORAL-PATCH CISTICOLA :Cisticole brune :Fuinha-castanha

11 :WING-SNAPPING (or Ayres's) CISTICOLA :Cisticole gratte-nuage :Fuinha de Ayres

12 :FAN-TAILED (or Zitting) CISTICOLA :Cisticole des joncs :Fuinha-dos-juncos

13 :SÃO TOMÉ PRINIA :Prinia de São Tomé :Prínia de São Tomé

14 :RIVER PRINIA :Prinia aquatique :Prínia-aquática

15 :TAWNY-FLANKED PRINIA :Prinia modeste :Prínia-de-flancos-castanhos

16 :WHITE-CHINNED PRINIA :Prinia à gorge blanche :Prínia-de-garganta-branca

17 :SIERRA LEONE PRINIA :Prinia du Sierra Leone :Prínia da Serra Leoa

18 :BANDED PRINIA :Prinia rayée :Prínia-barrada

Plate 83

1 :BUFF-BELLIED WARBLER :Phyllolaïs à ventre fauve :Felosa-das-acácias

2 :CRICKET WARBLER :Prinia à front écailleux :Felosa-de-testa-malhada

3 :RED-FRONTED WARBLER :Apalis à front roux :Apalis-de-testa-ruiva

4 :STREAKED SCRUB WARBLER :Dromoïque vif-argent :Fuinha-dos-espinheiros

5 :BLACK-COLLARED APALIS :Apalis à col noir :Apalis-de-colar-preto

6 :BLACK-CAPPED APALIS :Apalis à calotte noire :Apalis-de-barrete-preto

7 :BLACK-THROATED APALIS :Apalis à gorge noire :Apalis-de-garganta-preta

8 :RWENZORI APALIS :Apalis du Ruwenzori :Apalis das Ruwenzori

9 :MASKED APALIS :Apalis masquée :Apalis-mascarado

10 :MOUNTAIN MASKED APALIS :Apalis à face noire :Apalis-de-faces-pretas

11 :YELLOW-BREASTED APALIS :Apalis à gorge jaune :Apalis-de-peito-amarelo

12 :BUFF-THROATED APALIS :Apalis à gorge rousse :Apalis-de-garganta-vermelha

13 :SHARPE'S APALIS :Apalis de Sharpe :Apalis de Sharpe

14 :GOSLING'S APALIS :Apalis de Gosling :Apalis de Gosling

15 :BAMENDA APALIS :Apalis de Bamenda :Apalis de Bamenda

16 :CHESTNUT-THROATED APALIS :Apalis à gorge marron :Apalis-de-garganta-castanha

17 :GREY APALIS :Apalis cendrée :Apalis-cinzento

18 :BROWN-HEADED APALIS :Apalis à tête brune :Apalis-de-cabeça-castanha

Plate 84

1 :GREEN-CAPPED EREMOMELA :Érémomèle à calotte verte :Eremomela-de-barrete-verde

2 :SENEGAL EREMOMELA :Érémomèle à dos vert :Eremomela do Senegal

3 :GREEN-BACKED EREMOMELA :Érémomèle grisonnante :Eremomela-de-dorso-verde

4 :RUFOUS-CROWNED EREMOMELA :Érémomèle à tête brune :Eremomela-de-barrete-castanho

5 :TURNER'S EREMOMELA :Érémomèle de Turner :Eremomela de Turner

6 :BLACK-NECKED EREMOMELA :Érémomèle à cou noir :Eremomela-de-pescoço-preto

7 :YELLOW-BELLIED EREMOMELA :Érémomèle à croupion jaune :Eremomela-de-ventre-amarelo

APPENDIX

8 :SALVADORI'S EREMOMELA :Érémomèle de Salvadori :Eremomela de Salvadori
9 :BLEATING WARBLER (or Grey-backed Camaroptera) :Camaroptère à tête grise :Felosa-de-cabeça-cinzenta
10 :MIOMBO WREN (or Stierling's Barred) WARBLER :Camaroptère du miombo :Felosa de Stierling
11 :YELLOW-BROWED CAMAROPTERA :Camaroptère à sourcils jaunes :Felosa-de-sobrancelha-amarela
12 :OLIVE-GREEN CAMAROPTERA :Camaroptère à dos vert :Felosa-de-dorso-verde
13 :GREEN CROMBEC :Crombec vert :Felosa-verde
14 :LEMON-BELLIED CROMBEC :Crombec à gorge tachetée :Felosa-de-ventre-amarelo
15 :WHITE-BROWED CROMBEC :Crombec à sourcils blancs :Felosa-de-sobrancelha-branca
16 :NORTHERN CROMBEC :Crombec sittelle :Felosa-de-ventre-ruivo
17 :RED-CAPPED CROMBEC :Crombec à calotte rousse :Felosa-de-barrete-vermelho
18 :LONG-BILLED CROMBEC :Crombec à long bec :Felosa-de-bico-comprido

Plate 85

1 :GREY-CAPPED WARBLER :-minie à calotte grise :Felosa-de-barrete-cinzento
2 :ORIOLE WARBLER (or Moho) :Noircap loriot :Felosa-de-ventre-amarelo
3 :RED-WINGED WARBLER :Prinia à ailes rousses :Prínia-de-asa-vermelha
4 :WHITE-TAILED WARBLER :Poliolaïs à queue blanche :Felosa-de-cauda-branca
5 :MOUNTAIN YELLOW WARBLER :Chloropète de montagne :Felosa-amarela-da-montanha
6 :AFRICAN YELLOW WARBLER :Chloropète jaune :Felosa-amarela-africana
7 :PAPYRUS YELLOW WARBLER :Chloropète aquatique :Felosa-amarela-do-papiro
8 :MOUSTACHED GRASS WARBLER :Mélocichle à moustaches :Felosa-de-bigodes
9 :GREEN LONGTAIL :Prinia verte :Prínia-verde
10 :GRAUER'S WARBLER :Grauérie striée :Felosa de Grauer
11 :BLACK-HEADED RUFOUS WARBLER :Bathmocerque à capuchon :Felosa-ruiva-de-cabeça-preta
12 :BLACK-FACED RUFOUS WARBLER :Bathmocerque à face noire :Felosa-ruiva-

de-faces-pretas
13 :KEMP'S LONGBILL :Nasique de Kemp :Felosa de Kemp
14 :YELLOW LONGBILL :Nasique jaune :Felosa-amarela
15 :GREY LONGBILL :Nasique grise :Felosa-cinzenta
16 :BOCAGE'S LONGBILL :Nasique de Bocage :Felosa de Bocage

Plate 86

1 :BROWN PARISOMA :Parisom brune :Felosa-castanha
2 :YELLOW-BELLIED (or -breasted) HYLIOTA :Hyliote à ventre jaune :Papa-moscas-de-barriga-amarela
3 :SOUTHERN (or Mashona) HYLIOTA :Hyliote australe :Papa-moscas-austral
4 :VIOLET-BACKED HYLIOTA :Hyliote à dos violet :Papa-moscas-de-dorso-violeta
5 :RED-WINGED GREY WARBLER :Prinia grise :Prínia-de-asas-vermelhas
6 :FLOWERPECKER WEAVER FINCH :Astrild fourmilier à gorge rousse :Papa-formigas
7 :RED-FRONTED FLOWERPECKER WEAVER FINCH :Astrild fourmillier à front rouge :Pica-formigas-de-testa-vermelha
8 :BLACKCAP :Fauvette à tête noire :Toutinegra-de-barrete-preto
9 :LESSER WHITETHROAT :Fauvette babillarde :Papa-amoras-pequeno
10 :GARDEN WARBLER :Fauvette des jardins :Felosa-das-figueiras
11 :COMMON WHITETHROAT :Fauvette grisette :Papa-amoras-comum
12 :BARRED WARBLER :Fauvette épervière :Toutinegra-gavião
13 :ORPHEAN WARBLER :Fauvette orphée :Toutinegra-real
14 :SARDINIAN WARBLER :Fauvette mélanocéphale :Toutinegra-de-cabeça-preta
15 :SUBALPINE WARBLER :Fauvette passerinette :Toutinegra-carrasqueira
16 :TRISTRAM'S WARBLER :Fauvette de l'Atlas :Toutinegra do Atlas
17 :SPECTACLED WARBLER :Fauvette à lunettes :Toutinegra-tomilheira
18 :MENETRIES'S WARBLER :Fauvette de Ménétries :Toutinegra de Ménétries
19 :RUEPPELL'S WARBLER :Fauvette de Rüppell :Toutinegra de Rüppell
20 :DESERT WARBLER :Fauvette naine :Toutinegra-do-deserto

Plate 87

1 :BEDFORD'S PARADISE FLYCATCHER :Tchitrec de Bedford :Papa-moscas de

Bedford

2 :AFRICAN PARADISE FLYCATCHER :Tchitrec d'Afrique :Papa-moscas-africano

3 :SÃO TOMÉ PARADISE FLYCATCHER :Tchitrec du São Tomé :Papa-moscas de São Tomé

4 :RUFOUS-VENTED PARADISE FLYCATCHER :Tchitrec du Congo :Papa-moscas-congolês

5 :RED-BELLIED PARADISE FLYCATCHER :Tchitrec à ventre roux :Papa-moscas-de-barriga-vermelha

6 :CASSIN'S FLYCATCHER :Gobemouche de Cassin :Papa-moscas de Cassin

7 :SWAMP FLYCATCHER :Gobemouche des marais :Papa-moscas-dos-pauis

8 :SPOTTED FLYCATCHER :Gobemouche gris :Papa-moscas-cinzento

9 :GAMBAGA FLYCATCHER :Gobemouche de Gambaga :Papa-moscas de Gambaga

10 :SOOTY FLYCATCHER, (African) :Gobemouche enfumé :Papa-moscas-sombrio

11 :USSHER'S FLYCATCHER :Gobemouche d'Ussher :Papa-moscas de Ussher

12 :ASHY (or Blue-grey) FLYCATCHER :Gobemouche à lunettes :Papa-moscas-de-lunetas

13 :OLIVACEOUS FLYCATCHER :Gobemouche olivâtre :Papa-moscas-oliváceo

14 :CHAPIN'S FLYCATCHER :Gobemouche de Chapin :Papa-moscas de Chapin

15 :AFRICAN DUSKY FLYCATCHER :Gobemouche sombre :Papa-moscas-castanho

16 :LITTLE GREY FLYCATCHER :Gobemouche cendré :Papa-moscas-anão

17 :YELLOW-FOOTED FLYCATCHER :Gobemouche à pattes jaunes :Papa-moscas-de-patas-amarelas

18 :DUSKY-BLUE FLYCATCHER :Gobemouche ardoisé :Papa-moscas-ardósia

19 :TESSMANN'S FLYCATCHER :Gobemouche de Tessmann :Papa-moscas de Tessmann

20 :BOEHM'S FLYCATCHER :Gobemouche de Böhm :Papa-moscas de Böhm

Plate 88

1 :SHRIKE FLYCATCHER :Bias écorcheur :Papa-moscas-picanço

2 :BLACK-AND-WHITE (or Vanga) FLYCATCHER :Bias musicien :Papa-moscas-músico

3 :WHITE-EYED SLATY FLYCATCHER :Gobemouche de Fischer :Papa-moscas-de-olho-branco

4 :SOUTHERN BLACK FLYCATCHER :Gobemouche sud-africain :Papa-moscas-sul-africano

5 :NORTHERN BLACK FLYCATCHER :Gobemouche drongo :Papa-moscas-preto-africano

6 :PALE (, Pallid or Mouse-coloured) FLYCATCHER :Gobemouche pâle :Papa-moscas-pálido

7 :YELLOW-EYED BLACK FLYCATCHER :Gobemouche de Berlioz :Papa-moscas-de-olho-amarelo

8 :NIMBA FLYCATCHER :Gobemouche noir de Nimba :Papa-moscas de Nimba

9 :FRASER'S FOREST FLYCATCHER :Gobemouche forestier :Papa-moscas-da-floresta

10 :WHITE-BROWED FOREST FLYCATCHER :Gobemouche à sourcils blancs :Papa-moscas-de-sobrancelha-branca

11 :SEMICOLLARED FLYCATCHER :Gobemouche à demi-collier :Papa-moscas-de-meio-colar

12 :EUROPEAN PIED FLYCATCHER :Gobemouche noir :Papa-moscas-preto

13 :COLLARED FLYCATCHER :Gobemouche à collier :Papa-moscas-de-colar

14 :GREY TIT FLYCATCHER :Gobemouche mésange :Papa-moscas-chapim

15 :GREY-THROATED TIT FLYCATCHER :Gobemouche à gorge grise :Papa-moscas-de-garganta-cinzenta

16 :RED-BREASTED FLYCATCHER :Gobemouche nain :Papa-moscas-pequeno

Plate 89

1 :BROWN-THROATED (or Scarlet-spectacled) WATTLE-EYE :Pririt à collier :Papa-moscas-de-olheiras-de-asa-preta-e-branca

2 :WHITE-FRONTED WATTLE-EYE :Pririt à front blanc :Papa-moscas-de-olheiras-de-testa-branca

3 :BLACK-THROATED WATTLE-EYE :Pririt à gorge noire :Papa-moscas-de-olheiras-de-asa-preta

4 :WHITE-SPOTTED WATTLE-EYE :Pririt à taches blanches :Papa-moscas-de-olheiras-maculado

5 :CHESTNUT WATTLE-EYE :Pririt châtain :Papa-moscas-de-olheiras-castanho

6 :RED-CHEEKED WATTLE-EYE :Pririt de Blissett :Papa-moscas-de-olheiras-de-faces-ruivas

7 :BLACK-NECKED WATTLE-EYE :Pririt à cou noir :Papa-moscas-de-olheiras-de-pescoço-preto

8 :JAMESON'S WATTLE-EYE :Pririt de Jameson :Papa-moscas-de-olheiras de Jameson

9 :YELLOW-BELLIED WATTLE-EYE :Pririt à ventre doré :Papa-moscas-de-olheiras-de-barriga-amarela

10 :RWENZORI BATIS :Pririt du Ruwenzori :Papa-moscas das Ruwenzori

11 :CHINSPOT BATIS :Pririt molitor :Papa-moscas-molitor

12 :SENEGAL BATIS :Pririt du Sénégal :Papa-moscas-senegalês

13 :GREY-HEADED BATIS :Pririt à tête grise :Papa-moscas-de-cabeça-cinzenta

14 :BLACK-HEADED BATIS :Pririt à jaunes noires :Papa-moscas-de-cabeça-preta

15 :ANGOLA BATIS :Pririt de l'Angola :Papa-moscas-angolano

16 :ITURI BATIS :Pririt de l'Ituri :Papa-moscas do Ituri

17 :VERREAUX'S BATIS :Pririt de Verreaux :Papa-moscas de Verreaux

18 :BIOKO (or Fernando Po) BATIS :Pririt de Lawson :Papa-moscas de Lawson

19 :MARGARET'S BATIS :Pririt de Boulton :Papa-moscas de Margaret

Plate 90

1 :WHITE-TAILED BLUE FLYCATCHER :Tchitrec à queue blanche :Papa-moscas-de-cauda-branca

2 :AFRICAN BLUE FLYCATCHER :Tchitrec bleu :Papa-moscas-azul

3 :WHITE-TAILED CRESTED FLYCATCHER :Tchitrec à queue frangée :Papa-moscas-de-poupa

4 :DUSKY CRESTED FLYCATCHER :Tchitrec à tête noire :Papa-moscas-sombrio

5 :WHITE-BELLIED CRESTED FLYCATCHER :Tchitrec à ventre blanc :Papa-moscas-de-barriga-branca

6 :CHESTNUT-CAPPED FLYCATCHER :Érythrocerque à tête rousse :Papa-moscas-de-barrete-vermelho

7 :BLUE-MANTLED CRESTED FLYCATCHER :Tchitrec du Cap :Papa-moscas do Cabo

8 :BLUE-HEADED CRESTED FLYCATCHER :Tchitrec noir :Papa-moscas-de-cabeça-azul

9 :YELLOW (,West African or Western) PENDULINE TIT :Rémiz à ventre jaune :Chapim-amarelo

10 :GREY PENDULINE TIT :Rémiz de Carol :Chapim-de-garganta-branca

11 :FOREST (or Yellow-fronted) PENDULINE TIT :Rémiz à front jaune :Chapim-de-testa-amarela

12 :SENNAR (or Sudan) PENDULINE TIT :Rémiz du Soudan :Chapim-sudanês

13 :TIT-HYLIA :Astrild-mésange :Titília

14 :SPOTTED CREEPER :Grimpereau tacheté :Trepadeira-malhada

15 :MIOMBO (or Norhtern) GREY TIT :Mésange à ventre gris :Chapim-do-miombo

16 :WHITE-WINGED BLACK TIT :Mésange à epaulettes :Chapim-de-asa-branca

17 :WHITE-BELLIED TIT :Mésange à ventre blanc :Chapim-de-ventre-branco

18 :RUFOUS-BELLIED TIT :Mésange à ventre cannelle :Chapim-de-ventre-vermelho

19 :STRIPE-BREASTED TIT :Mésange à ventre strié :Chapim-de-cabeça-preta

20 :DUSKY TIT :Mésange enfumée :Chapim-sombrio

Plate 91

1 :YELLOW WHITE-EYE :Zostérops jaune :Olho-branco-amarelo

2 :PRÍNCIPE WHITE-EYE :Zostérops becfigue :Olho-grosso de São Tomé e Príncipe

3 :ANNOBON WHITE -EYE :Zostérops D'Annobon :Olho-grosso de Ano Bom

4 :FERNANDO PO SPEIROPS :Zostérops de Fernando Po :Olho-branco de Fernando Pó

5 :BLACK-CAPPED SPEIROPS :Zostérops de São Tomé :Olho-grosso

6 :PRÍNCIPE SPEIROPS :Zostérops de Principé :Olho-branco do Príncipe

7 :PYGMY SUNBIRD, (Southern) :Souimanga pygmée :Beija-flor-pigmeu

8 :VARIABLE (Yellow-Bellied) SUNBIRD :Souimanga à ventre jaune :Beija-flor-de-ventre-amarelo

9 :WHITE-BELLIED SUNBIRD :Souimanga à ventre blanc :Beija-flor-de-ventre-branco

10 :COPPER SUNBIRD :Souimanga cuivré :Beija-flor-cúpreo

11 :WESTERN OLIVE SUNBIRD :Souimanga olivâtre de l'Ouest :Beija-flor-oliváceo

12 :BATES'S SUNBIRD :Souimanga de Bates :Beija-flor de Bates

13 :LITTLE GREEN SUNBIRD :Souimanga de Seimund :Beija-flor-verde

14 :BROWN SUNBIRD :Souimanga brun :Beija-flor do Gabão

15 :FRASER'S (or Scarlet-tufted) SUNBIRD :Souimanga de Fraser :Beija-flor de Fraser

16 :ANCHIETA'S (or Red-and-blue) SUNBIRD :Souimanga d'Anchieta :Beija-flor-azul-e-vermelho

17 :WESTERN VIOLET-BACKED SUNBIRD :Souimanga violet :Beija-flor-de-dorso-violeta

18 :VIOLET-TAILED SUNBIRD :Souimanga

à queue violette :Beija-flor-de-cauda-violeta
19 :GREEN (or Yellow-chinned) SUNBIRD :Souimanga à bec droit :Beija-flor-de-queixo-amarelo
20 :COLLARED SUNBIRD :Souimanga à collier :Beija-flor-de-colar

Plate 92

1 :PRÍNCIPE SUNBIRD :Souimanga de Hartlaub :Beija-flor do Príncipe
2 :NEWTON'S (Yellow-breasted) SUNBIRD :Souimanga de Newton :Beija-flor-de-peito-amarelo
3 :CAMEROON (Blue-headed) SUNBIRD :Souimanga à tête bleue :Beija-flor-camaronês
4 :BUFF-THROATED SUNBIRD :Souimanga à gorge rousse :Beija-flor-de-garganta-amarela
5 :MIOMBO DOUBLE-COLLARED SUNBIRD :Souimanga du Miombo :Beija-flor-do-miombo
6 :RWENZORI (or Stuhlmann's) DOUBLE-COLLARED SUNBIRD :Souimanga de Ludwig :Beija-flor de Stuhlmann
7 :NORTHERN DOUBLE-COLLARED SUNBIRD :Souimanga de Preuss :Beija-flor de Preuss
8 :EASTERN DOUBLE-COLLARED SUNBIRD :Souimanga du Kilimandjaro :Beija-flor-de-colar-duplo
9 :OLIVE-BELLIED SUNBIRD :Souimanga à ventre olive :Beija-flor-de-ventre-oliváceo
10 :TINY SUNBIRD :Souimanga minule :Beija-flor-minúsculo
11 :REGAL SUNBIRD :Souimanga royal :Beija-flor-real
12 :ROCKEFELLER'S SUNBIRD :Souimanga de Rockefeller :Beija-flor de Rockefeller
13 :URSULA'S (Mouse-Coloured) SUNBIRD :Souimanga d'Ursula :Beija-flor de Ursula
14 :REICHENBACH'S SUNBIRD :Souimanga de Reichenbach :Beija-flor de Reichenbach
15 :ORANGE-TUFTED SUNBIRD :Souimanga de Bouvier :Beija-flor-de-tufos-laranja
16 :PALESTINE (or Northern Orange-tufted) SUNBIRD :Souimanga de Palestine :Beija-flor da Palestina
17 :SHELLEY'S SUNBIRD :Souimanga de Shelley :Beija-flor de Shelley
18 :PURPLE-BANDED SUNBIRD :Souimanga bifascié :Beija-flor-de-peito-violeta
19 :SPLENDID SUNBIRD :Souimanga éclatant :Beija-flor-esplêndido
20 :JOHANNA'S SUNBIRD :Souimanga de Johanna :Beija-flor de Johanna

21 :SUPERB SUNBIRD :Souimanga superbe :Beija-flor-soberbo

Plate 93

1 :MALACHITE SUNBIRD, (Yellow-tufted) :Souimanga malachite :Beija-flor-verde
2 :BRONZY SUNBIRD :Souimanga bronzé :Beija-flor-bronzeado
3 :BOCAGE'S SUNBIRD :Souimanga de Bocage :Beija-flor de Bocage
4 :SCARLET-TUFTED MALACHITE SUNBIRD :Souimanga de Johnston :Beija-flor-de-tufos-escarlates
5 :GOLDEN-WINGED SUNBIRD :Souimanga à ailes dorées :Beija-flor-de-asa-dourada
6 :PURPLE-BREASTED SUNBIRD :Souimanga à ventre pourpre :Beija-flor-púrpura
7 :RED-CHESTED SUNBIRD :Souimanga à ceinture rouge :Beija-flor-de-peito-vermelho
8 :GIANT SUNBIRD, (São Tomé) :Souimanga de São Tomé :Beija-flor-preto de São Tomé
9 :BLUE-THROATED BROWN SUNBIRD :Souimanga à gorge bleue :Beija-flor-de-garganta-azul
10 :BLUE-HEADED SUNBIRD :Souimanga d' Aline :Beija-flor-de-cabeça-azul
11 :BANNERMAN'S SUNBIRD :Souimanga de Bannerman :Beija-flor de Bannerman
12 :GREEN-HEADED SUNBIRD :Souimanga à tête verte :Beija-flor-de-cabeça-verde
13 :CONGO (Black-bellied) SUNBIRD :Souimanga du Congo :Beija-flor-congolês
14 :BEAUTIFUL SUNBIRD :Souimanga à longue queue :Beija-flor-rabilongo
15 :CARMELITE SUNBIRD :Souimanga carmélite :Beija-flor-carmelita
16 :SCARLET-CHESTED SUNBIRD :Souimanga à poitrine rouge :Beija-flor-de-peito-escarlate
17 :AMETHYST (or Black) SUNBIRD :Souimanga améthyste :Beija-flor-preto
18 :GREEN-THROATED SUNBIRD :Souimanga à gorge verte :Beija-flor-de-garganta-verde

Plate 94

1 :WHITE HELMET SHRIKE :Bagadais casqué :Picanço-branco
2 :RED-BILLED HELMET SHRIKE, (Northern) :Bagadais à bec rouge :Picanço-de-bico-vermelho
3 :YELLOW-CRESTED HELMET SHRIKE :Bagadais d'Albert :Picanço-de-crista-amarela

4 :RETZ'S (Red-billed) HELMET SHRIKE
:Bagadais de Retz :Picanço de Retz
5 :BRUBRU :Brubru africain :Picanço-
pintadinho
6 :BLACK-COLLARED BULBUL SHRIKE
:Bulbul à collier noir :Picanço-de-colar-
preto
7 :BLACKCAP (Marsh) TCHAGRA
:Tchagra des marais :Picanço-anão
8 :BROWN-CROWNED (or Three-
streaked) TCHAGRA :Tchagra à tête
brune :Picanço-de-barrete-castanho
9 :BLACK-CROWNED TCHAGRA
:Tchagra à tête noire :Picanço-de-barrete-
preto
10 :NORTHERN PUFFBACK :Cubla de
Gambie :Picanço da Gâmbia
11 :BLACK-BACKED (or southern)
PUFFBACK :Cubla boule-de-neige
:Picanço-de-dorso-preto
12 :RED-EYED (or Black-shouldered)
PUFFBACK :Cubla à oeil rouge :Picanço-
de-ombros-pretos
13 :PINK-FOOTED PUFFBACK :Cubla à
pieds roses :Picanço-de-patas-rosadas
14 :SABINE'S PUFFBACK :Cubla à gros bec
:Picanço de Sabine
15 :SOOTY BOUBOU :Gonolek fuligineux
:Picanço-sombrio
16 :MOUNTAIN SOOTY BOUBOU
:Gonolek de montagne :Picanço-preto-
da-montanha
17 :BOCAGE'S (or Grey-green) BUSH
SHRIKE :Gladiateur à front blanc
:Picanço de Bocage
18 :YELLOW-THROATED NICATOR
:Bulbul à gorge jaune :Tuta-de-garganta-
amarela
19 :WESTERN NICATOR :Bulbul nicator
:Tuta-malhada

Plate 95
1 :TURATI'S BOUBOU :Gonolek de Turati
:Picanço da Guiné
2 :TROPICAL BOUBOU :Gonolek
d'Abyssinie :Picanço-tropical
3 :SWAMP BOUBOU :Gonolek à ventre
blanc :Picanço-bicolor
4 :MOUNT KUPÉ BUSH SHRIKE
:Gladiateur du Kupé :Picanço de Kupé
5 :GORGEOUS (or Perrin's) BUSH
SHRIKE :Gladiateur vert :Picanço de
Perrin
6 :DOHERTY'S BUSH SHRIKE :Gladiateur
de Doherty :Picanço de Doherty
7 :LUEHDER'S BUSH SHRIKE :Gonolek de
Lühder :Picanço de Lühder
8 :YELLOW-CROWNED GONOLEK
:Gonolek de Barbarie :Picanço-de-
barrete-amarelo
9 :BLACK-HEADED GONOLEK :Gonolek

à ventre rouge :Picanço-de-cabeça-preta
10 :YELLOW-BREASTED BOUBOU
:Gonolek à ventre jaune :Picanço-de-
peito-amarelo
11 :PAPYRUS GONOLEK (or Bush Shrike)
:Gonolek des papyrus :Picanço-dos-
papiros
12 :ORANGE-BREASTED BUSH SHRIKE
:Gladiateur soufré :Picanço-de-peito-
laranja
13 :BLACK-FRONTED BUSH SHRIKE
:Gladiateur à front noir :Picanço-de-testa-
preta
14 :MANY-COLOURED BUSH SHRIKE
:Gladiateur multicolore :Picanço-
multicor
15 :FIERY-BREASTED BUSH SHRIKE
:Gladiateur ensanglanté :Picanço-peito-
de-fogo
16 :LAGDEN'S BUSH SHRIKE :Gladiateur
de Lagden :Picanço de Ladgen
17 :GREEN-BREASTED BUSH SHRIKE
:Gladiateur à poitrine verte :Picanço-de-
peito-verde
18 :GREY-HEADED BUSH SHRIKE
:Gladiateur de Blanchot :Picanço-de-
cabeça-cinzenta
19 :MONTEIRO'S BUSH SHRIKE
:Gladiateur de Monteiro :Picanço de
Monteiro

Plate 96
1 :YELLOW-BILLED (or Long-tailed)
SHRIKE :Corvinelle à bec jaune
:Picanço-rabilongo-ruivo
2 :EMIN'S SHRIKE :Pie-grièche à dos roux
:Picanço de Emin
3 :SOUZA'S SHRIKE :Pie-grièche de Souza
:Picanço de Souza
4 :RED-BACKED SHRIKE :Pie-grièche
écorcheur :Picanço-de-dorso-ruivo
5 :ISABELLINE (or Red-tailed) SHRIKE
:Pie-grièche isabelle :Picanço-de-cauda-
ruiva
6 :MASKED (or Nubian) SHRIKE :Pie-
grièche masquée :Picanço-nubiano
7 :WOODCHAT SHRIKE :Pie-grièche à
tête rousse :Picanço-barreteiro
8 :MACKINNON'S SHRIKE :Pie-grièche de
Mackinnon :Picanço de Mackinnon
9 :LESSER GREY SHRIKE :Pie-grièche à
poitrine rose :Picanço-pequeno
10 :GREY-BACKED FISCAL :Pie-grièche à
dos gris :Picanço-de-dorso-cinzento
11 :SOUTHERN GREY SHRIKE :Pie-grièche
méridionale :Picanço-real
12 :FISCAL SHRIKE :Pie-grièche fiscale
:Picanço-fiscal
13 :SÃO TOMÉ (or Newton's) FISCAL :
Pie-grièche de São Tomé :Picanço de São
Tomé

Plate 97

1 :EURASIAN GOLDEN ORIOLE :Loriot d'Europe :Papa-figos-europeu
2 :AFRICAN GOLDEN ORIOLE :Loriot doré :Papa-figos-africano
3 :BLACK-WINGED ORIOLE :Loriot à ailles noires :Papa-figos-de-asa-preta
4 :SÃO TOMÉ ORIOLE :Loriot de São Tomé :Papa-figos de São Tomé
5 :WESTERN BLACK-HEADED ORIOLE :Loriot à tête noire :Papa-figos-de-cabeça-preta-ocidental
6 :MOUNTAIN ORIOLE :Loriot de Percival :Papa-figos-montês
7 :EASTERN BLACK-HEADED ORIOLE :Loriot masqué :Papa-figos-de-cabeça-preta
8 :WESTERN JACKDAW :Corneille des tours :Gralha-de-nuca-cinzenta
9 :CAPE (or Black) CROW :Corneille du Cap :Gralha do Cabo
10 :PIED CROW :Corneille pie :Gralha-africana
11 :BROWN-NECKED RAVEN :Corneille brun :Corvo-do-deserto
12 :PIAPIAC :Piapiac africain :Gralha-rabilonga
13 :HOUSE CROW :Corneille familier :Gralha-das-casas
14 :FAN-TAILED RAVEN :Corneille à queue courte :Corvo-de-cauda-curta
15 :WHITE-NECKED RAVEN :Corneille à nuque blanche :Corvo-de-nuca-branca

Plate 98

1 :RED-WINGED STARLING :Rufipenne morio :Estorninho-de-asa-vermelha
2 :CHESTNUT-WINGED STARLING :Rufipenne de fôret :Estorninho-do-bosque
3 :SLENDER-BILLED STARLING :Rufipenne à bec fin :Estorninho-de-bico-fino
4 :WALLER'S STARLING :Rufipenne de Waller :Estorninho de Waller
5 :PRÍNCIPE GLOSSY STARLING :Choucador de Príncipe :Estorninho do Príncipe
6 :EMERALD STARLING :Choucador iris :Estorninho-esmeraldino
7 :SPLENDID GLOSSY STARLING :Choucador splendide :Estorninho-esplêndido
8 :RUEPPELL'S GLOSSY STARLING :Choucador de Rüppell :Estorninho de Rüppell
9 :PURPLE GLOSSY STARLING :Choucador pourpré :Estorninho-purpúreo
10 :BRONZE-TAILED GLOSSY STARLING :Choucador à queue violette :Estorninho-de-cauda-bronzeada
11 :COPPER-TAILED GLOSSY STARLING :Choucador à queue bronzée :Estorninho-cúpreo
12 :SHARP-TAILED STARLING :Choucador à queue fine :Estorninho-de-cauda-afilada
13 :LESSER BLUE-EARED STARLING :Choucador de Swainson :Estorninho-pequeno-de-orelha-azul
14 :GREATER BLUE-EARED STARLING :Choucador à oreillons bleus :Estorninho-grande-de-orelha-azul
15 :CAPE GLOSSY STARLING :Choucador à épaulettes rouges :Estorninho do Cabo
16 :LONG-TAILED GLOSSY STARLING :Choucador à longue queue :Estorninho-rabilongo
17 :PURPLE-HEADED GLOSSY STARLING :Choucador à tête pourprée :Estorninho-de-cabeça-púrpura

Plate 99

1 :SHINING DRONGO :Drongo de fôret :Drongo-resplandecente
2 :SQUARE-TAILED DRONGO :Drongo de Ludwig :Drongo-de-cauda-quadrada
3 :FORK-TAILED DRONGO :Drongo brillant :Drongo-de-cauda-forcada
4 :YELLOW-BILLED OXPECKER :Piqueboeuf à bec jaune :Pica-boi-de-bico-amarelo
5 :RED-BILLED OXPECKER :Piqueboeuf à bec rouge :Pica-boi-de-bico-vermelho
6 :WATTLED STARLING :Étourneau caronculé :Estorninho-carunculado
7 :COMMON STARLING :Étourneau sansonnet :Estorninho-malhado
8 :GREY-NECKED PICATHARTES :Picatharte à cou gris :Pega-calva-de-cabeça-vermelha
9 :WHITE-NECKED PICATHARTES :Picatharte à cou blanc :Pega-calva-de-pescoço-branco
10 :STUHLMANN'S STARLING :Rufipenne de Stuhlmann :Estorninho de Stuhlmann
11 :NARROW-TAILED STARLING :Rufipenne à queue étroite :Estorninho-de-cauda-fina
12 :SHARPE'S STARLING :Spréo de Sharpe :Estorninho de Sharpe
13 :VIOLET-BACKED (, Amethyst or Plum-coloured) STARLING :Spréo amethyste :Estorninho-de-dorso-violeta
14 :CHESTNUT-BELLIED STARLING :Choucador à ventre roux :Estorninho-de-barriga-ruiva
15 :WHITE-COLLARED STARLING :Rufipenne à cou blanc :Estorninho-de-peito-branco

APPENDIX

Plate 100

1 :WHITE-BILLED BUFFALO WEAVER :Alecto à bec blanc :Tecelão-de-bico-branco

2 :CHESTNUT-MANTLED SPARROW WEAVER :Moineau-tisserin à dos roux :Tecelão-de-dorso-castanho

3 :CHESTNUT-CROWNED SPARROW WEAVER :Moineau-tisserin à couronne marron :Tecelão-laranja

4 :IAGO SPARROW :Moineau d'Iago :Pardal de Cabo Verde

5 :SPANISH SPARROW :Moineau espagnol :Pardal-espanhol

6 :HOUSE SPARROW :Moineau domestique :Pardal-comum

7 :TREE SPARROW :Moineau friquet :Pardal-montês

8 :GREY-HEADED SPARROW :Moineau à tête grise :Pardal-de-cabeça-cinzenta

9 :RUFOUS (or Great) SPARROW :Moineau grand :Pardal-grande

10 :DESERT SPARROW :Moineau du désert :Pardal-do-deserto

11 :YELLOW-SPOTTED PETRONIA :Moineau soulcie à taches jaunes :Pardal-cinzento

12 :BUSH PETRONIA :Petit moineau soulcie :Pardal-do-mato

13 :SOUTHERN YELLOW-THROATED PETRONIA :Moineau soulcie d'Afrique du Sud :Pardal-de-garganta-amarela

14 :SUDAN GOLDEN SPARROW :Moineau doré :Pardal-dourado

15 :SPECKLE-FRONTED WEAVER :Moineau quadrillé :Pardal-de-testa-ponteada

16 :GROSBEAK WEAVER :Gros-bec à front blanc :Tecelão-de-bico-grosso

17 :BRAMBLING :Pinson du Nord :Tentilhão-montês

18 :CHAFFINCH :Pinson des arbres :Tentilhão-comum

19 :CUT-THROAT FINCH :Cou-coupé :Degolado-africano

Plate 101

1 :LARGE GOLDEN WEAVER :Tissirin doré :Tecelão-dourado-grande

2 :PRÍNCIPE GOLDEN WEAVER :Tissirin de Príncipe :Tecelão do Príncipe

3 :ORANGE WEAVER :Tissirin orangé :Tecelão-laranjo

4 :SPECTACLED WEAVER :Tissirin à lunettes oriental :Tecelão-de-lunetas

5 :BAGLAFECHT WEAVER :Tissirin de Baglafecht :Tecelão de Baglafecht

6 :BANNERMAN'S WEAVER :Tissirin de Bannerman :Tecelão de Bannerman

7 :HEUGLIN'S MASKED WEAVER :Tissirin masqué de Heuglin :Tecelão de Heuglin

8 :SLENDER-BILLED WEAVER :Tissirin de Pelzeln :Tecelão-de-bico-fino

9 :LITTLE WEAVER :Tissirin minule :Tecelão-pequeno

10 :VILLAGE (or Black-headed) WEAVER :Tissirin des villages ou gendarme :Tecelão-de-dorso-malhado

11 :NORTHERN BROWN-THROATED WEAVER :Tissirin à gorge noir du Nil :Tecelão-de-garganta-castanha

12 :BOCAGE'S WEAVER :Tisserin de Bocage :Tecelão de Bocage

13 :BATES'S WEAVER :Tissirin de Bates :Tecelão de Bates

14 :VITELLINE (,African or Southern) MASKED WEAVER :Tissirin masqué d'Afrique occidentale :Tecelão-de-mascarilha

15 :LESSER MASKED WEAVER :Tissirin masqué d'Afrique :Tecelão-pequeno-de-mascarilha

16 :NORTHERN MASKED WEAVER :Tissirin masqué du Nil :Tecelão-grande-de-mascarilha

17 :YELLOW-BACKED WEAVER :Tissirin à tête noire :Tecelão-de-cabeça-preta

18 :RUWET'S MASKED WEAVER :Tissirin de Ruwet :Tecelão de Ruwet

19 :KATANGA'S MASKED WEAVER :Tissirin de Katanga :Tecelão de Katanga

20 :STRANGE WEAVER :Tissirin Alien de montagne :Tecelão-de-babete-castanho

Plate 102

1 :BROWN-CAPPED WEAVER :Tissirin à cape brune :Tecelão-de-barrete-castanho

2 :YELLOW-CAPPED WEAVER :Tissirin à cape jaune :Tecelão-de-barrete-amarelo

3 :BLACK-CHINNED WEAVER :Tissirin à menton noir :Tecelão-de-queixo-preto

4 :PREUSS'S GOLDEN-BACKED WEAVER :Tissirin de Preuss :Tecelão de Preuss

5 :WEYN'S WEAVER :Tissirin de Weyns :Tecelão de Weyn

6 :YELLOW-MANTLED WEAVER :Tissirin tricolore :Tecelão-de-dorso-amarelo

7 :BLACK-NECKED (or Western Spectacled) WEAVER :Tissirin à cou noir :Tecelão-de-pescoço-preto

8 :DARK-BACKED WEAVER :Tissirin bicolore :Tecelão-de-dorso-escuro

9 :BLACK-BILLED WEAVER :Tissirin noir à tête jaune :Tecelão-de-barriga-preta

10 :MAXWELL'S BLACK WEAVER :Tissirin à nuque blanche :Tecelão de Maxwell

11 :VIEILLOT'S BLACK WEAVER :Tissirin noir de Vieillot :Tecelão-preto

12 :YELLOW-LEGGED WEAVER :Tissirin-malimbe à pieds jaunes

:Tecelão-de-patas-amarelas
13 :BAR-WINGED WEAVER :Tissirin-
malimbe à nuque blanche :Tecelão de
Angola
14 :SÃO TOMÉ WEAVER :Tissirin de São
Tomé :Tecelão de São Tomé
15 :LOANGO SLENDER-BILLED WEAVER
:Tissirin à bec grêle :Tecelão-de-bico-fino
de Loanga
16 :COMPACT WEAVER :Tissirin compact
:Tecelão-compacto
17 :GOLDEN-NAPED WEAVER :Tissirin à
nuque d'or :Tecelão-de-nuca-amarela
18 :GIANT WEAVER :Tissirin géant
:Tecelão-gigante

Plate 103
1 :RED-CROWNED MALIMBE :Tissirin-
malimbe couronné
:Tecelão-de-coroa-vermelha
2 :CASSIN'S MALIMBE :Tissirin-malimbe
de Cassin :Tecelão de Cassin
3 :RACHEL'S MALIMBE :Tissirin-malimbe
de Rachel :Tecelão de Rachel
4 :GOLA MALIMBE :Tissirin-malimbe de
Gola :Tecelão de Gola
5 :RED-VENTED MALIMBE :Tissirin-
malimbe à queue rouge
:Tecelão-de-barriga-vermelha
6 :GRAY'S (or Blue-billed) MALIMBE
:Tissirin-malimbe à bec bleu :Tecelão-de-
bico-azul
7 :IBADAN MALIMBE :Tissirin-malimbe
d'Ibadan :Tecelão de Ibadan
8 :RED-HEADED MALIMBE :Tissirin-
malimbe à tête rouge :Tecelão-vermelho
9 :RED-BELLIED MALIMBE :Tissirin-
malimbe à ventre rouge
:Tecelão-de-barriga-vermelha
10 :CRESTED MALIMBE :Tissirin-malimbe
huppé :Tecelão-de-poupa
11 :RED-HEADED WEAVER :Tissirin-
malimbe écarlate
:Tecelão-de-cabeça-vermelha
12 :RED-HEADED QUELEA :Travailleur à
tête rouge :Quelea-de-cabeça-vermelha
13 :RED-BILLED QUELEA :Travailleur à bec
rouge :Quelea-de-bico-vermelho
14 :CARDINAL QUELEA :Travailleur
cardinal :Quelea-cardinal
15 :PARASITIC WEAVER (or Cuckoo
Finch) :Tisserin coucou :Tecelão-
parasítico
16 :BOB-TAILED WEAVER :Travailleur
anomale :Tecelão-de-cauda-curta

Plate 104
1 :LONG-TAILED WHYDAH :Veuve
géante :Viúva-de-cauda-comprida
2 :YELLOW-SHOULDERED WHYDAH

:Veuve à dos d'Or :Viúva-de-manto-
amarelo
3 :MARSH WHYDAH :Veuve des marais
:Viúva-dos-paúis
4 :RED-COLLARED WHYDAH :Veuve
ardens :Viúva-de-coleira-vermelha
5 :WHITE-WINGED WHYDAH :Veuve à
ailles blanches :Viúva-de-asa-branca
6 :RED-SHOULDERED WHYDAH :Veuve
à épaulettes orangées :Viúva-de-ombro-
vermelho
7 :BLACK-WINGED RED (or Fire-
crowned) BISHOP :Euplecte
Monseigneur ou à tête rouge :Bispo-de-
coroa-vermelha
8 :NORTHERN RED BISHOP :Euplecte
franciscain du Nord :Bispo-laranja
9 :BLACK BISHOP :Euplecte de Gierow
:Bispo-negro
10 :YELLOW-CROWNED (or Golden)
BISHOP :Euplecte à tête jaune :Bispo-de-
coroa-amarela
11 :RED BISHOP :Euplecte franciscain ou
ignicolore :Bispo-vermelho
12 :GOLDEN-BACKED BISHOP :Euplecte à
dos doré :Bispo-de-dorso-amarelo
13 :YELLOW(-rumped) BISHOP :Euplecte
noir et jaune :Viúva-de-uropígio-amarelo

Plate 105
1 :CRIMSON- (or Red-)WINGED PYTILIA
:Pytilie à ailes rouges :Aurora-de-asas-
vermelhas
2 :RED-FACED (or Yellow-winged)
PYTILIA :Pytilie à ailes jaunes :Aurora-
de-faces-vermelhas
3 :ORANGE-WINGED (or Golden-backed)
PYTILIA :Beaumarquet à dos jaune
:Aurora-de-dorso-amarelo
4 :GREEN-WINGED PYTILIA (or Melba
Finch) :Beaumarquet melba :Aurora-
melba
5 :WHITE-BREASTED BLACKFINCH
:Bengali nègre à ventre blanc :Negrito-de-
peito-branco
6 :CHESTNUT-BREASTED
BLACKFINCH :Bengali nègre à ventre
roux :Negrito-de-peito-castanho
7 :PALE-FRONTED BLACKFINCH
:Bengali nègre à front jaune :Negrito-de-
testa-clara
8 :GREY-HEADED (or -Crowned)
BLACKFINCH :Bengali nègre :Negrito-
de-cabeça-cinzenta
9 :FERNANDO PO (or Little) OLIVEBACK
:Bengali vert de Shelley :Dorso-musgo-de
Fernando Pó
10 :GREY-HEADED (or White-cheeked)
OLIVEBACK :Bengali vert à joues
blanches :Dorso-musgo-de-cabeça-
cinzenta

11 :WHITE-COLLARED OLIVEBACK
   :Bengali vert à collier blanc :Dorso-
   musgo-de-colar-branco
12 :BLACK-BELLIED FIREFINCH :Sénégali
   à ventre noir :Granadeiro-de-barriga-
   preta
13 :BAR-BREASTED FIREFINCH :Sénégali
   à poitrine barrée :Granadeiro de Fraser
14 :BROWN FIREFINCH :Sénégali nitidula
   :Granadeiro-castanho
15 :RED-BILLED FIREFINCH :Sénégali
   amaranthe :Granadeiro-de-bico-
   vermelho
16 :AFRICAN (or Blue-billed) FIREFINCH
   :Sénégali à bec bleu :Granadeiro-de-bico-
   azul
17 :ROCK FIREFINCH :Sénégali de roche
   :Granadeiro-das-rochas
18 :KULIKORO (or Mali) FIREFINCH
   :Sénégali du Mali :Granadeiro de
   Kulikoro
19 :PALE-BILLED FIREFINCH :Sénégali de
   Landana :Granadeiro-de-bico-pálido
20 :JAMESON'S FIREFINCH :Sénégali de
   Jameson :Granadeiro de Jameson
21 :BLACK-FACED FIREFINCH :Sénégali à
   face noire :Granadeiro-de-faces-pretas

Plate 106

1 :CRIMSON SEEDCRACKER :Gros-bec
   ponceau à ventre brun :Bico-grosso-
   escarlate
2 :BLACK-BELLIED SEEDCRACKER
   :Gros-bec ponceau à ventre noir :Bico-
   grosso-de-barriga-preta
3 :BLUEBILL, (Western) :Gros-bec sanguin
   :Tecelinho-de-bico-azul
4 :GRANT'S BLUEBILL :Gros-bec rouge-
   noir à bec bleu :Tecelinho de Grant
5 :RED-HEADED BLUEBILL :Gros-bec à
   tête rouge :Tecelinho-de-cabeça-
   vermelha
6 :DYBOWSKI'S DUSKY TWINSPOT
   :Bengali tacheté à ventre noir
   :Pintadinho de Dybowski
7 :DUSKY TWINSPOT :Bengali tacheté
   sombre :Pintadinho-sombrio
8 :PIN-TAILED WIDOW :Veuve
   dominicaine :Viúva-de-cauda-fina
9 :LONG-TAILED PARADISE WIDOW
   :Veuve à collier d'Or :Viúva-rabilonga
10 :TOGO'S PARADISE WIDOW :Veuve du
   Togo :Viúva do Togo
11 :UELLE'S (or Exclamatory) PARADISE
   WIDOW :Veuve d'Uelle :Viúva interject
12 :SAHEL PARADISE WIDOW :Veuve de
   paradis :Viúva do Sahel
13 :BROAD-TAILED PARADISE WIDOW
   :Veuve à large queue :Viúva-de-cauda-
   larga
14 :JOS PLATEAU INDIGOBIRD

:Combassou du Plateau de Jos :Bico-de-
prata do planalto Jos
15 :VILLAGE INDIGOBIRD :Combassou
   bleu ou du Sénégal :Bico-de-prata do
   Senegal
16 :VARIABLE INDIGOBIRD :Combassou
   noir :Bico-de-prata de Wilson
17 :GOLDBREAST (or Jambandu)
   INDIGOBIRD :Combassou jambandu
   :Bico-de-prata de Jambandu
18 :DUSKY INDIGOBIRD :Combassou
   cendré :Bico-de-prata-sombrio
19 :CAMEROON INDIGOBIRD :Combassou
   du Cameroun :Bico-de-prata-camaronês
20 :BAKA INDIGOBIRD :Combassou Bakra
   :Bico-de-prata de Baka
21 :QUAIL FINCH INDIGOBIRD
   :Combassou du Nigéria :Bico-de-prata da
   Nigéria
22 :WILSON'S INDIGOBIRD :Combassou
   noir :Bico-de-prata de Wilson

Plate 107

1 :GREEN-BACKED TWINSPOT :Bengali
   vert tacheté :Pintadinho-verde
2 :RED-FACED CRIMSONWING :Bengali
   de Reichenow :Asa-rosada-de-faces-
   vermelhas
3 :ABYSSINIAN CRIMSONWING
   :Bengali de Salvador :Asa-carmim-pálido
4 :DUSKY CRIMSONWING :Bengali de
   Jackson :Asa-carmim-escuro
5 :SHELLEY'S CRIMSONWING :Bengali
   de Shelley :Asa-rosada de Shelley
6 :BROWN TWINSPOT :Bengali tacheté à
   ventre roux :Pintadinho-castanho
7 :PETER'S (or Red-throated) TWINSPOT
   :Amaranthe enflammé :Pintadinho-de-
   garganta-vermelha
8 :LAVENDER WAXBILL :Astrild gris-bleu
   :Cauda-vinagre
9 :BLACK-TAILED GREY WAXBILL
   :Astrild à queue noire :Bico-de-lacre-de-
   cauda-preta
10 :CINDERELLA WAXBILL :Astrild de São
   Tomé :Bico-de-lacre-são-tomense
11 :YELLOW-BELLIED (or Swee) WAXBILL
   :Asrild à ventre jaune :Bico-de-lacre-de-
   queixo-preto
12 :ANAMBRA WAXBILL :Astrild
   d'Anambra :Bico-de-lacre de Anambra
13 :FAWN-BREASTED WAXBILL :Astrild à
   poitrine fauve :Bico-de-lacre-de-cabeça-
   cinzenta
14 :ORANGE-CHEEKED WAXBILL :Astrild
   à joues orangées :Bico-de-lacre-de-faces-
   laranja
15 :CRIMSON-RUMPED WAXBILL :Astrild
   à croupion rose :Bico-de-lacre-de-
   uropígio-vermelho
16 :BLACK-RUMPED WAXBILL :Astrild

cendré :Bico-de-lacre-de-uropígio-preto

17 :COMMON WAXBILL :Astrild ondulé ou bec-de-coral :Bico-de-lacre-comum

18 :BLACK-FACED WAXBILL :Astrild à masque noir :Bico-de-lacre-de-faces-pretas

19 :BLACK-CROWNED WAXBILL :Astrild à couronne noire :Bico-de-lacre-de-barrete-preto

20 :BLACK-HEADED WAXBILL :Astrild à tête noire :Bico-de-lacre-de-cabeça-preta

Plate 108

1 :AFRICAN QUAIL FINCH :Astrild caille :Freirinha de Ansorge

2 :BLACK-CHINNED QUAIL FINCH :Astrild caille a gorge noire :Freirinha-de-queixo-preto

3 :LOCUST FINCH :Astrild caille à gorge rouge :Freirinha-gafanhoto

4 :AFRICAN (or Warbling) SILVERBILL :Spermète bec d'Argent :Bico-de-prata

5 :BRONZE MANNIKIN :Spermète cucullata :Bico-de-chumbo-bronzeado

6 :BI-COLOURED (, black-and-white or Red-backed) MANNIKIN :Spermète à bec bleu :Bico-de-chumbo-de-dorso-preto

7 :MAGPIE MANNIKIN :Spermète pie :Bico-de-chumbo-de-dorso-castanho

8 :ZEBRA WAXBILL (or Goldbreast) :Astrild à flanks rayés :Ventre-laranja

9 :CORDON-BLEU (or Blue Waxbill) :Bengali cordon bleu méridional :Peito-celeste-de-faces-azuis

10 :RED-CHEEKED CORDON-BLEU :Bengali cordon bleu à joues rouges :Peito-celeste-de-faces-violetas

11 :GOLDEN-BREASTED BUNTING :Bruant à poitrine dorée :Escrevedeira-de-peito-dourado

12 :CABANIS'S BUNTING :Bruant de Cabanis :Escrevedeira de Cabanis

13 :HOUSE BUNTING :Bruant striolé :Escrevedeira-das-casas

14 :LARK-LIKE BUNTING :Bruant impétuan :Escrevedeira-cotovia

15 :BROWN-RUMPED (or Nigerian) BUNTING :Bruant à ventre jaune :Escrevedeira-de-uropígio-castanho

16 :CINNAMON-BREASTED (Rock) BUNTING :Bruant cannelle :Escrevedeira-de-peito-canelado

17 :ROCK BUNTING :Bruant fou :Cia

18 :CORN BUNTING :Bruant proyer :Trigueirão

19 :ORTOLAN BUNTING :Bruant ortolan :Sombria

20 :CRETZSCHMAR'S BUNTING :Bruant cendrillard :Escrevedeira-cinzenta

Plate 109

1 :ORIOLE FINCH :Pinson-loriot :Bico-grosso-de-cabeça-preta

2 :LINNET :Linotte mélodieuse :Pintarroxo-comum

3 :GREENFINCH :Verdier :Verdilhão-comum

4 :TRUMPETER FINCH :Bouvreuil githagine :Pintarroxo-trombeteiro

5 :SÃO TOMÉ GROSBEAK :Gros-bec de São Tomé :Enjolo

6 :YELLOW-RUMPED (or Black-throated) SEEDEATER (or Canary) :Serin à croupion jaune :Canário-de-garganta-preta

7 :WHITE-RUMPED SEEDEATER (or Canary) :Serin à croupion blanc :Canário-de-uropígio-branco

8 :STRIPE-BREASTED SEEDEATER :Serin de Reichard :Canário-de-peito-estriado

9 :STREAKY-HEADED SEEDEATER :Serin gris à tête blanche :Canário-de-cabeça-estriada

10 :YELLOW-CROWNED CANARY :Serin à couronne d'or :Canário-de-nuca-cinzenta

11 :AFRICAN CITRIL :Serin d'Abyssinie :Canário-africano

12 :PAPYRUS CANARY :Serin de Van Someren :Canário-dos-papiros

13 :BLACK-FACED CANARY :Serin à masque noir :Canário-de-faces-pretas

14 :YELLOW-FRONTED (or -eyed) CANARY :Serin à front jaune :Canário-de-testa-amarela

15 :BRIMSTONE (or Bully) CANARY :Serin de Shelley :Canário-grande

16 :BLACK-EARED SEEDEATER :Serin à oreillons noirs :Canário-de-faces-pretas

17 :THICK-BILLED SEEDEATER :Serin de Burton :Canário-de-bico-grosso

18 :STREAKY SEEDEATER :Serin strié :Canário-estriado

19 :PRÍNCIPE SEEDEATER :Serin roux :Canário do Príncipe

INDEX OF COMMON NAMES

Numbers refer to the relevant plate, followed by the number of the bird on that plate.

INDEX OF SCIENTIFIC NAMES

The *genus* in which a bird species is placed is written with the first letter in capital. Numbers refer to the relevant plate, followed –in case of the species- after the dot by the number of the bird species on that plate.

INDEX OF SCIENTIFIC NAMES

BIBLIOGRAPHY AND FURTHER READING

OTHER FIELD GUIDES

C. Barlow, T. Wacher and T. Disley, *A Field Guide to the Birds of The Gambia and Senegal* (Mountfield, 1997)

L. Johnsson, *Birds of Europe with North Africa and the Middle East* (London, 1992). For migrants and North-African Birds

W. Serle, G. J. Morel & W. Hartwig, *A Field Guide to the Birds of West Africa* (London, 1986)

L. Svensson & P. J. Grant, *Collins Bird Guide* (London, 1999). For migrants and North-African Birds

HANDBOOKS

The Birds of Africa (Academic Press, London)

L. H. Brown, E. K. Urban & K. Newman, (Eds) (vol. I) *Ostrich – Raptors* (1982)

U. K. Urban, C. Hillary Fry and S. Keith, (Eds) (vol. II) *Guineafowl – Doves* (1986)

C. Hillary Fry, S. Keith & E. K. Urban, (Eds) (vol. III) *Parrots – Woodpeckers* (1988)

S. Keith, E. K. Urban & C. Hillary Fry, (Eds) (vol. IV) *Broadbills – Chats* (1992)

E. K. Urban, C. Hillary Fry & S. Keith, (Eds) (vol. V) *Thrushes – Puffbacks Flycatchers* (1997)

C. Hillary Fry, S. Keith, E. K. Urban & (Eds) (vol. VI) *Picathartes – Oxpeckers* (2000) (vol. VII Last vol., not yet published)

African Handbooks of Birds (Longman, London and New York)

C. W. Mackworth-Praed & C. H. B. Grant, *Birds of West Central and Western Africa*, Volumes I and II (1981)

Handbook of the Birds of the World (Lynx Editions, Barcelona)

J. del Hoyo, A. Elliott, J. Sargatal, (Eds)
(Vol. I)   *Ostrich – Ducks* (1992)
(Vol. II)   *New World Vultures – Guineafowl* (1994)
(Vol. III)   *Hoatzin – Auks* (1996)
(Vol. IV)   *Barn-owls – Hummingbirds* (1997)
(Vol. V)   *Sandgrouse – Cuckoos* (1999)
(Vol. VI)   *Mousebirds – Hornbills* (2001)

Other volumes yet to be published.

OTHER IMPORTANT LITERATURE

R. A. Cheke, J. F Walsh, *The Birds of Togo* (B.O.U. Checklist no 14, 1996)

J. H. Elgood et al, *The Birds of Nigeria* (B.O.U. Checklist no 4, 1994)

M. E. J. Gore, *Birds of the Gambia* (B.O.U. Checklist no 3, 1981)

L. G. Grimes, *The Birds of Ghana* (B.O.U. Checklist no 9, 1987)

W. Gutter, *Birds of Liberia* (Pica Press, 1997)

C. J. Hazevoet, *The Birds of the Cape Verde Islands* (B.O.U. Checklist no 13, 1995)

Leon Lippens, Henri Wille, *Les oiseaux du Zaïre* (Tielt, 1976)

BOOKS ON BIRD GROUPS

Pica Press, Mountfield:

C. Byers, U. Olsson and J. Curson, *Buntings and Sparrows* (1995)

P. Chantler and G. Driessens, *Swifts* (1995)

N. Cleere and D. Nurney, *Nightjars* (1998)

F. Lambert and M. Woodcock, *Pitta's, Broadbills and Asities* (1996)

N. Lefranc and T. Worfolk, *Shrikes* (1997)

K. M. Olsen and H. Larsson, *Skuas and Jaegers* (1997)

B. Taylor and B. van Perlo, *Rails* (1998)

H. Winkler, D. A. Christie and D. Nurney, *Woodpeckers* (1995)

A & C Black, London:

K. Baker, *Warblers of Europe, Asia and North Africa* (1997)

P. Clement, A. Harris and J. Davis, *Finches and Sparrows* (1993)

C. Feare and A. Craig, *Starlings and Mynahs* (1998)

C. H. Fry, K. Fry and A. Harris, *Kingfishers, Bee-eaters and Rollers* (1992)

T. Harris and K. Franklin, *Shrikes & Bush-shrikes* (2000)

P. Harrison, *Seabirds* (1983)

S. Harrap and D. Quinn, *Tits, Nuthatches & Treecreepers* (1996)

J. Hancock and J. Kushlan, *The Herons Handbook* (1984)

A. Turner and C. Rose, *Swallows and Martins* (1998)

S. Madge and H. Burn, *Wildfowl* (1988)

S. Madge and H. Burn, *Crows and Jays*

Oxford University Press, Oxford:

Kemp, *The Hornbills* (1995)

Houghton Mifflin Company, Boston:

P. Hayman, J. Marchant & T. Taylor, *Shorebirds* (1986)

AFRICAN BIRD SOUNDS

C. Chappuis, *African Bird Sounds* (volumes 1 & 2)

Volume 1: contains 4 discs, covering North West Africa, Canaries & Cape Verde with sounds of 423 species.

Volume 2: contains 11 discs, covering West and Central Africa with sounds of 1043 species.

THE BIRDLIFE AFRICAN PARTNERSHIP

BirdLife International is a global alliance of national conservation organisations working in more than 100 countries worldwide. The BirdLife International Partnership strives to conserve birds, their habitats and global biodiversity, working with people towards sustainability in the use of natural resources. In Africa, national BirdLife Partners provide a focus for bird conservation activity in 18 countries across the continent. This BirdLife African partnership currently has over 300 staff and 30,000 members in 17 autonomous organisations. Over 200,000 children from 5000 wildlife clubs are involved in activities with the African Partnership every year. Information on African national BirdLife Partners can be obtained on the BirdLife website www.birdlife.net/africa or by contacting BirdLife International, Wellbrook Court, Girton Road, Cambridge, CB3 0NA, UK.

BirdLife's Important Bird Areas programme has published a regional directory of IBAs in Africa in 2001 which lists 1228 priority sites for bird conservation and makes recommendations for their conservation. The programme has also seen national guides to IBAs published in Ethiopia, southern Africa (including Botswana, Lesotho, Namibia, South Africa, Swaziland and Zimbabwe), Madagascar, Egypt , Kenya and Uganda.

WEST AFRICAN ORNITHOLOGICAL SOCIETY

The West African Ornithological Society aims to promote scientific interest in the birds of West Africa and to further the region's ornithology, mainly by means of its journal Malimbus.

Applications for membership are welcomed.

Correspondence should be addressed to the Treasurer, 1 Fisher's Heron, East Mills, Fordingbridge, Hampshire, SP6 2JR, U.K.